Chaplin in the Sound Era

Chaplin in the Sound Era

An Analysis of the Seven Talkies

by

Eric L. Flom

McFarland & Company, Inc., Publishers

Jefferson, North Carolina, and London

Frontispiece: Chaplin as lady-killer, from *Monsieur Verdoux* (1947).

Photographs from *A Countess from Hong Kong* © 1967 by Universal City Studios, Inc. Courtesy of Universal Studios Publishing Rights. All Rights Reserved.

British Library Cataloguing-in-Publication data are available

Library of Congress Cataloguing-in-Publication Data

Flom, Eric L., 1968–
    Chaplin in the sound era : an analysis of the seven talkies / by
Eric L. Flom.
        p.   cm.
    Includes bibliographical references.
    ISBN 0-7864-0325-X (library binding : 50# alkaline paper) ∞
    1. Chaplin, Charlie, 1889–1977 — Criticism and interpretation.
I. Title.
PN2287.C5F58   1997
791.43'028'092 — dc21
[B]   96-29890
                                                    CIP

Manufactured in the United States of America

McFarland & Company, Inc., Publishers
  Box 611, Jefferson, North Carolina 28640

For Angie —
my best friend and loving spouse,
whose companionship and support
is prized above all and
whose tolerance knows no bounds.

Table of Contents

Acknowledgments

There are many, many people who have helped make this book possible. First, Stephanie Ogle, whose history of cinema class at the University of Washington inspired this undertaking in the first place, and whose store — Cinema Books — profited handsomely in my quest for research materials. Mary Corliss at the Museum of Modern Art deserves special thanks for graciously accommodating my tight schedule while selecting photographs for this work, as does Charles Maland of the University of Tennessee, for sharing his valuable insight on Chaplin. Additionally, I would like to thank the many helpful individuals from the Seattle Public Library, Everett Public Library and the University of Washington Library system, most of whom managed to get me pointed in the right direction when I needed it.

Closer to my own circle, I would especially like to thank my Mom and Dad, Arden and Cathy, not only for their lifelong support but, in this case, for their excellent proofreading skills as well. Additionally, my sister Kristen deserves praise for helping obtain some of the reference material for this book, especially considering that I pretty much made her participation compulsory.

Finally, no one deserves more thanks than my wife Angie, who has somehow managed to live with me throughout this entire ordeal. Though marrying me meant marrying my project as well, that she stuck around through all the high points, low points, late nights, early mornings and spontaneous tantrums is an accomplishment in itself. She's my greatest source of love and support, and my best friend to boot; I'm very fortunate.

Preface

From one perspective, little can be written about Charles Chaplin that hasn't already been said. In *Charles Chaplin: A Guide to References and Resources* (G.K. Hall, 1977), author Timothy J. Lyons catalogues upwards of 2,000 sources on Chaplin and his works, from a diverse array of languages and cultures around the globe. While such a list is indeed impressive, denoting Chaplin's influence on world cinema and modern culture throughout the twentieth century, it in no way can account for all the written works on the comedian. Also, as the book was published in 1977, Lyons cannot account for many additional works that have been put forth during the ensuing period. Events such as the comedian's death (also in 1977) and the centennial celebration of his birth in 1989, as well as ongoing re-evaluation of his works by film scholars and enthusiasts, continue to multiply the amount of information currently available. Perhaps no list could accurately record every written account of Charles Chaplin, who for a good portion of his professional life, under the guise of his cinematic character, the Tramp, stood as one of the most recognized figures on the face of the earth.

Consequently, writers on Chaplin have a tough task finding fresh approaches to viewing his life and art. With David Robinson's exhaustive biography in 1985, that author (the first writer with privileged access to Chaplin's personal papers and studio records) tapped perhaps the last large cache of new information. While there might be new interpretations of this material if it were made available to others, the hope of finding something new and of far-reaching importance about the comedian's life and craft seems slim indeed.

As such, future writers are left with concentrating on more specialized aspects of the comedian's career; this work on his sound era films is in that vein. Chaplin's commercial popularity and influence on the film industry had already made him an enduring figure by the time talking pictures became the norm in Hollywood. Had the comedian simply hung up his derby, cane and oversized boots late in the 1920s rather than continue working, the argument could be made that his importance as an artist would have been only slightly diminished in the realm of history. But Chaplin's creative drive was too great for him to simply abandon the medium, and although his sound films were less successful in terms of aesthetic and technical achievement — and in some cases, popular acceptance — they are nonetheless an important facet of his long career, and helped further solidify his significance as a motion picture and world figure.

These films have tended to occupy a rather underappreciated position in discussions of Chaplin's motion picture work. Books concerning film history, and even some Chaplin biographies, have often concentrated on the importance of his early work, particularly the influence and appeal of his Tramp character, yet have not given the same attention to his creative projects in the sound era. Generally, *City Lights* (1931) and *Modern Times* (1936) have been exceptions, as Chaplin not only kept Charlie as a screen persona for these films, but waged his own private battle against sound technology as well. To a lesser degree, *The Great Dictator* (1940) also remains of interest, though primarily because of its political and historical significance. But to diminish or dismiss Chaplin's sound films is to overlook an important portion of his career when the artist and the art became invariably close, and when the essential character of the man more overtly asserted itself in his screen images than in his earlier work.

With this in mind, I undertook the writing of this book with the goal of exploring this portion of Chaplin's film career. While many books have done an excellent job depicting Chaplin's sound era projects, most focus on the comedian's influence as a silent film artist, which to some degree Chaplin himself never escaped during this latter portion of his career. While no book could address Chaplin's sound films without consideration of his silent shorts and features, this book attempts to place the spotlight directly on those works produced after 1930.

One problem in doing this, however, is the nature of the comedian himself. One cannot simply address Chaplin's films, nor the events during this later period, and get a full picture of the man. Indeed, as David Robinson expressed in the preface of his work, to concentrate on any one aspect of Chaplin's life necessitates an understanding of his whole life, including both personal and professional endeavors.[1] Internal and external catalysts made marks upon his personal character, which in turn influenced the nature of the films he produced. To fully understand the comedian, one must chronicle, catalogue and decipher his life as well as his films, for they are closely linked; this is particularly true for Chaplin's post–1930 output. For this manuscript's purpose, I have chosen not to dwell on every detail of his childhood and development as an artist, as he came up through the English music hall circuit and his early films. Instead, I have focused on those points necessary to understand why Chaplin rose to such prominence in the motion picture industry, as well as the influences that directly affected his work, especially his sound films. Thus, beginning with the discussion of 1931's *City Lights*, the reader should have a reasonable understanding of Chaplin as a creative artist and personality — an ample foundation from which to view his first sound era film.

Similarly, each chapter, divided by individual films, begins with a biographical sketch of Chaplin's activities between projects. Events in the comedian's life immediately preceding a film project, particularly during the sound era, tended to influence the tone or character of that picture greatly. These biographical sections, too, are by no means exhaustive, but should move the reader toward understanding Chaplin's creative inspiration and concerns while framing the narrative of a particular film.

As I noted before, several outstanding books have chronicled Chaplin's life and work. Without question, David Robinson's *Chaplin: His Life and Art* (McGraw-Hill, 1985) is the foremost volume on the comedian, and succeeding generations will be hard-pressed to challenge its thoroughness. Working with Chaplin's personal papers, Robinson not only puts into perspective the nature of the man and his creativity, but also dispels a good number of falsehoods that have been handed down from earlier written works. More importantly, Robinson fills in many of the gaping holes left from Chaplin's own memoirs, particularly with regard to the details of particular films and his production methods. As such, it was impossible for me to write this work without using Robinson's publication as a "Chaplin Bible" of sorts, so invaluable is his research.

Charles Maland's *Chaplin and American Culture* (Princeton University Press, 1989) is another outstanding publication, and this book is also indebted to that investigation. Like the present work, Maland's focuses on a more narrow theme in Chaplin's career: his public/critical perception and reception in his adopted homeland of America. As the comedian became a lightning rod for controversy late in his career, Maland's study is an interesting look at how Chaplin's films and public endeavors at first raised him to prominence, then later left him falling out of favor in the United States, only to regain his stature, to a degree, toward the end of his life.

Several other aspects make Maland's work unique and indispensable: his study of a film's promotion and reception, including reviews from liberal, conservative and alternative publications; his extensive probe of government documents on Chaplin, particularly relating to the comedian's paternity trial in the 1940s and ban from the United States in 1952; his efforts in detailing Chaplin's sustained popularity through the continuation of the "Charlie" image in the comedian's later years; and his identification of an "aesthetic contract" of audience expectations (which he defines as a mixture of comedy, romance and pathos) to be found in almost every picture — characteristics that audiences began to know and expect from his work. I generally dislike using his aesthetic contract as a template for all of the sound era films, for its definition seems too narrow in addressing outside influences or smaller trends within Chaplin's work. If used too broadly, the term could also suggest that its elements were a blueprint for popular and critical success. But as each element of the aesthetic contract can be found, in varying degrees, in most of Chaplin's films, and because the analysis works extremely well in discussing *City Lights* and *Limelight* (1952), it is hard to ignore.

While I have found Robinson's and Maland's, as well as many other works, integral sources of material for this book, I have not attempted to imitate their level of scholarship. Rather, this work was undertaken for a more general level of readership, one that may be unfamiliar with the full scope of Chaplin's creative work or unaware that he continued to produce films long after the advent of sound. Analysis of each picture addresses some of its broader themes, utilizing a mixture of my own observations and interpretations as well as arguments from the plethora of other scholarly or biographical works currently available. Thus, this volume was not intended to be a major re-evaluation of Chaplin's comedic films, but rather a collection of pertinent information from many diverse sources, gathered into a single volume on the subject of his sound era films.

The book, I hope, will present a more clear understanding of Chaplin's later film projects, but if readers come away with but one feeling from this text, I would hope it would be the desire to view Chaplin's films, silent and sound. While a book may offer more insight on the man and his craft, offering a better understanding and appreciation of his work, the films themselves speak for their timelessness as art. Whereas some films or even styles of comedy can seem strangely dated after a few years, Chaplin's work has delighted audiences and generated critical attention for decades. With continued appreciation and preservation of his works, they will continue to do so.

1

Prologue

As the days of silent film become more and more distant, the names that first brought notoriety to Hollywood and the film industry have become relics of the past. Very few people can remember someone like D.W. Griffith, let alone recall that he made two of the most important pictures in the history of film, *The Birth of a Nation* (1915) and *Intolerance* (1916), in addition to his early groundbreaking work with the Biograph Company. The names of Douglas Fairbanks and Mary Pickford may be more recognizable, but few are familiar with their motion pictures. When various lists categorizing the best films of all time are published, often only a handful of silent films are included, despite the fact that well over one-third of cinema's history took place before the advent of sound. The pioneers of the motion picture industry, as well as their technical and artistic achievements, have been largely forgotten in the collective mind.

Except for Charlie Chaplin.

His name is synonymous with a general, though perhaps misleading, perception of what silent film (or more precisely, silent comedy) had been — rough and tumble, crudely simplistic films, which commonly featured some mixture of custard pies and slapstick chases. In Chaplin's case, it was a world set in the lower echelon of society — the back alleys, cafés, saloons and flop houses — very much, it would seem, a cartoon world.

But it was the moviegoing public's fascination with this cartoon world, and specifically the popularity of "Charlie" as a screen character, that helped boost motion pictures from an entertainment novelty to a legitimate art form. As the film industry expanded its complexity in aesthetic and business terms, attracting new and more diverse audiences, Chaplin found his screen image crossing cultural, economic, gender and age barriers in its appeal. With his character, the Tramp, who tried so nobly to rise above his impoverished status, Chaplin captured the hearts and imaginations of the world. He attained such a phenomenal, sustained popularity that he was able to cultivate his filmmaking talents and evolve both his screen characterizations and subject matter far beyond the broad comic style most generally associated with the silent era. So large was his creative drive, wealth and popularity, in fact, that Chaplin remained active in the industry for over half a century — far outlasting the age when simple slap-stick reigned as a popular industry genre.

But while Chaplin's most prolific period and perhaps his best works came in the silent era, mostly in the form of short two-reel (approximately twenty minute) comedies, his artistic work extended well beyond this period. Though his production of films had slowed (he would produce only seven feature films after 1930, as opposed to the 74 shorts and features prior to the introduction of sound to film), his creative drive extended well beyond the era which had immor-talized him.

His sound era films provide a unique glimpse into the work and inspira-tion of one of the world's most acclaimed and recognized artists. These films find several distinct trends running through Chaplin's work. Many were rooted directly in the sentiments, events and experiences of the comedian himself, affecting his subject matter, his characters and his cinematic style.

But to fully understand them, one must begin by looking at the artist's background; from his boyhood in London, through the old music halls of Eng-land the Vaudeville houses of America, and his initial work in the film indus-try. The development of his own character through these years, as well as after vaulting to international stardom, had a profound effect on the man and his creative work.

I. THE BOYHOOD

April of 1889 was a month that would figure momentously in the history of the twentieth century. On the 20th, in the small Austrian town of Braunau, a baby boy was born to Alois and Klara Hitler. The child, baptized Adolfus, would eventually become one of the world's most influential figures — a little man with a toothbrush mustache who would rise from the poverty and obscu-rity of his childhood, ascending to great heights in an adopted country. The boy, as we know, would change the course of history.

Just four days prior to the birth of Adolfus Hitler, on April 16, in London, another baby boy had been brought into the world. This boy, Charles Spencer Chaplin, would also become an influential figure of the twentieth century. He too would find fame as a little man with a toothbrush mustache. He too would leave the poverty and hopelessness of his childhood and ascend to great heights in an adopted country. This boy too, in his own unique way, would change the course of history.

Both of Charles Chaplin's parents were employed in the entertainment business, the English music halls. His father, Charles Chaplin, Sr., was a dash-ing singer and comedian of 26 at the time of his son's birth. He was an up-and-coming star of the stage, but would vanish from Chaplin's life early, gradually sinking deeper into the alcoholism that would cut short not only his career but his life as well. He would stay barely a year with mother and son; Chaplin himself would recall very little of his father in his memoirs, mostly fragments of information he remembered gathering from his mother. Even so, he spoke fondly of him. "I was hardly aware of a father, and do not remember his having lived with us. He too was a vaudevillian, a quiet, brooding man with dark eyes. Mother said he looked like Napoleon. He had a light baritone voice and was considered a very fine artist. Even in those days he earned the considerable sum of £40 a week. The trouble was that he drank too much, which Mother said was the cause of their separation."[1] Chaplin's parents split up shortly after Charlie's birth; Charles, Sr., took his flourishing music hall act to America for a brief tour, while mother Hannah, then only 22, found herself in the company of another vaudevillian, a singer named Leo Dryden. This brief relationship, lasting not even two years, would see the birth of a baby boy — Wheeler Dryden, born to Hannah Chaplin on August 31, 1892. When the unwed pair split suddenly, Wheeler was taken by his father, a source of considerable grief for Chaplin's mother.

Hannah, often performing under the stage name of Lily Harley, also sang in the music halls, and occasionally burlesqued contemporary public figures as part of her act. Her career on the stage was much less successful than Charles, Sr.'s, though for a short period in young Chaplin's life she managed to maintain it as well as play the role of mother to Charlie and his half-brother Sydney, four years older and the product of a previous relationship. Voice trouble effectively halted Hannah's career when Chaplin was only five, though she would at various times attempt to return to the stage. As romantic accounts went, Hannah was said to have been onstage one evening when her voice broke, and she was yelled off the stage by a particularly boisterous crowd. The stage manager, having seen Charlie perform little songs and routines in the wings of the theater, promptly brought the five-year-old out to try his luck as a filler; Chaplin himself recalled that he sang a song titled "Jack Jones." The boy's act was treated to a shower of money and applause from the audience, at which point little Charlie received a tremendous laugh by stopping the song and announcing that he would begin singing again once he had retrieved all of the coins. The event, it seems, marked the end of Hannah's professional stage career, although she would perform intermittently over the next few years. Chaplin had fond memories of both Hannah and her performing abilities; she would often entertain her children for hours with her whimsical impersonations and songs.

"I was hardly aware of a crisis," Chaplin would recall of his London childhood, "because we lived in a continual crisis."[2] With Hannah's stage career on the decline, the family relied heavily on Charles, Sr.'s support payments to make ends meet. But regardless of the so-called substantial sum his father made on the music hall circuit, obtaining these payments was always a problem. This income would not only be limited but intermittent, and Charles,

Sr.'s touring schedule made him difficult to locate when payments were not being made. The few legal remedies available to Hannah to enforce payment were cumbersome and worked only temporarily; even then, Chaplin's father made them under protest. He was particularly incensed that London officials treated the boys as legitimate brothers — thus he was forced to pay for Sydney, who wasn't even his own child. With such unreliable support, Hannah and her two sons quickly sank into extreme poverty. As a single mother in Victorian London, she labored at various tasks to bring in enough money to support herself and the boys.

But it was a losing battle, for Chaplin, Sydney and Hannah spent much of the 1890s in and out of London workhouses as they struggled to gain a stable financial foothold. This was a revolving door for the family for a number of years — their stays in local infirmaries followed by equally brief stays living independently. In May of 1896, after officials forced Sydney and Charlie into an unsuccessful living arrangement with Charles Chaplin, Sr., and his live-in girlfriend (whose own alcoholism and strong dislike for Sydney made living insufferable), the boys were admitted to the Newington Workhouse. In June, both were transferred to the Hanwell Schools for Orphans and Destitute Families, some 12 miles outside London. About the same time, Hannah was admitted to the Champion Hill Infirmary.

The move would separate Sydney and Charlie not only from their mother but, because of Hanwell's segregation of boys on the basis of age, from each other as well. Hanwell was not unlike the many similar institutions Chaplin would see in his life, though his experiences there had a profound impact on his life, ironically providing him with one of the most secure, if temporary and wholly unpleasant, memories of his boyhood.

> Although at Hanwell we were well looked after, it was a forlorn experience. Sadness was in the air; it was in those country lanes through which we walked, a hundred of us two abreast. How I disliked those walks, and the villages through which we passed, the locals staring at us! We were known as inmates of the "booby hatch," a slang term for the workhouse.[3]

Particularly horrifying were Chaplin's memories of the poor living conditions in such institutions. At Hanwell, outbreaks of ringworm were commonplace (Chaplin got it once) and the comedian vividly recalled the eerie sight of the quarantined boys peering from windows onto the courtyard below, their heads shaved and smeared red with iodine.

If there was any sort of bright spot throughout his stay at Hanwell, it was that he and Sydney grew closer, despite the separation of the older and younger boys. A feeling of mutual dependence formed, which helped the brothers persevere. But overall the stay at Hanwell would forever etch the memory of Chaplin's boyhood poverty and broken family condition in his conscience; throughout his career in motion pictures, his comedy often reflected the painful degradation and embarrassment of being poor, perhaps no more explicitly than in the very character he would come to play.

While the Chaplin boys grew closer at Hanwell, their co-dependence was not entirely of their own doing; both Charles, Sr., and Hannah were slowly deteriorating in their own right, leaving the boys more and more to their own devices. Their father was a heavy drinker and spotty provider; Hannah began to show increasing signs of mental instability, sometimes necessitating hospital care above and beyond that which a workhouse was able to provide. This was not the first such illness in the Chaplin lineage, as Mary Ann Hill, Hannah's mother, had also been institutionalized for a similar condition, a fact which Hannah seems to have concealed from her boys.[4]

Even during the periods when she was on her own and healthy, Hannah still faced the trouble of providing for the family. Working as a seamstress in their modest lodgings, her income had to be augmented by whatever could be earned by the boys. At Hanwell, Sydney had been selected as part of a program to train young boys for a career at sea. In late 1896 he became a bugler on the training ship *Exmouth* on its runs between England and South Africa. Charlie, on the other hand, took numerous small jobs throughout London during this period. But for the youngest Chaplin, his ultimate sights, and ultimately those of Sydney as well, were set on following his parents onto the music hall circuit. "I had been a news vendor, printer, toymaker, glass blower, doctor's boy, etc., but during those occupational digressions, like Sydney, I never lost sight of my ultimate aim to become an actor. So between jobs I would polish my shoes, brush my clothes, put on a clean collar and make periodic calls at Blackmore's theatrical agency in Bedford Street off Strand. I did this until the state of my clothes forbade any further visits."[5] (Chaplin's elaboration of the casting practices in the Blackmore waiting room would eventually find their way into his 1952 film *Limelight*. In the picture, a similar lobby, filled with smartly dressed entertainers, would quickly empty as a representative enters, pointing to each individual and announcing coldly, "Nothing for you, nothing for you," etc.)

Though his parents were indeed gifted performers, there was certainly nothing to hint at young Charlie's future success, and the music halls perhaps seemed only to hold a little more opportunity than did the streets of London. For he and Sydney, two young boys who were proving to be more steady providers than their own parents, any chance for a better life was a welcome one.

II. THE ENGLISH STAGE

Through a happenstance meeting with his father, Charlie was able to take his first steps toward becoming an actor when he joined a touring music hall group called the Eight Lancashire Lads in December, 1898. Managed by William Jackson, who had a number of his own boys in the troupe (Chaplin would recall four, though this figure includes a daughter with a rather boyish haircut), the Lads provided a stable, family-type environment as well as a small income. Further, it was Mrs. Jackson's policy to enroll the boys in local schools where the Lads played, though their education was certainly limited by such guest appearances. (Chaplin would characterize schooling throughout his early life as an "ogre," an attitude which no doubt lessened the positive benefits he could have received from Mrs. Jackson's piecemeal education plan.)

Lasting from Christmas 1898 to Christmas 1900, Chaplin's experiences with the Eight Lancashire Lads fired his interest in the stage even further. Touring had allowed him to become more familiar with the life that both his father and mother had known, and the opportunity to witness some of the more acclaimed performers of his age — Dan Leno, whom Chaplin lauded as the greatest comedian of the vaudeville stage; comedians Harry Lauder and Frank Tinney; dramatic specialists Marie Doro, William Gillette, Herbert Beerbohm Tree and Constance Collier. At the tender age of 11, the young Chaplin was quickly gaining both knowledge and experience in the music hall business, training that would be instrumental in catapulting him to fame once in Hollywood.

On May 9, 1901, Charles Chaplin, Sr., died at St. Thomas' Hospital in London from cirrhosis of the liver. This was not an uncommon end for many a music hall artist. Most theaters were adjoined by bars, and performers commonly shared drinks with patrons following shows. Although Chaplin respectfully claimed that a wealthy uncle financed a proper burial of his father, Charles, Sr., was actually buried as a pauper the day after his passing.[6]

Though the death of his father was a blow to the young boy, it did not undermine his own business enterprise: According to Chaplin's recollection, he ran a profitable weekend trade as a flower salesman following his father's death. Wearing a black armband in memorial, he earned many tips purely out of sympathy from his customers. Hannah eventually put an end to the endeavor; she was not particularly angry with her son's method of sales, he remembered, but did not approve of his entering the many pubs in which he plied the trade at such a young age.[7]

Following his departure from the Eight Lancashire Lads, Chaplin's next stage experience was in 1903, when the Blackmore agency offered him the plum role of Billie, a pageboy, in the touring production of *Sherlock Holmes*,* which even earned him some critical recognition in the process. The tour, beginning in late July of 1903 and running for some ten months throughout England, earned Charlie the sum of two pounds and ten shillings per week. In addition,

---

*Chaplin would warm up for the part in a short-lived and poorly received production, Jim, the Romance of a Cockayne. Though Charlie himself was singled out for critical praise in his role as Sammy the newsboy, the production disappeared from the stage shortly after its debut.

through Charlie's insistence, Sydney, after returning from an extended trip at sea, joined the ensemble during its first run in a small supporting role.

Before the Chaplin boys made their way about England, however, Hannah took a turn for the worse. In May, 1903, shortly before the beginning of Charlie's stint with *Sherlock Holmes*, her sporadic mental instability degenerated to the point where she was formally institutionalized and diagnosed as insane. Chaplin himself was forced to commit his mother to the Cane Hill Asylum; later, he would ominously recall Hannah's comment to him that, if only he had thought to prepare her a cup of soothing tea that day, she would have been quite all right.[8]

Ironically, Hannah's institutionalization perhaps couldn't have been more timely. Just as her boys were gaining some measure of stability and independence in their performing careers, their mother and primary care giver had to relinquish almost all control over them. Beginning with the Cane Hill stay, Hannah Chaplin would be institutionalized almost continually from 1903 through 1912, when her boys, by then earning sufficient wages from their vaudeville endeavors, moved her to a private nursing home.

Onstage, the youngest Chaplin would go on to three separate revivals of the *Sherlock Holmes* tour, spanning from late 1904 through 1906. Shortly thereafter he joined a troupe Sydney was working with, a Wal Pink comedy sketch entitled *Repairs*, featuring a rather inept group of paper hangers. It would be a brief layover for Charlie, from March to May of 1906, but the sketch would provide an excellent introduction to the type of comedy material Chaplin would later build upon during his early motion picture days at the Keystone Studios. The recurring characters of repairmen and paper hangers ran throughout his film career.

Though briefly reunited in *Repairs*, the brothers would again go their separate ways in the theater. Sydney landed a position with the Karno Silent Comedy Troupe, one of the top vaudeville comedy organizations in England, while Charlie spent a year with another show, *Casey's Court Circus*. The stint with *Casey's* offered Chaplin the chance to learn and improve on the caricature skills his mother had taught him as a young boy, though he himself considered the show awful.[9] Impersonations Charlie had perfected included a send-up of Dr. Walford Brodie, the famed music hall hypnotist who was a popular attraction of his day.

Meanwhile, Sydney quickly rose to be one of Karno's top comedians, allowing him to return Charlie's earlier favor with *Sherlock Holmes* by securing a position for his younger brother. In February of 1908, Charlie Chaplin was signed to a three-year contract with the Karno troupe, though owner Fred Karno had some last-minute hesitation over Sydney's diminutive and young-looking brother.

But, with time, Chaplin not only proved to be a comedian of great skill and ingenuity, but an employee of comparable value to Sydney. Charlie's first real success with Karno, a troupe that specialized in wordless comedy sketches, came with his role as a drunken theater patron in *Mumming Birds*, where an inebriate foils the presentation of a fictional vaudeville performance from a box seat near the stage. Chaplin, though only 19 at the time, was made up to look much older, and his natural pantomimic skills vaulted him to one of Karno's prized artists. *Mumming Birds* would prove such a success over the course of his stay with Karno that Chaplin would often build on the character of the drunk in his later film years.

Chaplin would achieve comparable success in sketches such as *The Football Match, Skating* (roles he inherited from his brother Sydney, who also co-wrote *Skating*) and *Jimmy the Fearless*. The latter sketch involved the heroism of a boy who, following his daring exploits, awakens to find his deeds only a dream. Initially, Chaplin disliked the lead role and surrendered it to his understudy, young Karno comedian Stanley Jefferson. But Jefferson lasted only one performance as Jimmy: Chaplin, seeing the sketch on its opening night, promptly demanded back — and received — the role. Ironically, Jefferson, like Chaplin, would also find considerable fame in the motion picture industry, though under the name Stan Laurel. To John McCabe, biographer of both Laurel and Hardy and Charlie Chaplin, Laurel later stated with ironic pleasure, as few could boast, that Chaplin had been his replacement.[10]

Eventually, Chaplin was encouraged to tour the United States by Alf Reeves, manager of Karno's vaudeville troupes in America. At the time, Sydney was considered the better comedic talent. This is not to say Charlie was not valued as a comedian; in fact, he was one of Karno's best. But Sydney had displayed a talent for writing as well as acting, whereas Charlie's first written sketch, a courtroom satire, was halted during pre-production due to its flimsy quality. Because both Karno and Reeves were leery of American attempts to snare their top comedians, a multi-talented prospect such as Sydney was destined to remain in England. However, Chaplin had talented company on the journey. His roommate for much of the tour would be Stanley Jefferson, and the group would also boast a young man named Albert Austin, who would later find a home at the Chaplin Studios during the comedian's most prolific period of filmmaking and become one of Chaplin's key creative advisors.

Chaplin opened at the Colonial Theatre in New York on October 3, 1910, playing the lead role in a sketch entitled *The Wow-Wows*. The run was a disaster. Fred Karno had the mistaken impression that America was filled with all sorts of secret societies, which *The Wow-Wows* satirized. Reaction from New York audiences was very cold, and though the troupe was experienced enough to switch to a more perfected sketch such as *Mumming Birds*, Karno refused to allow them to do so. Though the situation improved over successive weeks, reception to the Karno troupe by New York audiences on this tour was less than impressive.

Between October, 1910, and May, 1912, Chaplin would make two separate tours of the United States with the Karno troupe. Following the troublesome presentation of *The Wow-Wows* during the New York leg of the first tour, the troupe finally resumed with *Mumming Birds*, which was renamed *A Night in an English Music Hall* for American audiences. Chaplin played the drunk, and once again earned critical raves for his performances.

Though both tours had proven successful not only for the Karno troupe but Chaplin personally, being away from England was beginning to take its toll on the young comedian. Upon his arrival in the United States, Chaplin had been filled with optimism regarding his prospects for success. His touring schedule, however, began to weigh heavily upon his attitude. Booked briefly into a run of smaller theaters, Chaplin would recount some 50 years later:

> Those cheap vaudeville circuits were bleak and depressing, and hopes about my future in America disappeared in the grind of doing three and sometimes four shows a day, seven days a week. Vaudeville in England was paradise by comparison. At least we only worked there six days a week and gave only two shows a night. Our consolation was that in America we could save a little more money.[11]

Even with the monetary prospects that American vaudeville may have provided, Chaplin apparently felt that it still could not provide the type of secure future he wished for. Competition in vaudeville was fierce, his peak days of performing would eventually pass him by, and audience interest in his act could fade, thus forcing him to leave the stage altogether. Chaplin was evidently worried about such possibilities, as he and another touring vaudevillian, Ralph Lohse, briefly hatched a scheme to move into the hog-raising business in Arkansas. The process of castrating hogs, Chaplin later claimed, turned him off to the enterprise, and he instead opted to stick to vaudeville for the time being, preferring to wait for some other opportunity.

As a relief from the doldrums in America, Chaplin returned to England from June to September of 1912, only to find things much different than before. Hannah was still in a fragile condition and Sydney had now taken a wife, another music hall performer named Minnie Constance. A brief tour of English music halls proved uneventful, perhaps even dreary, since the result was his re-evaluation of his prospects in America. Despite his earlier morose feelings, he once again placed his hopes and dreams of success there. "I was just a kid out from England," he would tell *New York Times* critic Bosley Crowther nearly half a century later, "with all sorts of fancies about the West and the frontier. So when we hit towns such as Denver, Tacoma, Minneapolis — places with rich American names — I felt I was right in the middle of a new and wonderful thing."[12]

III. THOSE MOVING PICTURES

Chaplin's second journey to the United States with the Karno troupe, again entailing two different tours around the country, was almost as uneventful as the first. Though he continued to get rave reviews at virtually every stop of the tour (by this point, his name was now being featured prominently in Karno's publicity campaigns), Chaplin was still concerned about his future.

During a layover in Philadelphia in May 1913, Karno tour manager Alf Reeves received a telegram that ultimately proved the answer to Chaplin's career concerns.

MAY 12, 1913

ALF REEVES MANAGER
KARNO LONDON COMEDIANS
NIXON THEATRE, PHILADELPHIA

THERE IS A MAN NAMED CHAFFIN IN YOUR COMPANY OR SOMETHING LIKE THAT STOP IF SO WILL HE COMMUNICATE WITH KESSEL AND BAUMANN 24 LONGACRE BUILDING BROADWAY.[13]

In his memoirs, the comedian remembered that the cable immediately sent his mind racing. Certainly he had come into an inheritance, since he understood New York's Longacre Building to be a bastion of lawyers. Chaplin recalled he had a wealthy aunt in the United States, and as she must have passed on, he set off to New York with high hopes of receiving a small fortune. To his disappointment, however, Adam Kessel and Charles Baumann — former book-makers — were not lawyers at all. Rather, they were engaged in the fledgling motion picture industry, the corporate office of several film companies, including Keystone Studios in California.

According to legend, Keystone Studio boss Mack Sennett had attended *A Night in an English Music Hall* the previous year and had found Chaplin's comic performance impressive. Ford Sterling, Sennett's current star comedian, had been rumored to be leaving Keystone shortly, and in thinking of possible replacements, Sennett remembered the performance of the "inebriate" he had seen earlier. In his efforts to track down the Karno Company, Alf Reeves thus received the telegram during the Philadelphia layover.

However, it is more likely that a representative of Kessel and Bauman witnessed Chaplin's performance and recommended the comedian for the stint out west. Further, it is not likely that Chaplin was meant to replace Sterling. Though he was a popular vaudeville performer, Chaplin was without a moment of screen experience to his resumé. It is more probable that he was actually a replacement for Fred Mace, another comedian slated to leave Sennett's nest soon; Chaplin biographer David Robinson's research uncovered a letter from Charlie to Sydney indicating that this was Chaplin's understanding at the time.[14] For Sennett to have anticipated that the appeal of this new, untested English comedian would even remotely rival that of the phenomenally-popular Sterling is unlikely.

At any rate, Sennett was looking for new talent at a time when Chaplin was questioning his long-term prospects on the vaudeville circuit. Both men would be rewarded many times over for the Keystone Company's decision to lure the English comedian to California.

"Had I seen a Keystone comedy?" Chaplin recalled being asked at the meeting. "Of course, I had seen several, but I did not tell [Mr. Kessel] I thought they were a crude melange of rough-and-tumble.... I was not terribly enthusiastic about the Keystone type of comedy, but I realized their publicity value. A year in that racket and I could return to vaudeville an international star."[15] The work, then, was a secondary concern; Chaplin found his opportunity to cash in on his talents. After signing a contract with Keystone, he set out to finish his tour with Karno before embarking on his new and, as he apparently anticipated, short career in motion pictures.

But when Chaplin arrived in Southern California for work in December 1913, he quickly began to have second thoughts about his decision. Not only did it take him three days to even summon the courage to enter the studio, according to his recollection, but once inside he found a largely foreign atmosphere that was terribly intimidating. To add to his woes, Sennett, for whatever reason, chose not to put him to work immediately, and after a few weeks of idleness, the comedian was seriously questioning his decision to leave the stage.

However, Sennett finally found a role for Chaplin to play. In a Keystone production entitled *Making a Living*, Chaplin was cast as a slicker, a man who flirts with a rival's girl and her mother, as well as seeks to out-hustle his competitor as a newspaper reporter. In short, he was cast as a villain.

In the Keystone tradition (a tradition which, based on his comments to Mr. Kessel at least, Chaplin dreaded), the film was short and packed with action. The performances of Chaplin and his counterpart, Henry Lehrman, also the director on the production, served almost entirely to facilitate a series of chases, while raising as much mayhem as possible in the process. Altogether, from the improvised script to the performances to the final product, Chaplin hated it. Most Keystone comics, in Chaplin's estimation, had no style of their own — everyone merely copied Ford Sterling, the studio's biggest star at the time. As he found during his first few films, there was little room in the Keystone structure for the type of comic pantomime that he had learned in the English music halls, which was far more subtle and leisurely by comparison. His attempts to insert such comic business largely ended up on the cutting room floor. David Robinson noted Chaplin's predicament:

> Karno taught his comedians other principles of comedy: that a slow delivery can often be more effective than hectic speed, but that in any event pace must be varied to avoid monotony; that humor lies in the unexpected, so it is funnier if the man is not expecting the pie that hits him in the face. The serious absurdity and the bizarre comic transpositions of the Karno sketches must often have resembled Chaplin gags.[16]

Although he earned some praise for his performance, Chaplin was dissatisfied with his first film and, perhaps looking for a scapegoat, he focused on *Making a Living* director Henry Lehrman, whom he felt had cut his most credible comic gags. The two immediately struck up a mutual discord.

As was Keystone's practice, films were produced with blazing speed, at least by today's standards. One-reelers, with a running time of roughly ten minutes, could be completed, from original inception to filming, cutting, printing and shipping, in a matter of days. Further, since the films tended to be based largely on formula, nearly always leading to a climactic chase, Keystone actors didn't need to begin a project with a clear vision of where they were headed. Essentially, one idea would spark another idea which would create another, and the resulting chaos was recorded on celluloid and spliced together. Production methods such as scripting and the shooting of retakes were almost unheard of. Coming from the exacting and well-rehearsed arena of vaudeville sketches, Chaplin's background was distinctly at odds with the requirements of the new medium.

It wasn't until Chaplin's second film with Keystone, *Mabel's Strange Predicament*, that his famous screen character made his first appearance on film. This auspicious moment in motion picture history has been recalled by a variety of people in a number of differing versions, not all of them truthful, least of all Chaplin's. With a good deal of nostalgia, the comedian remembered the moment thusly:

> [Mack Sennett] was standing there with Mabel [Normand], looking into a hotel lobby set, biting the end of his cigar. "We need some gags here," he said, then turned to me. "Put on a comedy make-up. Anything will do."
> I had no idea what make-up to put on. I did not like my getup as the press reporter. However, on the way to the wardrobe I thought I would dress in baggy pants, big shoes, a cane and a derby hat. I wanted everything a contradiction: the pants baggy, the coat tight, the hat small and the shoes large. I was undecided whether to look old or young, but remembering Sennett had expected me to be a much older man, I added a small mustache, which, I reasoned, would add age without hiding my expression.
> I had no idea for the character. But the moment I was dressed, the clothes and the make-up made me feel the person he was. I began to know him, and by the time I walked onto the stage he was fully born.... As the clothes had imbued me with the character, I then and there decided to keep this costume, whatever happened.[17]

Richard Attenborough's 1992 film biography *Chaplin* satirizes the comedian's tendency to over-romanticize the birth of the Tramp, as Chaplin certainly does in his memoirs. In that film, as Robert Downey, Jr., portraying an elderly Chaplin, speaks to the fictional editor of his autobiography (Anthony Hopkins), the film moves backward in time to find a young Chaplin in the Sennett dressing room. The trademark hat and cane begin "calling" to the comedian, as if by some divine force. The situation is ludicrous, and the flashback is promptly interrupted by Hopkins, who uses a fitting expletive to describe Chaplin's account. A more credible scenario follows, one that has been put forth by a number of the comedian's own colleagues during the Keystone period: In the heat of the moment, Chaplin merely put on whatever pieces of an outfit he could find handy in the dressing room. Thus, one of cinema's most enduring figures was born quite by accident — much less dramatic, but perhaps more factual. Chaplin's own version of the event, in fact, has prompted at least one scholar to describe it as a "marvelous piece of retrospective fakery."[18]

Along with distinct influences from Chaplin's childhood poverty, his experiences in the English music halls may also have played an integral role shaping the character. "Grotesquely ill-fitting clothes, tiny hats, distasteful mustaches and wigger-wagger canes were the necessary impediments of the [music hall] comedian," notes David Robinson. "Some of Dan Leno's stage costumes hint at Chaplin's; and Chaplin's old Karno colleague, Fred Kitchen, used to complain gently that it was he who first originated the costume and the splay-footed walk. Elements of the character had been predicted in Chaplin's own stage career. His make-up in the single surviving photograph of Wal Pink's sketch *Repairs* somewhat resembles that of Charlie; and there is said to have been much of the costume in his get-up as a rag-and-bone man in Karno's *London Suburbia*."[19]

The effect of Chaplin's seemingly insignificant wardrobe and characterization choices was, as we now know in hindsight, momentous. As the comedian must have recognized early on, establishing audience identification in film after film would require distinctive costuming. But Chaplin, unknown to anyone at the time, would eventually develop this character into an "everyman"—a modest screen persona that people could genuinely identify with. Eventually, as the appeal and popularity of Chaplin's character soared, an effect similar to that which he witnessed at Keystone, with the performers aping of Ford Sterling, impacted the nature of silent screen comedy. Silent comedian Harold Lloyd recalled in an interview with Kevin Brownlow:

> "I didn't like [Lonesome] Luke,"* said Lloyd. "Luke was a semi-imitation character. I tried my best to stay away from anything Chaplin did, and my clothes were really the reverse of Charlie's, being too small instead of too big. All the same, Charlie had the corner on comedy clothes. Lonesome Luke was a broad comedy character, and Charlie had the corner on that too. He was king in that department."[20]

Mabel's Strange Predicament would mark Chaplin's debut performance as Charlie, but it was not, according to most Chaplin biographers, the first public appearance of the Tramp in a Keystone film. While *Predicament* was being

---

*Lonesome Luke was Lloyd's second comic character, Willie Work being his first and the famed "glasses" character being his third. Luke, however, was the first to earn him a true niche in comedy, launching his film career.

edited and printed, Chaplin was dispatched to Venice Beach, the site of a local soapbox derby event and an ideal setting for an off-the-cuff Keystone comedy. He was again under the direction of Lehrman, who would direct Chaplin's first four films at Keystone. Such were Sennett's production methods: His studio pictures were often augmented by "quickies," often coinciding with parades or other public gatherings that would provide an interesting backdrop. *Kid Auto Races at Venice*, a half-reel film purportedly shot in 45 minutes, essentially dwells only on Lehrman's attempts to film the races, while an annoying, shabby little gentleman does everything in his power to sneak into the film. Given the five-minute running time, *Kid Auto Races* was able to be cut, printed and distributed in almost no time (sharing half a reel with a documentary on the production of olive oil), and thus beat the release of *Mabel's Strange Predicament* by two days.

Recent scholarship, however, has not only differed from this long-accepted account but may be even more precise in pinpointing the birth of Chaplin's Tramp. Bo Berglund, writing in the Spring 1989 edition of *Sight and Sound*, notes that silent films were typically shot on open air stages with muslin overhead to diffuse sunlight, and bases his theory on this aspect of early filmmaking in Hollywood. Tracking the weather patterns in Los Angeles and Venice, Berglund cross-referenced this material with the newspaper advertisement for the auto races, and backed by later accounts from other Keystone performers, he contends that *Mabel's Strange Predicament* could not have been shot prior to *Kid Auto Races*— in part or in whole — due to poor weather around the Keystone Studios. Berglund pinpoints the birth of the Tramp to Saturday, January 10, 1914, at approximately 1:30 P.M., shortly before the start of the *auto races*.[21] It is likely that the comedian still had to create his character on the spur of the moment, but regardless, Chaplin seemed taken with this Tramp character, enough to keep the same basic garb and mannerisms through his first few films with the company, perhaps in an effort to become familiar to motion picture audiences. It didn't take long for him to be noticed; "We do not think we are taking a great risk in prophesying," wrote *Exhibitors World* after the release of *Kid Auto Races*, "that in six months Chaplin will rank as one of the most popular screen comedians in the world."[22]

Though Chaplin was initially turned off by the motion picture business, he was a quick learner, and as he found himself becoming more comfortable creating comedy for the screen, he also began to feel confident with his ability to direct Keystone films as well. This is less presumptuous than it at first seems. Given that the Keystone staff and performers built their stories as they went along, Chaplin's comedic suggestions were at least as good as anyone else's, and with his many years on the English vaudeville circuit, he certainly had plenty of material to draw from. Further, with short productions, and as Keystone was certainly more centralized than today's huge and highly specialized

Chaplin, seated at lower left, with fellow Karno vaudevillians near Butte, Montana. Seated at the far right is Stanley Jefferson, aka Stan Laurel; standing behind Chaplin is Albert Austin, who would later become an integral member of the comedian's comedy troupe.

studios, Chaplin had the opportunity to learn the technical essentials of filmmaking, such as staging and editing, at a relatively quick pace. These skills would eventually serve him well in asserting creative control over his later projects.

Furthering his desire to step behind the camera were his ongoing problems with the Keystone directors. After completing 12 shorts in two months, Chaplin had firmly established himself as a problem actor — one who felt he knew more about the principles of comedy than any director assigned to him. The problem finally came to a head after Chaplin was put under the direction of Sennett's leading lady and girlfriend, Mabel Normand. Her youthful age of 22, in addition to her gender, had as much to do with Chaplin's dissatisfaction with her work as Normand's professional competency. Though the pair remained friendly, even sharing directorial responsibilities on a number of early films, Chaplin clearly felt the need to guide his own productions.

The Keystone "atmosphere," so foreign to him when he arrived, had begun to stir creative curiosity. [Sennett's] remark that first day at the studio: "We have no scenario— we get an idea then follow the natural sequence of events …' had stimulated my imagination…. It was this charming alfresco spirit that was a delight — a challenge to one's creativeness. It was so free and easy — no literature, no writers — we just had a notion around which we built gags, then made up the story as we went along."[23] The comedian was insistent, and after some hesitation, Sennett relented and let his star direct. Chaplin would later recount, however, that he had to put up $1500 of his own money to guard against the film's failure.[24]

But like the comedian's account of the Tramp's first appearance, this too is probably the stuff of legend rather than fact. Allowing Chaplin to direct was likely more than simply appeasing a temperamental actor, since Sennett most likely had the business impacts of such a decision to weigh as well. As their popularity was growing rapidly among theater patrons and exhibitors, Kessel and Baumann were clamoring for more Chaplin releases. After only 17 shorts with Keystone, the Tramp's films were being billed exclusively as Charlie Chaplin pictures — notoriety that took the comedian years to achieve on the stage. If Sennett did ask for an up-front payment in order for Chaplin to direct, it was probably more a symbolic demand for Sennett to maintain the upper hand over his opinionated young talent.

Though both Sennett and the comedian recall the Keystone short *Caught in the Rain* (released May 4, 1914) as Chaplin's directoral debut, versions of this event, too, have not corresponded with recent scholarship. Sifting though Chaplin's personal papers, David Robinson discovered a letter dated August 9, 1914, to Sydney in which Chaplin lists the films he had appeared in to date. There, Chaplin cites *Twenty Minutes of Love*, released some two weeks before *Caught in the Rain*, on April 20, as his first directoral effort.[25]

Neither *Twenty Minutes of Love* nor *Caught in the Rain* displays characteristics that would distinguish them from the typical Keystone product. In *Rain*, taking place in a hotel (the same setting as *Mabel's Strange Predicament*), Charlie is inadvertently caught in a woman's bedroom by a jealous husband who's not open to excuses, which leads to predictable mayhem. Hotel comedies, together with park comedies like *Twenty Minutes of Love*, were standard fare for the Keystone folks. Nonetheless, these tried-and-true settings provided a firm comedic base for Chaplin's initial forays into acting/directing.

Public reaction to Chaplin's initial directoral efforts proved positive. The comedian's increasing popularity started the ball rolling, and when his first few films as actor/director continued to draw large audiences, Keystone saw no reason to tamper with success. Following the release of *Caught in the Rain*, Chaplin only collaborated as a director/scenarist on two more Keystone films, aside from making a guest appearance as a boxing referee in the Fatty Arbuckle film *The Knockout*, released on June 11, 1914, and playing in Sennett's six-reel slapstick feature *Tillie's Punctured Romance*, released on November 14.

In all, Chaplin's work at Keystone, with release dates spanning from early February to early December of 1914, saw the production of 35 individual motion pictures, almost one-half of the 81 films Chaplin would make during his lifetime. Many were very near the sort of rough-and-tumble shorts that Chaplin initially disliked, based on his skepticism in the Kessel and Baumann offices. Though his stay at the studio was short, it was instrumental in launching his film career and developing his character of the Tramp. Contrary to Chaplin's assertion of "knowing and feeling" the Little Fellow once he hit upon his famous costume, the comedian had really only laid the foundation for his screen character at Keystone. Often, Charlie, largely remembered for his sentimentality and kindness, was quite a mean and vindictive character in his early shorts, defending himself against the chaotic world depicted in many Keystone films. In terms of historical reference, it is clear that Chaplin the actor was only beginning to learn about the Little Fellow. Keystone's emphasis on action, leaving subtleties behind, coupled with the comedian's efforts to learn the medium of film as an actor and director, did not allow Chaplin to grow much beyond a very basic cinematic caricature.

Over such a short span, Chaplin progressed from a novice film comedian to a cameraman, director, scenarist and editor. These technical skills enhanced the range and effect of his comedic sensibilities, and helped move him toward becoming more singularly responsible for the quality of his work. In building on this basic education, Chaplin would begin to develop his own, less frantic style of slapstick comedy, a move that contributed not only to his popularity but longevity in the film industry. The gems of the Keystone films are few and far between — the Chaplin-directed *Dough and Dynamite* (October 26, 1914) is often praised as the comedian's first real classic — but it cannot be overstated how important this tutorial period was in helping establish and maintain his long career in motion pictures.

IV. ESSANAY AND MUTUAL

At the close of the comedian's first contract, Chaplin shocked Sennett by asking for $1000 per week (more than Sennett himself made at the time) to renew his contact with Keystone. When the company refused the offer, Chaplin began to consider moving elsewhere. Sydney, who had left the Karno Company late in 1914 to join his brother at Keystone, found his astute business sense put to work shopping his brother's talents about the motion picture industry. With the comedian's popularity amongst both exhibitors and the public, there was much interest, but few studios were either willing or able to meet Chaplin's rumored (and inflated) salary demands.

Finally, the Essanay Film Manufacturing Company, a Chicago-based outfit that produced the popular Bronco Billy Anderson westerns, came forward with a 12-picture deal. Anderson, whose real name was Max Aronson, had been a part of the industry since the nickelodeon days; one of his earliest roles was in Edwin S. Porter's landmark of early cinema *The Great Train Robbery* (1903). Now a star in his own right, he was the co-owner of Essanay with George K. Spoor — a hybrid of their last names forming the title, S. & A.

Jessie Robbins, negotiating the contract on behalf of Anderson, made an offer of $1250 per week to the comedian. Unfortunately, he was under the mistaken impression that Chaplin had also demanded a signing bonus in his prior negotiations with Keystone; when Robbins also offered $10,000 on the signing of an Essanay contract, no one from the Chaplin camp, naturally, spoke against it. Additionally, Robbins and Anderson made the offer without consulting Spoor, who, in an effort to delay paying Chaplin's bonus, took a leave of absence when Essanay's new comedian arrived at the Chicago studio.

Though Chaplin shot his first Essanay production, appropriately titled *His New Job* (released February 1, 1915), in Chicago, he was uncomfortable in the confines of the company's downtown studio. Essanay was a true factory environment — not only did the company utilize almost every cost-cutting measure available in producing films, but it even had a scenario department that handed out rudimentary scripts to each of its film companies. The Chicago studios seemed to Chaplin less of a creative climate than a cinematic assembly line.

Accordingly, the comedian moved west once again, and for his next five Essanay releases, he was based out of Essanay's studio in Niles, California, where Bronco Billy filmed most of his productions. There too, he was unhappy with his surroundings. One humorous story involves his letdown upon moving into Anderson's studio bungalow, a shanty that would have proved a fitting abode for the Little Fellow, but hardly so for film stars of Anderson's or Chaplin's caliber.*

---

*Ironically, Chaplin's own dressing room in later years would prove disappointing to others. (See Maurice Bessy; Charlie Chaplin; page 414; Alistair Cooke; Six Men; page 22.) (continued on next page)

After the five films at the Niles Studios, Chaplin did one in the Bradbury Mansion Studio in Los Angeles, and his final five films for Essanay at the Majestic Studios.

As with Keystone, Chaplin would stay with Essanay for only one year, 1915. The year, however, was as crucial to his artistic and technical development as his stint under Sennett, for several reasons. First, Chaplin utilized his departure from the formulaic Keystone environment to further develop the character of Charlie. Sentiment, or pathos, was slowly becoming a recognizable feature in Chaplin's comedy repertoire, especially in releases such as *The Tramp* (April 11) and *The Bank* (August 9). Both films found Chaplin moving away from the chaotic slapstick of Keystone. "In the Keystone days the Tramp had been freer and less confined to plot," Chaplin would recall. "His brain was seldom active then — only his instincts, which were concerned with the basic essentials: food, warmth and shelter. But with each succeeding comedy the Tramp was growing more complex. Sentiment was beginning to percolate through the character. This became a problem because he was bound by the limits of slapstick."[26]

With *The Bank* in particular, Chaplin borrowed from elements from the Karno production of *Jimmy the Fearless*. The Tramp here, as the janitor in a bank, bravely rescues his love interest, a secretary, from a band of bank robbers, only to awaken to find his heroic deeds a dream and the girl in the arms of a co-worker. *The Bank* was not the only Karno-inspired production, either. Chaplin also revived and elaborated the *Mumming Birds* sketch, his version released as *A Night at the Show* on November 20. The comedian played dual roles in the film version, one as the inebriate, as he had in his Karno days, and one as a boisterous lout in the gallery of the theater.

Two particular factors that aided Chaplin's development of the Tramp were the expanded format of his films (now almost always all two-reelers) and the greater amount of production time he utilized. At Keystone, most films were only one reel in length, which almost necessitated quick narrative action (hence the chases and/or fights) and lacked substantial character development. With Essanay, Chaplin not only had the luxury of making pictures nearly twice as long, but took upwards of several weeks to deliver them. At Keystone a brand new Chaplin comedy had been released roughly every ten days, but at Essanay the comedian had a new picture in theaters approximately every month. The quality of Chaplin's Essanay pictures benefited greatly from the additional time spent on each production, especially when compared to the pictures the comedian was making only a year before.

As well as creating more polished films, the year with Essanay also helped

---

(continued) *"'If I had a room like that,' Charles Chaplin, Jr., recalled his father saying of Douglas Fairbanks' opulent dressing room, 'I couldn't possibly portray the Little Tramp. I need a place that looks like him.'" (Charles Chaplin, Jr.; My Father, Charlie Chaplin; page 30.)*

Chaplin establish a core group of comedic actors who would become integral parts of his creative team. Most notably, Chaplin was introduced to Edna Purviance, a young woman from Lovelock, Nevada, working as a secretary in San Francisco, who became his leading lady. Though she had no specific acting abilities, Chaplin nonetheless found Edna both attractive and an attentive pupil for his often exacting directoral methods. She would play opposite Chaplin regularly for the next eight years. Her first appearance with Chaplin was in *A Night Out*, the comedian's second Essanay production and first at the Niles Studio.

Edna Purviance's talent for acting was dubious at best, though most of Chaplin's supporting characters in his two-reelers at this point relied on established comic stereotypes. Edna may not have been a seasoned performer, but Chaplin was taken with her charm and sense of humor, and she did prove easy to work with. Eventually, as she and Chaplin began to develop their own romantic relationship offscreen, the comedian's portrayal of romance within his films began to change as well. More consistent with the popular memory of Charlie, the Tramp slowly began to idealize love, almost engaging in a form of feminine worship, the inklings of which were especially apparent in films such as *The Bank*, where the Tramp longs for Edna's character from afar.

Leo White, Bud Jamison, Billy Armstrong, Paddy McGuire, Wesley Ruggles and John Rand, among others, provided a seasoned group of actors with whom to work during this period. All had comedic experience from stage and/ or screen, and their skill and versatility (many of Chaplin's supporting cast played multiple roles in a given production) also helped solidify the quality of his film output.

Essanay offered Chaplin another 12-picture deal for $350,000 toward the end of 1915, but balked at his demand for a signing bonus of $150,000. Thus, Sydney once again found himself negotiating with other film companies on behalf of his brother. Interest in the industry's hottest property was high, and Sydney found a willing taker with the Mutual Film Corporation — a package deal worth $670,000 for 12 films, and which included yet another signing bonus.

Taken together, the Mutual films would find Chaplin's early work at its peak, both in terms of narrative construction and the evolution of Charlie as a character. Chaplin's themes at Mutual began to take on a more situation-type comedy — the Tramp as a fireman or policeman, for instance — that broadened the notion that Charlie was an "everyman," as he found himself placed in countless different situations. He also produced at least three outright masterpieces during this period: *Easy Street* (January, 1917), *The Cure* (April, 1917) and *The Immigrant* (June, 1917), in addition to a host of other finely-executed screen comedies.

Continuing to enhance his creative team, Chaplin engaged cameraman Rollie Totheroh, who would remain in the comedian's service into the 1950s. Totheroh and Chaplin first met at Essanay's Niles Studio, where Totheroh had been filming a number of Bronco Billy's pictures. Though they never worked together at Essanay, Totheroh did follow the comedian to Mutual, where their long collaboration began.

Chaplin's company would be further augmented with other stock characters, most notably Karno veteran Albert Austin, Henry Bergman and Charlie's gigantic menace, Eric Campbell. The additions gave Chaplin a very capable and enthusiastic set of advisors (Austin and Bergman, in particular) with whom to work out his comic bits. As Chaplin continued to shoot most of his films more or less off the cuff (in 1967 he described the method as "plac[ing] yourself in a labyrinth and ... find[ing] your way out"[27]), he often floated potential ideas with his colleagues about possible gags or story directions. A strong-willed performer, as evidenced by his early troubles at Keystone, Chaplin often disregarded criticism to his ideas, utilizing men such as Bergman and Austin as sounding boards rather than equal contributors. During productions, the comedian maintained strong control over his project. The most successful Chaplin advisors, it seems, particularly in terms of longevity, were those who were much more patient and much less opinionated than their boss.

Chaplin's increasing production lengths were more apparent at Mutual than they had been at Essanay. This, again, is a contributing factor to the enhanced quality of the comedian's Mutual pictures. However, instead of meeting his contract deadline within a year, as had been the anticipation of both Chaplin and Mutual, the comedian had to extend his stay an extra four months in order to finish all 12 releases.

But despite the slowing output by the comedian, Chaplin's popularity continued to grow exponentially with every Essanay and Mutual release. In 1915, writer Charles McGuirk dubbed the craze a national epidemic of "Chaplinitis."[28] The comedian had arrived at Keystone at the beginning of the Hollywood star system, and quickly became one of the industry's most recognizable talents. Earlier, the names of principal actors and directors were not given, and therefore were unknown to audiences; Florence Lawrence, for instance, was simply known as "the Biograph Girl" during her days under the direction of D.W. Griffith. Chaplin emerged at a time when the movies were broadening their appeal demographically, and many studios were beginning to recognize the value of exploiting the images of their popular actors and actresses.

Aiding Chaplin's professional standing at this time was an increase of studio public relations, an outgrowth of the budding star system, particularly while he was with Essanay. Look-alike contests, comic strips, dolls and even songs inundated an eager public. At one point the Chaplin brothers, concerned that many products were capitalizing on the Charlie likeness without the proper rights, found they could do little in securing the comedian's fair share of the merchandising profits. So prolific was the profiteering that the cost of tracking down most would not have been cost-efficient.[29] Denis Gifford and Mike Higgs' book *The Comic Art of Charlie Chaplin* provides a glimpse as to the amount of money that was made by capitalizing on the Charlie image at the

Chaplin signing his Mutual contract, February 1916. Sydney Chaplin (center) looks on, Mutual President John Frueler at left.

time. The book is crammed full of memorabilia, ranging from comic books to dolls to musical sheets, all taking advantage of Chaplin's screen persona. A good portion of these items were no doubt using the Tramp image illegally.

Even from within the film industry itself, capitalizing on Charlie's persona was commonplace. As Harold Lloyd indicated, many screen comedians found it difficult to establish unique characters because of Charlie's wide appeal with audiences. Other, less scrupulous performers didn't adopt a different character at all. There were numerous imitators; one was Billie Ritchie, a former colleague of Chaplin's at Karno who insisted that he in fact originated the Tramp character. Ritchie produced a number of one- and two-reel films that attempted to cash in on the comedian's popularity, all fashioned in the Chaplin vein.

Other industry schemes occurred as well. Some clever distributors found they could retitle old Chaplin films, advertise them as new Chaplin releases, and dupe motion picture audiences into paying first-run theater prices for a previously-released film. Following Chaplin's move to Mutual, even Essanay, in a move that typified their emphasis on maximizing profits, assembled a number of outtakes from Chaplin's films, padded them with additional shots, and released them as new pictures. *Charlie Chaplin's Burlesque on Carmen*, a two-reeler when it was released in December, 1915, suddenly became a four-reel feature when Essanay re-released it in 1916. Similarly, *Life*, an Essanay comedy that Chaplin abandoned in 1915, became the two-reeler *Triple Trouble* when recut with material from other films and released in 1918. Though Chaplin instituted legal proceedings against Essanay with respect to the *Carmen* re-release, he was not successful in stopping its exhibition.[30]

This period also saw the first "official" biography on the comedian: *Charlie Chaplin's Own Story*, by San Francisco journalist Rose Wilder Lane, which appeared in 1916. Lane had interviewed Chaplin for her publication *The Bulletin*, and after padding the material with some rather creative accounts of the comedian's early life, the property was snapped up by an entrepreneur and published by the Bobbs Merrill Company in September. The comedian, through his lawyers, halted mass publication of the book. Scattered copies of the original still exist, and the manuscript was reprinted in 1985.

Accordingly, the comedian himself was clearly attuned to his own bankability as his Mutual contract drew to a close. With all this popular attention, Chaplin recognized the opportunity to be compensated even more for his worth, and, more importantly, to become decidedly more independent as a producer of motion pictures. As the owner of his own studio, Chaplin felt he could work uninterrupted on his film projects, relatively (save for financially) free of outside control. Working in familiar surroundings, and accompanied by an entourage of skilled personnel catering to the comedian's needs, the quality of his pictures could only improve.

Unfortunately for Mutual, Chaplin was no longer willing to consider another contract with the company. Though they offered $1 million for Chaplin's next eight motion picture releases (a salary that would have made Chaplin Hollywood's first million dollar star), the contract failed to offer the independence he sought. The comedian again began to look toward other companies.

V. FIRST NATIONAL

At the end of 1917 I joined First National, for whom I made eight films during the next five years. It was not a happy time: the company was inconsiderate, unsympathetic and short-sighted.[31]

— Charles Chaplin

As Chaplin recalled in his memoirs, the Tramp had been slowly developing away from the chaotic slapstick of Keystone during the Essanay and Mutual periods, and pathos began to play a more prominent role in his characterization of the Little Fellow. To this end, consistent with his desire to expand the role of the Tramp, Chaplin was also becoming interested in expanding his narratives beyond the two-reel format, elaborating his stories toward possible feature length, which was then becoming an industry trend. This of course would require more elaborate sets, and would increase the cost of productions and slow his output even more than it had before. So when the recently-established First National Corporation stepped forward with a generous eight-picture, $1.2 million offer, Chaplin seemed to have found the organization in which to achieve his professional goals.

First National was set up by a conglomeration of motion picture exhibitors and was designed to compete with the increasing power asserted by the major studios. By attempting to attract the biggest names in show business, the organization sought to have exclusive access to the industry's brightest talent. Nabbing the top comedian in motion pictures only two months after being established was certainly a major coup.

Under the First National setup, Chaplin would receive $125,000 for each two-reeler, from which he was to draw his salary and pay for the picture's production costs. An additional sum of $15,000 was to be given for each reel over two, with the company and the comedian splitting the profits. More important than the monetary agreements, however, the move to First National guaranteed Chaplin the opportunity to construct a visual symbol of his popularity and independence in the film industry — his own studio.

A site was selected, well out of the traditional studio section of Hollywood, on a five-acre plot on the corner of Sunset and La Brea. The outside of the buildings took the form of quaint English cottages, most of which served as offices and dressing rooms for the studio. Designed to placate the concerns of local residents, the architecture also may have paid homage to the star's humble roots as well. Alf Reeves, Chaplin's tour manager during his days in the American arm of the Karno troupe, joined the studio shortly after its opening. By 1920, he would become studio manager, a position he held for the next quarter-century.

In commemoration of the new studio, a short picture entitled *How to Make Movies* was shot. It offered a tongue-in-cheek glimpse of studio life with Chaplin, and was undertaken primarily as a record for posterity and never released to the general public.*

Chaplin's tenure at First National would be his longest at a studio during his early career, lasting from 1918 to 1923, though his total output in that time would be only eight films. As during his days with Mutual, Chaplin again relied primarily on situations to guide the Tramp's comedy. He was also able to move beyond the two-reel format; his first picture, *A Dog's Life* (January, 1918), ran

---

*Parts of How to Make Movies *can be viewed in the introduction to Chaplin's 1959 compilation film* The Chaplin Revue, *as well as in Kevin Brownlow and David Gill's documentary* Unknown Chaplin, *the latter containing several outtakes from Chaplin films that had never seen the light of day. Snippets from* How to Make Movies *include stop-action footage of the studio construction and a whimsical look at Chaplin directing his crew in the art of assaulting stock character Loyal Underwood.*

roughly four reels — his longest film to date (barring *Tillie's Punctured Romance* at Keystone), yet not quite feature-length.

He followed this with the first comedy dealing directly with the theme of war, *Shoulder Arms* (October, 1918). Though the film appeared very near the end of World War I, the topic was nonetheless daring at the time. Many felt that the hostilities in Europe were too horrible and gruesome to make light of, but *Shoulder Arms* shows Chaplin's skillful handling of the topic. In the film, Charlie is going to serve his country, if his awkwardness can find a place in the Army's regimentation. Despite this problem, the Tramp is an inadvertent dynamo on the battlefield, capturing an entire trench of German soldiers. In explaining how it was done single-handedly, he simply shrugs and confesses that he surrounded them. Later, Charlie rescues a French girl (Edna Purviance) and captures the Kaiser (Sydney Chaplin), delivering him to the U.S. command. But alas, as in *Jimmy the Fearless* and *The Bank*, the hapless Charlie awakens from a dream — in the same boot camp where the story began.

One interesting aspect of *Shoulder Arms* is its avoidance of anti-German propaganda. Instead of exploiting the enemy soldiers as vicious cutthroats, Charlie instead treats his captured prisoners with gentlemanly respect, even offering them cigarettes. Only the feisty little German officer (Loyal Underwood), who shows his indignation by throwing a child-like tantrum upon capture, is dealt with differently. Charlie takes the little man over his knee and proceeds to give him a spanking, much to the delight of the German soldiers, who appreciate seeing authority treated with disrespect. War films were not new to this era, but *Shoulder Arms* stays away from stirring up anti-German sentiment as did D.W. Griffith's *Hearts of the World* (1918) and many other pictures released during World War I.

Though released quite late in the battle, the film was viewed by some as a fine contribution by the comedian to the national war effort. In addition, Chaplin joined Douglas Fairbanks and Mary Pickford to help promote the national sale of Liberty Bonds for a brief period, and produced a split-reel promotional film entitled *The Bond*, distributed free of charge to theater exhibitors throughout the United States. *The Bond* was also fashioned with the Liberty Loan Drive in mind.

On a personal note, the First National period saw Chaplin's first marriage, on October 23, 1918, to 16-year-old Mildred Harris. (Chaplin's previous romantic relationship with Edna Purviance never worked out, though they were certainly on friendly terms and continued to work together.) Miss Harris was an up-and-coming starlet who had worked in pictures since the age of ten. Chaplin found her youthful looks attractive, though he was never particularly taken with the girl intellectually. Rather, he was forced into the marriage when Mildred suspected that she was pregnant, though this ultimately was not the case.

It was a mismatch from the beginning, and Chaplin's unhappiness surfaced almost immediately. Mildred wanted her new husband to take more of an interest in her career, but with Chaplin's singular devotion to his own films, this was simply not possible. At times when his home life was unhappy, the studio became Chaplin's hideaway. Relations eventually became so frosty in the Chaplin household that even his work became negatively affected. *Sunnyside* (June, 1919), Chaplin's follow-up to the success of *Shoulder Arms*, has been generally considered, even by Chaplin himself, to be one of his weakest films of the period. Creatively and emotionally, the comedian was drained; Chaplin described the ordeal of creating the film as tantamount to pulling teeth.[32]

Mildred became pregnant in actuality during the course of their short marriage, though the malformed boy born to them on July 7, 1919, had little chance of surviving. The child lived barely three days; Norman Spencer Chaplin was buried four days following his birth. His headstone read "The Little Mouse," as was Mildred's wish. Chaplin wept at the death of his first-born, but it effectively severed any remaining bond between the couple. "Although I had grown fond of Mildred," he would recall, "we were irreconcilably mismated. Her character was not mean, but exasperatingly feline. I could never reach her mind.... After we had been married a year, a child was born but lived only three days. This began the withering of our marriage. Although we lived in the same house, we seldom saw each other, for she was as much occupied at her studio as I was at mine."[33]

In the midst of his failing marriage, however, Chaplin would embark on the project that would prove his greatest triumph of the First National period. *The Kid*, begun under the working title *The Waif*, would become one of the biggest films of the silent period, and would mark Chaplin's fullest and most effective use of pathos to date. It was an ambitious undertaking — his longest in production and in running time, and the most expensive project thus far in his career. His selection of the talented young Jackie Coogan to play the title role catapulted the boy to international stardom.

Though *The Kid* proved to be a phenomenal smash hit when it was released, Chaplin suffered under horrible working conditions while making it. Created without the benefit of a shooting script, the film was complex and Chaplin was filled with persistent self-doubts, both about the creative decisions he was making and the picture's chance for success. To make matters worse, First National executives became concerned when the project, burgeoning to a full six reels, continued to drag on during production. Later, during the editing stage, Mildred attempted to attach the film in her divorce suit. The First National people were handled by extending them an open invitation to the Chaplin Studios one afternoon to witness some of the shooting. Mildred's unsuccessful move necessitated that Chaplin steal away in the night with the uncut film to Salt Lake City, and later to the East Coast, where he and a few assistants were able to assemble a rough version of the picture while hidden away in hotel rooms. Despite the comedian's fears, *The Kid* was a tremendous hit upon its release.

While preparations to release *The Kid* were underway, Chaplin — anxious to complete his stint with First National — undertook a pair of rather uneventful two-reelers, *The Idle Class* (September, 1921) and *Pay Day* (April, 1922). Both show a progressing technical polish in his productions, but considering the films that preceded and followed them, were not the most challenging pictures Chaplin had attempted. The comedian was beginning to sour on the First National organization as a whole. Among a host of squabbles, the company had sought to consider *The Kid* contractually as three two-reel films, a move that would have completed Chaplin's stint with the company sooner but would have been financially detrimental to the comedian, who had invested some $500,000 in the film. Chaplin came out on top during negotiations concerning *The Kid*, though doing so only lengthened his stay with a company with which he was growing increasingly dissatisfied.

Following completion of shooting on *The Idle Class* and of initial production on *Pay Day*, Chaplin abruptly halted shooting and decided to accompany *The Kid* on its European premieres. After nearly five years of non-stop work, this was the comedian's first real vacation following his motion picture fame, a homecoming that meant increased attention and publicity for his cherished film. The whirlwind tour lasted almost six weeks, during which he was able to visit much of war-torn Europe, all the while hounded by thousands of enthusiastic fans and eager members of the press. *The Kid* proved as successful in Europe as it had in the United States. Later he would record his thoughts about the tour in the book *My Wonderful Visit* (1922) — or, as it was published in America, *My Trip Abroad*.

The comedian's final release at First National, *The Pilgrim* (February, 1923), was a four-reeler; Chaplin portrayed a prisoner who assumes the identity of a minister while making his escape. Ironically, the implication of Chaplin's depiction of the Tramp in the film, as an escaped convict, has not been lost among several commentators on Chaplin's work. Given his eagerness to part ways with his employer, Chaplin probably felt as if he were escaping from the First National prison. The role also allowed Chaplin to deliver a pantomimed sermon of the David and Goliath story, which the comedian was known to have performed previously in games of charades.

It is interesting to note that the finale for *The Pilgrim* was one that would have particular significance in Chaplin's later life, when the comedian fell out of favor with many people, particularly in the United States. In the final reel, Charlie, having been discovered by the town sheriff, is taken to the U.S./Mexican border. As a humanitarian gesture to reward Charlie's previous good deeds, the sheriff asks Charlie to cross into Mexico and pick him some flowers, hoping the Little Fellow will recognize that he is free to go. However, Charlie, oblivious to the sheriff's intentions, promptly returns to the U.S. side with the requested flowers. Finally, the Tramp is made to realize that he is not wanted in the U.S. But before he can enjoy his freedom, some bandits appear on the

Mexican side, yelling, shooting guns and creating chaos, making Mexico an equally perilous spot for the Little Fellow to stay. As the camera irises out, Charlie hustles off into the distance, one foot on American soil, one on Mexican soil, as neither country can provide a safe haven for the Tramp.

Also of note is the discovery of a few rudimentary working notes and gag sequences for the production. Though this may have been Chaplin's practice for some time, *The Pilgrim* is the first of Chaplin's pictures to have such documentation survive the years.[34] As his productions moved toward feature-length, the comedian seemed to be approaching his films with more than just a single idea or situation in which to place the Tramp. He didn't write formal scripts until the late 1930s, but such a method of note-taking, which he used to varying degrees for the remainder of his career, is indicative of the growing complexities of both the film industry and the nature of Chaplin's comedy.

Chaplin's five-year stint with First National was the longest with a studio thus far in his film career, yet the period saw relatively few releases. Again, Chaplin was slowing his output, though unlike his time with Mutual, where the comedian made consistently excellent two-reel comedies, many of the First National films fail to display the same polish. With pictures such as *Sunnyside, A Day's Pleasure, The Idle Class* and *Pay Day*, half of the comedian's eight First National releases, Chaplin almost seemed in a creative rut. All are relatively uneventful, particularly in terms of creativity — it's as if the comedian, to borrow D.W. Griffith's characterization of some of his own less-inspired pictures, was simply "grinding out sausages." Chaplin's unhappiness with the First National organization, coupled with the personal difficulties during his failed first marriage, were likely contributors to his creative malaise.

But these lifeless qualities weren't apparent in the comedian's other four First National releases. In all four, Chaplin was expanding the length of his pictures — initially to three reels (*A Dog's Life, Shoulder Arms*), then moving to his first full-fledged feature (*The Kid*), and finally rounding out his contract with a four-reeler (*The Pilgrim*). For these projects, the comedian was considerably more challenged, and the inventiveness and spontaneity of each is apparent onscreen. Like Chaplin's shift away from the chaotic slapstick of Keystone, gradually portraying the Tramp as a sympathetic figure whose adventures combined both comedy and pathos, the effort to expand the length of his pictures not only capitalized on an evolving industry trend toward feature filmmaking, but afforded an even more intricate background in which to develop his stories. The shift would slow his output considerably, but his films would also show an increasing sophistication in terms of technical detail and narrative complexity, both of which — after such films proved successful with the public — solidified his status as a comedic genius. Some comedians of the era didn't yet have the range necessary to go beyond the two reel length — even Buster Keaton had a false start with his seven-reeler *The Saphead* (1920), after which he returned to shorts for three years honing his talents. Chaplin had the popularity and certainly the resources (thanks to the construction of the Chaplin Studios) to move in this direction, and was determined to take his work to the next logical level.

Although pictures such as *The Kid* and *The Pilgrim* stood out as exceptional pieces of work, at the close of the First National period it was clear that Chaplin's foremost concern was to again change companies. This time, however, his choice of studios would help him take that final step toward becoming a truly independent feature filmmaker; it would be a new studio that Chaplin had an instrumental part in forming — United Artists.

VI. UNITED ARTISTS

The story of Chaplin's involvement with United Artists actually predates his work on *The Kid*. In January of 1919, rumors were rampant throughout Hollywood that Paramount boss Adolph Zukor was engineering a merger with the First National Exhibitors Circuit. The increasing salary demands of their big name performers (to which Chaplin contributed heavily) were a cause of tremendous studio concern, and Zukor was said to be contemplating a consolidation of studios and exhibitors — control designed to minimize the clout of the individual film star. Tipped off to such a prospect, some of the heavyweights of the Hollywood community — Mary Pickford, Douglas Fairbanks, William S. Hart, D.W. Griffith and Chaplin — hastily arranged a dinner in the Alexandria Hotel in Los Angeles to kick the industry rumor mill into high gear. This public outing, Chaplin later contended, was designed only to give the impression that the stars were contemplating forming their own distribution network, and to scare off the potential consolidation between Paramount and First National. Without stars, there would be little profit, they reasoned, and hence all five looked to bluff their way into killing a possible Zukor/First National deal.

However, word eventually got out about the meeting, and when several studio heads expressed an interest in the project (including, some said, Zukor himself), only then, according to Chaplin, did the group begin to seriously consider forming their own studio. As a result, in February of 1919 United Artists was officially born, with the foursome of Pickford, Fairbanks, Griffith and Chaplin signed on. (Hart had withdrawn, opting to stay with his studio.) "The lunatics have taken over the asylum," went one famous commentary on the new organization.

United Artists looked to offer its filmmakers a higher degree of control over the production, distribution and exhibition of their pictures. For Chaplin, who viewed United Artists primarily as a distribution entity, it offered a much more amenable situation than did his contract with First National, or that of any other studio. He would be able to take as much time as he needed to complete a picture, and would be free of completing a predetermined number of films during a contractual period. With the business aspects of filmmaking generally in place, Chaplin may have been thinking, he could then fully devote his time to the creative aspects of his work.

After its incorporation in 1919, however, it had been the work of Fairbanks and Pickford that supported United Artists, which consistently failed to show a profit. Griffith did not come over to the new organization right away, and Chaplin was bound to complete his contract with First National.* Though Doug and Mary's films were proving profitable, they alone could not support United Artists fiscally. The company began losing money, and, accordingly, they placed a lot of pressure upon Chaplin, one of the industry's biggest box office draws, to bring his first UA picture to the screen.

Following *The Pilgrim*, Chaplin was freed from his obligations with First National. But instead of beginning with a comedy featuring the Tramp, he chose instead to pursue an interest in straight drama. *A Woman of Paris* (1923) exercised the comedian's growing desire to establish his talents outside of his comic persona, as well as help provide Edna Purviance with the opportunity to launch her career as a dramatic leading lady. Chaplin concentrated primarily on conceiving the scenario and directing, but he also played a small uncredited role as a porter in a train station, with only a few seconds of screen time.

The story follows Marie (Edna), a starry-eyed country girl in France, as she ascends and descends the Parisian social ladder, at her height becoming the mistress of the wealthy socialite Pierre Revel (Adolphe Menjou). Her character allegedly had its origins in Peggy Hopkins Joyce, an aspiring European actress in the early 1920s who became known during her stay in the United States more for the series of wealthy men she married and divorced than for her performing abilities. She and Chaplin had been briefly linked following Chaplin's divorce from Mildred Harris.

Edna did her best to establish her dramatic talents throughout the film, though ironically it would be Menjou's career that would be launched by the picture. As a producer, Chaplin would arrange only one more film starring Edna, Josef von Sternberg's abandoned project *Sea Gulls* (1926).† Upon the

---

*Unlike the other stars that formed United Artists, Griffith was not in a position to finance the production of his own pictures at the time, and continued to secure production money through contracts with other companies. While he continued to achieve high artistic quality with some of his longer films, as with Broken Blossoms (1919), and scored the second-highest grossing film of his career with Way Down East (1920), Griffith was often forced to make relatively modest pictures between his more ambitious outings to achieve profitability. While some of this shorter work during the late 1910s, such as True Heart Susie (1919), were indeed impressive, many of his shorter works in the early 1920s were half-baked pot-boilers that did little to enhance his reputation as a genius in the motion picture industry or further his career.

†No copy of the film exists today, and accounts vary on the quality of the picture. Chaplin was apparently so disappointed with the film that he would not allow it to be released theatrically and stored it away in his vaults for a number of years. In 1933, as federal tax authorities and the Chaplin Studios

completion of *A Woman of Paris*, Edna and Chaplin would part after over eight years of working together. Though she would never again work in a Chaplin film, he always retained a sense of concern for her well-being, and the comedian kept Edna on the studio payroll until the 1950s.

Though *A Woman of Paris* received a warm reception by critics and other filmmakers (particularly Ernst Lubitsch), many of whom hailed its subtle and innovative use of suggestion, the picture was very unlike anything Chaplin had released before, and audiences did not embrace it. At this point in Chaplin's career, the public was not willing to accept Chaplin without Charlie. Though the comedian would cherish the film as one of his best ("The film was a great success with discriminating audiences," he would protectively assert in his memoirs[35]), in terms of public reaction *A Woman of Paris* would be one of Chaplin's most disappointing feature films.

But Chaplin returned to the character of the Little Fellow for his next United Artists release. *The Gold Rush* (1925) is the motion picture Chaplin is most remembered for, a film which wins consistent recognition as one of Chaplin's greatest and ranks as one of the best of the silent era.

Inspired by slides of miners traversing Chilkoot Pass as well as a macabre interest in the Donner Party incident, Chaplin again placed the Little Fellow in an unfamiliar environment, this time the frozen Klondike. Like *The Kid* before it, Chaplin's blend of comedy and pathos is woven intricately. Charlie's romantic interest, played by the lovely Georgia Hale, stirs the Tramp's emotions, and we feel for him as he is stood up for a hard-earned New Year's Eve dinner. The film also contains two classic screen moments: Charlie's boiled shoe dinner and, in a dream sequence, his dance of the dinner rolls. Chaplin's comedy was sharp, his use of pathos and romance delicately constructed, and the nuances of his pantomime brilliantly conceived. In a period when Chaplin had still not yet utilized a full shooting script, the artistic achievement of *The Gold Rush* was quite impressive. And, fortunately for the struggling United Artists, it was a financial blockbuster as well.

During the filming of *The Gold Rush*, Chaplin married for a second time, under circumstances similar to the first. Since his divorce from Mildred Harris, he had been seen in the company of numerous young Hollywood starlets, and was the subject of much gossip concerning possible nuptials. Chaplin was in fact engaged for a short period in 1923, during the filming of *A Woman of Paris*, to actress Pola Negri, who had recently arrived in Hollywood from her native Germany. They had met earlier, during the comedian's European tour

---

(continued) *tangled over the extent of the comedian's holdings, an agreement was reached such that the film had to be destroyed for Chaplin to claim it as a total business loss. (David Robinson;* Chaplin: His Life and Art; *page 451.) Von Sternberg was understandably angry with Chaplin's decision to scrap* Sea Gulls, *though his frustration would not linger. By the time he penned his memoirs, von Sternberg had only the highest praise for the comedian, and considered his work on* Sea Gulls *to be beneficial if only for the experience. (Josef von Sternberg;* Fun in a Chinese Laundry; *page 33.)*

in 1921. It was a tempestuous relationship, however, and lasted only five months. During the entire ordeal, Chaplin appeared uncharacteristically quiet and sheepish alongside the publicity-hungry Negri, who was the subject of a considerable amount of studio-generated hype at Paramount.

When the comedian married a second time, it was to 16-year-old actress Lillita McMurray, whom Chaplin had given the stage name Lita Grey. Previously, she had been engaged by the Chaplin Studios as an extra; ironically, she played an "angelic vamp" who tempts Charlie in The Kid, as well as a bit role, along with her mother, in The Idle Class, as one of Edna Purviance's valets. She was the comedian's initial choice to play the dance hall girl in The Gold Rush, which ultimately went to Georgia Hale.

As before, his bride was quite young, though when Lita's contract signing for The Gold Rush was announced to the press, Chaplin's publicists made sure she had aged an additional three years. And, as had been the case with Mildred, a pregnancy scare — this one real — prompted the nuptials. On the pretense of filming sea scenes for The Gold Rush, even bringing with him his film crew to complete the charade, Chaplin evaded the Hollywood press by marrying Lita in Guaymas, Mexico, on November 25, 1924.*

Lita gave birth to Charles Chaplin, Jr., on May 5, 1925, though the arrival would not be announced for nearly two months, as the comedian did not wish to add to the scandal of his unusually young bride by proving that it had been a forced marriage. Accordingly, Lita and baby went into hiding, and with the help of a falsified birth certificate, Charles Jr.'s birth was announced on June 28. The pair would have another boy, Sydney, on March 30 of the following year.

As was the case with Chaplin's first marriage, the union would not prove successful. Chaplin was again unhappy with his romantic predicament, and attempted to stay as far away from his Summit Drive, Hollywood mansion as possible, leading to a breakdown in the marriage. While working on his next film, The Circus, released in 1928, Lita filed for divorce, in what would prove to be an extremely hostile (and largely public) affair. Work on that picture would be halted for a full eight months until the dissolution was final. And, adding insult to injury, claims for over $1.1 million in back taxes were also filed by the United States government at approximately the same time. It was a pattern that would repeat itself at virtually every juncture when Chaplin ran into trouble publicly. Chaplin settled the tax matter for $1 million in April of 1927, nearly four months after Lita had filed her divorce affidavit. Two-thirds of the amount was assessed personally against Chaplin, with the remainder against his studio.

---

*The Gold Rush does contain sea scenes at the end of the film, when Chaplin and Georgia Hale are reunited on their way back to the mainland United States. This footage, however, was not shot in Mexico.

D.W. Griffith, Mary Pickford, Chaplin and Douglas Fairbanks at the formation of United Artists, February 1919.

Lita's lurid court document, which found itself circulating as popular underground literature, alleged that Chaplin had been in the company of several women throughout the course of their two-year marriage (an assertion that was likely correct), and that he was also attempting to abandon his children. Further, the document contained detailed information about Chaplin's preferred sexual practices, acts that seemed shockingly lurid when put into print during the late 1920s. The affidavit painted Chaplin as a selfish and uncaring man, and with the sexual revelations, at least, one with an inclination for perversion and abuse. It was clearly an attempt to damage the comedian's reputation as much as possible, not only in an effort to move Chaplin towards a quick settlement but perhaps to tarnish his career in the way comedian Fatty Arbuckle's had been during his murder trials some years earlier.

Lita's lawyers (relatives of hers) played the headlines for sympathy, but with only moderate success. Many people denounced the obvious character assassination being perpetrated on Chaplin; nonetheless, the accusations were devastating to him personally. Rumors of a nervous breakdown by the comedian surfaced, coupled with unconfirmed reports that Chaplin was possibly suicidal.

Chaplin may not have been in such rumored danger, but the ordeal did affect him. Not surprisingly, this marriage and its aftermath are dismissed in a mere two sentences in his autobiography, an omission that, acknowledged Chaplin, he made on account of his two sons. Eventually a final divorce agreement was reached in which Lita would receive $600,000 in addition to a $100,000 trust fund for each of the two boys. At the time, it was the largest dissolution settlement in history.

Further troubles kept Chaplin's mind occupied during this period of his career. First, in late September of 1926, eight months into work on his next project, *The Circus*, a fire at the Chaplin Studios destroyed the set and many pieces of filmmaking equipment. Though the studio would be up and running again by mid–October, it was nonetheless a disheartening blow to the production. David Robinson's Chaplin biography contains a photo of the comedian, dressed as Charlie, surveying the damage, which is perhaps one the saddest-looking pictures of the famed comedian, his round, melancholy eyes seemingly on the verge of tears.[36]

Later, on August 28, 1928, seven months following the release of *The Circus* and during preparations for his first sound era film, Hannah Chaplin passed away in Glendale, California. Her final days were spent in the company of private nurses and assorted friends, in the quaint home her boys had purchased for her after her arrival in America in 1921.

Though Chaplin had the opportunity to be closer to his mother during her final years, Hannah's condition seemed to be a hidden source of anguish for him, and he was constantly bothered by the notion that perhaps he, too, would suffer from some sort of mental imbalance later in life.[37] Though she had been near her boys during the period in which Chaplin created some of his greatest film work, Hannah was never to fully understand the nature of the film industry or the amazing popularity and wealth his success had garnered. One story concerns her visit to the set of *The Gold Rush*, where Chaplin greeted his mother clad in his traditional Tramp costume. Hannah became somewhat upset by his appearance, despite her son's reminders that she had seen some of his films and should be familiar with the character he played. It was no use; "Charlie," she fretted, "I've got to get you a new suit."[38] Like so many of Chaplin's films, the story is both humorous and, paradoxically, tragic as well. Though he and Sydney had made every provision for her comfort, Chaplin could nonetheless become very upset over her varying mental condition, and was filled with grief after she passed away.

The strain of Chaplin's personal difficulties was again evident in *The Circus*, as it had been before with *Sunnyside*. Though it would earn Chaplin an honorary Oscar at the first ceremonies held, in May of 1929, for the "versatility and genius in writing, acting, directing and producing *The Circus*," the film clearly showed the tensions of the preceding months.

In it, Charlie befriends the daughter of a menacing circus ringmaster, and inadvertently finds himself drawn into the circus as a clown. (The girl was played by Merna Kennedy, one of Lita's childhood friends and, according to her, one of Chaplin's partners in infidelity as well.) Charlie eventually loses the girl to Rex (Harry Crocker), a tightrope artist, but valiantly puts his own feelings for the girl aside and helps the young couple wed over the objections of Merna's abusive father.

Though the film seemed to lack some of Chaplin's usual comic spark, it was nonetheless warmly received at the box office, an indication to the comedian, perhaps, that after the scandalous revelations of the Lita Grey divorce suit, he had been vindicated with the public. Interestingly, Chaplin may have anticipated that the damage to his reputation had possibly ruined his career altogether. In the finale of the film, as the circus rolls out of town, the Tramp is left alone in its wake as dust swirls about. At his feet lies a scrap of paper, emblazoned with a star, a torn souvenir from the passing show. Charlie reflects on the paper, as well as on the circus star he briefly was. After a slight moment of contemplation, the Tramp suddenly crumples the paper in his hand, kicking the relic aside. He then walks away into the sunset, his jaunty shuffle indicating that he is happy just being the Little Fellow. The symbolism had obvious parallels to his own personal situation at the time, and is one of the most direct autobiographical elements employed by Chaplin during his silent film career. Stardom, both for the Tramp and for Chaplin (or so he would have us believe), was ultimately not important.

Based on popular reaction to *The Circus*, it may have seemed to the comedian that any damage done to his reputation as a result of the divorce was deflected by his stature as a popular film artist. This no doubt encouraged Chaplin after a long period of self-doubt. The Tramp came roaring back; however, the changing nature of the film industry still conspired to put his future in question. During the production of *The Circus*, sound had come to film. Within a matter of months, this so-called new cinematic technique began to turn all of Hollywood upside down, posing a direct threat to silent screen actors, particularly silent comics, and proving a potentially serious blow to Chaplin's ability to remain a top box-office draw. As Chaplin faced the sound era, he was at a crucial crossroads of his career: The talkie revolution was changing Hollywood dramatically, and despite a dwindling few who felt otherwise, silent cinema, the very medium Chaplin had mastered and helped make popular the world over, was fast disappearing.

VII. CHAPLIN'S DEVELOPMENT AS A FILM ARTIST

Genius has its own rules, and Chaplin's is generally regarded as a manager of the most peculiar kind, his method begins to set at naught all of the methods usually taken for granted.[39]

— Elsie Codd

I was Chaplin's assistant [director, on *A Woman of Paris* and *The Gold Rush*] so I said "camera" and "cut." And, I made suggestions like everybody else, but don't let anybody tell you they ever directed Chaplin. Chaplin directed himself.[40]

— Eddie Sutherland

Charlie was God, you forget. Everyone forgets that in his studio he was the only person whose opinion mattered in any way.[41]

— Virginia Cherrill

Before taking a look as Chaplin's sound era films, it is important to briefly move away from chronicling the comedian's life and concentrate specifically on aspects of his creative personality, as the coming of sound would eventually change the techniques Chaplin had employed to create comedy up to that time.

As we have seen, Chaplin entered the film industry with an extensive background in comic acting for the stage, in which he had developed his sense of rhythm and timing, particularly with the Karno troupe. Part of Chaplin's early troubles at Keystone were directly related to the conflict between the nature of early film comedy and Chaplin's own music hall experience. With Sennett's emphasis on short narratives and physical action, many of the comedic subtleties Chaplin had developed on the stage had little place in the popular Keystone formula. One-reel shorts and fast pacing necessitated the use of character stereotypes, instantly recognizable to audiences of the day, and almost never allowed for the extensive development of any particular role.

Much of the comedian's time at Keystone, then, found him more or less learning the most basic filmmaking skills, both as an actor and director, rather than developing his screen character or altering the pace and structure of the Keystone style. Few of Chaplin's early films show a remarkable advancement over the studio's typical fare, though the comedian certainly found a little more leeway to develop scenarios and gags to his liking once he had taken over the director's helm.

Not surprisingly then, Chaplin's initial cinematic style reflected this early screen tutelage. The camera remains fairly distant from the performers, allowing a variety of full-body, broad action to be undertaken simultaneously. Settings tend to revolve around the typical Keystone places — parks, hotels, saloons, and the like — and standard comedic characters such as buffoonish cops, flirtatious men, jealous spouses and overbearing bosses are everpresent. As Chaplin averaged a new release every ten days during 1914, much more of his effort was put into completing pictures with regularity than in discovering his own technique or furthering the development of his screen character.

At Essanay in 1915, Chaplin was afforded a key element in the expansion of his skills as a performer and directorm by moving to an almost strictly two-reel format. Even doubling the length of his films did not totally change the nature of Chaplin's comedy, as the comedian's first few Essanay deliveries are

The Chaplin Studios at 1416 N. La Brea in Hollywood, circa 1922.

still distinctly rooted in the Keystone style. But Chaplin was beginning to establish his own creative ground, both with his screen character and with directorial duties.

Beginning with *The Tramp* and (in particular) *The Bank*, Chaplin began to expand Charlie's range, helping establish his character as both a pathetic and comic figure, longing to be loved and to fit in with the rest of society. An element of vulnerability, unique among silent comics of the time, was ultimately to become one of Charlie's signature attributes, helping endear him to audiences around the world. At first, it wasn't a consistent portrayal by any means, but the traits that distinguished the Charlie of the feature length comedies began to take shape beginning with Chaplin's Essanay shorts. However, such moments are often sandwiched between the type of broad and chaotic slapstick proceedings that reflect a lingering Keystone influence.

Additionally, with nearly 15 months elapsing between his first and last releases with Essanay, Chaplin distinctly slowed his output. This was partly due to adopting the two-reel format, which necessitated greater preparation and development than a simple one-reel scenario. Another contributing factor may have been Chaplin's astronomical popularity, which showed no signs of letting up. His films garnered high praise, and the public was thronging to theaters with every new release. As one of the industry's top box office draws, his popularity led to a touch of self-consciousness, even more apparent later when artists and critics of high caliber began lauding Chaplin's work. Each release had to top the last one, and Chaplin naturally became more of a perfectionist, using only what he considered his best material in each film and taking additional time to complete projects when needed. (As we will see later, this aspect of Chaplin's work habits would find some of his most inspired works lost on the cutting room floor, only saved for posterity by pure luck.)

While working at Mutual, Chaplin seemed to tie many of the remaining loose ends together, as evidenced by the strength of releases such as *The Pawnshop, Easy Street, The Cure* and *The Immigrant*. Here, several factors come into play. Unlike his stints at Keystone, Essanay and First National, Chaplin did not have a host of grumbles with the company throughout his 17 month stay. He was thus free to explore the limits of his comedy, and not concern himself as much with some of the more troublesome aspects of creating for film. In fact, he considered the Mutual period to be his happiest in motion pictures.[42]

His stock set of performers, assembled at Essanay but refined and enhanced at Mutual, also helped bring his filmmaking to a higher level. Performers like Albert Austin, Henry Bergman, Edna Purviance, Leo White and Eric Campbell, among numerous others, provided the comedian with a steady group of performers on which to draw upon. These individuals provided consistency and continuity from picture to picture, offering similar faces in similar roles — Campbell as the menace or bully and Edna Purviance as the object of Charlie's love, for instance.

Chaplin's work with Purviance, in particular, altered the pattern of Charlie's romantic encounters on film and shaped how he would address the subject in his sound era projects. Aside from Keystone actresses such as Alice Davenport and Phyllis Allen, both perfect as domineering wives or mothers, women in Chaplin's films primarily worked as comic foils. But with time, perhaps as their own relationship grew, Chaplin dealt with Edna's characters with a much more idealized form of romanticism; the roles that Edna herself played expanded very little, but the Tramp's relationship to her characters grew significantly. Charlie began to place beauty and charm on a pedestal, longing for the opportunity to prove himself a worthy suitor for the affections of another. While this kind of romance was certainly not depicted throughout all of Chaplin's silent shorts, one can see the beginnings of the romance and pathos the comedian would later develop more fully in features such as *The Gold Rush* and *City Lights*. Onscreen, Edna often provided the ideal, yet perhaps unattainable mate, and when in *Sunnyside* we see the Little Fellow's vain attempt to duplicate the dress and mannerisms of Edna's wealthy suitor in an effort to compete for her hand, we recognize the earnest and pathetic qualities that became indelible marks of the Tramp character.

With such a solid, dependable cast behind him, Chaplin was afforded the opportunity to emphasize the role of the Tramp, making him the central, most well-developed character in each picture. Chaplin, too, benefited from utilizing the same character from film to film, since the Tramp's exposition, motivation and manner were already established with audiences. But with Charlie as the sole focus in Chaplin's comedy, this trait has been viewed as a double-edged sword. While he firmly established the character of the Little Fellow over the years, adding a considerable depth to the character's vast screen popularity, many commentators have been critical of Chaplin's focus on himself through-out his pictures, a notion that has helped bolster the reputation of the consid-erably less self-conscious works of Buster Keaton and Harold Lloyd.

But, during the silent period at least, Chaplin's focus on developing the Tramp helped solidify the comedian's popularity with audiences. Whether con-scious of the change or not, Chaplin's efforts to develop his screen character were affecting the nature of his films structurally, moving him to lengthen his pictures, add narrative and emotional complexity, and move away from the purely slapstick environment practiced at Keystone. It was a factor that added to his longevity, as screen comedy in general become more sophisticated throughout the silent era. Sennett, whose principles of comedy matured com-paratively little during the same period, eventually lost his early stature, as audiences began to expect more from comedic films (at least in terms of pol-ish and length). Chaplin was fortunate in this sense, discovering and evolving his screen capabilities throughout the silent period and moving creatively in more or less the same direction as motion picture audiences.

Courtesy of *Unknown Chaplin*, the outstanding documentary by Kevin Brownlow and David Gill, we can also get an insider's view of some of the Mutual films, and a better understanding of how Chaplin actually worked as a director. Preserved outtakes from several productions, most notably *The Floor-walker*, *The Cure* and *The Immigrant*, indicate a distinct creative method for the comedian.

First, Chaplin tended to rehearse gags on film, many times without any clear narrative or comedic direction whatsoever, as he waited for inspiration to guide his filmmaking. He worked ideas over and over, it seems, improvis-ing a little here and there. He kept mannerisms or actions that he liked in suc-cessive takes, and discarded the rest. Working without a script, Chaplin achieved results that are impressive in terms of his comic inventiveness. But such a practice was both time-consuming and expensive, considering the amount of film being exposed. That Chaplin had many run-ins with profit-con-scious parent companies during the course of his early career is certainly no surprise.

Occasionally, while groping to find a direction in which to take a story or a way to perfect a scene, Chaplin could take his onscreen rehearsals to mad-dening lengths. In *The Cure*, for instance, it took the comedian a full 84 takes, and a reconstruction of the set, in order to find a comfortable starting point for his film. Other films, particularly in the sound era, would take many years of production time, with total exposed film sometimes running up to 40 times the amount used in the final print.

Chaplin's stint at First National allowed him to experiment with the feature or near-feature length format, although he did return to two-reelers such as *Pay Day* and *The Idle Class* late in his stay when he was anxious to finish his contact. With these early efforts into lengthier films, Chaplin tested himself in the areas of motion picture form and character development, as the industry's trend (both from an artistic and economic sense) necessitated a more concerted effort toward expanding comedy to feature length. "I was beginning to think of comedy in a structural sense," Chaplin would recall of the First National period, "and to become conscious of its architectural form. Each sequence implied the next sequence, all of them relating to the whole."[43] Contrasts began to become more prevalent in his work. In *A Dog's Life*, Chaplin cuts between parallel scenes of the Tramp and Scraps, the mutt, both of which are similar in composition and tone. This not only links the characters as soulmates but helps identify the level of their existence as well — both are outcasts, and therefore made for each other. In his first two sound era films, *City Lights* and *Modern Times*, contrasts would be utilized even more profoundly. But while this architectural form of filmmaking added visual and narrative complexity to Chaplin's films, it also slowed his production time even further.

Aside from the comedian's move toward feature film length, the most significant event of the First National period was the construction of the Chaplin Studios. Just as his steady crew of actors and technicians helped Chaplin maintain consistently high quality in his films, the creation of the studio proved to be an important factor in his success as well. Essentially, its back lots would become Charlie's home. Sets could be utilized and interpreted in a number of different ways (some backdrops become recognizable, for instance, from film to film), and virtually anything he would ever need could be constructed right there to his exacting specifications. But perhaps even more than the studio's filmmaking advantages, it stood as a symbol of Chaplin's phenomenal popularity, as well as his rising independence in the film industry. "Building his own studio was one of Chaplin's shrewdest acts of foresight," Charles Maland noted, "enabling him to control his productions and own the rights to his films, an independence almost unheard of in Hollywood, before or after."[44]

The jump to United Artists was Chaplin's final triumph over the creative struggles that had followed him throughout his career. The comedian now had everything necessary for true artistic freedom. He was his own scenarist, director, actor, producer, studio owner and, thanks to his role in the founding of United Artists, distributor as well. In fact, Chaplin's first film for United Artists, *A Woman of Paris*, can be viewed from one perspective as a symbolic act of the comedian's newfound freedom. At eight reels (his longest film to date), it wasn't a comedy and didn't even feature him in a credited role.

The move to United Artists found Chaplin working exclusively on feature length projects, and the beginning of the UA era found him concentrating more and more on the romance and pathos in his films. However, another interesting trend was at work in Chaplin's films as well. Though poverty had been one of the founding elements of his screen character, it had grown to become a more conspicuous aspect of Charlie's nature with each successive release — as Chaplin's personal wealth grew with each new contract, the Tramp conversely became more and more indigent. This is certainly true in the later features *The Gold Rush* and *The Circus*, and is also evident in his first two sound films, *City Lights* and, particularly, *Modern Times*. Likewise, as the allegations about Chaplin's personal life became public, both before and after his ill-fated marriage to Lita Grey, the comedian's alter ego became increasingly moral and romantic.[45] This was quite a contrast from Charlie's early Keystone and Essanay days, where the Tramp could be quite aggressive in both romantic and physical situations, and is symptomatic of the softening Chaplin's character underwent as the creator himself grew older. The same Charlie who would regularly throw bricks at authority figures at Keystone, for example, would do so only accidentally to a police officer in 1936's *Modern Times*.

In all likelihood, Chaplin did not consciously set out to make many of these changes to his screen character. Rather, he was instead reacting to personal and artistic influences around him. As Chaplin changed, his alter ego of the Tramp also changed. Eventually, so did the nature of the comedian's screen narratives. As we shall see later, Chaplin would be especially sensitive in reflecting new aspects to his life and the world around him during his sound era work.

Chaplin, of course, altered his creative personality during his silent film years as well, though such change does not always lend itself to any particular period of studio involvement. As evidenced by his early troubles with directors at Keystone, Chaplin was a headstrong comedian who felt that he alone knew how best to utilize his talents. While this was perhaps a reaction to Sennett's comedic style, so different from the background Chaplin had experienced on the English vaudeville circuit, the comedian's forceful reaction nonetheless indicates a strong will and a tremendous self-confidence in his own abilities.

As Chaplin's films quickly garnered a large public following and wide-scale critical success, the young Englishman became one of Hollywood's most respected individuals, and his level of assuredness grew. Many began to feel, in fact, that Chaplin's ego rivaled his immense public popularity. Chaplin's press agent Carlyle Robinson recalled that each morning, upon the comedian's arrival at the Chaplin Studios, a cry would go up all over the lot, "He's here!", and virtually all activity would cease while Chaplin rode triumphantly through the studio gates. While such an entrance was completely unnecessary, it wasn't discouraged by the comedian either, for Robinson speculated that Chaplin enjoyed the pomp and circumstance of his daily arrival.[46]

As Chaplin's move toward creative autonomy found him taking more and more responsibility for his pictures — from acting, directing and editing to financing and doing numerous behind-the-scenes tasks — this awesome respon-sibility also affected his personality. Confidants such as Albert Austin and Henry Bergman were not so much collaborators or advisors as they were sounding boards for Chaplin's various bits of inspired mayhem. Over the years, former members of Chaplin's cast and crew would often remark that his word was vir-tually law unto itself. His sometimes volatile nature prompted employees with disagreements to be very delicate in presenting their particular concerns. And for good reason, too. As the pressures of filmmaking fell squarely upon his shoulders, Chaplin could become quite temperamental at times, a trait that was already apparent during his comedic performances with Karno. Employees at the Chaplin Studios, it was said, could tell his daily mood by the color of suit he wore upon his morning arrival. "He was the most lovable, likable person in the world," cameraman Rollie Totheroh later recalled, "when everything was going right. He could be like a Jekyll and Hyde. One day he's a swell man and then he would be mean. All he had to do is give you a look; you could feel he hated your guts."[47]

The documentary series *Unknown Chaplin*, for instance, contains an out-take from *The Immigrant* in which Chaplin explodes with anger at a crowd of extras. A revolving door episode from *The Cure* shows Chaplin becoming so fed up with his cane after it sticks unexpectedly in the door that he throws it violently to the ground. Ironically, his anger with the mishap became comic inspiration — he managed to utilize the stuck cane gag in the final film.[48]

But if Chaplin's moods weren't enough to cause occasional rifts between him and his studio staff or friends, his creative urges certainly were. In his early days, at least, he was a creature of whims, whether at work or at play. Though Chaplin was a sporadic worker himself, he would require all studio per-sonnel to be ready and made-up each morning by nine. Chaplin, however, would sometimes not arrive to begin work until the afternoon, if he arrived at the studio at all. The entire production of *City Lights*, for example, would take a total of 683 working days to complete. Yet a full 504 of those days were idle days at the studio, meaning that no actual filming was done. Though these idle days included story conferences and set construction, there were plenty of days considered idle because Chaplin simply chose not, or was "unable," to work. Considering the fact that all studio employees were being paid regardless of what was being done on the lot, the amount of money wasted due to Chaplin's creative whims was enormous. Sydney, his business senses much sharper than his brother's, was always troubled by such wasteful habits.

When Chaplin was on the set, his unceasing energy was another source of frustration for those who worked with him. When inspired, he would work feverishly throughout the day, and might push his crew late into the evening. Rehearsing gags onscreen, he often preferred the inspiration of a particular moment to mapping out an entire sequence in advance, an expensive and wasteful working method regardless of the results. D.W. Griffith, in contrast, utilized extensive rehearsals prior to filming to plan every scene, thus minimizing the amount of takes necessary. Chaplin's directorial methods were not nearly so organized or efficient; often times, they were simply counter-productive.

Quite often, Chaplin's direction found him acting out various roles between shots, carefully articulating exactly what he wanted to see from another performer, whether that actor was in a principal role or merely an extra. Then he would film take after take, wearing a performer's patience thin, sometimes in order to achieve some relatively insignificant gesture, facial expression or movement. Horror stories abound regarding Chaplin's excessiveness on the set, which also contributed significantly to production delays and cost overruns. It took two days of shooting, for instance, and some 90 individual takes, for Edna Purviance to master the art of discarding a cigarette and deciding not to go out for the evening in *A Woman of Paris*.[49] Virginia Cherrill, Chaplin's leading lady for *City Lights*, had similar experiences:

> He didn't care how many takes it took. In fact, I often thought that if he couldn't think of what he was going to do next, he simply went on doing the same shot over again until he thought of it. But he was a perfectionist, and to us [each take] often seemed to be exactly the same. But to him, it was not.[50]

With his own performance, Chaplin could be equally harsh. The boiled shoe dinner in *The Gold Rush* required some 63 takes; Chaplin shot and reshot the scene with Mack Swain despite the fact that the boots, made of licorice, were making both men ill. While filming *The Circus*, Chaplin's perfectionism led to over 200 takes of the Tramp bumbling into a lion's cage.[51]

Sometimes such methods cost more than time and money, however. The character of Charlie was constantly on the screen in Chaplin's comedy films; there are relatively few scenes without him, and little comedy that does not extend, in some way, from him. Accordingly, while editing, Chaplin often selected takes for the master print on the basis of his performance, since the audience, he felt, would be attuned to Charlie's antics. While his rationale was sound, Chaplin left the door open for continuity errors, which he made with some frequency.

Because so many scenes were improvised, or shot over and over, they might be performed in an entirely different manner on each take. During this process, Chaplin sometimes had no concern about changing the position of a prop in the background, or adjusting something on someone's costume — whatever suited his needs at the moment. When the editing process brought together scenes shot on different days and under different conditions, Chaplin may have been successful in building his own best performance, but often overlooked some of the smaller details in his pictures. Most errors are often not strikingly apparent but they nonetheless become apparent upon repeated viewings.

Take the cane/revolving door gag in *The Cure* that Chaplin incorporated after blowing up at his inability to negotiate the door as planned. While displaying comic inspiration by accident, the scene also demonstrates that the comedian concentrated on the comedy, and not the continuity, while editing the sequence. Early in the gag, Charlie is thrown out of the revolving door rather violently, losing both his hat and cane in the process. He re-enters the door, only to become hopelessly trapped once again when the character played by Eric Campbell, also in the door, gets his foot stuck and traps both men in the enclosed portions. Suddenly, Charlie raises both his hat and cane into the frame, despite clearly losing them only moments earlier.

A similar instance can be found in *The Vagabond*. Early on, tempers flare in a saloon between Charlie and some rival street musicians, and a chase ensues both inside and outside of the establishment. At one point, outside the saloon, Charlie trips over a drum, sprawling on the ground and losing his derby. This shot is followed by one of Charlie dashing into the building, and it clearly shows the Little Fellow clutching his hat as he hurriedly makes his way for the back door. Then, outside the bar once again and returning to the original long shot, the Tramp attempts to elude his pursuers by darting into the saloon a second time, though not before stooping to grab his lost derby. A very similar hat problem occurs early in *A Dog's Life*, as the Little Fellow is playfully tormenting a policeman.

In each case, the sudden disappearance or reappearance of certain props is a clear error in the film's continuity; Chaplin had either missed or was relatively unconcerned about these occurrences during editing. Perhaps each shot — one before and one after his inspiration for the stuck cane gag, for instance — constituted the best take, and thus Chaplin opted for these.

Again, the comedian operated this way because it suited his particular needs. Since Chaplin never worked from a full script or completed scenario during the silent era, always leaving room for spontaneous comic invention or inspiration as he went along, successfully integrating comedy and a suitable storyline became increasingly difficult, and sometimes downright aggravating, especially when he moved into feature filmmaking. Continuity problems were an outgrowth not only of the comedian's occasionally careless editing, but also his desire to create the best product his talents could muster.

Production delays could also be viewed in this manner. But it was also true that Chaplin used idle days as a diversionary tactic at times. Since his productions were derived primarily from his own talents, the comedian was susceptible to creative blocks that could cause shooting to grind to a halt as he searched for a picture's next logical direction. In addition to his moodiness, Chaplin's absence from the studio often had much to do with his inability to find a way out of the proverbial corner he may have painted himself into. "Chaplin was making one of his pictures," Konrad Bercovici wrote after spending some time with the comedian on the set of *The Circus*, "but he could not always resist the temptation to run away and try to forget he was working. A hundred men and women were walking about impatiently as the 'lot,' all dressed up for their respective parts. The cameramen had trained their apparatuses and were waiting at their posts; for no one knew when Charlie would suddenly appear and begin to work as if nothing had happened, as if he had left off just a few minutes before."[52]

Chaplin would also use other methods of buying himself time during these situations. Sometimes, he recalled, he would order a set built with little or no idea of how he was to use it comedically.[53] Stuck in a bind, Chaplin knew that he could order sets to be constructed which would take a number of days to finish, thus affording him more time to plan for a particular film or scene.

Chaplin also solved immediate cinematic problems by starting on an entirely new production. During the middle of shooting *Sunnyside*, he suddenly became unhappy with the project, and abandoned it to work on a new film, which would eventually be released as *A Day's Pleasure* (1919).[54] He would go back to *Sunnyside* after roughly a week and continue until the film was completed some two and one-half months later. He then moved back to *A Day's Pleasure*, only to leave that production for some preliminary work on *The Kid*. He then returned to *A Day's Pleasure* and finally saw it to completion, some three months after he abandoned it the second time. At times, the staff at the Chaplin Studios must have been pushed to their limits. The comedian's flighty nature required them to abandon projects, start new ones, then pick up where they left off on the old ones and finish them, as if no change to the production schedule had ever occurred.

Despite these traits, however, there was no questioning Chaplin's dominance in the film industry. Not only did he have a loyal following of fans around the world, guaranteeing an enthusiastic response to his films, but he also enjoyed consistently excellent critical response as well. He was one of the movie industry's premier figures, and found a host of press reporters, fans and prominent world figures all clamoring for an audience with the biggest celebrity that motion pictures had yet produced. At the dawn of the sound era, Chaplin had survived many challenges to his motion picture work — troubles with studios, creative strains, personal problems and the like. Following the release of *The Circus*, yet another challenge lay ahead for the comedian, that of confronting the new technology employed in Hollywood.

2

City Lights

In undertaking the production of *City Lights*, his follow-up to *The Circus* and first sound era film, Chaplin began a gradual metamorphosis that would not only change the nature of his films altogether, but change the public's perception of him as an artist as well. Part of this change would see the eventual demise of his famous screen character, the Tramp. However, for his first two productions at least, the Little Fellow stayed. While *City Lights* is not a true silent picture (Chaplin would adapt sound technology to achieve his own artistic ends), he nonetheless defied conventional Hollywood wisdom at that time and produced a feature film without dialogue. Using sound technology as an enhancing rather than essential component of the production, he ultimately utilized the new technology to augment the elements of his silent features — his nuanced pantomime and slapstick — that had made him one of Hollywood's most popular figures. *City Lights* would also mark Chaplin's last attempt (or, at least, last successful attempt) for almost two decades to utilize overt pathos as an element of his comedy, in the tradition of *The Kid* and *The Gold Rush* before it. The picture would become a favorite with many critics, rivaling even *The Gold Rush* in its sustained popularity, despite its tremendously sentimental finale. Theodore Huff acknowledged "the equivocal ending of the film, ironic and vibrant with the tragic sense of life, seldom fails to bring tears ... [it] is one of the most poignant scenes ever photographed,"[1] and critic James Agee referred to it as "... enough to shrivel the heart to see, and it is the greatest piece of acting and the highest moment in movies."[2]

But before Chaplin could concoct a rough scenario for the film, he first had to seriously consider the changing landscape of cinema technology. Following Warner Brothers' release of *Don Juan* in August, 1926, and *The Jazz Singer* the following year, Hollywood had moved quickly into the sound era.

I. THE EMERGENCE OF SOUND TECHNOLOGY

... I don't think the voice is necessary, it spoils the art as much as painting a statuary. I would as soon rouge marble cheeks. Pictures are a pantomimic art.[3]

— Charles Chaplin — 1921

Although the idea to mesh sound with the moving image was afoot long before Chaplin even entered the motion picture industry, the technology had been slow in its development. Thomas Edison envisioned a direct link between his phonograph and his early experimentation with film; he was not alone. In the pre–Griffith era of filmmaking, Edison and many other visionary entrepreneurs successfully developed numerous processes by which this marriage of sight and sound could be achieved, though almost all were unsuccessful for large-scale and consistent exhibition. Most early attempts at sound film focused on Edison's phonograph notion, or a sound-on-disk technology. The problem, however, was obvious: Amplification to a large audience was extremely difficult, synchronization with screen movement was less than perfect, and the length of even a short film could exceed that of a single disk, necessitating a change mid-film. While many companies advertised and exhibited so-called "new" technological inventions throughout the traveling exhibition and nickelodeon eras, their practical application was quite limited. Work on perfecting the synchronization of sight and sound was ongoing, and as silent motion pictures began to develop their own system of production, exhibition and distribution, the majority of sound film techniques became little more than curiosity pieces.

After World War I, experimentation with a sound-on-film process began in earnest. While this method proved far more successful than sound-on-disk, with several short subjects undertaken during the early to mid–1920s, many at the time saw the process as both imperfect and too expensive for serious consideration. Silent films were quite successful, and there was nothing to suggest that the viewing public yearned for sound with their pictures.* Sound, then, though available for industry experimentation, was considered to be a film curiosity during the early to mid–1920s, or at best a potential enhancement to the silent screen with respect to the addition of sound effects.†

Sound did play an important role in silent film, even though the medium itself could not bring such sounds to an audience. On the set, many silent film directors, Chaplin being a notable exception, employed the services of trained musicians directly off-screen, primarily for two reasons. First, music would help set the tone for a particular scene, especially in dramatic films, stirring emotion in the actors and actresses and achieving, theoretically, the greatest authenticity in their performances. Opinions vary on the effectiveness of the

---

*Some ingenious early exhibitors went as far as hiring actors to provide dialogue for silent films from behind the screen. Most audiences, however, found this effect very humorous, and the technique never caught on. The practice is seen today as more reflective of the kind of showmanship required of early motion picture exhibitors than as a serious effort to combine sound with the moving image.

†True to his reputation as an innovator in world cinema, D.W. Griffith experimented with a very simple version of the sound process in his film Dream Street (1921); Griffith himself even introduced the picture in a spoken prologue. The process failed to achieve the desired effect, and the film was soon playing widely in a silent version.

practice; some directors, such as William Wellman and King Vidor, praised the method and felt it added measurably to a film's believability. Edward Sloman, on the contrary, felt the method was merely a crutch for untalented performers.[4] Second, the method could also help overcome the inherent noise problem on some silent film sets. Early cameras, clackity contraptions hand-cranked by cameramen, could be a distraction to some. This was evidently not a problem for Chaplin (he claimed to have found the rhythmic noise an excellent sort of pace to follow through his comic routines), but other performers sometimes found it affected their concentration. With a set-up as simple as a violin or piano off-screen, this noise could be mitigated.*

Film exhibitors also had a noise problem to overcome, since the projection of a motion picture could be equally distracting. Exhibitors, like the moviemakers themselves, had found a similar solution: Musical accompaniment in the theater became the norm in virtually every motion picture house, not only to drown out the projection noise but to enhance the onscreen action as well. The successful silent film exhibitor had to be a true showman, and he was hard-pressed to distinguish his movie house from those of his competitors. Music, whether a simple or lavish affair, depending on the size and nature of the particular house, was often an exceptional distinguishing feature.

Live musicians were highly successful at overcoming the two major deficiencies in mechanical sound at the time, synchronization and amplification. The number of musicians utilized could vary from a simple piano in many small theaters to a full-blown orchestra in the most grandiose movie palaces. Sometimes, as Kevin Brownlow noted, the picture was not always the best attraction at the local theater.

> During the Golden Era, the reputation of a theatre often depended on its orchestra. People sometimes claimed that they went to the movies "just for the music."
> A first-class orchestra could make the dullest picture bearable, and careful scoring, combined with good playing, could provide an extra dimension to the magic of the movies.... (M)otion picture theatre orchestras brought classical music to the ears of many who had never heard it.[5]

By the 1920s, pipe organs had also became popular fixtures in some movie houses. Companies such as Wurlitzer offered not only high quality, reverberating music throughout a theatre, but also had the ability to provide unique

---

*David Robinson has noted, however, that Chaplin did use music when necessary, specifically during the filming of The Gold Rush when he employed a string quartet while filming the cabin scenes with Mack Swain. He also concludes that the infamous "Oceana Roll" dance must also have been filmed to music, as each of the existing outtakes flow with a precise synchronicity. (David Robinson; Chaplin: His Life and Art; pages 353–354.) Additionally, a photograph from The Circus, capturing Chaplin in a bit of clowning before performing one of his many takes inside a lion's cage, distinctly shows that the comedian used musical accompaniment in this situation as well, considering there is a piano to the immediate right of several of the technicians.

sound effects to coincide with the action. With an orchestra, specific individuals could be assigned specific sounds, if the exhibitor was able to obtain a film in time for his musicians to plan and practice; often this was not the case and, in a bind, improvisation was common. With an organ, one person could effectively create an entire musical and sound effect score, often with greater ease than an orchestra. But organs tended to be cost-prohibitive for all but the largest motion picture houses, and most theaters were relegated to more simple, less expensive orchestral accompaniment.

Though matching sound to film would significantly change motion pictures, only a select few visionaries felt that sound could supplant silent film in industry dominance. Many critics of the new technology, particularly studio heads, observed that silent features had been improving significantly in both aesthetic and artistic quality. Initially, most of those in the motion picture industry believed sound to be a costly and superfluous folly.

Warner Brothers, one of the industry's smaller studios looking for a niche in a crowded marketplace, was not satisfied with the status quo. In 1926, the studio leased a process called Vitaphone, developed by Western Electric and the Bell Telephone Laboratories, as a tool for enhancing the company's pictures by adding simple, unobtrusive sound effects. Vitaphone was a more sophisticated and reliable form of sound-on-disk, and a much more cost-effective innovation than the sound-on-film processes then available. It still wasn't cheap: Installation of Vitaphone technology in theaters could cost upwards of $25,000 per screen. Further, an engineer was required to be present in a specially-wired seat during screenings to ensure sound quality. As the technology was fallible, it had to be constantly monitored and altered throughout each performance.[6] But Warners was committed to expanding the variety of the studio's offerings to exhibitors, and they helped provide the push the motion picture industry needed to test sound technology.

Despite reports to the contrary, Warner Brothers was not financially strapped at the time it leased the Vitaphone process. Fighting to increase its operations to compete with the top-level studios, the expansion effort only left Warner Brothers tight on money for the short term.[7] Since they had only a small network of theaters in which to distribute their pictures, unlike larger studios, sound offered a unique (albeit risky) means to distinguish themselves from the competition. Their first release, *Don Juan*, synchronized music with film, primarily in the accompanying shorts on the program. The process was not perfect, nor was it warmly received by critics, but in retrospect it did mark the beginning of the end for the silent era.

Never ones to let a new innovation put them behind the times, many Hollywood production units, such as Fox's Movietone, began their own experimentation with sound film. However, until Warner Brothers released *The Jazz Singer* in 1927, sound had yet to form an intregal component of narrative expression.[8] Even with Jolson's feature — essentially a silent picture in terms of direction and staging—actual synchronization of voices was limited to only a handful of scenes, and the transition between silent and sound portions sometimes appeared rather awkward and clumsy. Nonetheless, the process continued to be utilized for succeeding films, and when box office receipts seemed to indicate the public's enthusiasm, other studios began developing their own sound techniques as well. Many moved quickly to wire their stages for sound production. Despite the still-primitive technology, industry attitude toward sound had begun to change drastically.

A box office downturn prior to large-scale application of sound had kept many studios at an earnings plateau, but financial prospects of the new medium, even after the considerable expense of installing it, showed great potential. While many observers and critics felt that silent and sound productions could co-exist, sound technology did at the very least offer the film industry a new and innovative method of expressing their stories.

The task of modernizing film studios and rewiring movie houses around the world for sound accompaniment was a costly and sometimes detrimental burden, even for established film companies. Studios took to quickly modernizing their theater chains on borrowed capital, hoping to recoup their expenses under the auspices of the promising technological advancement.

Box office receipts from the early all-dialogue films, such as Warner Brothers' *Lights of New York* (1928), seemed to prove that the public was indeed enthusiastic about the new medium, despite the primitive nature of early talkies. Initially, all-dialogue films tended to be just that—all dialogue. The subtlety of the silent era was gone, the pace of films slowed considerably (in deference to concealed microphones), camera angles and mobility were limited, and actors could often appear strangely stiff. Slapstick, with its lively and spontaneous qualities, was very much at odds with the rigidity of early sound; successful film comedy was gravitating toward the verbal and away from the physical.

These early sound features, however, with their rather inflexible characteristics, were part of the aches and pains of the technology's growth, and only after filmmakers began to discover methods of freeing early talkies from their stagebound nature did sound film firmly begin to push the silents aside. Box office receipts rose by nearly 50% immediately prior to the Depression, which may have saved many studios from financial ruin, what with the expense of rewiring theater chains throughout the nation.[9] Some intellectuals and critics (as well as performers such as Chaplin) held that the silent format had more artistic value—a persuasive argument in light of some early dialogue features—but the box office popularity of these films seemed to justify the sudden studio conversion to the talkies. (Chaplin was heavily influenced by the opinions of intellectuals, as many had embraced his films as high art and had consistently lauded the comedian's talents. Psychologically, Chaplin also may have been closely attuned to such highbrow commentary to compensate for his lack of formal education, a fact he seemed quite conscious of.)

Chaplin had many salient considerations of his own on why *not* to plunge into producing sound films. There was certainly no lack of quality to silent films during the last half of the 1920s; Chaplin's own films, for instance, showed a vast improvement in picture quality, production values and theme development in the decade preceding the advent of sound. But the possibility of failing to deliver what the public seemingly wanted, even with the popular Tramp character, forced the comedian to weigh the drawing ability of Charlie against that of the new technology.

For Chaplin, there were economic considerations as well. The addition of spoken dialogue meant an increase in planning time and production costs, both in order to equip his studio and to over-dub prints for foreign markets. The pantomime of the silents was a universal language of sorts, understood and popular the world over. With the increasing importance of foreign revenues to offset the production costs of film projects, maintaining profit margins would be even more difficult.

Chaplin, by this time financing his own films, would ultimately bear the economic brunt of a failed effort in the talkies. Whereas a major studio could bounce back from financially disastrous projects with other releases, Chaplin may have felt that he had to guarantee a bankable first effort in the sound era if he wished to continue serious filmmaking. He could not simply churn out another film as he had done during his one- and two-reel days a decade earlier. Given the fact that the Lita Grey settlement and the government tax problems were resolved around the same period of time, the argument can be made that Chaplin's financial situation at the onset of sound film was quite tenuous indeed.[10]

In this case, the financial and creative independence that Chaplin had fought so long to achieve, which in part led to the formation of United Artists in 1919, was now working against him. A substantial cinematic failure would be a financial loss both for Chaplin and for United Artists. And, although his creative direction was already in place at the time of the October stock market crash of 1929, the Depression only furthered his need for an immediate success with his first sound era project.

Chaplin was also quite aware of the effect that sound would have on his style of comedy. Cinema was seeing less and less importance placed on what many considered to be the comedian's strongest asset. Chaplin's pantomime required a great degree of subtlety and timing — elements that were steamrolled by the barrage of words in early talkies, which he later recalled as more laughable than revolutionary.[11] The comedian's techniques, highly improvisational and subject to rapid changes, were far too varied to limit his movements to the vicinity of a hidden microphone. But if he did utilize dialogue, there were many inevitable questions: How would critics and the public react to Charlie in a speaking role? Would Chaplin's own voice have its intended effect on the audience? Could Chaplin provide dialogue becoming of his artistic stature, without sacrificing the traditional elements of a Chaplin comedy—pantomime, pathos, romance and the like?

Chaplin was indeed troubled by the dilemma. *The Circus* was released just as the silent period was receiving its first real challenge from sound, and though the film proved a critical and financial success, there remained the distinct possibility that screen pantomime was a dying art. That he must clearly establish the style of his next film before he undertook possible narrative ideas was obvious, since his approach to any picture would be dependent on the medium he chose to shoot in. Sound required not only the purchase of new and expensive equipment for his studio, but the unfamiliar element of extensive pre-production planning as well. For a man who was still shooting feature-length films from only minuscule notes, relying on creative inspiration to fill gaps in perhaps only a thinly-sketched story, such regimentation ran directly counter to a working method he had developed over the previous 15 years.

To speak or not to speak was further complicated by the fact that some of Chaplin's contemporaries made the move quickly and successfully. Comedian Harold Lloyd took the completed silent feature *Welcome Danger* (1929) and dubbed in dialogue during post-production, although at great expense.[12] Buster Keaton, too, then under contract to Metro-Goldwyn-Mayer, had made the transition, though the loss of independent status, coupled with his worsening alcoholism, left him under the direction of studio management and their projects. He found himself playing second fiddle to Jimmy Durante, a comedian whose gifts were better suited for talkies. Following Lloyd's example perhaps would have made the most logical step, since Chaplin would have been able to gauge audience reaction to the popular silent comedian in a speaking role. Lloyd's sound debut was a stunning success (*Welcome Danger* would be the second highest grossing film of Lloyd's career), perhaps suggesting that the move could be made effectively, but Chaplin was not convinced.[13] In the end he resisted allowing the Tramp to make a similar jump; as one critic put it, Chaplin's status afforded him the unique position of being "the only [silent comic] who was rich, proud and popular enough to stay silent."[14]

The growing amount of time between Chaplin films proved a benefit while planning what would become *City Lights*. The period between *The Gold Rush* and *The Circus*, two- and-a-half years, was his longest absence from the screen to date, and there were no indications that sound was propelling him to speed production on a follow-up. Thus, Chaplin was allowed the luxury of monitoring the progress of talking films. Should they become permanent fixtures, he could have conceivably altered his project, as Lloyd had. But Chaplin ultimately found a way to undermine conventional wisdom by having the best of both worlds, sound and silent, in the creation of *City Lights*. Though he would concede to using a synchronized soundtrack and would include some simple sound effects, the film would remain a non-dialogue picture and would rely on Chaplin's characteristic physical humor and sentimentality.

The comedian felt that the Little Fellow was a fixture of the silent era, and owed his popularity essentially to the pantomimic skills of his creator. In a pure sound medium, Charlie would be robbed of much of his balletic grace and charm. Just as very early film audiences were enthralled by the simple spectacle of motion on a screen, so too did it seem to Chaplin that the new talkies were capturing audiences under the spell of sound.

When Chaplin did finally take the plunge into talking films, with *The Great Dictator* in 1940, he reflected upon the consequences of finally capitulating to the new medium. "I had thought of possible voices for the Tramp — whether he should speak in monosyllables or just mumble. But it was no use. If I talked I would become like any other comedian."[15] For Chaplin to "diminish" his famous screen character to simple jabbering, as Chaplin felt many early sound comedies did to performers, would be a disservice to himself, his public and his art. The silent format was not only Charlie's natural environment, but offered a guaranteed following of loyal fans, and Chaplin banked on his longtime popularity to carry the film's financial prospects. Regardless of conventional wisdom, as long as the Tramp remained a cinematic fixture, Chaplin would continue to spurn dialogue films as long as he could afford to do so.

II. CONCEIVING *CITY LIGHTS*

Chaplin toyed with several potential scenarios for the Tramp, the most prominent of which looked to combine elements of *The Kid* and *The Circus*. Charlie would be a circus clown with failing eyesight, a condition which he would valiantly attempt to hide from his little daughter. In retrospect, it is odd that Chaplin would have considered the circus and children's themes again. Though Chaplin often re-interpreted individual gag sequences throughout his film career, the concept seems to be too clearly rooted in situations he had already utilized. With the importance that the new film would have in regard to its technical style, Chaplin perhaps felt the need to create a scenario characteristic in tone, yet more independent of his recent work. He therefore discarded the blind clown idea.[16]

He appears to have been looking for a theme with obvious sentimental qualities. As a result, a new idea emerged — one that kept the device of blindness, but discarded both the circus and child themes. Charlie would instead meet a blind flower peddler (a heroine similar to Harry Langdon's in 1926's *The Strong Man*), a beautiful girl whom he would fall in love with and attempt to nurture with his help. Comedically it was not his most inspired scenario, though it would become one of the most poignant and moving narratives Chaplin had ever conceived. The period both before and during the filming was one of the most strenuous of his life, and yet the finished product would become one of the most memorable of his motion pictures.

With a basic plot in mind, integrating the new technology was likely the comedian's next concern. In retrospect, *City Lights* indicates how innovatively sound could work in motion pictures. Yet, because of its use, the picture cannot be considered a true silent film. The addition of a musical soundtrack (composed by Chaplin himself) and sporadic sound effects separates *City Lights* from his previous silent features. True, audiences would have been able to hear both at the theater had *City Lights* been released in the silent era, but not as the artist himself had originally envisioned it. But neither can the film be billed as a true sound film, since its use was limited to only specific background or enhancing effects. Instead, what Chaplin achieved was a maximization of the new medium to suit his own artistic needs — recognizing those areas of film comedy where sound could be of benefit, and exploiting the technology in those situations. Otherwise, Chaplin's film was conceived, shot and even marketed as if it were one of his silent features. Pantomime — the comedian's strength — took precedence.

This approach was altogether innovative (and some said foolhardy) for the period. By the time shooting for *City Lights* was underway, there was no mistaking that sound films would replace the silents as the new method of filmmaking. Despite his numerous public statements to the contrary, most of which can be considered as part of the tremendous promotional campaign undertaken for *City Lights*, Chaplin knew that the silent era was finished by the time the film was eventually released. Still, *City Lights*, as well as his next film, *Modern Times*, remained in essentially silent form, relying on pantomime rather than dialogue.

Chaplin's own personal experiences may give a clue as to his adamant refusal to include dialogue in both pictures. The comedian recalled that his first starring role with Karno, in a vaudeville comedy sketch titled *The Football Match*, ended after only two performances because nagging voice troubles — shades of what was said to have doomed Hannah Chaplin's stage career — necessitated that his understudy take over the role.[17]

Outside of performing, too, the comedian was weary of his voice. *My Trip Abroad*, published in 1922, notes the anxiety he felt prior to public speaking, as does *My Autobiography* some 42 years later, this time concerning his speeches promoting a Second Front during World War II. Charles Chaplin, Jr., recounts that his father vomited before one of his Second Front speeches, so nervous and unsure was he of his own voice. Only cameraman Rollie Totheroh had any recollection of the comedian appearing at ease before large crowds.[18]

City Lights, then, as well *Modern Times*, serves as a bridge in the comedian's artistic transformation toward sound. Chaplin would give up the silent medium, albeit slowly, and, courtesy of his unique financial and artistic independence, on his own terms. A clear jump into sound would not only attract potentially negative critical attention to the film but perhaps alienate longtime Charlie fans, as well as intellectuals who felt strongly about Chaplin's artistic significance. Given the comedian's fear of failure, a quick and clean break from his roots may have seemed too much of a creative risk. What Chaplin did was construct for himself a gradual transition to sound, gradually accepting the medium into his film repertoire and gauging its success.

Hand in hand with placing a growing emphasis on sound, Chaplin must have also felt that he would have to move toward retiring his persona from the screen — the pantomimic Tramp would ultimately have to surrender to the age of his creator and escalating film technology.

III. THE NARRATIVE OF *CITY LIGHTS*

The film opens in a bustling urban center, with a number of citizens awaiting for the unveiling of a new sculpture. The portly mayor (Henry Bergman) is about to address the crowd gathered for the dedication. When he speaks, however, his voice is but the whimsical sound of a kazoo, as are those of the other speakers on the podium — an effect that not only pokes fun at the dignitaries, but at talking films as well. Following their remarks, a hideous piece of public art entitled "Peace and Prosperity" is unveiled. The statue, however, has provided a suitable refuge for Charlie, dreamily nestled in the cradling arms of — ironically — "Prosperity."

After creating pandemonium while making his exit, the Little Fellow moves through the city to begin his day. Crossing a street congested with automobiles, Charlie, in an effort to avoid a nearby policeman, takes a shortcut directly through the backseat of a limousine, and finds himself emerging before a lovely girl (Virginia Cherrill) selling flowers on the street corner. Captivated by her beauty, Charlie offers perhaps the only money he has to purchase a flower, which accidentally drops to the sidewalk. While she gropes for the lost goods, the Little Fellow realizes that she is without sight, and his heart goes out to her. But when she hears the limousine pull away from the curb, the Flower Girl thinks that the Tramp has left without his change, and Charlie does not spoil her assumption of his wealth, as he quietly slips away.

Later that evening, as Charlie wanders to a spot by the river in search of a place to sleep, he comes across a heavily intoxicated and suicidal Millionaire (Harry Myers). Charlie gallantly rushes to the rescue as the stranger attempts to throw himself into the river with a rock tied around his neck. The Tramp champions the will to live, but is inadvertently tossed into the water during the melee, rock attached. The Tramp himself is saved and the Millionaire, impressed with Charlie's heroism, invites his new friend to accompany him home.

The pair spend a long night of drinking and nightclubbing, and when they return to his spacious townhouse the next morning the Millionaire, still fully inebriated, offers Charlie his expensive car. Spying the Flower Girl heading toward her street corner to begin her day, the Tramp sets off to see her. She is flattered by the return of her "rich benefactor," and is quick to accept Charlie's generous offer for all of her flowers, as well as a ride home in what she believes to be his own car.

When Charlie returns, however, the Millionaire has sobered up from his evening of excess, and fails to recognize him. The Little Fellow is rudely pushed aside, as the rich man departs the townhouse in the car he had so recently given away. Bewildered, the Tramp wanders off.

It is not long, however, until Charlie again crosses paths with the Millionaire. Once again drunk, he is now friendly again toward the Tramp, and offers to throw a party at his townhouse in Charlie's honor. While there, the Little Fellow inadvertently swallows a small whistle, which begins to sound every time he hiccups — the first audible noise uttered by the Tramp on film. He disrupts a tenor's song, summon a taxi, and attracts a number of neighborhood dogs with the shrill pitch of the whistle.

But when morning arrives, a sober Millionaire is once again unaware of his friendship with Charlie, and is shocked to find the shabby man sleeping in the same bed. The Little Fellow is promptly thrown out into the street.

Again bewildered, the Tramp departs for the Flower Girl's house and, while innocently peering through her window, finds she has fallen gravely ill. Desperately wanting to help, Charlie resolves to find a job so that his earnings can assist her and her Grandmother.

He takes a job as a street cleaner, though his work ethic leaves something to be desired. At one point, he attempts to avoid a herd of horses traveling on Main Street only to come face-to-face with a passing circus elephant. When he is finally allowed to break for lunch, Charlie quickly buys what little groceries he can afford and races to the girl's meager flat. There he finds her alone, as she has been forced to relinquish the daily flower-peddling to her Grandmother while she recuperates.

Charlie kindly cares for her needs, even reading to her an article from the newspaper about a surgical procedure that could perhaps restore her sight. The Flower Girl is excited, proclaiming how wonderful it would be to finally see her benefactor, whom she still believes to be wealthy. The Tramp is hesitant to share her optimism: What would she think if she knew the truth? But he is quick to shrug off the thought, for she is ill. Later he stumbles upon an eviction notice addressed to the girl and her Grandmother. Possessed with optimism, yet most assuredly without the means, Charlie announces that he will return the following day with enough money to pay off the balance of their owed rent. Unfortunately, he is late to return from his lunch break, and is promptly fired from his job.

A crooked boxer from across the street, noticing the commotion at the street cleaning offices, pulls Charlie aside and convinces him to fight for a $50 purse, but to throw the bout so they can split the prize.* Just before fight time, however, the boxer must skip town in order to avoid the cops, leaving Charlie with a new boxing adversary. This character, played by Hank Mann, is not about to honor the previous set-up. In desperation, Charlie follows the lead of another boxer by rubbing his body with a lucky rabbit's foot. Unfortunately, that same boxer is soon dragged back into the dressing room unconscious. Charlie then watches as his ring foe and the victorious fighter begin to argue, and the victor is promptly leveled by Mann with a single blow. The Tramp makes vigorous efforts to rid his body of the secret charm, but it is to no avail; Chaplin's beautifully choreographed fight scene does not go in Charlie's favor.†

Battered, literally, but not beaten, the Tramp again runs into his old pal the Millionaire, who is characteristically brimming with liquor. They return to the townhouse, where Charlie is able to share with him the plight of the Blind Girl over a drink. Touched, the Millionaire offers Charlie more than enough to cover both the rent and the operation, and Charlie is ecstatic with this luck.

There are, however, two burglars in the house, who knock out the Millionaire and attempt to do the same to Charlie. He narrowly escapes and notifies the authorities. But when the police arrive, the thugs have disappeared and Charlie is found to have a large sum of cash in his possession. What's more, the Millionaire, reeling from the blow to his head, again cannot remember the

---

*The scene is a variant of a fight-fixing gag depicted in Kevin Brownlow and David Gill's Unknown Chaplin documentary series that was ultimately discarded from The Circus. Hassled by a boxer in a café, Charlie privately pays the gentleman $5, urging him to take a dive in a staged fight in order to impress the girl, Merna Kennedy. The boxer is soundly "beaten," and exits. The scheme has worked— that is, until the boxer's twin brother enters and sits. Charlie, thinking his nemesis has returned for another beating, finds the second brother to be a bit more formidable than the one he paid off. Luckily, Charlie's rival for the girl's affections, Rex (Harry Crocker), is able to rescue a battered Charlie by knocking the newcomer out. Thoroughly confused, the Little Fellow leaves the café, though not before retrieving "his" money from the body.

†This scene also contains a comic gag quite unlike those which Chaplin traditionally used. Generally, the Tramp was the comedic focus of every film, and supporting characters did little in the way of participating in gags that didn't somehow involve him — they were, essentially, props for the comedian to use. Here, Hank Mann actually gets his own, albeit brief, piece of comic business. As Mann enters the arena, he singles out one particularly exuberant fan and knocks him upside the head, which all but silences him. Later, as Mann is leaving the ring after his victorious bout, he again looks menacingly at the fan, who this time cowers in fear. Filmed in a long shot, with a tremendous amount of activity in the sporting arena, as well as coming at the beginning and end of the sequence, the gag is very easily lost amid a blaze of other activity. However, perhaps in deference to his long association with Mann, a former Keystone Cop, Chaplin keeps this uncharacteristic little piece in the picture.

The gag is reminiscent of the type Chaplin remembered having to devise early in his days with Mack Sennett, while under the direction of Henry Lehrman. Feeling that his best business was ending up on the cutting room floor, Chaplin took to making comic entrances or exits, which, together with running gags throughout many scenes, were often too hard to cut during post-production. Either the comedian constructed a similar gag for Mann to execute, or Mann had learned the same lesson during his film career and found it useful here.

Little Fellow. Instinctively, Charlie bolts for the door, eluding the police. Knowing he will be caught, he goes to the home of the Blind Girl, turns over the money, and sadly announces that he must go away for a period, and may never see her again. He leaves and is eventually apprehended. Thus, jail awaits the Tramp, but he enters its doors only after giving a defiant back kick to his cigarette, signifying that his spirit, at least, will carry on.

Nine months pass, and the Tramp emerges — not the brave soul who entered, but with the look of a truly broken man. His shuffle is one of tired defeat, and his clothes are quite ragged, even by the Little Fellow's standards. Following a bout with some pesky street corner newsboys, Charlie turns to look directly into the face of the Flower Girl, now cured of her blindness and operating a flower boutique with her Grandmother. She is taken aback by the strange man's gaze, but kindly offers him a flower for his lapel and some money. Charlie quickly shuffles away, too afraid to think of her reaction should she know the truth. But she stops him and presses the coin into his palm. Then she pauses, recognizing his touch as the hand of her wealthy suitor, and tearily asks, "You?" Charlie nods, noting that she can see. "Yes," she replies. "I can see now." The camera cuts to a close-up of Charlie's face, a mixture of happiness and anticipation, unsure whether she is happy to finally meet him or appalled by his identity. As Chaplin fades out on the scene, the outcome of the encounter is still up in the air.

IV. THE RESISTANCE TO SOUND

Because the silent or nondialogue picture has been temporarily pushed aside in the hysteria attending the introduction of speech by no means indicates that it is extinct or that the motion picture screen has seen the last of it. *City Lights* is evidence of this.[19]

— Charles Chaplin — 1931

In approaching an analysis of *City Lights*, it is important to focus on Chaplin's rejection of a full-fledged talking film, considered by Gerald Mast as "the most brilliant decision of his career,"[20] and to consider his desire to ensure a critical and popular success for his first sound era project.

Though the comedian had defied conventional wisdom by making an essentially silent film, *City Lights* is, in retrospect, less a look to the past than it is a look to the future for Chaplin as a screen artist. A successful sound era debut would not only allay some of his fears about the new medium but reinforce his stature as a film artist and not merely a silent comedian. As Chaplin was advancing in age (he would turn 42 the year of *City Lights'* release), it would not be long before he would be forced to abandon both the silent comedy format and the sprightly man that was his famous screen character. *City Lights*, in this sense, plots an interesting course for his entry into the talkies.

Out with the Millionaire (Harry Myers) in *City Lights*.

Predictably, much of the film's initial hype centered on Chaplin's spurning of sound technology. But regardless of how he claimed throughout the promotion of *City Lights* to abhor it, sound did in fact serve Chaplin well in many areas of the film. Substituting a kazoo for the voices of public speakers or swallowing the whistle enhances the humor of these situations without detracting or proving obtrusive to his screen pantomime. The use of sound effects throughout the picture is calculated to enhance slapstick rather than supplant it. If *City Lights* had been produced in the silent era, similar sounds likely would have been added via musical accompaniment, especially in larger metropolitan-area theaters, so in this respect he was not dramatically altering how his picture would have been received by a considerable portion of the viewing public.

In at least one respect, Chaplin *had* to incorporate sound in some form. By 1931, most theaters had long since given up providing musical accompaniment as a result of the switch to sound — the addition of film soundtracks took care of this. With fewer and fewer motion picture theaters still able to screen a silent feature without special (and potentially expensive) arrangements, the comedian had little choice but to incorporate the new medium to some extent in his new production. But while this may seem a reluctant concession, the technology offered Chaplin complete control over not only what was seen but what was heard in his film as well.

City Lights marked the director's first effort to completely score a film himself, and although Chaplin did have a hand in this aspect of production for nearly a decade prior to the release of *City Lights*, it provided him the opportunity to showcase his musical talents to the public. With all of Chaplin's feature-length films from *The Kid* onward, a musical score (in the form of recommended cue sheets) was to be composed and performed with the completed picture. However, Chaplin could never guarantee the musical content or quality throughout a film's general run. Given the varying size and caliber of movie houses across the United States and abroad, the ability of each to provide comparable musical accompaniment was virtually impossible. Cue sheets were only suggestions; if they were used at all, parts could be moved, altered or omitted at the exhibitor's or musical director's discretion. Sound technology changed this, and *City Lights* would be the first of Chaplin's films to be circulated in the exact manner in which the comedian had both visually and musically conceived it.

Chaplin had long fancied himself a musician. During his music hall days, he became proficient as a violinist (the strings on his violin had to be strung backwards to accommodate his left-handed bowing), and the instrument would be a constant companion throughout his early career. In 1916's *The Vagabond*, he even had the Tramp appear as a wandering musician playing a violin. Chaplin's musical aspirations took an official form when, in the same year, the Charlie Chaplin Musical Publishing Company was established. The endeavor seems to have been poorly organized (Chaplin recalled the organization was "collegiate and quite mad"[21]), and during the company's brief operation only three songs composed by the comedian are known to have been published: "There's Always One You Can't Forget," "Oh! That Cello" and "The Peace Patrol." Later, in 1925, Chaplin would publish two additional songs, "Sing a Song" and "With You Dear in Bombay."[22]

Chaplin's musical skills have been subject to varying degrees of interpretation. Many writers have looked upon his composing as yet another interesting element of his tremendous creative drive. Alistair Cooke, who began an acquaintance with the comedian shortly after the release of *City Lights*, would consider Chaplin's scoring "brilliantly amateur," borrowing a bit from the styles of a number of classical composers.[23] The music Chaplin wrote for his films isn't particularly distinguished, though it was well-suited to his scoring needs.

According to David Raksin, who worked on the musical accompaniment to *Modern Times* (1936), Chaplin's skill as a composer was indeed limited. Since the comedian could not read musical notes, he would dictate themes or fragments of songs. Raksin would elaborate from there, but only under

Chaplin's strict and sometimes unending supervision.[24] "If the people in his studio had suffered from Dad's perfectionist drive," Charles Chaplin, Jr., commented, "the musicians who now began working with him endured pure torture."[25] The score for *City Lights* was a collaboration with Alfred Newman, which developed through very long and occasionally very strained sessions.

In terms of using sound to create comedy, the opening of the film is interesting in that, with Bergman and company emanating the hum of a kazoo when speaking, the effect is a parody of early dialogue films: simple noise. The scene constitutes the film's best use of sound as a comedic device — other sequences also utilize some sound, yet this opening sequence will be long remembered as his first use of sound technology. This was the opening scene as Chaplin originally envisioned it. But interestingly, a forced layover at the studio for outside road construction brought Chaplin a different inspiration.[26] Despite having shot the opening of *City Lights* in its entirety, Chaplin set out in August of 1929 to shoot a new opening sequence which would end up being one of his most simple and impressive scenes of screen comedy, and one which would remain hidden for years.

Charlie is seen alone on a bustling city street, and notices a small block of wood stuck in the grating at his feet. Rather casually, he attempts to knock the wood through the grate with his cane, only to find it hopelessly stuck, rotating with each successive stab. His interest is piqued, and soon what began as an offhand curiosity becomes a full-blown fixation; the piece of wood envelops Charlie's total concentration. In the process, Charlie's obsession soon becomes everyone else's entertainment, attracting the attention of a window store clerk, stopping foot and automobile traffic, and, naturally, drawing the attention of police as well.

With only minimal cuts to the sequence, the unused film stands alone as a shining example of Chaplin's ability to extract comedy from the most simple premise, and sustain it almost single-handedly. (It recalls his solo two-reel performance as a drunk in the Mutual release *One A.M.* [1916], which culminates in another battle with an inanimate object, a bed.) Unfortunately, the new opening was a casualty of Chaplin's meticulous perfectionism. Despite shooting and cutting the scene in its entirety, he discarded the piece for some unknown reason and went back to the statue unveiling, with its barbed putdown of dialogue filmmaking. The stick sequence was simply placed in a canister, stored away and forgotten for some 50 years. Not until Kevin Brownlow and David Gill's efforts in creating the documentary series *Unknown Chaplin* did the seven minute, completely cut version finally surface. "I was absolutely sick with excitement," David Gill recalled on seeing the sequence for the first time, "realizing what we were doing at that moment, seeing a film which Charlie had shot, cut, put together — a little scene that ran about six or seven minutes, complete with a beginning, middle and end — perfect in all its ways and lying on a shelf unknown to anyone outside of Charlie's immediate circle for

50 years! It felt like opening the door to Tutankhamen — an emotional moment."[27]*

Considering the creative challenge posed by sound at the time, the film's current opening seems the most fitting in retrospect, with its parody of talking films. Though Chaplin was indeed troubled by the rapid move to sound by the film industry, he was confident enough in his skills not only to fly in the face of conventional wisdom by producing a non-dialogue picture, but arrogant enough to mock the new format in the first scene as well. Consistent with that opening, *City Lights* continues to utilize sound as an enhancing, yet not entirely integral element of the film's narrative. The comedian skillfully maintained those elements of his work that brought him fame. His use of a recorded soundtrack did offer a considerable advantage in the uniform presentation of the picture, but rather than simply adjust his material to accommodate sound, as the motion picture industry had done, Chaplin adjusted sound to compliment his material.

V. CONTINUING THE CHAPLIN TRADITION

In terms of narrative structure, *City Lights* utilizes themes that were typical for a Chaplin feature, or, as Charles Maland has asserted, it fulfills an "aesthetic contract" with the audience — fulfilling an expectation of comedy, romance and pathos.[28]

Comedy, of course, was Chaplin's mainstay. As with his earlier work at Essanay and Mutual, where the Tramp often found himself placed in different environmental or employment situations, he used a similar approach in *City Lights*. Oftentimes, scenes tend to comprise a collection of ideas and concepts that related to character development. For instance, Chaplin's opening sequence, with the statue unveiling and some comic business featuring a nude statue in a storefront window, helps depict Charlie's life on the streets, and establishes the Tramp as a wanderer in this cinematic city. The situational approach can also be seen in other sequences — Chaplin imagines how the Little Fellow would react in a boisterous Prohibition-era nightclub or as a prize

---

There is yet another missing element from City Lights, also related to the opening moments, one which seems to have gone no further than the planning stage. As Chaplin once envisioned it, the Little Fellow would appear at first as a distinguished gentleman — a prince about to woo his princess. Charlie's romantic overtures are met with approval, but as he and his love kiss, the Tramp, resting in a doorway, is rudely awakened from a dream. The wetness he feels is not from the lips of a beautiful maiden, but from a stray dog. Photographic stills taken in preparation for the sequence, along with a rough film test preserved in Unknown Chaplin, show the comedian garbed in European-style military attire in what looks to be a serio-comic version of Erich von Stroheim. The dream sequence has obvious parallels with films such as The Bank and Shoulder Arms, and even the earlier Karno sketch Jimmy the Fearless, but Chaplin seems never to have developed this idea for City Lights beyond the testing phase.

fighter, among many others. At the same time, these vignettes rarely stray too far from the main dramatic theme, Charlie's efforts to help the Blind Girl.

Other sequences also help define the Tramp as a character. Charlie's attempts to raise money for the girl, for instance, whether as a street cleaner or boxer, underscore the notion that the Little Fellow is ill-suited for work despite his good intentions. Charlie is the classic fish out of water; comedy arises from the fact that he's attempting to do something — work — that is as alien to him as submitting to the Army's regimentation in *Shoulder Arms*. The same principle holds true of Charlie's outings with the Millionaire, for the Little Fellow is distinctly out of place in such opulent surroundings, despite his comical attempts to blend in. Themes such as "the streets" or "employment" were not new to Chaplin's repertoire, for variations on these and other motifs appear throughout his silent film work. Here these aspects serve not only as comedic episodes but as character exposition, even suggesting the social and economic differences that may ultimately keep Charlie and the Blind Girl apart at the end of the film.

Charlie's relationship with the Millionaire also provides noteworthy comic ground for Chaplin. Though he is clearly a plot device to help the Tramp rescue the Girl via his money, the Millionaire is used as a primary comedic inspiration as well.

Interestingly, the Millionaire's situation holds a lot of parallels to that of Chaplin at this point of his life: Both are wealthy men whose wives have left them and, based on popular rumors of Chaplin's earlier condition, both were moody and suicidal. Though Chaplin did not have a drinking problem (he was never much of a drinker, perhaps due to recollections of his father's alcoholism), the situations appear eerily similar. "In the creation of comedy," Chaplin wrote in explaining his inspiration for *The Gold Rush*, "it is paradoxical that tragedy stimulates the spirit of ridicule, because ridicule, I suppose, is an attitude of defiance: we must laugh in the face of our helplessness against the forces of nature — or go insane."[29] In later films, Chaplin would deal more directly with such concerns — his politics, his morality and his waning popularity, defiantly (to use his term) addressing his personal concerns on the public arena of the screen. It is not outlandish, then, to suggest that the Millionaire may have been a therapeutic device, as well as a comedic one, for Chaplin.

It was ample ground from which to work, but it was not new material — just uniquely interpreted. Charlie's various drunken escapades with the millionaire harken back to the comedian's inebriate in Karno's *Mumming Birds*, with Fatty Arbuckle in *The Rounders* (1914) or Ben Turpin in *A Night Out* (1915), his solo performance in *One A.M.* (1916) or his portrayal of the Millionaire drunk in *The Idle Class* (1921), among many others. Such scenes are played almost strictly for comedic purposes. There is no attempt to extract pathos from the situation, though the backdrop of the Millionaire's affluent world does provide a stark contrast to that of the modesty of the Blind Girl's, particularly with respect to their residences.

Romance and pathos are also key elements of *City Lights*, and both are so closely inter-related that they should be considered together. Romance, of course, is personified in the character of the Blind Flower Girl. Like the romances depicted in several earlier films with Edna Purviance, Georgia Hale in *The Gold Rush* or Merna Kennedy in *The Circus*, it would take the form of an almost singular devotion, a romantic affection that guides the Little Fellow's moves throughout the film.

The romance in *City Lights*, however, contains two aspects that make it unique. First, though Charlie is certainly taken by the Flower Girl's beauty, and longs for her affections, his relationship with her is somewhat paternal in nature. The same could be said of the Tramp's relationship with Merna Kennedy in *The Circus*— though there is a definite romantic attraction, Charlie displays a more nurturing side of his character that wasn't as apparent in *The Gold Rush* or in Chaplin's earlier films. While some hope of love between the Flower Girl and the Tramp remains throughout *City Lights*, the Little Fellow appears more as a provider and caregiver than a romantic equal in the film. Perhaps due to Chaplin's own advancing age, especially in relation to the ages of his leading ladies, he was altering his depiction of romance, which would become even more clear with his next two films, *Modern Times* and *The Great Dictator*, while working opposite his third wife, Paulette Goddard.

Second, Virginia Cherrill's character, unlike most of Charlie's previous screen heroines, is taken with the Tramp immediately. She feels the very same emotions as he, though the pathos of the film's finale hinges on the notion that her mental image of Charlie is grossly idealized. One feels that their romance could not have occurred, in fact, without the girl's blindness. In past films, Charlie's love interests were often just friendly acquaintances, mostly one-sided infatuations that (initially, at least) offered little realistic hope for the Tramp to have his love returned. Thus, the further the relationship develops between the Tramp and the Flower Girl, the more the audience can feel the inevitability of Charlie being "found out," and the possibility that Cherrill will reject him as a result of her shattered perceptions.

This aspect helps mesh the romance of *City Lights* with its pathos, which comes to a head in the final scene of the film. The Little Fellow and the Girl gape at one another almost indefinitely — he ashamed, she astonished. Both characters are attempting to judge the reaction of the other, their humble conversation on Chaplin's printed titles forming a sort of double entendre ("Yes," Cherrill says to the Tramp, "I can see now.") that gives no indication where the emotion-filled moment will lead. The impact of the scene is heightened by Chaplin's decision to iris out without a clear resolution. How the Girl ultimately react to Charlie and his poverty, either with acceptance or rejection, is left up to the viewer. Unlike *The Gold Rush* or *The Circus*, where the Tramp's

romantic endeavors were clearly resolved by the end of the film, the ending of
City Lights allows both romance and pathos to hang in the balance.

Crucial to the effectiveness of both the romance and pathos of *City Lights*
was the casting of the Blind Girl. In Virginia Cherrill, Chaplin found a suitable
player. Like Edna Purviance, Georgia Hale and Merna Kennedy before her,
Cherrill was a relatively unknown and inexperienced girl playing opposite
Chaplin as the Tramp's object of affection.

Cherrill, then only 20 years old, had been discovered ringside at a Los
Angeles boxing match (a favorite sporting interest that the comedian picked
up during his days at the Keystone studios); Chaplin quickly convinced her
to screen test for the role of the Blind Girl. Despite the auditions of more
experienced actresses (including Georgia Hale), Cherrill won the part, perhaps, ironically, due to her unfamiliarity with acting. Trained stage presence,
at least in Chaplin's mind, made it difficult for many actresses to not only
appear blind, but also accept his shouted (and often exacting) directoral com-
mands. The comedian was not willing to waste time undoing technique that
did not suit his needs.

But Cherrill was not an actress at heart, and her inability to devote herself fully to Chaplin's production became apparent almost immediately after
filming began. Cherrill was coming off a recent divorce in Chicago, where she
had circulated in prominent social circles. Her lifestyle in Los Angeles not particularly different. In fact, the new environment merely opened an entirely new
set of social opportunities on a far more grand and glamorous scale. Often she
would arrive at the Chaplin Studios in the morning looking ragged and terribly under the weather, much to the dismay of her irate director. As Cherrill had
not come to Hollywood desiring a film career as such, and as her divorce settlement was providing a suitable income, she was not as concerned about applying herself as fully to her acting as Chaplin would have wished. The comedian's
shooting methods also did not help endear the profession to his new starlet.
There were long delays between scenes that involved her character, coupled with
Chaplin's on-again, off-again work habits. This meant that there were long
periods when Virginia was not really required on the set at all, though she, like
everyone at the studio, was expected to report for work and prepare for possible shooting every day. Thus, she may have felt inclined to seek more entertaining endeavors within the glamorous Hollywood night life.

Unfortunately, Cherrill's most important scene, the one most pivotal to
establishing the romance and pathos aspects of the film, was the same one that
caused Chaplin the most difficulty: the Tramp's first meeting with the Blind
Girl. Chaplin had placed himself in yet another narrative tight spot concerning
this first encounter: How could she be convinced that Charlie was a wealthy
aristocrat when she could not see? The problem was vexing. Ultimately, the
device Chaplin utilizes, having the Tramp pass through a limousine to avoid
a nearby policeman, with the slamming car door a signal to Cherrill of Charlie's

"status," came some 534 days into production and after several unsuccessful attempts at depicting the scene. Prior to this moment of inspiration, the comedian had spent nearly three agonizing months of shooting, story conferences and long absences from the studio attempting to solve his dilemma.

As a consequence, his patience was thin. He had hit upon his method of framing the sequence, but perhaps looking to buy himself some more creative time, or perhaps just frustrated in general, Chaplin found Virginia's simple efforts to raise a flower and hand it to the Tramp totally inadequate. Over and over Chaplin re-took the scene, showing Cherrill exactly how she was to perform the seemingly simple task, and over and over she could not satisfy her director.

Ralph Barton, a prominent cartoonist and friend of Chaplin's, took some interesting 16mm home movies of Chaplin working, quite unsuccessfully, on the Flower Girl scenes (preserved in *Unknown Chaplin*). "He'd take it over and over again," Virginia Cherrill would recall, "and when he'd finally say 'It's a take,' we'd breathe a sigh of relief and then he'd say `Well, perhaps just one more time.'"[30] It was, according to Chaplin, attributable to his tireless perfectionism,[31] but privately he acknowledged that during the sequence, "I was a terror to be with …"[32]

Eventually, the difficulties with Cherrill and the pressures of an exhausting shoot came to a head. In November of 1929, some eleven months into shooting, Chaplin fired Virginia from the production after she allegedly expressed her desire to leave work early for a hairdresser's appointment. Although this seems both drastic and unusual, this was not the first time Chaplin had resorted to such actions. *The Gold Rush*, for instance, had begun preliminary shooting when Lita Grey was abruptly dropped as the leading character in favor of Georgia Hale. The 16-year-old Lita, of course, did not lack in devotion as Miss Cherrill would, but her pregnancy surely could not have been hidden for the duration of the shoot. Luckily, Chaplin had begun shooting *The Gold Rush* with scenes in which Lita was not required, so switching leading ladies proved to be a minor distraction.

City Lights was also not the first time that Chaplin became unhappy with a performer. Henry Clive was originally to play the role of the Millionaire, but he was dropped in June of 1929 when he balked at performing the suicide scene, arguing that the water was too cold. Clive was quickly replaced by Harry Myers, who proved far more receptive to Chaplin's directorial wishes. Though Clive had been with the production for over a year, and Chaplin was a full six months into shooting, the actual time spent on the Millionaire/Tramp scenes constituted a mere three days at the time of his dismissal. Thus, Chaplin's brash move was not as detrimental to the production as some earlier biographers have alleged.[33]

Though it came relatively late in the production, dismissing Virginia also came early enough to allow for the possibility for reshooting her scenes with another actress.[34] As in *The Gold Rush*, Georgia Hale was once again brought on board to assume the role of leading lady, even though Chaplin pressman Carlyle Robinson argued strongly against her employment, clearly favoring Cherrill's screen work.[35] Hale's stay would be brief, barely two weeks, and outtakes appear in Brownlow and Gill's *Unknown Chaplin*. Most interesting is to see her in an early version of *City Lights*' conclusion, one which clearly shows that Chaplin had not yet defined either his directorial approach or the emotional backdrop for this scene. The clip is particularly rough, rudimentary in its staging and lacking the performance quality that eventually graced the finished print.

Chaplin's problems only seemed to mount following the dismissal of the actress. Unsatisfied with the material being shot with Georgia, he briefly entertained thoughts of others for the role, but finally opted to resume shooting with Virginia once again. Cherrill, in fact, even found her dismissal to be a blessing in disguise. Marion Davies pointed out that she had been one year shy of legal age when she signed her first contract with Chaplin and, hence, could use this as leverage when the comedian asked her to return to the production; armed with such information, she was able to double her weekly salary to $150.[36] Following a heated catharsis between the pair after Cherrill's immediate return, *City Lights* proceeded without further problems between its male and female leads.

By the time Chaplin got down to shooting the pivotal final scene again, it is clear that he had more fully contemplated the narrative and emotional climax, far more than he had in the dry run with Georgia Hale. Several additional factors helped heighten the finale's impact, contributing to the tension of that fateful meeting. For instance, Charlie has been unjustly incarcerated for robbing the Millionaire, and when he is released nine months later, the Little Fellow is clearly shaken by this sacrifice. His clothes are extremely tattered and his slow shuffle clearly indicates a battered and defeated soul. A pair of pea-shooting newsboys, a nuisance whenever the Little Fellow has run into them, gain the upper hand as Charlie has clearly lost the will to battle their mischief. Further, the meeting in front of the flower shop proves a complete role reversal from their initial encounter. This time, it is Charlie who needs the helping hand, with the Flower Girl in a position to lend it. Clearly frightened by the prospect of Virginia discovering his identity, a battered flower that the Tramp has retrieved from the gutter symbolically comes apart when he lays eyes upon her. From the moment the Tramp is released from jail, Chaplin clearly stacks the deck against his character, purposely extracting as much pathos from this situation as possible.[37]

But when Virginia insists he take her gifts of a flower and coin, she recognizes the touch of Charlie as she presses the coin into his hand. At once she is taken aback, but her look is ambiguous. One hopes that Charlie is not turned away, and apparently this is what Chaplin intended, based on his early notes

The Tramp as romantic — with Virginia Cherrill from *City Lights* (1931). Charlie demonstrating feminine worship from afar.

on the story.[38] Virginia was to lead the Tramp into the flower shop as the scene fades out, much as Edna Purviance did in accepting the Little Fellow at the end of *The Kid*, or earlier in *The Vagabond*. But Chaplin, perhaps to heighten its emotional impact, opted for the ambiguous ending, not an uncommon occurrence in his filmography.[39]

Chaplin was most satisfied with the conclusion of *City Lights*. "I had several takes and they were all overdone, overacted, overfelt," he recalled years later. "[In the print cut] I was looking more at her, interested to see that she didn't make any mistakes. It was a beautiful sensation of not acting, of standing outside myself. The key was exactly right — slightly embarrassed, delighted at meeting her again — apologetic without being emotional about it. [Charlie] was watching and wondering what she was thinking and wondering without any effort. It's one of the purest inserts — I call them inserts, close-ups — that I've ever done. One of the purest."[40]

VI. *CITY LIGHTS* AS SOCIAL COMMENTARY

Given the period in which City Lights was released, at the height of the Depression, one is bound to be struck by the juxtapositions between the carefree life of the Millionaire and the genuine struggles of both the Blind Girl and the Tramp. Such vast contrast in lifestyles, particularly in a period of profound economic crisis around the world, is bound to raise questions about Chaplin's intended social commentary. Are we to assume that its intent is to point at the growing disparity between the rich and the poor, highlighting the struggles of the less privileged?

On the surface, this may seem to carry some validity, but it is not entirely true. In many of Chaplin's films, poignant contrasts between rich and poor are commonplace. The comedian often drew the humor and pathos of his character directly from his struggle to assume the posture of more wealthy, educated and sophisticated men. This was the case, for instance, in 1919's *Sunnyside*, when the Tramp attempts to become a gentleman to win the hand of Edna. Actually, City Lights has much in common with the scenario for *The Idle Class*. In that particular film, Chaplin played the dual role of the Tramp and a drunken millionaire, either one of whom, depending on one's interpretation, could constitute the "idle class." As the rich man, Chaplin's drinking drives his wife (Edna Purviance) to leave him and vow not to return unless he gives up the bottle (which, of course, he does not). The comparison to Harry Myers' Millionaire is easily made; City Lights, in this respect, could be the continuation of the drunk's story, a theme abandoned in *The Idle Class* to focus on Charlie's infatuation with the Millionaire's wife. Additionally, employing the plot device of mistaken identity in *The Idle Class*— which would resurface in 1940's *The Great Dictator*— the Tramp inadvertently assumes the role of the drunken Millionaire (at a costume ball), a humorous scenario that also contrasts the rich and the poor through the Tramp's attempts to bluff his way as a socialite.

For a film released at the height of the Depression, it is easy to draw similar parallels between the social conditions of the era and what the comedian depicted in his narrative. But Chaplin seems to have had the general plot for City Lights conceptualized and was almost ten full months into shooting when the October Crash helped plunge the world into economic chaos. Instead, as Charles Maland has argued, it may be more accurate to consider *City Lights* as a commentary on the Roaring Twenties in general, when carefree optimism and prosperity ran rampant for many, but not all; a period when the disparity between the world's millionaires and the world's tramps grew steadily.[41]

To this extent, the Crash, unexpected as it was, amplified Chaplin's intended narrative scope, and was likely not — initially at least — the object of his commentary. The comedian's off-the-cuff shooting methods certainly afforded him ample opportunity to change the tone or direction of his films; the length of the *City Lights* shoot alone lasted 22 months, ending in October of 1930, and gave him plenty of opportunity to make a social statement if he wished. But given the threat to Chaplin's stardom posed by the introduction of sound to film, he was probably little concerned with making the type of social or political observations that would mark his later film work. Though aspects of his personality and politics are evident throughout his filmography, his emphasis in *City Lights* was clearly elsewhere. Producing a silent picture in a rapidly advancing age forced Chaplin to seek to insure its artistic and commercial success. It is therefore tempting to offer a far more symbolic analysis of *City Lights* than the artist likely intended.

Nonetheless, the depiction of the rich and the poor makes for some interesting comparisons. Many of the contrasts in *City Lights* center around money. With the Millionaire, cash is never a worry and is used as an escape from dealing with the real world — a shield behind which the troubled or unhappy can hide and yet still feel, at least superficially, accepted. Money is a convenience that can purchase happiness and friendship, and provides a simple escape from the despair of his failing marriage. His wealth supports his empty lifestyle; the Millionaire spends a good portion of his days drinking or recovering from such excesses. In the days of Prohibition, not only was he breaking the law, but enjoying a luxury only the well-off could afford day in and day out. When contrasted with the Blind Girl's struggle, the Millionaire does indeed appear shallow and care-free. Myers' Millionaire is a rich man with no soul; Virginia Cherrill, on the other hand, as Chaplin depicts her in *City Lights,* is rich in soul but poor in terms of material wealth.[42]

For the Blind Girl, money represents not escape, but hope. Between herself and her Grandmother, there is hardly enough income to cover even the basic necessities. Chaplin romanticizes the plight of the struggling Blind Girl, a theme he usually reserved for the Little Fellow. Despite her impoverished exterior and yearning for a better life, the inner goodness of the Girl's character is genuine enough that we can believe there may be room for a Blind Girl-Tramp romance at the film's conclusion. With such richness in her heart, she wants only for a stable life. Charlie's "stolen" money provides not only that, but also the opportunity to restore her sight. Money, to this end, while representing hope, has not voided her compassion and love for her faceless suitor. Money has allowed her to embark on a brighter and more stable future, in direct contrast to its flawed and selfish use in the hands of the Millionaire.

As for the Tramp, Chaplin never leaves the viewer with any confusion where his sympathy lies; it becomes evident in a brief scene with Charlie in the Millionaire's limousine that harkens back to an earlier gag. In the conclusion of *The Gold Rush*, the now-wealthy Little Fellow, dressed in his shabby garb for the benefit of reporters, stoops to retrieve a discarded cigar butt, proving that old habits die hard. Charlie not only creates a comic irony but also displays his humanistic sympathies with the audience. Regardless of his wealth or status, the Little Fellow's humble roots will not be soon forgotten, and success has not changed him at heart.

In *City Lights*, the scene is repeated. Charlie, bestowed with the gift of the limousine by the Millionaire, is quick to follow a sharp-looking gentleman down the street in hopes that he will soon part with the remainder of his cigar. When the man does, Charlie quickly vaults from the luxury car to retrieve the prize before a competing street tramp can make off with it. Victorious, the Little Fellow proudly retreats behind the wheel of his automobile, much to the confusion of the tramp who saw his cigar butt lifted from him by an apparent upper classman. The situation is comedic in and of itself, but it also portrays the schism many saw in society — the growing gap between those who rode the wave of prosperity and those who were drowned in its wake. He had not forgotten his own childhood poverty, and like the character Chaplin portrayed, he has the ability to commingle with the highest social set without losing touch, so it seemed, with the values of the common individual.

Thus it seems clear that in *City Lights* the role of money is one of opportunity rather than necessity. It is not ultimately important whether the Blind Girl becomes wealthy with her flower shop; nor, do we believe, is it wealth that will determine whether she is accepting of Charlie as her kindly benefactor. Although it is her hope and dream that Charlie will turn out to be that dashing young man of prosperity and influence, this is nothing more than a common fantasy. It is ultimately genuine love and kindness that she is seeking, the plausibility of which heightens the tension of the finale. Money, with the Blind Girl, can be liberating in its ability to offer a broader range of opportunities, whereas its selfish misuse by the Millionaire merely buys a superficial and temporary form of idle satisfaction.

VII. RESPONSE TO *CITY LIGHTS*

City Lights is remembered as one of Chaplin's greatest feature-length motion pictures, but ironically, his preview for the film was a disaster.[43] Chaplin had arranged for an unannounced screening at the Tower Theatre in Los

Angeles less than two weeks before the film was slated to open, only to find a small and rather unenthusiastic crowd in attendance. With all that seemed to be riding on the picture, the lukewarm response was terrifying to the comedian. He had worked increasingly hard to guarantee the film's success, from the actual production time (the longest of his career) to an extensive promotion and advertising campaign, but his hard work nonetheless gave way to insecurity as the official opening approached. Chaplin was pitting the popularity of Charlie against the public's apparent love affair with sound technology, with no sure guarantee of success.

But when Chaplin attended the gala premiere on January 30, 1931 with date Georgia Hale, accompanied by his guests Mr. and Mrs. Albert Einstein, *City Lights* awed the crowd at the newly-constructed Los Angeles Theatre. The premiere was not without its glitches; the film was stopped midway through the screening and the house lights raised so that the audience, according to an announcement, could marvel at the theater's palatial surroundings, much to Chaplin's anger. Nonetheless, reaction to the film that evening was tremendous, and served to boost his confidence in its ultimate success.

Following the Los Angeles premiere, Chaplin made directly for the East Coast with his film, which was to settle into the George M. Cohan Theatre in New York. There, Chaplin became upset with what he considered a lack of adequate publicity, and took control of the promotional aspects himself. What may have been the root of the problem, however, was Chaplin's personal demand for half of the gross on *City Lights*, a figure that United Artists felt would discourage many exhibitors from showing it. How the public would react to an essentially silent film, coupled with Chaplin's wish to raise ticket prices, were additional factors that could possibly hurt the film's financial prospects. However, Chaplin was not satisfied with these arguments, and oversaw the New York opening in order to ensure compliance with his original demands.

His efforts paid off: Reaction in New York was no less enthusiastic than in Los Angeles. After a host of glowing critical reviews greeted the film's appearance, *City Lights* would break all house records at the Cohan, generating over half a million dollars during its 12-week run. For Chaplin's fans, it seemed, the novelty of sound had worn off. *City Lights*, with the return of Charlie, not only recalled a more nostalgic era, but provided a unique form of entertainment, with far more energy than many sound releases of the day. The public, en masse, would support *City Lights* to the tune of approximately $2 million throughout its highly successful run.

By and large, Chaplin, the darling of critics and world intelligentsia, was praised for his new film. But not everyone was satisfied with *City Lights*. One of the few truly negative reviews came from *Nation* critic Alexander Bakshy, who noted in his March 4, 1931, column that *City Lights* was perhaps the feeblest of Chaplin's feature films to date, and particularly derided the film's "three years of publicity." Bakshy further objected to the film's over-sentimentality and silent format, and suggested that Chaplin may be losing some of his comedic brilliance.[44] He also alludes to the glowing reviews of others as partially descending from Chaplin's status as one of Hollywood's greatest stars, making him a personal favorite of many critics, which hence may have clouded their reactions to the film.

Writing long after the film's premiere, George Jean Nathan was another who conceded that Chaplin's talents were many, but that the excess of artistic praise heaped on him obscured a truly perceptive view of his pictures. This was especially true for the filmmaker's first sound era release. "In *City Lights*," he wrote, "Chaplin had a rich opportunity to make use of sounds, both for their own valuable collaborative effect and in the way of travesty, which he did not take advantage of. After the first few moments within the imitation of the talking screen's voices in terms of musical instruments — a fetching idea — there was no use of sound that was not stale and obvious."[45]*

On the needling of Chaplin's critical success, the comedian was — to a degree — guilty as charged. He had not only helped define screen comedy for the previous 15 years, but his popularity as a screen figure had a substantial impact on the acceptance of film as a mode of mass entertainment and as an art form. Critics certainly recognized the importance of each new Chaplin release, especially *City Lights*, in light of his challenge to film's newest technology. Chaplin had grown from the relative simplicity and vulgarisms of his early Keystone pictures to an artist of high respect, wealth and status — aspects that undoubtedly weighed, however unconsciously, in critics' minds as they discussed his works at the time.

But at this point in Chaplin's career, pointed criticism from mainstream writers was few and far between; though Bakshy and Nathan certainly demonstrate that dissenting voices were heard, they were swamped by zealous accolades for the comedian's work. While lauding Chaplin's newest release, equating the mixture of comedy and pathos with his features of the past, *New York Times* critic Mordaunt Hall was typical in his praise. Not only had the old Charlie returned, he noted, but even though the comedian chose to spurn

---

*Ahead of its time, Nathan's sound effects argument is insightful, and is perhaps best seen in light of later history. In the 1940s, 1950s and 1960s, when silent films was undergoing a revival of sorts, many companies snapped up copies of older comedy films to duplicate and redistribute, particularly those of Chaplin's Keystone, Essanay and Mutual periods. In an effort to make the films seem less antiquated, they were often "enhanced" with musical accompaniment and sound effects. Unfortunately, this practice often failed to appreciate film form or an artist's intent, and many soundtracks appeared horribly mismatched and sound effects inserted haphazardly for random laughs. In addition to the poor print quality of many films, the overall appearance of these releases was sometimes very sloppy and, in retrospect, may have damaged silent comedy somewhat by giving it the appearance of crudeness.

Upon reflection, the comedian's use of sound effects could appear at times to be very similar to the type added to many films during the 1950's. To be sure, Chaplin exercised considerably more thought and care than did the small film distribution companies of a generation later, but Nathan's criticism, in retrospect, is quite valid.

dialogue, "Mr. Chaplin's shadow has grown no less."[46] Chaplin's cinematic legacy with the Tramp, coupled with both critical and popular success from the farthest corners of the globe, made his work difficult to argue against persuasively.

City Lights has also received great praise since the time of its release, especially during subsequent revivals and throughout critical assessments of Chaplin's works. While certainly not unassailable as a film (Bakshy's comments on Chaplin's predilection toward sentimentality are indeed prophetic[47]), it would nonetheless prove to be one of Chaplin's most remembered films, perhaps *because* of its sentimentality. Chaplin had proven to himself and to motion picture audiences the world over that his brand of comedy, lined with the crucial elements of romance and pathos, still had a place in world cinema. *City Lights* won both popular and critical acceptance, proving the comedian's contention that the public had not tired of silent films.

With respect to the body of Chaplin's work, *City Lights* was a tremendous achievement, especially in light of the issues he was facing during the period — rapidly changing film technology, a vicious public divorce, tax troubles, the death of his mother and a long and arduous shoot, all occurring within the span of a few years. Chaplin was under enormous pressure from both his public admirers and from within to prove his worth on the screen once again, almost as if he were some sort of heralded newcomer to the Hollywood scene.

Sound film did not automatically mark the demise of every silent film star, as has sometimes been popularly expressed. It did, however, pose a brand new challenge for many in the film industry to quickly adapt to a medium requiring skills — acting or otherwise — far different from its previous form. Some met with success, others didn't. Chaplin was determined to succeed, both financially and artistically. He felt that the best way to do so was to capitalize on his strengths, utilizing a familiar narrative structure not unlike the types that had secured his fame.

The unobtrusive use of a soundtrack and simple sound effects were concessions to sound, but represent only a minor deviation from the physical presence of a theater orchestra. Chaplin pitted the familiar appeal of Charlie against the popularity of a new medium, and his success moved him into a new era in his filmmaking.

Yet, *City Lights* would also mark an end of sorts to the traditional Chaplin feature. He had already produced one successful "silent" film in the sound era, but knew he could not toy with the inevitable for long. At some point he would have to embrace sound. And, the comedian perhaps felt, it certainly could not be done with the Tramp.

Virtually all of his popularity, however, rested on the Little Fellow, and to suddenly purge him from the screen would no doubt be a cinematic risk equal to, if not greater than, catapulting into the medium of sound. Perhaps he remembered his experience with *A Woman of Paris*, where audiences abandoned a Chaplin film that failed to feature the Little Fellow. The comedian was in no hurry to break with his trade persona. As we shall see, he would ease the audience out of the elements of a traditional Chaplin film and his screen character, allowing him to move on to projects with distinctly different tones and characteristics. At the same time, Chaplin would also look to utilize more and more sound techniques. Thus, his next motion picture, *Modern Times*, would demonstrate a fuller acceptance of sound technology, and portray a story which minimized the role of Charlie.

But before pondering his next film project, Chaplin still had the matter of continuing to promote *City Lights*, which provided an opportunity to turn business into an extended vacation. As he had following the American release of *The Kid*, Chaplin accompanied his new film to Europe and attended gala premieres on that continent. Chaplin would again recount the trip in print, this time in a five-part magazine article for *Woman's Home Companion* (entitled "A Comedian Sees the World"), which begins to show Chaplin's flirtation with the political and social beliefs that would become a dominant trait in his film projects for the remainder of his career. It was also during this trip that Chaplin would find part of the inspiration for his next film, a picture that would touch upon the poverty and suffering he would witness in Depression-era Europe.

3

Modern Times

Both before and after the premiere of *City Lights*, Chaplin devoted much time and effort to the promotion of the film, almost a necessity given the public's acceptance of sound film. He felt that he had to generate an unprecedented amount of excitement for *City Lights* in order to guarantee its box office success. Accompanying the film to Europe was an ideal promotional tool. His appearances would spur a tremendous amount of publicity as the press recorded his various comings and goings. Also, he could utilize the trip for some much-needed relaxation. The strain of creating and promoting the film was great, and the comedian could certainly benefit from a few months of rest.

I. HIS TRIP ABROAD

I want to live my youth again, to capture the moods and sensations of childhood, so remote from me now — so unreal — almost like a dream. I need to turn back time; to venture into the blurred past and bring it into focus.[1]

— Charles Chaplin, recalling
his 1931 world tour

Even with the overwhelming critical and promising financial success of *City Lights* in the United States, Chaplin showed no reservation toward embarking on the extended foreign tour. Staffer Carlyle Robinson was instructed to make the necessary arrangements for him to set sail for Europe on February 13, 1931, just one week after *City Lights* premiered at New York's George M. Cohan Theatre.

He documented his thoughts on the journey in the magazine *Women's Home Companion*, thanks to the efforts of managing editor Willa Roberts, who tailed him on part of his trip and convinced him to write the piece. The articles would eventually run in monthly installments from September, 1933 to January of 1934, and are instrumental in understanding his thoughts and concerns during this period, as well as the inspiration for his next film, *Modern Times*.

However tentative Chaplin may have felt about his stature as a box office draw in the sound era, this tour of Europe would assure a great response to his latest film. The media eagerly kept in step with Chaplin's public appearances, providing numerous reports and updates on nearly every outing, thought and gesture he communicated throughout his vacation. Chaplin cashed in on his personal popularity, as he did during his 1921 visit — attention which translated into box office receipts for *City Lights*.

Originally, the Chaplin entourage was only to include himself, Robinson and Kono, Chaplin's Japanese servant and his "man Friday." During his stay in New York, however, Chaplin met up with a friend, cartoonist Ralph Barton, who at the time was despondent over his failed relationship with a young actress and deeply troubled over the direction of his career (issues that Chaplin himself had tangled with not long before). Barton had already made one suicide attempt. At the last minute, Chaplin graciously invited his friend to accompany him to Europe. If the journey was truly to be as enjoyable as the comedian hoped, perhaps both he and Barton could recuperate from the pressures to be found in America.

When the passenger ship *Mauretania* pulled into Portsmouth, England, on February 19, 1931, there was certainly no question as to whether Chaplin's popularity had waned during the decade since his previous visit, judging by the mass of human bodies gathered at the dock. His arrival by train in London found police frantically attempting to contain a crowd of thousands, all well-wishers seeking just one glimpse of their native son. "They are frenzied with excitement and I am enjoying it all," Chaplin wrote. "We are being carried along in the crush and they are all pushing and shoving. But I love it! It feels like an affectionate embrace."[2]

Soon Chaplin launched full swing into the promotional and social itinerary that would consume virtually all of the rest of his stay in Europe. Lady Astor, John Maynard Keynes, George Bernard Shaw, Winston Churchill, Prime Minister Ramsay MacDonald and H.G. Wells were just a few of the personalities Chaplin met with in England alone. His audience with Shaw is interesting because a meeting of the two on Chaplin's previous visit had fallen through; the comedian was so nervous at the prospect of meeting the famed playwright that he couldn't muster the courage to call upon him.

As with his visit in 1921, Chaplin found a great spiritual and emotional uplift in revisiting the areas of London where he had grown up as a boy. This was to be a recurring source of energy for Chaplin — Jerry Epstein, an assistant to the comedian late in his career, accompanied him on many such visits to London throughout the 1950s and 1960s, and remarked how rejuvenated Chaplin would become following such outings.[3] One notable visit on the 1931 tour was a return to the Hanwell Schools, the institution that seemed to have the most impact on Chaplin as a boy. (While Chaplin was deeply touched by his visit, a promised return trip never materialized — he sent Kono and Robinson in his place. Viewed by some as a snub to the orphans, it would become one of many so-called social blunders reported by the press during his visit.)

After premieres of *City Lights* in both London and Paris proved successful, the burden of promotion had been lifted off Chaplin's shoulders, and he began to concentrate on enjoying the rest of his stay. Before leaving England, however, Chaplin bid farewell to Ralph Barton, who was clearly not finding Europe as healing as the comedian was. In "A Comedian Sees the World," Chaplin recounted the erraticness of Barton's behavior as the excitement following their initial arrival died down, including his snipping the wires of the clock in their shared suite, ostensibly to escape the noise of the second hand. Chaplin wished him the best and was fairly confident of Barton's recovery from acute depression. The cartoonist would end his life a mere two months following his return.

Next came trips to Vienna and Berlin, the latter indicating the universality of the Tramp's appeal. On his 1921 tour, Chaplin was virtually unrecognized in Germany, since a government ban on American films there extended back to World War I. *The Rink*, which saw its American premiere in December, 1916, had been the first Chaplin film released in Germany, and debuted only a few weeks prior to Chaplin's 1921 visit. Now, a decade later, Berlin crowds easily rivaled those of London, Paris or any other large European city. But the crowds weren't the lasting impact of his visit. Chaplin was very distressed by the social and economic ills he witnessed in Germany, ones that were lending to the rise of Adolf Hitler and the Nazi Party.

The German trip also allowed Chaplin to pay a visit to the flat of physicist Albert Einstein and his wife. The Einsteins, who had been Chaplin's special guests at the Los Angeles premiere of *City Lights*, were genteel hosts in their modest apartment. Chaplin, who had already had a smattering of Depression-era political debate during his stay in England, used the visit with Einstein to float some of his own theories on the crisis.

> The recovery of past economic depressions may have been due to inventions and new enterprises, but since those days the necessity of man power has been rapidly decreasing because of modern machinery, and whatever new enterprises crop up in the future, they will not require the man power that was necessary in the past. Therefore as man's only means of consuming what machinery produces is by work, our problem becomes a difficult one ...

Continuing later, this time on economics:

> These two mediums of exchange — credit and gold — will never stabilize prices, for credit is more elastic than gold. Therefore the value of all our enterprises built up by credit will always be at the mercy of the gold standard which can reduce those values at will.[4]

Professor Einstein remained a polite host throughout Chaplin's commentary. Though he perhaps had a much more credible background to discuss theories in economics and politics, the physicist nonetheless declined to take issue with any of Chaplin's statements. "You're not a comedian," he remarked to Chaplin later. "You're an economist."[5]

Chaplin left the Rhineland for further excursions into France, including a rather slapstick attempt at boar hunting in Normandy, and finally to the French Riviera to reunite with his brother Sydney, who had then retired from the filmmaking business. Another trip found the Chaplin entourage in Algiers — a land that Chaplin was evidently taken with, as Alf Reeves, back at the Chaplin Studios in Hollywood, announced to a journalist that the country would provide an opportune setting for Chaplin's next film.[6] According to Reeves' account, the Little Fellow would be donning the garb of an Arab sheik, perhaps trading the snow of the Klondike for the sand of Algiers in Chaplin's search for an exotic setting. It was, of course, never utilized, but nonetheless one can imagine the fumbling Little Tramp invoking the satirical image of Rudolph Valentino.

Following an excursion through Spain, Chaplin made his way back to London where he had hoped to relax for a few months before his eventual return to California. There, Chaplin received the unusual invitation to meet Mahatma Gandhi at the home of a prominent London doctor. The request was unusual because Gandhi did not know who Chaplin was, having never seen a motion picture in his native India. And as if returning the favor, Chaplin knew relatively little about Gandhi or his cause. Nonetheless, at the meeting, Chaplin took the opportunity to engage the Indian leader in a conversation of what little he knew about Gandhi's movement, specifically regarding an avoidance of modern technology, as he would later recall:

> I should like to know why you're opposed to machinery. After all, it's the natural outcome of man's genius and is part of his evolutionary progress. It is here to free him of the bondage of slavery, to help him to leisure and higher culture. I grant that machinery with only the consideration of profit has thrown men out of work and created a great deal of misery, but to use it as a service to humanity, that consideration transcending everything else, should be a help and benefit to mankind.... You must progress like the western world. Sooner or later you will adopt machinery.[7]

Gandhi was gracious in accepting Chaplin's criticisms, perhaps out of politeness for the guest he hardly knew and for the comedian's obvious unfamiliarity with the nature of Gandhi's home rule campaign.

Similar to his conversation with Einstein, Chaplin's comments to Gandhi, particularly regarding "machinery with only the consideration of profit," would serve as the foundation for his next film, *Modern Times*. At virtually every stop on this European tour, Chaplin was circulating through the highest circles of government officials and celebrities. The economic, labor and political conditions that Chaplin found throughout Europe left lasting impressions. How many times Chaplin's ideas and comments were treated with kid gloves out of respect for his stature we can only speculate. What may have been common courtesy on the part of many statesmen may have been interpreted by Chaplin as validation of his opinions. Whether or not this was the case, Chaplin, who had long held strong feelings about political and social causes, was becoming much more socially conscious through his artistic and political associations, and these opinions would find an increasing importance in his work for his next three films.

Upon his return to London from an excursion to Northern England, Chaplin accepted an invitation from Douglas Fairbanks to travel to St. Moritz, Switzerland, for two weeks of skiing. Sydney Chaplin also joined the entourage there. Although acknowledging he wasn't much of a skier, Chaplin nonetheless could not pass up the opportunity to spend time with Fairbanks, one of his few close friends among Hollywood contemporaries. The original two-week period became two months before he finally left Switzerland.

His extended European vacation was obviously enjoyable, but Chaplin had begun to find himself eager to return to Hollywood. Arrangements were made for him to leave Italy by boat and travel through the Orient en route to his home in California. Before sailing, however, the Chaplin party attempted to arrange a meeting with Mussolini while they were in Rome. Chaplin had only two days before his ship was scheduled to depart and, predictably, Il Duce refused to make special arrangements to accommodate an American entertainer. Thus, the comedian was deprived of the opportunity to actually meet Mussolini some eight years before he would write a burlesque of the Italian leader, Benzino Napoloni, into *The Great Dictator* (1940).[8]*

Chaplin sailed from Italy to the Orient, making brief stops in both Ceylon and Singapore. Bali, a land that Sydney had spoken of to his brother, was his only other major layover. During the journey, Chaplin was taken with the stories of two American boys on the ship who were traveling to Bali in part because of its affordability, a rare find in the throes of the world-wide depression. "It's no use going back to the states now," they told him. "We'd only join the ranks of the unemployed."[9]

From Bali the ship traveled towards Japan. Kobe, Chaplin's city of arrival, was jammed with Japanese admirers, and airplanes inundated the crowds from above with leaflets welcoming the comedian to the country.

An interesting anecdote to a scene in this film, however, stems from a visit Chaplin had during his European tour with the King of Belgium. The comedian, already quite short in comparison to the King, found himself seated in an abnormally short chair that only further accentuated their differences in size. Chaplin would use the gag — this time to his own advantage — when Benzino Napaloni arrives at Hynkel's (Hitler's) palace in The Great Dictator. Garbitsch, Hynkel's Minister of the Interior, arranged for the seat to be abnormally low, attempting to psychologically emphasize the differences in stature between the two vain dictators.

But the friendly enthusiasm of the Japanese people did not seem to last for long. By the time Chaplin had reached Tokyo, a strange aura of mysteriousness had begun to envelop his visit. Kono, Chaplin's servant, who had entered Japan some time earlier to make arrangements concerning their arrival, was acting a bit strangely. While driving through the city, Chaplin recalled, Kono urged the limousine driver to stop the car, and asked Chaplin to exit and bow before the Palace, citing tradition as the reason.[10] This was done, but not without a good deal of suspicion by members of the traveling party. Later, Sydney would express the feeling that his belongings had been searched.

As it turned out, during their stay, Japan's Prime Minister Tsuyoshi Inukai was assassinated in the Palace by members of the Black Dragon, a band of conspirators looking to restore authority to Japan's imperial tradition. At the time of the murder, Chaplin and his entourage were attending a sumo wrestling match as the guest of the Prime Minister's son, and were never in harm's way.

But in his memoirs, Chaplin clearly relishes the notion that he was somehow involved in Japan's dark political intrigue, and attempts to put the conspiracy into perspective. He attributes Kono's behavior as being influenced by the Black Dragon; bowing before the palace was not tradition, but an unknowing tribute to the revolutionary group. Further, Chaplin claims that he may have figured in an early version of the assassination plot — a plan that would have trapped Chaplin and other government officials on the floor of the Japanese parliament. The conspirators, he claims, planned to launch explosive devices from the galleries above, while other Dragon members were to be stationed near the exits and gun down survivors as they scrambled for safety. Killing Chaplin would serve as a direct blow to America, members of the Black Dragon felt, as he was one of its most beloved Hollywood stars.

The true threat to Chaplin during his Japanese trip is debatable; his gift for dramatization is clearly evident in his recollection of these events. However, he does offer one comically macabre postscript to his supposed brush with death: "I can imagine the assassins having carried out their plans, then discovering that I was not an American but an Englishman — 'Oh, so sorry.'"[11]

Although Chaplin's stay in Japan was not without delightful experiences (he was particularly taken with kabuki theater), he looked forward to the arrival of his sailing date for home. On June 2, 1932, some 16 months after leaving the United States, he set sail. The journey home offered the film star plenty of time to reflect on all that he had seen, and he directed his thoughts toward the economic and social ills that he had witnessed throughout the tour. Chaplin capped the trip home by penning his so-called *Economic Solution*, which outlined his philosophy on aiding the recovery from the world-wide depression — though his actual grasp of economic complexities was rooted more in his own idealism. Characterizing the plan as "capitalist utopianism," biographer David Robinson respectfully noted, however, that regardless of its merit as a legitimate

The Tramp as an inadvertent radical — picking up the red flag in *Modern Times*.

economic agenda, "it serves to illustrate the range and ingenuity of his intellectual effort."[12]

As Chaplin closed his thoughts in "A Comedian Sees the World," he took the images of poverty he had seen throughout Europe and Asia and focused on his adopted homeland. On his journey back to California, he noted that America had become, contrary to his early feelings during his vaudeville days, a place of uncertainty. No longer did the country seem to hold the promise it once did. Somehow, as the whole world had been brought down by economic chaos, even the brightness of the United States had been dimmed since his departure. As with his conversation with Gandhi, his commentary in *Women's Home*

Companion would become the conceptual seed of what would become his next motion picture project, *Modern Times.*

> Something has happened to America since I've been away. That youthful spirit born of prosperity and success has worn off and in its place is a maturity and sobriety.
> As I journey from Seattle to Hollywood, passing through the rich farmlands of Washington, the dense pine forests of Oregon and on into the vineyards of California, it seems impossible to believe ten million people wanting when so much real wealth is evident.[13]

Later, in his memoirs, Chaplin characterized his 1931-32 world tour similarly. "My holiday came to an end," he noted, "and although I had enjoyed many aspects of it, some had been depressing. I saw food rotting, goods piled high while people wandered hungrily about them, millions of unemployed and their services going to waste ... [t]he depression was deeply cruel."[14]

II. ANALYSIS OF HIS TRIP

> [Chaplin's] contact with the social ideas of distinguished men, particularly in 1931, intellectualized his view of himself and in a sense alienated the emotional-moral content of the Tramp.[15]
> — Parker Tyler

> It was in the 1930s that Chaplin's critics — often the best disposed of them — began to complain that he was getting above his station. The clown was setting himself up as a statesman and a philosopher. He had mingled so much with world leaders (they said) that he had begun to think of himself as one.[16]
> — David Robinson

Chaplin's series of articles, "A Comedian Sees the World," demonstrates his emerging penchant for addressing social issues, a trait that would cross over into his films as well. As Parker Tyler contends, Chaplin's contact with the leaders of business and government, not to mention an occasional brush with royalty, helped attune his mind toward the political and economic crisis plaguing the globe. A basic observation on "A Comedian Sees the World" is Chaplin's distinct tendency for name-dropping (a charge that would also plague him later with the publication of his memoirs). More importantly, however, the series also contains snippets of real and tangible political discussion, however idealistic or naive Chaplin's personal views may have been. The effects of his trip, coupled with observations of Depression-era America and a growing progressivism in his own social, critical and political circles, were some of the major factors that lead Chaplin away from his traditional film material. With increasing frequency, Chaplin was being considered by many to be something more than simply a popular film comedian — rather, he was becoming looked upon as an influential world figure and artist.[17]

Perhaps the most significant of his observations of the trip were his comments on England and Germany. England, of course, held its own sentimental value for him. As in 1921, he used the opportunity to revisit the places of his youth, particularly his former dwellings (his visit to the Hanwell Schools, for example) and the old English music halls where he used to travel with *Sherlock Holmes, Casey's Court Circus* and Karno's Silent Comedians. All but the grandest of the old halls had fallen into disrepair (many others had been converted into movie theaters), and Chaplin found his treasured memories had been somewhat tarnished. Ironically, motion pictures, which Chaplin helped lift to an art form and mode of popular entertainment, had had a profound effect on the decline of the English music hall circuit.

Even so, Chaplin looked forward to visiting his old haunts once again, and in the process, seems to have held a sort of macabre sense of curiosity toward them. He was particularly drawn towards familiar areas from his boyhood that were rumored to be the hardest hit by the Depression. "I had been told that conditions were desperate in the north," Chaplin recalled at one point about visiting Manchester, "and that it was hardly safe to be seen in an automobile."[18] No doubt Chaplin utilized a bit of creative danger in writing such passages; he certainly would not risk his own life for the sake of sight-seeing. But they nonetheless indicate his desire to witness first-hand the type of conditions described to him throughout the trip.

In Germany, too, Chaplin was able to see the devastating effects of the world's economic crisis. In 1921, Chaplin observed that the citizens of Germany possessed a noble determination, exhibited through their tireless efforts to rebuild following the First World War. In 1931, however, Chaplin saw a society that had almost pulled itself up by the bootstraps, only to be plummeted into economic and political chaos.

Taking tea with several prominent officials at the Reichstag, Chaplin was able to hear harrowing accounts of a German government scrambling to hold the country together despite numerous concerns, including the rise of the Nazi Party. "Even if we get through this year," Chaplin was told, "... we shall have trouble. Just think of the condition of our universities. We have young men graduating in qualified professions and passing their examinations, only to leave college and stand in the bread lines with the rest of the unemployed. These things are bound to create trouble and it does not look as though conditions will improve."[19] No doubt Chaplin was reminded of this comment later when he encountered the American boys traveling to Bali, who were looking to escape similar conditions in the United States.

As evidenced by his conversations with various government officials, or eminent men such as Gandhi and Einstein, Chaplin was indeed becoming caught up in the economic and political issues of his day. His naiveté about the complexities of these crises was perhaps apparent, but he nonetheless used these opportunities to talk seriously of world issues throughout his tour — opinions that were greeted, at the very least, with respect. Upon his arrival back in North America, on June 13, 1932, in Vancouver, British Columbia, Chaplin felt bold enough to assert to the gathered press: "I am reputedly a comedian, but after seeing the financial conditions of the world I have decided I am as much an economist as financiers are comedians."[20] Business, Chaplin said, would have to increase production and take less profit in order to help right the current conditions. It was a pompous statement, but one which indicates a new focus to his thoughts, and this concern would find Chaplin moving towards more socially and politically oriented subject matters in his next three film projects.

Yet another interesting development of Chaplin's trip was the growing amount of unfavorable publicity he received as his tour wore on. The incident at the Hanwell Schools, where Chaplin sent Kono and Carlyle Robinson as stand-ins for himself on a second planned visit, was only one of several so-called snubs widely reported, not only in European but in the American papers as well.

For instance, it was reported that Chaplin had rather tactlessly turned down a dinner invitation with England's Prime Minister Ramsay MacDonald and several members of the House of Commons. Later, on his return visit to London, he declined to attend a Royal Variety Performance, which was interpreted by some (quite incorrectly) as an affront to the King.[21] For the comedian, who had been rumored to be considered for a knightship early in his visit, such offenses did not endear him to certain sections of English society, regardless of his boyhood roots.

He also had a bit of legal trouble on his trip. Chaplin had hired a secretary in London to deal with an influx of mail to his hotel suite, but she was simply overwhelmed by the amount of correspondence arriving daily and demanded a raise for her services. Stubbornly, Chaplin dug his heels in and attempted to hold her to the original contract. Eventually he relented, though not before the squabble had garnered some critical press in the process.[22] While it was a relatively minor flap, it nonetheless holds particular significance in view of Chaplin's future troubles. First, it would not be the only time he would have publicized troubles with a personal secretary. But more importantly, the manner in which Chaplin dealt with this problem revealed an intractable side of his personality — one willing to stand firm when he believed he was right, regardless of how he was portrayed in the press. Though Chaplin eventually knuckled under — uncharacteristically, in light of his future legal problems — he was nonetheless willing to push the issue as a matter of principle rather than resolve the relatively small dispute quietly.

Though Chaplin's initial arrival in Europe was greeted with tremendous accolades, the novelty wore off the longer he chose to stay. Whereas the public and the press first embraced him wholeheartedly, over time Chaplin showed his human side and became more and more a target for criticism. But even these instances could hardly tarnish his reputation at this time; by and large, the comedian's world tour proved that the masses still loved Charlie Chaplin unconditionally.

III. THE RETURN

Just as Chaplin found that America had changed since his departure almost 18 months earlier, so too had Hollywood. "Most of the silent screen stars had disappeared," Chaplin would lament; "only a few of us were left. Now that the talkies had taken hold, the charm and insouciance of Hollywood were gone. Overnight it had become a cold and serious industry."[23] The artistic medium that he and others had mastered suddenly seemed a sprawling, rigid factory of technology. The delightful spontaneity of filmmaking seemed to have been lost.

At this point, during the summer of 1933, Chaplin claims to have seriously contemplated leaving the film industry altogether, vanishing to the quiet obscurity of either China or Hong Kong.[24] The argument isn't convincing; Charles Jr. recalled that it was somewhat of a tradition for his father to announce privately at the conclusion of a picture that it would be his last, only to once again become inspired by a new subject.[25] For a man who was still contemplating another film project in the 1970s, while in his late eighties, it is hard to believe that Chaplin could have simply walked away from the industry altogether, as his brother Sydney had.

But he didn't have a clear idea as to what his next project would be. The "sheik" idea, floated by Alf Reeves during Chaplin's European trip, went no further than its release to a sole journalist. Even if he did have a scenario in mind, he still faced the sound-or-silence dilemma once again. To stick with the lovable Tramp would require adherence to the old ways.

At this point, at least, the comedian had no clear direction. Chaplin was still obligated to complete the article series for *Women's Home Companion*, which quickly became his foremost concern upon returning to America.

One thing that was missing from Chaplin's life at this point in time was a relationship. He had been seeing Georgia Hale off and on before his trip. His neglect to contact her during the months he was away, however, not to mention some widely reported love interests during his journey, effectively ended any potential romance between them. In Europe, Chaplin had been in the company of many women. The longest and most significant liaison was with May Reeves, a woman the film star originally employed while in the South of France to tend to his correspondence, and whom Chaplin began seeing shortly after their initial introduction. Throughout their travels, however, Chaplin never seemed to be as taken with her as she was with him. Amicably, the pair parted ways shortly after Chaplin's retreat to St. Moritz.

During the affair, Sydney and Carlyle Robinson were understandably nervous regarding Chaplin's interest in Reeves. Following the aftermath of the Lita Grey marriage, and with growing publicity given the two as they continued to appear together, they perhaps found themselves more cautious regarding her actual intentions than may have been necessary. Nonetheless, an end to the relationship was attempted. Robinson informed Chaplin that Sydney had previously had an affair with Reeves, a move that frosted relations not only between Chaplin and Reeves but, for reasons not quite clear, between Chaplin and Robinson as well. Soon after, Robinson would be reassigned from the Chaplin entourage in Europe to New York, becoming Chaplin's East Coast representative. Chaplin had been growing tired of his longtime employee, who used to openly joke that his job was actually that of being a "sup-press" agent for the comedian. The reassignment was only a prelude to his dismissal shortly thereafter.

Though Chaplin does speak of meeting several women throughout the trip, most upon his original excursion through England, Miss Reeves is not mentioned by name in "A Comedian Sees the World." She may warrant a few comments in *My Autobiography*— Chaplin neglects to identify her but leads into, ostensibly, a discussion of their time together by recalling sentiments expressed to him by H.G. Wells. "There comes a moment in the day," Wells is said to have remarked to Chaplin, "when you have written your pages in the morning, attended to your correspondence in the afternoon, and have nothing further to do. Then comes that hour when you are bored; that's the time for sex."[26] Though Chaplin seems to have been taken somewhat with Reeves' free-wheeling spirit, it was a relationship that couldn't progress further. Fleeting as their romance may have been, however, it was long enough for both Reeves and Chaplin to capitalize on it in literary form: Reeves' *Charlie Chaplin Intime* was published in France in 1935; Chaplin would later develop a screenplay based, in part, on his experiences with her.

Back in Hollywood, however, Chaplin seemed very isolated. Douglas Fairbanks and Mary Pickford, who had greatly influenced Chaplin's social itinerary throughout his early Hollywood years, had split, and the comedian was waning in his enthusiasm for socializing with the William Randolph Hearst/Marion Davies crowd at Hearst's infamous San Simeon estate. Lita was still an occasional nuisance in Chaplin's life. Shortly after his arrival back in the United States, she was looking to start Charlie, Jr. and Sydney in motion pictures, and began arranging for a film contract. Chaplin and his lawyers spent a good part of the late summer and early fall of 1932 in court attempting to block Lita's exploitation of the boys, which the comedian felt would cause unnecessary harm to them as they grew to adulthood. Chaplin was ultimately successful in his efforts to block the contract.

On a more favorable note, Joseph Schenck invited Chaplin for a week-end excursion on his yacht around Catalina Island. One of the girls with them that weekend was Paulette Goddard (her real name was Paulette Levy), a young actress with only minimal screen experience who at the time was under contract at the Hal Roach Studios. According to his memoirs, Chaplin was immediately taken with the blonde 21-year-old, whose spunk and youthful zeal seemed one of the few bright spots in an otherwise uneventful home-coming.

Paulette, although young, had been recently divorced, and was contemplating plunking a good portion of her settlement money into a dubious film project. Over the weekend, Chaplin promptly talked her out of what he felt was a foolish endeavor and, somewhere in the process, won her heart as well. In the months to come, the pair saw each other on a regular basis, much to the delight of the Hollywood gossip press. Unlike May Reeves, Paulette was someone who could stir his interest intellectually as well as romantically. Paulette's contract with the Hal Roach Studios was soon purchased by the Chaplin Studios.

The relationship seemed to revitalize Chaplin both emotionally and creatively, for he began to turn his attention toward a new film project by March of 1933. Influenced by the extreme images of poverty he had witnessed during his tour, Chaplin set forth constructing the scenario that would become *Modern Times*, a film set in a typical Depression-era city and highlighting the valiant struggle of people to survive during a time of economic blight.

Additionally, in opting to utilize the Tramp once more for *Modern Times*, Chaplin again spurned the use of full sound technology. In keeping with his distrust of sound film, the picture found Chaplin blurring the boundary between a silent and sound production for a second time. Like *City Lights*, *Modern Times* would utilize a recorded soundtrack, again composed by Chaplin. Sound effects, used only sparingly in his previous motion picture, would become much more pronounced, including some sound-dependent gags and the first spoken dialogue in a Chaplin film. The comedian also devised a finale to the picture that would thrust the Little Fellow into the position of using his own voice, captured onscreen for the first and only time.

Although Chaplin was primarily concerned with the financial and artistic prospects of *Modern Times*, initial word concerning the film seemed to signal a change in the typical Tramp scenario. The Depression had given strength to a number of socialist and communist political movements, which had in turn influenced aesthetic discourse on film, focusing on more socially-conscious art forms.[27] Bolstered by an increase in liberal, sometimes even leftist political thought, the people and images seen on his world tour and the growing view of Chaplin as a world figure rather than just a popular entertainer, the comedian seemed intent on moving toward more socially and politically oriented themes. Such a shift in focus would not only shape *Modern Times* but also his next two films, *The Great Dictator* (1940) and *Monsieur Verdoux* (1947).

Much more than with his previous films, Chaplin was tight-lipped during production, and speculation about its content ran high. Though little was known about the film's outline, some errant reports claimed the film would be called *The Masses*, and as *New Masses* was the title of the publication of the American Communist Party, a few ventured to suggest that Chaplin was fashioning an explicit social document rather than simply another comedy.[28] Such anticipation regarding the picture's content had many wondering, and also greatly influenced critical reaction to *Modern Times*, which varied greatly in interpretations of Chaplin's artistic intent.

Chaplin's more socially conscious themes in the picture limited the traditional role of the Tramp, and foreshadowed the demise of this trademark character. Fragments of the Little Fellow can be found in a number of Chaplin's future screen roles, but when cameraman Rollie Totheroh finally faded out on Charlie at the end of *Modern Times*, it would mark the end for the most popular figure in screen history.

IV. THE NARRATIVE OF *MODERN TIMES*

In the administrative offices of the Electro Steel Corporation, in some nameless Depression-era city, we find the company president (Allen Garcia) lazily reading the comic pages, after abandoning the jigsaw puzzle strewn on his desk. Bored, he turns to a giant television monitor behind him, and booms over the loudspeaker to the factory foreman: "Section Five, speed 'er up; four-one." The foreman, following orders, shifts the gears of the machinery that will increase the pace of production.

On the assembly line, Charlie, a hapless worker in Section Five, monotonously tightens the bolts on the conveyor belt in front of him, but the Tramp consistently lags behind his co-workers. When it finally comes time for Charlie to have a break, with a relief man assuming the Tramp's position on the line, the Little Fellow continues to twitch violently in bolt-tightening fashion as he escapes to the restroom to sneak a cigarette. But his brief moment of relaxation is interrupted when the president suddenly dials into the restroom over an Orwellian television monitor and chastises the Tramp for not being at his post. Charlie returns as instructed, only to again fall behind.

Meanwhile, the company president is entertained by a group of salesmen offering a revolutionary new invention called the Bellow's Feeding Machine. The invention allows an employee to continue working at breakneck speed, while being fed automatically at his post — increasing production by eliminating the lunch hour. Intrigued by its possible applications, the entourage moves to the factory floor in search of the ideal test subject.

Not surprisingly, the Little Fellow soon finds himself strapped to the machine. But the system is not without its glitches, all of which seem to rear their ugly heads with poor Charlie attached. Seeing the Little Fellow messy with food and thoroughly battered by the experience, the president is displeased with the test results — not because the feeding machine malfunctioned, but because, as he notes, "it isn't practical."

Later in the day, stress has made Charlie unable to continue work. He has a nervous breakdown, frantically tightening every bolt in sight — pursuing them through the cogs of the factory's machinery, chasing a secretary with bolt-like buttons on the back of her dress, and dangling wrenches from his ears. He runs about the factory, halting all production by flipping levers and buttons at will, and squirting oil into the faces of co-workers. Eventually he's apprehended and is taken away in a waiting ambulance.

Elsewhere in the city, down by the docks, a street-wise Gamin (Paulette Goddard) is nearly caught stealing bananas from a boat to feed herself and some hungry street children. When she returns home with her bounty, she is quick to feed her two younger sisters, and eventually her father when he returns home. It is clear from the helplessness of his facial expression that her father is a desperate man, humiliated by his inability to find work and provide for his family.* They all share the bananas, knowing that it may be their only meal for some time.

At the hospital, Charlie is informed that his ailment has been cured, as long as he can avoid stress and excitement. With nowhere to go, the Little Fellow is shuffling down the street past a boarded-up factory when he spies a red safety flag that has fallen from a passing truck. Being a good Samaritan, Charlie retrieves the flag and heads down the center of the street, waving it about in a vain effort to attract the driver's attention. Unbeknownst to the Tramp, however, a mob of angry strikers rounds the corner behind him, many of them holding banners with leftist slogans. The police storm in to break up the demonstration and Charlie is rounded up as a Communist leader, based on his possession of the red flag.

Ironically, incarceration doesn't prove so bad, providing Charlie with a comfortable place to live, far from the mayhem of the outside world. Unfortunately, the Little Fellow finds himself thrust in the midst of a jailbreak, and must outwit several other inmates before restoring order to prison officials. As a result, the warden not only upgrades his model prisoner to a more luxurious cell, but arranges for his early release, coupled with a recommendation to help Charlie get work on the outside.

Meanwhile, tragedy strikes the Gamin and her family. Another demon-

---

The scene recalls Chaplin's earlier comments from the world tour: "Look into the faces of the masses in our large cities and you will see harassed defeated souls and in the eyes of most of them weary despair." (Charles Chaplin; "A Comedian Sees the World," from Woman's Home Companion, *January 1934; page 22.)*

Charlie and Big Bill from *Modern Times*. Unlike this curious still, Bill and his break-in cohorts are not in the department store to steal, but are portrayed sympathetically as unfortunate victims of economic chaos.

stration of workers in the streets turns violent, and the Gamin's father is slain by an unruly mob, leaving the daughters to fend for themselves. Since all are underage, juvenile authorities arrive to take charge. The Gamin flees, leaving her sisters behind. Now alone, she walks the streets tired and hungry.

After failing as a general laborer in a local shipyard, the Little Fellow once again wanders the streets. He runs into the Gamin, literally, as she attempts to escape a baker from whom she had stolen some bread. She is apprehended, yet Charlie chivalrously accepts responsibility for the stolen goods, mesmerized by her youthful beauty and, quite likely, looking to return to the comfortable life he had known in jail. His ploy doesn't work, however, and the Gamin is hauled off for petty thievery.

Determined to get back to the easy life behind bars, the Tramp promptly enters a local café, where he proceeds to consume enough food for several people in a single sitting. Then, just before visiting the cashier, Charlie summons a policeman passing along the street and presents him with the check. Not amused, the policeman is quick to cuff the contented Little Fellow and call for a paddy wagon.

Also in the wagon is the Gamin, visibly upset and ashamed at the crime hunger forced her to commit. Looking to escape, she rushes the guard at the back of the van, Charlie in tow, and all three plummet to the street. She and Charlie are able to make their getaway.

The two retreat to a residential street where they begin to get acquainted, and even share an idealized daydream of how wonderful life would be if they owned their own home, with plenty of money and food to guarantee a worry-free existence. It is only when a policeman spies them loitering that they must end their fantasy and hustle off.

Later, Charlie finds a job as a night watchman for a large downtown department store, and is quick to let the Gamin inside once the staff has left for the evening. They share food at the lunch counter and rollerskate in the toy department, and the Gamin spends a luxurious night of sleep among the home furnishings while Charlie attends to his duties throughout the store.

But they are not alone inside. Some gun-toting intruders corner the Tramp and take him hostage. But the Little Fellow is recognized by one of the burglars, Big Bill, a workmate from Charlie's factory days. The men are not in the store to steal, they explain, but merely to get a decent meal from the lunch counter, since they cannot make ends meet even though they are employed.

Unfortunately, a long night of revelry leaves Charlie the worse for wear the next morning, as he has passed out underneath a pile of fabric. Once discovered by store managers, he is fired and carted off to jail.

The Gamin is there to meet him when he is released, and gleefully announces that she has found a home for them both. The place is merely a dilapidated shack, but it is nonetheless greeted with enthusiasm.

The following morning, headlines in the local paper have announced the re-opening of a local factory, which sends Charlie hustling off for a job, fighting the crowd to be the last to enter the gates and gain a day's employment.

Inside, Charlie is put to work as an assistant to a line foreman played by Chester Conklin, an old comic partner from Chaplin's Keystone days. Both are charged with the duty of tuning the factory's machinery for the eventual start of production. Chester, through no fault of his own, becomes tangled in the mechanized beast, much as Charlie had been in the opening of the film, and the Tramp spends most of their lunch hour attempting to feed him.* After Chester is finally freed, they are informed that the workers are going on strike, only hours after the factory re-opened. Both men gaze at each other with complete bewilderment.

Thrust out of work once more, Charlie inadvertently manages to launch a brick in the direction of a police officer outside the factory, which lands him

---

*This scene, and the Little Fellow's conveyor belt entrapment at the beginning of the film, may have been inspired by an event from Chaplin's childhood, when he bluffed his way into a job as a Wharfdale printing press operator. He had never operated one, and vividly recalled its colossal size and his fear that it would somehow swallow him. (Charles Chaplin; My Autobiography; page 61.)

in jail yet again. When he is set free, the Gamin is there to greet him, only this time dressed in finery. She has found work as a dancer in a local café, and promises to plead with the owner so that Charlie, too, can get a steady job.

The café owner (Henry Bergman) agrees to give Charlie a trial run as a waiter — a singing waiter, that is. The Gamin enthusiastically vouches for the Little Fellow's vocal ability, despite the visible apprehension on his face.

Ultimately, Charlie's table-waiting skills aren't up to snuff, and Bergman gives his trainee a firm warning that he better deliver as a singer if he wants to keep his job. The Little Fellow practices in the wings, yet his inability to remember the words forces the Gamin to write them on his paper cuffs — a gimmick that the Tramp can call upon later when he takes the stage.

When that time does come, Charlie shuffles out to the floor of the café, and enthusiastically dances to the applause of the crowd. Unfortunately, his dance is so exuberant that it manages to send his paper cuffs sailing. From the wings, the Gamin implores Charlie to continue with whatever he can improvise.

Through his motions, Charlie assures us that he will sing. However, his tune is not in English. Instead, the song he belts out takes the form of a European gibberish, from languages both real and imaginary. Charlie vigorously pantomimes throughout, improvising the story of a young girl being courted by an older gentleman.* In the end, the patrons greet the performance with a standing ovation. Impressed, Bergman is quick to overlook the Tramp's shortcomings as a waiter and offer him a permanent position.

However, as the Gamin takes the floor for her number, she is recognized by juvenile authorities in the audience. She and Charlie have to make a quick getaway and leave behind the opportunities that both had in working at the café.

Morning arrives and the pair are sitting beside a road in the country. The Gamin is clearly dejected, but Charlie (as he did for the Millionaire in *City Lights*) expresses his boundless optimism, pleading for her to carry on, head held high. His pleading works, for she is roused from her state of depression and the two proudly start off down the lonesome road toward an unknown, but presumably better future.

V. THE SECOND BATTLE WITH SOUND

Every day he was forcefully reminded of how he was sticking his neck out. His silent picture making was the gossip of the town. There were

---

*In this sense, the paper cuffs served a dual purpose. Not only were they a device for Chaplin to heighten the comedic tension of the café scene by losing them, but having Paulette write on them tipped off the audience to the basic thrust of the pantomime in the song. (Dan Kamin; Charlie Chaplin's One-Man Show; page 119.)

lugubrious headshakes from his fellow producers and friends and tongue-in-cheek speculations by columnists. Sometimes he must have been appalled himself at his own conservatism.[29]

— Charles Chaplin, Jr.

Although *City Lights* was a great triumph, ... I felt that to make another silent film would be giving myself a handicap — also I was obsessed by a depressing fear of being old-fashioned. Although a good silent film was more artistic, I had to admit that sound made characters more present.[30]

— Charles Chaplin —1964

In terms of format, *Modern Times* is consistent with Chaplin's evolving cinematic technique of employing sound as an enhancing, rather than imperative form of movie-making. It is quite apparent that Chaplin placed far more emphasis on the medium for this production than he had in *City Lights*. But *Modern Times* was still essentially silent, and in some respects was even more daring a leap than *City Lights*. Producing a non-dialogue picture in the mid–1930s posed the definite risk of alienating audiences who by then would have viewed the silent format as a complete anachronism, with or without the Tramp.

Although Chaplin had again opted to work in a virtually silent medium, *Modern Times* may not have begun that way. Among the comedian's records, a small portion of which is on display at the Museum of the Moving Image in London, is a partially written scenario— a first for Chaplin — which outlines the plot from the opening scenes through the department store sequence, and includes dialogue.[31]

While this is certainly a significant break from Chaplin's traditional working methods, it was perhaps a necessary one as well. Complete improvisation of another feature film may well have met with predicaments similar to these encountered on *City Lights*— creative blocks, excessive shooting delays, re-shooting, etc. Chaplin must have realized after *City Lights* that these old ways significantly lengthened production time and increased costs, and felt the need for greater efficiency in planning his production. There would still remain some degree of flexibility for Chaplin to improvise his comic turns, but *Modern Times* seems to find him beginning to revise and streamline his creative methods, an outgrowth of his ongoing transformation toward feature filmmaking in the sound era.

According to David Robinson's assessment of the early *Modern Times* script, the dialogue Chaplin originally planned was quite simple and designed to present the Tramp as aloof and softspoken, modeled more along the lines that Chaplin would use in creating his Barber character in his first full talkie, *The Great Dictator* (1940).[32] In preparation, the Chaplin Studios underwent a modernization to enclose its open-air stages (the last remaining in Hollywood) prior to the film's production, and both Chaplin and Paulette took voice tests for the film in December of 1934, some nine months after the filming had begun. At that point, sound was to have played a critical role in the shooting of the jail scenes. Robinson remarks, however, that the scenes, and perhaps the whole context of sound within the film, could never quite satisfy the comedian. "Chaplin was evidently dissatisfied with the results," Robinson comments. "The unit had been told that the Dream House sequence would be shot the following day [also] with sound. In fact no more dialogue scenes were to be shot for *Modern Times*."[33]

First and foremost on Chaplin's mind would have been audience reaction to a speaking role for Charlie, regardless of the nature or extent of that dialogue. While such a twist would spur the curiosity of many, it could also have had the opposite effect by increasing the chances of failure for the film, bringing the Tramp to the level of a simple talking comedian — a concern Chaplin had while approaching *City Lights*.

Perhaps he didn't feel comfortable filming in sound. More likely, the early rushes may not have measured up to his standards, and thus he reconsidered how he wished to shoot the entire picture. We can only speculate about the reasons, but Chaplin reassessed his work early in the production and found some sort of artistic justification for producing another essentially silent feature, discontinuing his brief flirtation with dialogue.

But even with the decision to shun the talkies for a second time, sound (including some speech itself) would play an important role in the construction of several comic scenes. Unlike in *City Lights*, Chaplin included several sound-dependent gags in the final print, a clear sign that he was both accepting and looking ahead to his eventual use of full sound technology.

Allen Garcia, playing the president of the Electro Steel Corporation in the opening sequence, received the dubious honor of speaking the first dialogue in a Chaplin picture. However, as Walter Kerr has observed in *The Silent Clowns*, Garcia's lines, as well as numerous other spoken parts in the film, are transmitted primarily through electronic mediums.[34] The effect gives such characters a cold and impersonal nature which, in effect, helps emphasize two of Chaplin's themes in the film, the breakdown of individual relationships and the dehumanizing effect of machines on people. Charlie turns machine-like from working on the production line and the president utilizes a close-circuit television to monitor production and to spy on his employees. In all other sequences Garcia speaks with the same title cards as would any other character.

The use of sound also seems reserved for specific situations. Generally, Chaplin's use of sound effects and dialogue coincides with the action on the screen, enhancing it in some way. For instance, the salesmen of the Bellow's Feeding Machine use a phonograph as an on-site spokesperson. While they surround their prized machinery, pantomiming its virtues, the phonograph goes to great lengths vocally extolling its production benefits and urging a test run on a typical employee, since "actions speak louder than words." Later, in the jail scenes, Charlie looks to cover up the echoing noise of his rumbling stomach by turning on a radio. In both scenes, sound emanates from electronic sources, but it is the screen action that takes center stage; the dialogue simply provides an enhancing background element for the humorous escapades.

Only the café scenes are different. Before Charlie begins his number, the singing waiters who precede him can also be distinctly heard. This is a particularly interesting moment of contrast in that while Chaplin and Goddard rehearse Charlie's song offstage with the help of titles, the song from the café floor continues to be audible. Clearly, Charlie's world is one of virtual silence, even when nearing the time to take the stage and cross into the new medium.

But Chaplin ingeniously gives his character an out in the finale of *Modern Times*. With the comic business of losing the words to his song, drawing out the introductory bars of the tune in anticipation, audience expectation is heightened: How will Charlie (or, perhaps, Chaplin) get out of this? Will he make up the words to the tune, as the Gamin instructs, or will he retreat to the wings of the café and risk losing his job?

The Tramp stays on the café floor, but instead of speaking outright and entering the sound era, his language is garbled between a number of real and fabricated dialects, which still leaves the audience dependent on Charlie's pantomime. And, since writing the intended words on Charlie's cuff has tipped off the audience in advance to the plot of the song, the pantomime display is easily comprehended.

Thus, nothing truly revealing about Charlie has been disclosed despite his talking. Without an intelligible word in the song, Charlie is able to speak freely on the stage without truly opening himself up to the movie audience. Hence, when he returns to the wings and again speaks via title cards, the effect is believable, and one of Charlie's mysteries has remained intact. Chaplin has devised a joke within a joke. The Tramp is solving his problem with the lyrics in a comic way, while Chaplin is solving his "voice before the public" problem in a comedian's way. And, as in the opening sequence of *City Lights*, Chaplin takes the opportunity to comment on sound technology at the same time — gibberish.

The scene in fact could have served, as Chaplin, Jr. felt, as his father's public sound test.[35] The nonsense tune was a narrative device that not only built suspense but got the inevitable out of the way — the public would hear Chaplin speak. Surely, the comedian knew his next feature would have to be a full-fledged talkie. The introduction of sound-dependent gags in *Modern Times* proves that Chaplin was becoming more comfortable with its application to his style of comedy. For instance, an extended sequence within the jail with Charlie's gurgling stomach is the clearest example of a gag that could not have worked without sound enhancement. Though the humor is derived purely from the actions of the characters, in silence, and while we may be able to imagine these sounds, the sequence without sound enhancement would lose its comic effect. Contrast the jail scene with its most recognizable counterparts from *City Lights*, the statue dedication and whistle sequences. To remove sound out of the statue dedication does leave behind the effect of mocking the talkies, yet the scene could conceivably stand on its own as a lead-in to Charlie's first appearance. Similarly, the swallowed whistle scene could also stand on its own. We have seen him swallow the whistle, and his exaggerated gestures certainly indicate that he is hiccoughing, but the sound of a whistle does not add anything crucial to understanding the gag nor enhance its comedic elements. Instead, sound for these two scenes, as for the rest of *City Lights,* was enhancing the pantomime of the screen rather than playing an integral role in the humor, as is the case in certain portions of *Modern Times.* "In retrospect," Julian Smith has aptly noted, "Chaplin's fabled resistance to sound appears to have been a game in which he talked endlessly about why he would not speak in movies while going about the business of making genuine sound films that tell us far more about the possibilities of film sound than most of the competition."[36]

Even while glancing toward the future with this utilization of sound technology, Chaplin created the bulk of his comedy sequences from traditional slapstick. They employ vestiges from both the earlier Tramp films and the vaudeville sketches and routines that had kept both Charlie and silent comedy popular for well over two decades. More so than in recent pictures, Chaplin returned to settings and themes that were common throughout his silent shorts. Cafés had always been a popular spot for the Little Fellow; rollerskating in the department store was a throwback to 1916's *The Rink* (and its inspiration, the Karno sketch *Skating*); the escalator in the store, from *The Floorwalker* (1916); and a doped-up Charlie manhandling society's criminal element, as the Tramp does in thwarting the jailbreak, from the classic *Easy Street* (1917). "My Father's interpretations are always unique," Charles Chaplin, Jr., remarked. "He has the ability to pull funny pieces of business right out of the air, so that with his clever innovations the hoariest gags look brand new."[37]

But increasingly dependent on sound, from occasional dialogue to sound-oriented gags and to Charlie's own solo, *Modern Times* is primarily a film that brought closure to the screen adventures of the Tramp, while pushing the comedian toward his first full-fledged sound project. Most significantly it was to be the final outing on the silver screen for the Little Fellow. "If *Modern Times* was not a revolutionary film," Gerard Molyneaux noted, referring to the picture's political overtones, "there is surely much evidence that it was an evolutionary movie which ultimately concluded the Tramp's journey."[38]

The character had become one of the most popular figures in motion pictures, a symbol of the new and powerful industry, and had been embraced by film audiences around the globe. Although he never trumpeted *Modern Times* as the Tramp's final picture, it was perhaps becoming apparent that Chaplin could not carry the character any further. The comedian knew he could not avoid sound a third time. Despite his early prediction, the technology had become the accepted norm, and even Chaplin had to admit that silence would likely never return as a popular or artistic competitor to talking films. The Tramp was a vestige of the past and, as the silent medium was cast aside, Charlie would have to be as well. Additionally, with Chaplin himself nearing 50, the comedian was certainly aware that his age was a factor that discouraged continuing with his screen character much further.

But while Chaplin looked to "retire" his longtime screen persona, he also brought a new characteristic to his filmmaking in *Modern Times* which would color virtually all of his remaining film projects. Though Chaplin's emerging penchant for social commentary is somewhat tentative with this particular picture, it nonetheless marked the comedian's first effort to build a feature film around a broader social or political theme.

VI. SOCIO-POLITICAL ASPECTS OF *MODERN TIMES*

If social commentary is, indeed, the main theme of *Modern Times*, then it certainly does lack unity. Chaplin's statement, plus viewing of the film, make it clear that social commentary is not the main theme. Such commentary is merely one manifestation of the larger theme. Like *The Gold Rush*, the theme of *Modern Times* is man's survival. The problems [Charlie] faces in *Modern Times* are sometimes due to big business, sometimes not. But all the problems are related to the "modern" world.[39]
                                                                    — John Paul Smead

In Chaplin's filmography, *Modern Times* served as a distinct bridge between the more traditional type of Chaplin feature (*City Lights*) and what would mark three of his next five films (*The Great Dictator, Monsieur Verdoux* and *A King in New York*), which featured highly politicized themes and confrontational postures. The addition of dialogue beginning with *Dictator* helped solidify this shift. But for *Modern Times*, at least, he was still attempting to balance his populist art with his emerging political beliefs.

Aside from the content of the picture itself, there were outside factors which made the film politically oriented. At one point during the production, the comedian hosted a delegation at the Chaplin Studios of Soviet film industry officials then touring Hollywood, and screened a rough cut of *Modern Times* for their enjoyment.[40] Later, Chaplin's work was highly praised for its "ideological content" by Boris Shumiatsky, who headed the delegation, in several articles which were reprinted in the American press. At the time of the visit, the comedian was aware that some in America would react suspiciously toward the tour, for he is said to have told the Soviet group that the visit would cause delays in the production of *Modern Times*, and the studio seems to have made efforts to downplay Shumiatsky's comments when they appeared.

Together with ongoing rumors about Chaplin's own leftist political sympathies, speculation ran high regarding his second sound era film. Before its debut, word had begun to spread (which, no doubt, enhanced publicity for the film) that Chaplin was concocting a motion picture more controversial than the typical Charlie scenario, and potentially lenient in its political sympathies towards the Left.

But the pre-release speculation and the actual content of the film ultimately did not match up. Much has been made of *Modern Times* in regards to Chaplin's commentary on the subservient relationship between man and machine, brilliantly satirized in incidents such as the Bellow's Feeding Machine and Chester Conklin's entrapment while reconfiguring the assembly line at the Jetson Mill. However, as John Paul Smead's earlier comment indicates, more basic human themes emerge in the midst of Chaplin's socially conscious depictions: that of the necessity for food and, to a lesser extent, shelter.

Time and again, *Modern Times* depicts the struggle for mere survival in a world of economic and social chaos. When we first meet the Gamin, for instance, she is stealing bananas from a boat on the waterfront — not only for her own family, but to feed some of the neighborhood's neglected children as well. This is one of four separate occasions where the Gamin must steal to combat starvation: She also snatches a loaf of bread, which facilitates her first encounter with Charlie; she makes a hearty meal from items left on the lunch counter at the department store where the Tramp is employed; and she has mysteriously acquired breakfast for herself and Charlie on the first morning in their "Hooverville shack." Similarly, when Big Bill and his cohorts break into the department store, they enter not to steal any merchandise but to partake, as the Gamin did, at the lunch counter. Big Bill cannot make ends meet despite being employed.

The grimness of Chaplin's assertion with these incidents cannot be overlooked. Everyone is impacted by the hardships of the Depression, even the employed, and the comedian additionally calls attention to the fact that some crime is driven not by want, but by need. His directorial hand is never too heavy, as such scenes are handled with a light, ironic touch, framing such gloomy topics as unemployment and starvation in comic terms, making them thought-provoking but perhaps more palatable. *The Gold Rush*, with its boiled shoe dinner and Mack Swain's cabin hallucinations, also satirizes starvation in such a manner.

In the department store, the theft of food is designed to create pathos, though it is distinctly less sentimental than in films past. The focus of the pathos in *Modern Times* is not only on Charlie's plight but on that of the general working class. Building upon the image of the "despairing eyes" of men like the Gamin's father, Chaplin creates desperate situations in which his characters must struggle for mere survival in a cruel world. It's a theme he would later explore in *Monsieur Verdoux* (1947) in a much more overt and, and to some audiences, more antagonistic fashion.

But like Chaplin's brief flirtation with full dialogue scenes in *Modern*

Times, he initially may have conceived the department store scene differently. One existing production still (see page 92) shows the Tramp and Big Bill in an unfamiliar (based on the final print of *Modern Times*, at least) part of the department store, featuring silverware and other serving items. The Little Fellow looks on in dismay as Bill, sack in hand, loads expensive silver items from a glass display case in the center of the room. Unlike the finished film, in the photograph Bill is depicted as actually stealing goods, which would not make him a particularly convincing object of pathos. No such scene exists in the film, nor does David Robinson, after accessing Chaplin's production notes, cite such a scene as forming a portion of the comedian's intended narrative.*

The room which Charlie enters immediately prior to being confronted by Big Bill and company does resemble somewhat the room depicted in the photo. The contents, however, have changed to china and the display cabinets, glass-fronted in the photograph, are wood in the film; Charlie skates haphazardly into this room perhaps attempting to achieve a laugh from the Tramp's care free jaunt through such hazardous surroundings. While it would not be unheard of to pose a still photo based loosely on events in the film, for Chaplin to have changed an entire set and establish a mood that runs directly counter to Big Bill's characterization in the finished film seems very unlikely. That Chaplin had a change of heart regarding the intruders and their motivation for breaking into the department store would seem more plausible. It would be consistent with his practice during this period of not working from a clearly defined script, leaving his narratives somewhat open for inspired alterations. Thus, it is conceivable that this odd photo is a visible example of Chaplin's improvisational methods, taken before the comedian hit upon the sympathetic treatment of Big Bill and his cohorts.

Shelter, too, plays an important role in *Modern Times*. The most obvious example is Chaplin's "dream home" fantasy in which the Tramp and the Gamin imagine themselves in some sort of suburban Shangri-La. However, when the Gamin does find shelter for the both of them, as she readily admits, "it's not Buckingham Palace." It is, in fact, a Hooverville shack, an effective contrast between his idealized desires and the cold reality of the Depression; the comedian was perhaps even satirizing the entire notion of the "American Dream." Similarly, the Little Fellow's employment at the department store, in addition to providing a quick meal, also provides a roof for the couple, though only for one evening.

But Chaplin's most effective commentary on shelter is the irony of Charlie's

---

Robinson does note, however, the fact that Chaplin did abandon some familiar material in the process of putting Modern Times *together. In particular, the discarded opening for* City Lights, *featuring the stick and the street grating, was originally planned for resurrection. So too was the twin fighter gag that was intended and shot for* The Circus *(this also can be seen in* Unknown Chaplin*). In Robinson's assessment, "Chaplin never wasted anything." (David Robinson;* Chaplin: His Life and Art; *page 460.)*

wish to return to jail early in the film. Both food and shelter are provided there free of charge and without the chaotic surroundings of the outside world. That Charlie would prefer a life behind bars to freedom is indeed a harsh criticism of these "modern times." Despite the upbeat ending to the picture, such images offer a decidedly bleak presentation of what individuals faced in the harsh Depression-era environment, and lent ammunition to critics who felt that the comedian was dabbling in issues too political.

Concern by some toward Chaplin's personal politics was not new (interest had arisen along with Chaplin's star image in the motion picture industry), though *Modern Times* was the first of his feature-length films to potentially delve at any great length into his personal views. Since embarking on his world tour following the premiere of *City Lights*, Chaplin had begun to more openly express his ideas on a number of issues and causes, many of which leaned toward the more liberal end of the political spectrum. One was supporting Upton Sinclair's candidacy for the governorship of California in 1934. (Sinclair ran under the socialistic banner of EPIC — "End Poverty in California.") Most of Hollywood's conservative studio bosses had mobilized under an anti–Sinclair banner, waging an expensive and often slanderous campaign against pro–Sinclair forces, even threatening to transfer production units to Florida in case of an EPIC victory. Staunchly conservative attacks on Sinclair brought out many of Hollywood's more liberally-inclined stars to his defense, including Chaplin, but they could not bring a gubernatorial victory. While it is likely that Chaplin supported Sinclair more because of their personal friendship than his actual policies, the two did have much in common politically. (It was Sinclair whom Chaplin credited for stirring his interest in the philosophy of socialism, and who also allegedly penned a script for the comedian in 1918 called *The Hypnotist*.[41]) Also, at the time, Chaplin was favoring Roosevelt's New Deal; uncharacteristically, he even made a small contribution to Roosevelt's first re-election campaign. "[Roosevelt's policies were] going too far," Chaplin recalled years later. "[T]his was socialism, the opposition shouted. Whether it was or not, it saved capitalism from a complete collapse. It also inaugurated some of the finest reforms in the history of the United States."[42]

It's clear from a viewing of *Modern Times*, however, that despite Chaplin's ties to so-called radicals such as Upton Sinclair and other liberal artists, he kept these associations at a distance when it came to his filmmaking or public endeavors. While perhaps sympathetic to the rhetoric of the American Left, Chaplin's narrative for *Modern Times* shows a flirtation with, but not a full embrace of, progressive political causes. Given the $1.5 million price tag for the film which Chaplin bore from his own pocket, and with the project once again in an essentially silent format, the comedian (as with *City Lights*) kept a careful eye on the picture's box office potential. Still tentative, it seems, about his work in the sound medium, Chaplin allows comedy to take center stage in *Modern Times*, and though the issues raised in the picture could be viewed as partisan in nature, he would keep his film politically ambiguous. As we will see later, it was primarily between films, when Chaplin was contemplating his next creative endeavor, that he would more actively concern himself with matters of politics. Nonetheless, the general plot of *Modern Times* led many conservative elements to question Chaplin's motives. Given the times, the subject matter seemed rife with propagandistic possibilities for the Left.

Chaplin's own account of the inspiration for *Modern Times*, particularly the factory scenes in which Charlie has his mental breakdown, seems to have been inspired by what he felt were the distressing conditions faced by the modern working man. "... I remembered an interview I had with a bright young reporter on the *New York World*," he recalled in his memoirs. "Hearing that I was visiting Detroit, he had told me of the factory-belt system there — a harrowing story of big industry luring men off the farms who, after four or five years at the belt system, became nervous wrecks."[43] Additionally, many of the conditions Chaplin saw throughout his world tour had also affected him. In Chaplin's conversations with Gandhi and Einstein, for instance, one can see the kinds of concerns that would influence *Modern Times*. Chaplin may have circulated in privileged circles throughout the trip, but these were not the images that seemed to have the biggest impact on him. Instead, it was the American boys traveling to Bali, or Reichstag officials literally confounded on how to reverse the perilous economic stagnation, in Germany, that he most vividly recalled. Chaplin's final comments in "A Comedian Sees the World" are evidence that he saw a similar discontent in America. Conditions in the United States were, in fact, hardly different than those he saw during his travels — America, like the rest of the world, was a nation of people who desperately wanted opportunity. Given these observations, one may have expected Chaplin to have been critical of business and, perhaps, government as well, but no such theme clearly develops in *Modern Times*. Instead, the comedian found hypocrisy in both the actions of business and labor; throughout the picture, he walks a middle ground that prevents *Modern Times* from being a clear product of either liberal or conservative doctrine.

As the narrative unfolds, there is ample territory for Chaplin to exploit the abuses of the industrial system, one that drives men to the brink of insanity in its insatiable desire to both produce and consume products. This would certainly reinforce the ideas he expressed to both Gandhi and Einstein, and may account for the fact that he neglects identifying the product that Charlie helps manufacture at the Electro Steel Corporation. The product is of no significance to the story — only the methods employed to create it. We do know that, whatever it is, it must be made at a rate that pushes the worker to his limit — the more the better — while management sits about idly and looks for ways to produce even more. The product omission amplifies the impact of the Tramp's breakdown. How callous could big business be to grind away at the human condition merely for the sake of increased profits?

This dehumanization becomes genuinely diabolical with the Bellow's Feeding Machine (according to Meyer Levin, "the greatest satiric commentary on mechanized civilization I have ever encountered"[44]), a depiction that certainly visualizes Chaplin's earlier comment about business for the sole purpose of productivity and profit. The device is a bust, but Allen Garcia, as president of Electro Steel, rejects it not on the basis of its performance, but merely because the technology "isn't practical."

Thus, with the opening scenes at least, *Modern Times* does indeed embark on a highly politicized narrative, one severely critical of both capitalists and industry in the 1930s. But Chaplin neither continues nor expands on this notion outside of the factory sequence — the factory sets, for instance, while certainly ominous and forbidding in appearance, could have been exploited further for propagandistic ends had Chaplin been concentrating on a strictly anti-business message. In fact, once removed from the factory, the film begins to back away from this stance, allowing the Tramp to engage in a variety of events that could be interpreted as being pro- or anti-capitalist. Many have no political significance at all. Therefore, in analyzing these various aspects of the film, a clear and concise ideology does not seem to come forward.

Contrast, for instance, the film's initial anti-business theme with the fact that the Gamin's father, humiliated in his failed attempts to provide for his motherless little girls, is slain by a desperate mob of unemployed workers. Chaplin, certainly a progressive thinker, would likely sympathize with the cause of their discontent. But the scene is also representative of how many Depression-era workers may have inadvertently contributed to the country's problems; if the comedian was continuing his narrative in an anti-capitalist vein, Chaplin draws no clear connection between worker violence and the policies of business.

An even better example comes when Charlie and Chester Conklin are informed that the Jetson Mill crew will be going on strike, despite the fact that they had all just earned the opportunity to work. Both stare at each other, dumbfounded by something so counter-productive to the well-being of both workers and business. Similar in tone is the jail sequence, where Charlie sits in his cell following his successful efforts to thwart the jail break. "Strikes and Riots," "Breadlines Broken by Unruly Mob" read the headlines of his newspaper, causing the Little Fellow to shake his head in disgust and discard it due to the insanity of it all. If Chaplin had conceived *Modern Times* as a propaganda piece to expose the failings of the capitalist system and lend credence to the struggles of the worker, he was indeed mixing his metaphors in the process.

As Charles Maland has pointed out, the film's opening montage is a classic example of the confusing duality of Chaplin's criticism.[45] The comedian depicts sheep heading through a chute, a shot which then dissolves to a shot of workers emerging from the subway and heading toward the Electro Steel

Corporation. But it's not clear what Chaplin was attempting to say by using this Eisensteinian technique.* Are we to infer that business treats its workers as simple livestock, herding them about without regard to anything but profits? Perhaps the sheep, in this context, are heading for slaughter. Or are we to think that the worker allows himself to be regimented as if some lower creature? In the picture there is clear evidence to support either interpretation. Like the film as a whole, what emerges from this montage is a feeling of ambiguity. It seems that Chaplin could not cast a blind eye towards absurdity at any level, either with the industrialist or the worker, regardless of his sympathy or antipathy toward either one.

Thus, rather than indicting American capitalism, as some feared that he might, Chaplin more accurately walks the middle ground with his criticisms. Neither business nor labor can act without genuine consideration of the other. In this sense, Chaplin's message to the worker and the capitalist is a plea for cooperation and cohesiveness, since both must co-exist. It is only when one acts in isolation — squeezing more production from the already ragged workers, or striking in the face of a genuine employment opportunity — that the symbiotic relationship grinds to a halt. The economic hardship besetting Chaplin's world in *Modern Times*, it seems, will only be overcome through the trust, understanding and cooperation of all parties, even if it means making temporary sacrifices toward the long range goal of economic recovery and maintenance of social order.

Such was the nature of Chaplin's humanist philosophy, or the "capitalist utopianism" coined by David Robinson. *Modern Times* does not overly sympathize with either side. If it was intended in such a manner, then Chaplin failed to present it distinctly throughout the narrative. As with authoring his so-called *Economic Solution* toward the end of his 1931 world tour, Chaplin perhaps intended *Modern Times* to rise above the various political and social arguments of the day and express the mutual concerns of all people, highlighting, through comedy, those actions that impede a full economic recovery. In the process, observed biographer Theodore Huff, the comedian provided only the sort of fodder to be considered an incidental propagandist.[46]

Chaplin even employed *Modern Times* at one point to satirize common perceptions about his own political beliefs. The sequence following Charlie's release from the hospital, when he is arrested as a Communist organizer, deliberately pokes fun at persisting notions about Chaplin's own political ideology.

In *My Trip Abroad*, written following his European tour promoting *The Kid* and in the midst of America's first Red Scare, Chaplin recalled fielding

---

Chaplin was a great admirer of Sergei Eisenstein, particularly of Battleship Potemkin *and* Ivan the Terrible. *The comedian struck up a friendship with the Soviet director during his brief sojourn in Hollywood, around the period of the* City Lights *production, and the montage in* Modern Times *is perhaps directly inspired by that relationship.*

many questions from reporters inquiring whether or not he was a Bolshevik, since the comedian's liberal (if not socialistic) views had been rumored. "I am an artist. I am interested in life," went a non-committal Chaplin response. "Bolshevism is a new phase of life. I must be interested in it."[47]

Chaplin was careful not to endorse the Communist system nor any of its concepts outright in 1921. At that point in time, he perhaps recognized the seriousness with which his public statements were taken, and how they could either enhance or detract from his celebrity status. Not until he was free of a studio contract and successfully producing his own features could he afford to dabble in political debates without fear of affecting his professional work. By the mid–1930s, and with one profitable sound era film under his belt, Chaplin perhaps felt much less constrained about expressing his thoughts.

Unfortunately, not only did the comedian's stature give more weight to his stated opinions, but his overwhelming popularity lent him a touch of arrogance, and Chaplin often clung stubbornly to his beliefs. Few people, if any, openly contradicted him in face-to-face encounters, least of all those who worked closely with him. Further, America was supposedly the land of the free, an ideal that Chaplin seems to have embraced in the most libertarian sense. Although he may have had to temper his public attitudes occasionally, Chaplin firmly believed that he could express whatever view he wished privately.* Such firmness in his beliefs would work against Chaplin later, when his public opinions began to run counter to American popular sentiment.

For now, however, the Tramp's march down the street waving a red flag in *Modern Times* was a comic incident designed to satirize the growing belief that Chaplin was a "parlor pink." Poor Charlie is rousted by the cops even though the audience is fully aware of his honest intentions. Chaplin's ideological critics, here in the form of belligerent city police, promptly rush in to cart him off to jail on circumstantial evidence.

Chaplin's point is taken a bit further when the Tramp thwarts the jailbreak and restores order to the rightful authorities. A true anarchist, as the comedian's harshest critics would wish to perceive him, would have reveled in such an uprising, but the Little Fellow does not. Deep down, the Tramp was a decent, respectable and honest character.

VII. THE TRAMP AND THE GAMIN

Unlike previous Chaplin films, pathos did not center on the Little Fellow in *Modern Times*, but rather on the millions of citizens who struggled for

---

*"...Charlie [was] a stubborn man," Buster Keaton would recall in his autobiography, "and when his right to talk favorably about Communism was challenged he simply got bullheaded about it." (Buster Keaton; My Wonderful World of Slapstick; page 270.)

The Tramp as working man, from *Modern Times* (1936).

survival in the Depression. Similarly, romance would also be depicted differently. Specifically, Chaplin didn't create his heroine as a mere object of affection, but as a female counterpart equal to and sometimes even more resourceful than the Tramp himself. In addition, rather than establish a relationship based on Charlie's infatuation with the Gamin, the comedian instead fashioned a more paternal relationship with his leading lady.

The change may have been motivated by the satisfaction Chaplin had with the state of his personal life. Paulette was easily the most compatible of his mates thus far, and the strength of their relationship is evidenced by a role in *Modern Times* that goes far beyond that of the traditional Chaplin heroine.

Chaplin even made efforts to comment on the pairing in the film; just as he made light of his personal politics, Chaplin also took the opportunity to poke fun at the stir in some circles over his budding relationship with Paulette. The comedian, then 44, had again been linked romantically to an actress much younger than himself. Accusations of impropriety were old hat by the time Paulette came into his life, since both of Chaplin's previous marriages had been to so-called child brides. He had worked with young female acting talent in every outing since *The Gold Rush*, also contributing to accusations regarding his questionable morals.

Given the publicity surrounding his previous relationships, the comedian had understandably become quite private about his personal affairs. But at least two scenes in *Modern Times* contain what seem to be overt references to Chaplin's publicized romances and look to portray Chaplin (in the guise of his screen character) as a man of high morality.

For instance, as Paulette and Charlie are thrown from the paddy wagon on their way to jail, the Gamin looks to escape. Before the policeman who also fell from the van can awake, she bolts for freedom and, as she rounds the corner, urges the Tramp to follow. The shot then moves to a medium one of Charlie, who acknowledges the camera and, therefore, the audience. His choice is to stay with the policeman and face jail, which we already know is an agreeable place for the Little Fellow, or go with the beautiful girl. Charlie knows what he should do, but his body sighs, indicating that he is powerless to resist her beck and call. The Tramp, who earlier showed respect for authority by thwarting the jailbreak, now disregards this respect and follows the girl, willing to accept the consequences of his actions. Charlie (and likewise, perhaps, Chaplin himself) could not resist the opportunity for companionship.

Yet another direct reference to Chaplin's personal life appears as the Gamin and the Little Fellow take up residence in their Hooverville shack. The film makes a point of showing the chaste relationship between them while they coexist under one roof—the Gamin on the floor; the Tramp ironically (or appropriately, depending on one's interpretation) in the adjoining dog house. We could assume from Charlie's romantic involvement in previous features that the pair have nothing immoral in mind. But it is the purposeful depiction of their respective sleeping quarters that lends credibility to the contention that Chaplin was at least aware of criticism about his association with young women such as Paulette.

Thus, the comedian established a relationship between the Tramp and the Gamin that is clearly non-sexual, and even unromantic in some respects. In previous films, Chaplin had created heroines who served as the Tramp's object of love and desire; while there is a similar, although less pronounced bond in *Modern Times*, it is more accurate to assess the Tramp/Gamin relationship as one that is fostered more from mutual need than from infatuation or desirous love.

This is perhaps because the two are so well matched. More distinctive than previous Chaplin heroines, the Gamin appears, in effect, to be a female version of the Tramp: She too is homeless, penniless, and longs for the comfort and security so readily available to the more fortunate. In this sense, she is more aggressive in pursuing these goals than Charlie. Throughout the film, it is she who precipitates their escape from the paddy wagon, finds their shanty home and arranges for Charlie's employment at the café. Driving her is a strong desire for stability, a modest hope that was no doubt shared by many of the world's peoples during the Depression.

This was certainly the most compatible and realistic coupling that the comedian had created since some of his early two-reel pairings with Edna Purviance. Although Virginia Cherrill's Blind Girl comes close to being Charlie's natural mate (they both suffer from respective disabilities, Virginia's blindness and Charlie's poverty), the emotional content of the ending requires a certain degree of disparity between the two to retain its sentimental qualities.

In Chaplin's evolution as a filmmaker, the role of the love interest was waning in its importance to his narratives. Where many previous motion pictures were guided by Charlie's pursuit of a girl, romance would play a less pivotal role in Chaplin's future projects. Beginning with his next film, *The Great Dictator*, Chaplin would establish an even more paternal relationship with his leading ladies, a trait that would continue throughout the remainder of his filmography — perhaps a factor attributable to Chaplin's own advancing age in relation to his choice of actresses.

Nonetheless, the Gamin holds a far more prominent and developed role than previous heroines. One has only to remember that Chaplin's failing marriages coincided with films such as *Sunnyside* and *The Circus*, and the strain was apparent in both pictures. Here, we see the Gamin in a distinctly elevated role by comparison, indicating not only a confidence by Chaplin in Paulette's acting abilities but in their relationship as well.

To this end, Charles Maland notes that the *Modern Times* pressbook broke with earlier tradition by featuring not only Charlie prominently but the Gamin as well.[48] This kind of equal billing, which did not extend to actual marketing of the film (where the traditional image of the Tramp dominated), is indicative of two things. First, Chaplin's intention was to establish Paulette's acting career in feature films. Like he tried unsuccessfully to do for Edna Purviance in *A Woman of Paris*, he looked to create a role that would display his leading lady's talent, an effort that naturally lead to the creation of a character stronger than the traditional Chaplin heroine. Second, the comedian, like Charlie in the film, had finally found a compatible mate. Even Edna's comedy characters, who often seemed most compatible for the Little Fellow, failed to develop much beyond the Charlie's yearning phase within films.[49] In fact, there is a valid argument to be made that the development of the Tramp's form of "feminine worshipping," beginning during Chaplin's stint at Essanay and culminating in features such as *The Gold Rush, The Circus* and *City Lights*, firmly established itself during the period in which he and Edna were maintaining their own off-screen relationship. Since we have seen how Chaplin's previous romantic troubles had negatively affected his work, it thus seems likely that his satisfaction with various relationships also helped shape the nature of his motion pictures.

David Robinson offers an interesting aside to the Tramp and Gamin relationship. Chaplin, it seems, originally conceived the role of the Gamin in terms more closely analogous to the Blind Girl in *City Lights*.[50]

In an early version of the scenario, then titled *Commonwealth*, the ending is entirely different; Chaplin looked to end on an emotionally sour note, having the Gamin enter a convent to become a nun. Accompanied by her Mother Superior, she returns to see Charlie, who had been recovering in a local hospital. It is a tense and awkward reunion, reminiscent of one of Chaplin's recollections from his world tour, when he accompanied Ralph Barton on an uncomfortable visit with the cartoonist's daughter, then living in a Hackney convent.[51] The pair must part, and as she watches the lonely figure of the Little Fellow wander away, her spirit — the youthful, bubbly part of her character — leaves her body to give chase. It flits about the Tramp, who cannot see the apparition, and he simply continues on his lonesome way. Paulette looks on as she realizes that a part of her is gone forever.

Though the ending was never used, studio records indicate it was shot during May and June of 1935.[52] Why it was ultimately discarded is not known, although Gerard Molyneaux has suggested that perhaps it may have somehow run into problems with the Hays Office, Hollywood's self-censorship body.[53]*

As it stands, the existing ending reinforces the relationship between Paulette Goddard and Charles Chaplin (both on and offscreen), which seems to have been stable and entirely compatible despite their differences in age. Their departure arm in arm, heading toward a future together, seems an appropriate image for the Tramp's last screen moment, particularly in light of his history of longing for companionship. It was certainly a different sort of relationship than Chaplin had created before on the screen, and marked an auspicious screen debut for the former Paulette Levy (who, unlike Edna Purviance, had proven herself a fine actress in her own right). Film historian William K. Everson considered her portrayal of the Gamin one of the best performances by an actress in all of silent cinema.[54] Not only had Chaplin gone a different direction with the element of romance, but he helped establish Paulette as a feature film actress; Modern Times made clear to many that she had definite potential in motion pictures apart from her association with the comedian.

VIII. RESPONSE TO *MODERN TIMES*

Chaplin previewed Modern Times on two separate occasions and, based on audience reaction, each screening suggested areas for cuts.[55] Nonetheless,

---

*The Hays Office, administered by Will B. Hays (later known as the Production Code Administration, or Breen Office while under the direction of Joseph Breen), was charged with the duty of monitoring the content of Hollywood films for the studios, a self-policing tactic that had its origins in the Fatty Arbuckle and William Desmond Taylor scandals of the 1920s. Either Hays, Breen or their representative would hold a pre-production meeting with members of the studio, carefully scrutinize the script, monitor production, screen the production, and at all times reserve the right to recommend scene or dialogue changes. If, in fact, Molyneaux's assertions are correct, Chaplin may also have had this as a second motivating factor behind clearly depicting the chaste relationship between the Tramp and the Gamin.

audience reaction to the film was very good, and it looked as if *Modern Times* would once again prove that silent film, even when spiced with ideological speculation, could still draw patrons to the theater.

But when the picture was finally released, initial reviews were mixed, and certainly did not match the anticipated public enthusiasm. Based on early reports about the film, many conservative reviewers were prepared to assail it as liberal propaganda. But Chaplin balanced his socially conscious material with pure entertainment, failing, as many expected, to take a strong and persuasive political stand. Generally, most critics, regardless of their ideological predispositions, downplayed the socio-political aspects.[56] The juxtaposition of old and new comic material tended to prove more memorable than most of the social implications the film sought to highlight or convey, and led critics searching for a political subtext to be deeply disappointed with the ramifications of Chaplin's project.

A good cross section of reaction to *Modern Times* can be found in Alistair Cooke's book *Garbo and the Night Watchmen* (1937), a collection of commentaries on film in the 1930s, which contains an extended section on Chaplin's second sound era production. Opinions are widely divergent, from Don Herold's contention that the comedy outweighed any political message, to John Marks' impressions that there was too much pathos, to Robert Forsythe's fear that comedy derived from situations such as hunger and unemployment made *Modern Times* far too real for the general public to embrace. Cooke himself adds that the film tends to be merely a collection of gag sequences, and specifically lamented that "... *Modern Times* is never once on the plane of social satire."[57] Critic Otis Ferguson (from *The New Republic*) disparaged the segmented narrative of the film, which could have taken the form of two-reelers entitled *The Shop*, *The Jailbird*, *The Watchman* and *The Singing Waiter* respectively.[58] In addition to citing a number of technical flaws, he also noted that the film harkened back to the days when Chaplin's comedy, and not his politics, took center stage.

Other contemporary reviewers downplayed the socio-political aspects of *Modern Times* as well. "Sociological concept?" Frank S. Nugent wrote in the *New York Times* the day after its Big Apple premiere. "Maybe. But a rib-tickling, gag-be-strewn jest for all that and in the best Chaplin manner ... This morning there is good news: Chaplin is back again."[59]

Though perhaps not readily apparent to critics of the 1930s, Chaplin had broken with the style of his earlier work and showed the potential, if not the willingness, to engage in overt socio-political commentary — the very direction he would take with his next two films, one successfully, one not. In retrospect, we can see that *Modern Times* was slightly more than a half-step toward the more politicized narratives that would embody three of his final five film projects. The absence of a specific political sympathy to the narrative manifested itself in some widely divergent discussions of the film. Chaplin's emphasis on gags and action generally outpaced the topical backdrop of the film, leaving his ultimate criticisms dulled and for the most part evenly distributed between business and labor. What stands out throughout the picture are the comedic qualities that would have proved attractive to general audiences, while only flirting with Depression-era social concerns.

Despite placing the Tramp into situations that many Americans would have felt closely attuned to during the 1930s, as well as forgoing a strong political theme, *Modern Times* was surprisingly disappointing at the box office. With only $1.5 million in domestic receipts, it took in more than a half-million less than the domestic draw for *City Lights*, released during the height of the Depression. In America, *Modern Times* took the dubious honor of being the least profitable feature starring the Little Fellow, and led at least one historian to conclude that the so-called threat of socially conscious material in the film, not to mention the avoidance of dialogue once again, may have made the picture appear outdated to the audiences of its day.[60] By no means, though, was *Modern Times* a total failure. Alistair Cooke, for instance, noted in *Garbo and the Night Watchmen* that it was one of the most popular films of 1936.[61] But its cool reception at the box office no doubt caused concern for Chaplin and his ability to draw the public to his films. Perhaps the message seemed clear to the comedian: Sound, for better or worse, was the public's artistic choice as the medium for film.

Possibly resulting from the film's less-than-enthusiastic reception, the period following the release of *Modern Times* was one of relaxation and reflection for Chaplin, an opportunity to spend time with Paulette and his two young boys as well as to contemplate his own future. He would not tour the world as he had following the release of *City Lights*, but would instead embark on a planned vacation to Honolulu with Paulette shortly after the premiere of *Modern Times*. Planned, that is, to the extent that any holiday with Chaplin could be. His vacationing methods, like his work methods, were always subject to sudden improvisation. This particular trip held to form, and Honolulu served only as a springboard to the Orient, where Chaplin and Paulette spent nearly four months of impromptu touring.

The Great Dictator

Although their plans were to have simply vacationed in Hawaii, Chaplin and Paulette's itinerary changed abruptly when the comedian suddenly wished to sail to the Far East. Following the *S.S. President Coolidge*'s arrival in Honolulu, where they were able to acquire adequate supplies for the journey, the couple embarked further east on the ship.

This particular vacation would not garner near the amount of documentation that either Chaplin's 1921 or 1931 tours had. In fact, even in *My Autobiography*, Chaplin reveals virtually nothing about the nature of the trip at all. The entire journey entails a scant three pages, two of which detail Chaplin's often futile attempts to avoid Jean Cocteau, a fellow passenger on the *Coolidge*. According to Chaplin, neither artist was particularly inclined to spending a lot of time with the other.

Cocteau, however, related a different scenario. He evidently found Chaplin quite solitary and occupied throughout the journey.[1] Aside from the comedian's visit to his cabin at the beginning of their voyage (where Cocteau's male companion made a shoddy attempt to bridge their uncomfortable French-English language gap), Cocteau relates that Chaplin spent much of his time indoors, working on yet another film idea.

Cocteau's could, perhaps, be the more authentic version. Chaplin, eager to create another vehicle for Paulette, used his Shanghai visit as inspiration for a script tentatively titled *White Russian* (or *Stowaway*, at one point). The story, which Chaplin would eventually resurrect as his final film in 1967 under the title *A Countess from Hong Kong*, centered on a former Russian countess (based, in part, on May Reeves, his companion for much of the 1931 world tour) who stows away in the cabin of an American diplomat returning by ship to the United States. The picture was intended to star Paulette opposite, in Chaplin's mind, Gary Cooper.

The film, like *A Woman of Paris* before it, would have been a sole writing and directing credit for Chaplin, with the comic making perhaps only a cameo appearance (he played a seasick purser in the 1967 film). The comedian also intended the project for full sound accompaniment. *White Russian* took up much of Chaplin's time following his return to Hollywood, with a rough version ready by October of 1936. But even with such swift progress, for reasons unclear the script would not hold Chaplin's interest long enough for actual pre-production work to begin.

Yet despite Chaplin's avoidance of detail concerning the trip in his memoirs, he does write in passing of the event that proved to be the greatest source of public attention Chaplin would receive during this period — his confirmation of marriage to Paulette, in Canton. Hollywood gossip columns were filled with speculation regarding their marital status following their return to Los Angeles, yet for some reason neither would disclose this information.

The arrangement was one that likely suited both individuals well. For Chaplin, a constant subject in gossip circles, jockeying by reporters to uncover "the story" no doubt provided a touch of ironic pleasure. He had not forgotten the sting of numerous columns devoted to his troubles in divorcing Lita Grey and, perhaps, wanted to keep his private affairs even more so this time around. This stubborn sense of privacy, like his sense of justice, would later prove to be his Achilles heel in the United States.

Paulette had an equal, albeit much more ambitious reward in keeping the marriage secret. Unlike her husband, Paulette had not yet fully established herself as an actress, despite her fine work in *Modern Times*. Though she would, in fact, be the only one of Chaplin's four wives to continue acting successfully following their marriage, at this point in her career she may have been conscious of being considered a leading lady merely on the basis of her famous husband.

Accordingly, it was Paulette who reaped the benefits as well as the brunt of the secretive relationship. Some conservative women's groups had expressed their dissatisfaction toward the couple's ambiguous living situation (Paulette had become a resident of the Chaplin household), especially in light of their age differences. But Paulette was shrewd enough at her young age to realize that this kind of attention — most of it positive, painting her in a glamorous light — not only built but maintained acting careers.

Their motivations for failing to disclose the marriage are, however, speculative. For reasons ultimately known only to themselves, the nature of their relationship was never revealed publicly during the 1930s.

The period between *Modern Times* and *The Great Dictator* also provided Chaplin more of an opportunity to be with his two sons from the Lita Grey marriage. Both Charlie, Jr., and Sydney had seen their father only sporadically since the August 1928 divorce. But by the latter half of the 1930s, Lita had become very unstable as a parent. Bouts with alcoholism, nervous breakdowns, health problems and tumultuous romances characterized her life. Occasionally, too, she suffered from paranoid delusions, feeling that her former husband had hired people to monitor and control her life, and she specifically warned Charles, Jr., of his father's seemingly inescapable power. Hence the comedian's sons welcomed the attention and stability offered by Goddard and Chaplin.

In *My Father, Charlie Chaplin*, Charles, Jr., vividly recounts how well Paulette treated both boys, as well as their famous father. For such a young woman, Paulette had an enormous amount of maturity as well as vitality. Her exuberance was a welcome addition to the Chaplin household; Paulette seems to have brought out everyone's playful side, and the boys have fond memories of their father's comical imitations and games. Their memories are, in fact, very similar to Chaplin's own recollections of his mother Hannah when he was a boy. Charles, Jr., is very generous in his praise of Paulette's warmth and caring toward the Chaplin boys, displaying an affection for her that eventually formed into a boyhood crush of sorts.

Even Lita Grey found Paulette charming and sincere. They met but once, Lita recalled, when Chaplin arrived to pick up his sons one Christmas morning. "In the years that followed," she remembered, "I was to admire [Paulette] even more and be in her debt for the endless kindness she showed my boys when I became helpless as a mother and a human being. She lavished affection on them ... When I entered a hospital for an operation more than a year after our short, single meeting, my room was flooded with baskets of flowers and other gifts. The card read, 'Get up and out of there fast. Love, Plain Paulette Levy from Long Island.'"[2]

A warm and generous spirit wasn't the only thing Paulette brought to the Chaplin household. She and Sylvia Ashley Fairbanks, Douglas Fairbanks' last wife, supervised a stunning modernization to the interior of the Chaplin mansion on Summit Drive. (The comedian, who had never really bothered to update his palatial surroundings, found the redecoration bothersome but tolerable.) Paulette also introduced dogs to the Chaplin grounds, much to the delight of Sydney and Charlie, Jr., though apparently not of Chaplin himself (though he had often kept one as a mascot at the Studio).

I. NAPOLÉON, SCARLET AND HITLER

Given the ambition of Paulette to attain stardom in her own right, she could not resign herself fully to such "idle" tasks as redecorating. Even with the attention she had been garnering, she was eager to return to the screen as soon as possible and prove her acting worth. Unfortunately, Chaplin's script for the *White Russian/Stowaway* story had lost its appeal after the fall of 1936. This was actually the second film idea that he had abandoned during this period. Coinciding with his production of *Modern Times*, Chaplin began, through the work of hired staff, to conduct research for a historical film on a character who had long interested him: Napoléon Bonaparte.

While looking for a dramatic vehicle in which to star Edna Purviance over a decade previous, Chaplin first tapped his desire to play this role. He felt it would make an outstanding dramatic film, with distinctly different types of characters for both he and Edna (as Josephine) to play. The film, of course, was not made at that time. Edna's star-making vehicles would be *A Woman of Paris* and the ill-fated *Sea Gulls*, both of which failed to establish her a film career outside of Chaplin's circle.

Shortly thereafter, French filmmaker Abel Gance produced his epic *Napoléon* (1927), on a scale much larger than anything Chaplin likely would have conceived. Though it is doubtful that Chaplin saw Gance's original version of the film (which was shown only in a handful of European cities), he may have been able to view the severely-edited version that played eventually in America.

Chaplin was hard-pressed to shake his Napoleon fascination through the succeeding years. At one of William Randolph Hearst's lavish costume balls, during the period of his marriage to Lita Grey, Chaplin was photographed in full Bonaparte splendor, complete with hand tucked into the waistcoat and a conqueror's scowl to boot. The costume also came in handy for a few undated test photographs for the proposed Napoléon project with Harry Crocker; Chaplin later reprinted some of them (along with the Hearst photos) in his pictorial autobiography, *My Life in Pictures*.[3]

In 1930, Chaplin finally stated his desire to play the military figure outright; in an article entitled "Roles I Would Like to Play," appearing in the magazine *Bravo*, he cited Napoléon and Jesus Christ as the two parts he longed to undertake. Although he felt playing Christ was perhaps too controversial for the United States, he was quite specific about how he envisioned himself as the Corsican general. "I would not portray Napoleon as a powerful general," he noted, "but as a sickly, taciturn, almost morose man, constantly plagued by the members of his family. For, you see, it was these people, especially his mother, Laetitia Ramolino, who played a considerable part in shaping the manner of his existence. It has always amused me to think of his efforts to marry off his brothers and sisters, and also his in-laws, in order to remain on good terms with his mother and his wife. And at the same time go about winning wars! What a lot of dramatic situations could be created out of all that!" His comments seem a bit comical, but he apparently envisioned the project as more serious in nature, even asserting that he had "a pile of notes" from which to build a scenario.[4]

On his *City Lights* tour, as well, Chaplin continued his fascination with Napoléon. While in England, he bounced the idea off future Prime Minister Winston Churchill, who responded enthusiastically. Chaplin even used his European stay to pay a visit to Napoléon's tomb. "One can hardly realize," Chaplin would recount of the moment, "that in that marble casket lies the most dramatic mortal that has ever lived. I think for sheer drama Napoleon comes first. As I glance over the balcony, I am reminded of the line in Gray's Elegy — 'The paths of glory lead but to the grave.'"[5]

Though Chaplin had obviously been flirting with the idea for a number

Slapstick diplomacy. Hynkel and Benzino Napoloni (Jack Oakie) on the brink of an international incident, from *The Great Dictator.*

of years, he had never committed to pursuing his Napoleonic ambitions. After *Modern Times*, however, the project once again began to stir his interest.[6] Sound technology could not be spurned again; hence his willingness to proceed with a project not featuring the Tramp. A move toward more dramatic features and roles would seem logical, given his developing predilection for more serious subject matter, even within his comedies. Also, casting Paulette as Josephine would provide a high profile dramatic part for her, a role that almost any actress would covet.

Chaplin actually embarked on initial research for the Napoléon script prior to committing to *Modern Times*. For historical background and initial preparations, he employed a young British journalist he had met in 1933 named Alistair Cooke, then on a scholarship from Yale and working in Hollywood as a correspondent for the *London Observer*. While Chaplin was concentrating on putting *Modern Times* together, Cooke had numerous meetings with Chaplin's staff, including Carter De Haven, assistant director on *Modern Times*, and Henry Bergman. In time, however, Chaplin became so fully involved with the Tramp's final screen adventure that the Napoléon project was shelved.[7] In return for his efforts, Cooke was offered an assistant directorship in *Modern Times*, as well as Chaplin's words of encouragement that Cooke would make an excellent light comedian. Cooke, as we know, declined the offer.

Now, working on ideas to follow-up *Modern Times*, Chaplin once again picked up his interest in the film. A new (and only surviving) version of the script had been completed early in 1936, primarily by writer John Strachey* (who inherited the project after Jean de Limur had attempted a draft), and incorporated a number of the comedian's own inventive devices. But just as work could have begun in earnest, Chaplin was focusing on the release of *Modern Times* and preparing for his trip with Paulette. When he returned, Chaplin, a true creature of whims, was fully involved with *White Russian*, and the *Napoleon* project fell by the wayside.

When neither *Napoleon* nor *White Russian* proved they could hold his creative interest, the London office of United Artists purchased (on behalf of the Chaplin Film Corporation) the rights to D.L. Murray's novel *Regency*, which the comedian also looked to develop for Paulette.

David Robinson notes that Chaplin wanted to alter the role of Regency, an already strong female role, by giving it some political (and hence, in Chaplin's mind, more contemporary) overtones. The novel centered upon the lively escapades of a uniquely independent aristocratic girl. Chaplin's version introduced a love interest for Regency — a commoner with a strong distaste for the upper classes — that would find Paulette's character being torn between her noble heritage and her heart.[8]

Chaplin threw himself into the script for *Regency*. From October 1936 to February of 1937, Chaplin collaborated on adapting the novel with another writer, Major Ronald Bodley, whose services were also obtained in conjunction with the purchase of the film rights to Murray's novel. However, just as *Napoleon* and *White Russian* had failed to hold Chaplin's interest, so too would *Regency*. A more contemporary subject, Chaplin suddenly announced to his secretary, would be sought out for his next film project.

This tinkering with possible film ideas kept the creative and personal aspects of his life in limbo. Maurice Bessy recalled a visit to the Chaplin Studios in 1938, almost a full three years since the studio had seen any activity.

> The sets were tatty, dilapidated, old painted flats; I discovered that the swimming pool where the drowning in *City Lights* was shot was not much more than a ditch; and there was "the street," always the same in all his films, the shop on the corner becoming a florist's in *City Lights*, a drugstore in *Modern Times*. An air of neglect hung over it all. The wooden panels were crumbling away, the paint was flaking. The refuse-bin was old and dented. The old dog that was the studio mascot could hardly stand on its four legs, and lived in a battered kennel ...
> Poverty fitted Charlie like a glove. You could feel it everywhere.[9]

Chaplin's idleness was felt not only at the studio. Paulette was without

---

Chaplin's desire to complete a full script, as well as the employment of outside writers, is indicative of his intention of leaving his filmic past behind after the release of Modern Times.

work during what was potentially her most productive years in Hollywood, and was growing restless. Eager to work again, with or without Chaplin's assistance, she signed with producer David O. Selznick and Paramount Pictures over the objections of her husband. (Selznick owned a home near Chaplin's and, apparently, was not one of the comedian's favorite neighbors.*) Chaplin perhaps couldn't appreciate that his sporadic working habits weren't aiding Paulette's career and may consequently have viewed Selznick as a creative rival for his wife.

But from Paulette's standpoint, placing herself under Selznick's wing at that time could not have been a more shrewd career move. Selznick, after all, had obtained the rights to Margaret Mitchell's *Gone with the Wind*. By signing Goddard, Selznick fueled speculation within the Hollywood community regarding the casting of the coveted part of Scarlet O'Hara. At the very least, it added Paulette's name to an already exclusive list of cinema's top actresses.

To his credit, Chaplin did make efforts, however reluctant, to support Paulette's blossoming career. Constance Collier, renowned actress and friend of Chaplin's, worked with Paulette at his request prior to her October 1, 1937, screen test for *Gone with the Wind*. Judging from Selznick's reactions (revealed) in Rudy Behlmer's *Memo from David O. Selznick*), Paulette fared extremely well against the competition. Even as late as November of 1938, only weeks away from the scheduled start of principal shooting, Paulette was still being seriously considered for the role. Selznick, corresponding with Paramount executives on the East Coast, commented:

> ... I saw the Paulette Goddard–Jeffrey Lynn test and thought there was an enormous improvement in her work — so much so that I think we ought to take the chance that if she doesn't play Scarlet, we will be able to find other engagements for her besides the Universal job ...[10]

Later that month, Selznick again wrote New York to express interest in obtaining Paulette's services.

> Incidentally, the point in [Goddard's] contract about which I have written you, concerning Chaplin's rights, should be straightened out immediately if it needs straightening out. It might be wise to make clear to Goddard that unless this point

---

Ironically, Selznick would join United Artists after Samuel Goldwyn left the company in 1941. When Selznick failed to deliver projects right away, Chaplin, looking to spur the producer into action, sued him in 1943 for not meeting the specifics of his initial contract. Tino Balio cites a letter from Mary Pickford to Chaplin in which she rather shrewdly countered that Chaplin himself took a good many years to produce his first picture for United Artists, as he first had to fulfill his contract with First National. (Cited by Tino Balio; "Charles Chaplin, Entrepreneur: A United Artist," from Timothy J. Lyons et al.; Journal of the University Film Association, Winter 1979; pages 17–18.) Chaplin never pursued the lawsuit beyond the initial filing, leaving the case in abeyance.

is straightened out ... and unless we get a further extension of the contract to a full seven years, she is not going to play Scarlet.[11]*

Up until Christmas 1938, Paulette was part of an elite group of finalists, which included Jean Arthur, Joan Bennett and Vivien Leigh for the coveted role. By New Year's it was Leigh, championed to Selznick by Laurence Olivier, who was slated to play Scarlet.

Despite the setback, Paulette's career made substantial gains before she again took a role opposite her husband. She had prominent roles in *The Women* (1938), *The Cat and the Canary* (1939) and *The Ghost Breakers* (1940), the latter two being mystery comedies that paired her with Bob Hope. By the time Chaplin was ready to commence with a feature film once again, Paulette had earned for herself respectability within the industry.

But while Paulette's career moved forward during the late 1930s, her relationship with Chaplin did not. Bolstered by the prospects of a bright career, Paulette's focus began to turn more and more toward work — work that Chaplin, though he planned to create a role for her in his next picture, was not providing. Other problems manifested themselves as well. New to the Hollywood scene, the youthful Paulette was eager to bask in its glamour, an important part of establishing herself as a viable starlet. Parties, nightclubs, designer clothes, jewelry — such things were new and exciting to her. Chaplin, on the other hand, had outgrown his wild youth, and now approaching his 50s, was content to simply settle into an easy, comfortable lifestyle. The pair were moving at different speeds, and the resulting friction would cause a brief separation in 1938, leaving Chaplin without a developable project for his next film and a failing marriage with which to contend.

It was at this time that the comedian looked began to branch out socially, and spent a good deal of time with Tim Durant, whom Chaplin had met through director King Vidor. Durant was a young, high-society type, affiliated with the social set in Carmel and Pebble Beach north of Los Angeles. Given that Chaplin had failed to follow through on several film projects and his relationship with Paulette was faltering, the time was ripe for a change of pace. Durant invited Chaplin up the coast on a number of occasions, introducing him to

---

*The reference to Chaplin's rights is an interesting notation. Joe Morella and Edward Epstein contend in their biography of Goddard that what was known as the "Chaplin Clause" formed part of Paulette's contract, and was negotiated to help allay some of the comedian's initial anger with her decision to stake out her own career path. (Joe Morella and Edward Epstein; Paulette: The Adventurous Life of Paulette Goddard; page 63.) In essence, the clause stated, she would be allowed to work on whatever project she wished, provided it did not interfere with the production of a Chaplin film. In such cases, Chaplin reserved the right to utilize his wife's talents for as long as would be needed. Given her yearning to continue working and establish herself on her own, such control by Chaplin over her future (if, in fact, the clause existed) no doubt was a contributing factor in the eventual breakdown of their relationship.

several of the monied residents in Pebble Beach, as well as in the more Bohemian seaside town of Carmel.

Through these visits, Chaplin met a young man named Dan James, son to millionaire D.L. James. With him the film star shared an idea he had been toying with: A satirical film based on Adolf Hitler. James, no doubt a sounding board for Chaplin's creative mind, expressed enthusiasm.

The seeds of *The Great Dictator* may have just been sprouting in Chaplin's mind, but the topic of Fascism was not at all new to the comedian. Unfolding events in Europe were on the minds of many. Artists and intellectuals in Hollywood, as elsewhere, were becoming increasingly concerned with news from abroad.[12] Stories of Hitler's purges, primarily against Jews, began to surface. Refugees from Nazi cruelty relocated to the United States; some of these figures, including Albert Einstein and Chaplin's own brother Sydney, touched Chaplin personally. Motion picture figures such as actor Peter Lorre and directors Billy Wilder, Otto Preminger and Fritz Lang, among numerous others, also made their way to Hollywood. Artists Thomas Mann, Leon Feuchtwanger, Hanns Eisler and Bertolt Brecht, individuals whom Chaplin would come to know later in the 1940s, would also have a profound impact on his life and work, as they brought with them stories of their struggles and plights. "The refugees arrived in waves," Larry Ceplair and Steven Englund note in their study of the film industry's political activism between 1930 and 1960, *The Inquisition in Hollywood*, "and each wave further vivified what Hollywood people had been reading in their newspapers.... Years later, testifying before HUAC*, the conservative film writer James K. McGuinness, hardly a man to be bowled over by 'liberal' causes, told the Committee that Hollywood 'offered refuge to many vocal, articulate people who escaped the lash of Hitler.... They were accustomed to expressing themselves, and they brought home very forcibly to Hollywood the dangers of the Fascist and Nazi regimes.'"[13]

Their stories were sometimes harrowing, and many in the United States, including a number of those in the American film industry, were taken with their beliefs and began to organize a variety of anti–Fascist organizations that became known collectively as the Popular Front. This diverse array of groups, appealing to a wide spectrum of political thought, including some Communists, was linked by a common intolerance for the Fascist system of government. Through fund-raising for humanitarian efforts and general awareness campaigns, these formal and informal groups attempted to raise public conscious-ness about the terrible events taking place in countries such as Germany and Italy.

Chaplin himself was not active in the Popular Front prior to his work on *The Great Dictator*, though he was certainly aware of the political situation

---

HUAC stands for the House Un-American Activities Committee, which investigated a number of American institutions, including Hollywood, for alleged Communist influences, most notably during the McCarthy era of American history.

abroad as well as familiar with many of the individuals participating in the Front's activities at home. Since Chaplin would eventually become a hostile critic of Fascism and would later become very close to artists such as Eisler and Mann, it seems clear that he was at least sympathetic to the goals of the Popular Front and aware of its humanitarian efforts.

Thus, Chaplin was well attuned to the situation in Europe. As he reflected on the idea of a Hitler satire, previously suggested him earlier by Alexander Korda,* a whole range of comedic opportunities began to open up. Further, he recalled later, the rough scenario he was contemplating offered yet another opportunity to smooth the transition into sound. "Then it suddenly struck me. Of course! As Hitler I could harangue the crowds in jargon and talk all I wanted to. And as the tramp I could remain more or less silent. A Hitler story was an opportunity for burlesque and pantomime."[14]†

But neither Chaplin nor Korda were the first people to notice the similarities between the two; cartoonists had long capitalized on the likenesses between Der Führer and the Tramp. Even German film critic Rudolf Arnheim had noted earlier that "... looking into Hitler's face [one] must remember Charlie Chaplin.... The style of mustache of the Third Reich is derived from Chaplin as the swastika originates from the orientals. It is not innate but he glues it on his lip as if he wants to represent the little man who is queer and comical because he wears his shabby wretchedness like a well-fitting coat."[15]

Michael Hanisch researched public reaction to Chaplin in Germany, and found other motivating factors for the comedian's satire. Not surprisingly, Hitler had banned Chaplin's films after taking the reins of the German government. Since that time, Chaplin became a target for Nazi propaganda, both in Germany and in the United States; Ivor Montagu, a companion of Sergei Eisenstein during the director's visit to Hollywood in the early 1930s, recalled sending the comedian some of the material he had come across.[16] An October, 1938 issue of the Berlin magazine *Film Kurier* reprinted an article (originally published in the American newspaper *Liberation*) entitled "Who's Who in Hollywood — Find the Gentile," which listed over 90 Hollywood personalities said to have Jewish origins. Heading up the list was comedian Jack Benny, followed by Chaplin, whose name was allegedly Karl Tonstein. (He was not without notable company, at least. At one point the Nazis also fingered fellow silent comedian Buster Keaton as a Jew.[17])

---

*The account listed here is Chaplin's. Where the idea for The Great Dictator *actually originated has been the subject of some speculation. Charles Maland cites the influence of both Ivor Montagu and Alexander Korda, as well as the numerous émigrés in Hollywood during this period. Also, Konrad Bercovici would eventually bring suit against Chaplin, claiming that he had instigated the idea shortly after the release of* Modern Times. *Chaplin would himself credit Korda for the original idea, coupled with the plot device of mistaken identity.*

†*Apparently, at least at the time of writing his memoirs (the source of this quotation), Chaplin drew no distinction between the Little Fellow and his character from* The Great Dictator. *However, there are fundamental differences, to be discussed later, that distinguish this persona from Charlie.*

This was not the first time Chaplin had been taken for a Jew. Speculation had existed as early as his two-reel days as to whether he had Jewish ancestry, which he never denied (this would "play directly into the hands of anti–Semites," he said later[18]). Adolphe Nysenholc researched the origins of the comedian and, backed by David Robinson's publication of the Chaplin family tree in his biography, concluded that he was likely not Jewish.[19] However, his screen persona of Charlie did display a considerable amount of Jewish characteristics throughout his motion pictures, and these, along with Chaplin's open admiration for the Jewish people, no doubt helped promulgate the ancestry theory that the Nazis and their sympathizers sought to expose.* There was, nonetheless, an appropriateness of Chaplin's playing a Jew in *The Great Dictator*, Nysenholc points out, as Chaplin's screen character had so long been a figure in the throes of injustice and persecution, albeit comic ones. Chaplin was quite sympathetic to the Jewish plight, especially as evidence of persecution began to surface throughout the war, and it was reported in 1939 that he had arranged for the European earnings from *The Great Dictator* to be donated to an organization in Vienna that was helping Jews emigrate from countries under Hitler's control.[20] Regardless of the report's accuracy, by the time the film was ready to be released, there was no large European market left, and hence few proceeds to forward.

However Chaplin conceived the Hitler burlesque, he embarked on the preliminary work with much zeal and enthusiasm. Dan James, his sounding board in Pebble Beach, suddenly found himself employed by the Chaplin Studios in late 1938, helping devise both the plot and gags for the project. Unsubstantiated reports also had author John Steinbeck (a Chaplin acquaintance from the Pebble Beach/Carmel social set) being presented with an offer to co-write the film.[21]

Work progressed quickly, with much of the narrative compiled, albeit in the most rudimentary form, by Christmas of that year. By January of 1939, Chaplin began with actual preparations at the studio, and familiar personnel such as Sydney, Chaplin's half-brother Wheeler Dryden (who had arrived in Hollywood in the early 1920s), and Henry Bergman once again found themselves active. Other studio regulars would begin employment as the year progressed.

By the beginning of September, 1939, an official shooting script (the first of Chaplin's career and a lengthy one at that), was completed. At 300 pages, the work was already two to three times the average length of a Hollywood script, forcing Sydney (his business instincts as strong as ever) to become concerned

---

*Chaplin recalled in his memoirs a point in his vaudeville career, between his stint with the Wal Pink sketch Repairs and joining the Karno troupe, in which he embarked on a solo comedy act as a Jewish comedian, a popular stage get-up at the time. Though he had practiced the routine with dedication, his one and only performance got him promptly booed off the stage. As the comedian recalled, his routine was not only poorly received, but much of his act was anti–Semitic, which he attributed to his own naiveté. (Charles Chaplin; My Autobiography; pages 96–97.)

The humble Barber and Hannah (Paulette Goddard), from *The Great Dictator.*

about the costs and technical burdens associated with producing it. Just nine days later, Chaplin would begin shooting his first full-fledged sound film, a full 12 years after the medium took Hollywood by storm.

In hindsight, Chaplin did more than simply devise an ingenious transition to full-dialogue filmmaking with *The Great Dictator.* "Commercial realities apart," Charles Silver noted, "Hynkel (as Chaplin would call his dictator in the film) is the solitary justification for *The Great Dictator* as a sound film, and sound — radio— probably the primary factor in Hitler's astonishing sway over Germany. In a sense, then, the dictator had used and was the creature of the technology that Chaplin had so despised and so long resisted. It is a kind of poetic justice that Chaplin was so skillfully able to turn this unfamiliar weapon (to him) against his ranting nemesis."[22]

So, too, did it seem appropriate that these two figures, Hitler and Chaplin, who had been born just four days apart in April of 1889, whose popular appearances were so similar, and who both rose to world-wide fame in adopted countries, but represented such opposite views on humanity, should somehow do battle against each other.

II. THE NARRATIVE OF *THE GREAT DICTATOR*

In the final stages of the First World War, we are introduced to the army of Tomania, about to unveil its ultimate weapon, a monstrous cannon named Big Bertha, poised to annihilate the Cathedral of Notre Dame some 70 miles away. The honor of firing the massive gun goes to Chaplin, a barber in civilian life — a simple little man wrought in the tradition of the Tramp. Bertha does not, however, claim accuracy as its highest virtue; the first shot destroys a nearby outhouse, and the next barely sputters out of the cannon barrel.

With the front line being overrun, the Barber and his outfit are moved to face the oncoming soldiers. But the Barber quickly loses his way in the smoke and mayhem. He comes across an exhausted officer who implores the soldier to commandeer a nearby plane so he can fly them both back to Tomania. They narrowly escape the advancing enemy forces, but in the confusion the pair take to the air only to find themselves flying upside down and running out of fuel. They crash somewhere behind Tomania's lines, but find that their efforts were in vain. An armistice has been reached — Tomania has lost the war. Badly injured, the Barber is taken to a military hospital.

Through a succession of newspaper headlines that propel the action ahead to the late 1930s, we are introduced to the Tomanian dictator Adenoid Hynkel, also played by Chaplin. In a radio speech to the "sons and daughters of the Double Cross" (the comedian's substitution for the swastika), Hynkel launches into a tirade of exaggerated Teutonic gibberish, outlining his vision for the country. Through the voice of an English radio translator, the film audience is coached through the gist of Hynkel's speech, which extols the virtues of Tomania's citizens and the Aryan race while denouncing the intolerable Jewish populace. Hynkel is cheered gloriously at the conclusion of his diabolical speech, although his Minister of the Interior, Garbitsch (Henry Daniell), feels that Hynkel's tirade was too soft on the Jewish issue.

The story moves to the Ghetto, the part of a Tomanian city where the Jewish population has been forced to live. Mr. Jaeckel (Maurice Moskovich), the father figure of the local neighborhood, is fearful of Hynkel's anti-Semitic policies. With him is Hannah (played by Paulette and named, no doubt, after Chaplin's mother), who stays with the Jaeckel family because she has no family of her own. She is a laundress by trade, and starts off to make a delivery only to be viciously pelted with vegetables by a band of Hynkel's marauding Storm Troopers, the so-called law and order in the Ghetto.

Meanwhile, back in the military hospital, the Barber, who still suffers from amnesia following the plane crash, is set to be released. But hospital officials find that he has escaped before they have had a chance to inform him of the drastic changes that have gone on in Tomanian society since his arrival years previous.

The Barber heads straight to his old shop, nestled next to the Jaeckels' courtyard, and finds a litter of kittens springing from the inside of his dusty workplace. The Barber is alarmed and bewildered to find his shop filled with cobwebs and such, unaware of the passage of time, but is even more confused by the sight of Storm Troopers painting "Jew" on his shopfront windows. While removing the paint, he is confronted by two, who immediately order him to replace the label. The Barber shouts for the police, oblivious to the fact that Storm Troopers are the law, and tries to resist their attempts to restrain him. From an adjacent window, Hannah appears with a frying pan, dispatching the Barber's antagonists with a few well-placed blows. Soon, however, there are more Storm Troopers than can be dealt with, and the helpless Barber is captured and nearly hung from a street lamp. Only upon the arrival of superior officer Schultz (Reginald Gardiner), does the Barber get a reprieve. Schultz, as fate would have it, was the Tomanian officer the Barber saved in the First World War, and he now holds a lofty position in Hynkel's military hierarchy. The Barber is spared on Commander Schultz's orders.

Back at the palace, Hynkel is busy running the Tomanian war machine. So busy is he, in fact, that the artists working on a bust and a painting of "Der Phooey" are spared less than ten seconds to use Hynkel as a model, and must work furiously in the short time they are allotted.

Always looking for improvements in his military equipment, Hynkel is urged by Field Marshal Herring (Billy Gilbert) to see the demonstration of a bullet-proof uniform, in which Hynkel promptly shoots its creator dead. Like the factory boss dismissed the Bellow's Feeding Machine, Hynkel simply walks away uttering, "Far from perfect."

Garbitsch informs Hynkel that they do not have the capital to embark on a planned invasion of neighboring Osterlich, as most foreign banks are refusing to do business with Tomania. They hatch a plan to borrow the money from a wealthy Jew named Epstein, and soften their anti–Semitic policies in an attempt to win his favor.

Much later, both Mr. Jaeckel and Hannah, now in the refurbished barber shop, are perplexed at the sudden turnabout in Hynkel's Ghetto policy. The Storm Troopers, once everyone's enemy, even help Hannah up when she falls, spilling an apron full of potatoes on the sidewalk. She turns to the camera and expresses her hopes, wishing for a life where everyone may live in peace together.

Back inside the Palace, Hynkel is informed of a strike at one of his munitions factories. Coldly, he demands that all of the strikers be identified and shot. Garbitsch, however, reminds Der Phooey of the need to keep up production. He offers his own distorted wisdom of executing only the strike organizers, and Hynkel is pleased to hear that this action has already been taken. The pair begin to talk of the Tomanian ideal, with Garbitsch speaking maniacally of the beauty of engineering a pure Aryan nation, to be led by Hynkel. Drunk with Garbitsch's vision of the future, Hynkel begs to be left alone, contemplating his plans for the subjugation of the earth's people. A solitary figure, Hynkel grasps a globe-shaped balloon and gracefully dances a ballet with his toy until, at the height of Hynkel's twisted revelry, it bursts in his face.

Following an ingenious pantomime sequence in which the Barber shaves Chester Conklin (the Tramp's factory supervisor in *Modern Times*) in perfect time to Brahms' "Hungarian Dance #5," he readies himself for an evening out with Hannah. If not for the anti-Semitic rage about to come from the Tomanian Palace, Hannah and the Barber perhaps would have been drawn together by mutual need, much as the Tramp and the Gamin were in *Modern Times*.

But Epstein is not deceived by Hynkel's sudden change in policy toward the Jews and refuses to loan the government money. Hynkel is furious. He calls for Commander Schultz, demanding immediate retaliation in the Ghetto for Epstein's decision. Schultz argues that violence against the Jews is splitting Tomania apart, which promptly gets him arrested and sent to a concentration camp. Hynkel then takes to the Tomanian air waves to denounce the Jewish people and call for immediate violence against them, as they are all enemies of the state.

As the people in the Ghetto hear the Dictator's violent tirade, many scurry for the protection of the Jaeckels' courtyard, but this proves no shelter from the murderous Storm Troopers. Remembering Commander Schultz's order not to harm the Barber, the Storm Troopers spare him, but they are quick to return after learning of Schultz's removal from the high command. Narrowly escaping their marauding clutches, the Barber and Hannah watch from an adjacent rooftop as the Storm Troopers set the barber shop ablaze.

Schultz's stay in the concentration camp is not long, as he manages to escape and seek refuge at the Jaeckels (who are also hiding the Barber). With the aid of the Ghetto elders, Schultz devises a plan whereby one of them will infiltrate the Palace with a bomb, hoping to rid Tomania of its tyrant. Five puddings are made, one of which contains a coin which will identify the man who must become a martyr and carry out the plans. Hannah learns of the proposal and places a coin in all the puddings to sabotage their desperate and foolish intentions.

Soon, however, Storm Troopers arrive at the Jaeckel home looking for the Barber and Schultz. They narrowly escape to the Ghetto rooftops, but their flight is to no avail; both are soon apprehended and sent to a concentration camp. Hannah and the Jaeckels flee with their modest possessions to the neighboring country of Osterlich, where they intend to rebuild their lives free of persecution.

The people of the Palace are already contemplating their next conquest — a military invasion of Osterlich. However, Hynkel is informed that the dictator of the neighboring country of Bacteria, Benzino Napaloni, has already placed his troops on the Osterlich border, presumably to take it before Hynkel and the Double Cross can. To avert a Bacterian attack, Hynkel invites Napaloni to the Palace, hoping to dissuade him from carrying out his invasion.

The esteemed dictator Napoloni (Jack Oakie) quickly establishes himself as a boisterous foil to Hynkel's efforts in demonstrating the power of the Tomanian war machine. A meeting in Hynkel's office, a visit to the Palace barber shop and a military review all prove to be dismal failures for the Tomanian dictator.

Chided by Garbitsch, Hynkel approaches a gala ball held in Napaloni's honor as the final chance to persuade the country of Bacteria to back away from the Osterlich border. Their diplomatic conversation escalates into a war of egos and ultimately a food fight, but ends with the signing of a treaty that will forestall a Bacterian invasion of Osterlich, thus setting the stage for the Double Cross to take the prize for themselves.

Unaware of the invasion plans, both Schultz and the Barber are able to don military garb and escape from the concentration camp. They head for what they think is safety, the Tomania/Osterlich border. There they encounter Tomanian troops who, mistaking the Barber for Hynkel, escort them under military protection to begin the invasion. Meanwhile, the real Hynkel, duck-hunting to throw off speculation about any proposed invasion, is apprehended by Storm Troopers who take him to be the escaped Barber.

The Tomanian army is victorious, and both Schultz and the bewildered Barber are shuttled to the speaking platform, a massive concrete monument where Hynkel is slated to announce his triumph and the subjugation of the people of Osterlich. Garbitsch introduces the new leader of the country, establishing firmly the views of the Tomanian government and the many personal freedoms that its policies will forbid, since they "stand in the way of action."

As the Barber is about to speak, Schultz implores him to put his fears aside, for his voice is freedom's only hope. "Hope," the Barber repeats as he timidly makes his way to address the newly conquered subjects of the Double Cross. Here, with his one chance to denounce the policies of the Tomanian government, the soft-spoken Barber suddenly launches into a seven-minute speech, laced with idealistic rhetoric that hope, peace, love and humanity can ultimately prevail over the demoralizing and dehumanizing threat of dictators. Concluding the emotional monologue, he directly addresses Hannah, who we see listening to his words. As he expresses his optimism that the people will soon recognize the right path, the film closes, without revealing the fate of either the Barber or Schultz, both of whom are caught in the center of Tomanian officials without chance for escape.

III. THE GREAT SATIRE

Had I known the actual horrors of the German concentration camps, I could not have made *The Great Dictator*; I could not have made fun of the homicidal insanity of the Nazis.[23]

— Charles Chaplin — 1964

During the film's production, Chaplin could in no way have imagined the extent of the atrocities that were taking place as the result of Hitler's Aryan policies. Only in retrospect (and chillingly so) does *The Great Dictator* attain the heightened interest with which audiences now view it. Chaplin's depiction of Jewish persecution and his desperate plea for humanitarian action have been greatly enhanced by the outcome of World War II, especially in light of the grisly discoveries of Hitler's so-called "final solution."

This is not to argue that a satire of Fascism was uncontroversial when it was released. Chaplin realized not only the importance of the picture but the sensitivity with which he would have to approach the subject. For most of the principal shooting, Hollywood insiders knew little of the film (*Production #6*, as it was obliquely referred to), and a strict code of silence seemed to surround the studio and those associated with it. So guarded was Chaplin's control over the picture that late in its production, in June of 1940, he filed a $1 million lawsuit against *Life* for publishing an unauthorized photograph of himself dressed as Hynkel — a move that ultimately halted *Life*'s use of the picture, but after well over half of the magazine's slated run had hit the newsstands.[24]

Clearly, Chaplin was well aware of the propagandist aspects of *The Great Dictator*, and wanted to keep his production as closely guarded as possible. The film was conceived when much of the world, and particularly America, held an isolationist foreign policy view toward events in Europe. Chaplin's film seemed to advocate direct intervention against the Nazis, and some felt that it may be too controversial to release in many countries, perhaps even the United States — a direct threat to its financial success. The British office of United Artists, Chaplin recalled, had very strong reservations about the acceptance of the film in England before hostilities broke out.[25] By the time it was ready for release, some argued, the threat of Hitler and Fascism would be all too real for people to laugh at.

But Chaplin failed to let such concerns alter the course of his filmmaking. While he was not ready to make a clear political or social statement about the Depression in *Modern Times*, Fascism was another matter altogether.

"There are people crowding in the fields, tilling the soil, working feverishly all the time ..." he recalled of his trip to Germany shortly after World War I. "Men, women, and children are all at work. They are facing their problem and rebuilding. A great people, [who had been] perverted for and by a few."[26] From Chaplin's perspective, a nation of good and honest people had been ravaged once within his lifetime, and he was committed to making *The Great Dictator* so that the same mistakes were not repeated. He also had to make the film, he claimed at the time, "for the Jews of the world."[27]

Naturally, when rumors about the nature of Chaplin's latest project got out, they aroused the anxiety of supporters of the Third Reich. Chaplin recounts in his memoirs that many threats were made against both the studios and himself by pro–Nazi sympathizers,[28] all of which seemed to only strengthen his resolve to continue the picture with its anti–Fascist message. The main danger to acceptance of the film was not the threat of bodily or property harm, but a quick resolution to the threat posed by Hitler before *The Great Dictator* could be released. If the situation in Europe were to be resolved in some way, removing Hitler as a threat to world peace, a significant factor to the film's acceptance would be taken away. However, Hitler himself saw to it that Chaplin's production could stay on track. As the picture wore on, isolationism began to prove an ineffective foreign policy tool, and the escalation of tension throughout Europe, with allies such as France and England poised on the verge of action, worked to increase the potency of the film. Perversely, the more threatening the Third Reich became to other nations during the process of shooting *The Great Dictator*, the better chances for the film's popular success. The picture garnered a host of studio-generated advertising when it appeared, but in actuality *The Great Dictator* had no better publicity than that which was being provided by Hitler in Europe itself.

While the German leader served as Chaplin's prime inspiration for the picture, two specific comedic aspects of *The Great Dictator* came directly from the comedian's own experiences. By far the most memorable scene of the film, barring the final speech of the Barber, is the globe ballet of Hynkel. The scene, which ingeniously captures Nazi Germany's designs on world domination, has been consistently lauded as a graceful and ironic satire of Hitler's aggressive military designs. The scene does, perhaps, owe its inspiration to a much earlier piece of comic business.

Among the numerous outtakes compiled for their documentary *Unknown Chaplin*, David Gill and Kevin Brownlow uncovered footage from a 1929 party at Pickfair, the Hollywood mansion of Douglas Fairbanks and Mary Pickford, which captures a bit of silliness by those in attendance. Chaplin, we can see, flits about wrapped in a sheet, a sort of Julius Caesar. At one point, mockingly, he dances about with a small globe, and places a German helmet atop his prize, as if the Kaiser himself had laid claim to the planet. Thematically, of course, but also in terms of physical movement, the piece is remarkable in its similarity to the globe scene in *The Great Dictator*. Though Chaplin has refined it to both more meaningful and graceful proportions in the latter production, it is nonetheless prophetic to witness what clearly seems at least part of Chaplin's inspiration for the scene even before Hitler's rise to the helm of the German government.

It is also interesting to note that Chaplin's turn with the globe (at least in his production notes) began as a scene where Hynkel cuts up a map of the world, arranging the countries to his liking. From this Chaplin tapped into the idea of the globe dance (which, though seemingly an improvised scene, was actually choreographed quite extensively).[29] This, perhaps, is indicative of the structure that utilizing sound film and pre-scripted narrative was imposing on Chaplin's art, though he certainly had ample opportunity to devise further balletic moves on the set itself. David Robinson discovered that Chaplin used six full work days on the globe ballet over a span of two months, not including three days of retakes during the same period. Even so, it remains remarkably free of rigid structure, and brilliantly captures the mood of a tyrant in a moment of power-drunk whimsy.

Not to be outdone by Hynkel in the film, the Barber has his own dance that immediately follows. Chaplin's equally graceful shaving scene with Chester Conklin is yet another piece of reincarnated inspiration. In the First National release *Sunnyside*, Charlie plays the handyman of a small hotel who is called upon to do almost everything necessary to keep the place afloat. In one discarded scene, again preserved in *Unknown Chaplin*, Charlie attempts — rather unsuccessfully — to shave Albert Austin. The scene, of course, is devoid of sound, but Chaplin nonetheless displays a number of the "Barberish" mannerisms that would accompany his musical pantomime with Conklin. Even now, with Chaplin embarking on his first sound era production, these scenes, both essentially pantomime in their conception, are a throwback to silent comedy, and are typical of how he approached much of the comedic material in the picture.

Even though Chaplin had finally made the official jump to talking pictures, the comedian had again adapted the use of sound to his own terms. The film's structure is, in fact, more closely aligned with that of a silent film than a sound film, with more emphasis on sight gags; verbal or sound-dependent gags are utilized minimally.[30] The three most highly praised sequences in *The Great Dictator* are all dependent upon Chaplin's pantomime: Hynkel's gibberish speech at the beginning, his dance with the balloon globe and the Barber's "shaving to music" scene. Another scene, when the men of the Ghetto partake of puddings designed to identify who will be the martyr to carry a bomb to the Palace, is also played to long stretches with only musical accompaniment, extracting humor from their nervous reactions. Furthermore, even when the comedian is utilizing dialogue, as with his confrontations with Napaloni, it is primarily the physical elements of these scenes (Hynkel and Napaloni dueling in barber chairs, for instance) that forms the basis for humor.

In terms of structure, the film's writing, acting, camerawork and editing are rooted in Chaplin's past. However, the comedian did attain two noteworthy accomplishments with *The Great Dictator*. First, he finally made a full-fledged sound film and erased the possibility of the work seeming anachronistic to contemporary audiences (which may have partially accounted for the box office failure of *Modern Times*). The picture stood on its own merits, without any degree of public or critical dissatisfaction toward its format. Second, by keeping the Tramp-like role of the Barber mostly silent (and nicely contrasted with the vocal and physical hysterics of Hynkel), he retained many of the more comic, endearing and emblematic characteristics of the traditional Chaplin character.[31] Once again, Chaplin found a way to integrate pantomime with sound. While *The Great Dictator* is the comedian's first true sound production in the traditional sense, he managed to design a number of the comedic sequences in terms of silent comedy, playing to his own strengths.

Sound brought many changes, both positive and negative, to the Chaplin Studios. Despite Rollie Totheroh's long relationship with Chaplin, he and his brother Sydney had doubts regarding Totheroh's ability to photograph *The Great Dictator*. While he was certainly skilled in the silent medium and accustomed to the comedian's working methods, the decision was made that he could not shoot the picture alone due to the added element of sound. For this type of experience, the studio engaged Karl Struss, a veteran cameraman who had worked previously with Cecil B. DeMille, on some of D.W. Griffith's later projects and, along with Charles Rosher, had photographed F.W. Murnau's *Sunrise* (1927). He and Totheroh shared credit for the photography on the film.

Struss was not the only new face at the studio. As a result of the influence of labor and labor unions within the film industry during the 1930s, making *Production #6* proved to be a far different and sometimes more inconvenient task than Chaplin had been used to. New industry-wide regulations improving work conditions for studio crews put additional restrictions on his work routine and brought a host of new faces onto the lot. Some of them had almost no function other than to comply with the new codes.

Though in theory Chaplin's own political philosophy might have endorsed the new production codes and the workers' rights they attempted to protect, it was nonetheless a case of his political idealism conflicting with his needs as a creative artist. What once had been a small and specialized crew of workers with a history of working with the studios now became, in the eyes of Chaplin, a throng of people that he considered both annoying and unnecessary. He could no longer push his crew into the late afternoon without lunch, nor work them well into the evening under their normal salary structure. Though he was slowly learning to streamline his production methods, the codes forced Chaplin to work in a much different environment that he was used to; creativity was coming at a price.

These new regulations helped make *The Great Dictator* not only the second longest shoot of Chaplin's career but also the most expensive production of all his sound era films. The new requirements, Chaplin felt, forced him to give up some of the creative freedom he had worked so hard to achieve. Jack Oakie would recall:

"Who are all these people?" [Chaplin would] ask, looking around at the hustle and bustle. He just couldn't get over the shock of having them around. "Who are these people?" he'd turn to me and ask over, and over, and over again.

"You have to have them, Charlie," I told him. Day after day his brother Syd explained the necessity. "It's the law, Charlie. If we don't use them, they'll close down production ..."

"But we don't need them!" he complained. "What's a makeup man?" he said, putting his finger up to his little mustache. "I've been putting this on my face long before he was born!" he said, pointing across the road at the young man sipping coffee and trying to stay out of Charlie's way.[32]

Chaplin's unhappiness with the new regulations seems somewhat frivolous in light of his many other concerns while filming *The Great Dictator*. His comments to Jack Oakie show a clear inconsistency between the development of his progressive political outlook and his true feelings as an artist and creator. Though he would grudgingly come to accept the addition of these new staff people on his production, it was an interesting paradox that Chaplin was never able to clearly resolve.

IV. THE BARBER AND THE TRAMP

In terms of mannerisms and costume, the character of the Barber appears to have completely assimilated the character of the Tramp. But are they one and the same? Chaplin, reflecting upon his career in his memoirs, seemed to make no distinction between the two, though the opinions of others are divided. Although visually this seems to be the Little Fellow, there are compelling arguments to assert that the character of the Barber was actually a slight variation on the little man Chaplin had created.

Throughout his film career, Chaplin regularly identified with the weak or the persecuted, a sympathy that most clearly manifested itself in the characterization of Charlie. With a somewhat macabre regularity, the Little Fellow was subjected to numerous injustices throughout his screen adventures, particularly after Chaplin's departure from Keystone, when the films began to develop more elements of pathos. Thus, it's perhaps fairly easy to view the Barber as a Jewish version of the Little Fellow. Further, because the Barber's ghetto world in Tomania is a humble and often harsh environment, it seems a place quite similar to one Charlie would have inhabited. Several factors in the characterization of the Barber, however, remain inconsistent with the nature of the Little Fellow.

Foremost is that we are aware of the Barber's back story: He is a simple Jewish barber whose injury during World War I has kept him confined in a Tomanian military hospital. The Tramp has no clear history; in fact, the Little Fellow could not accurately be placed in any culture. Part of Charlie's appeal, and indeed part of his rapid rise to fame, was his ability to assimilate into the culture of virtually any viewing audience; in the United States he was American; in England, helped by Chaplin's own ancestry, he seemed British; and in France, "Charlot," as they called him, was French. Chaplin is said to have nearly always covered the production costs of his films from rentals in Japan alone, so popular were his comedies.

Charlie's life in the world of film — the bars, bunkhouses and streets — was so familiar yet culturally nondescript that they could have had their origin anywhere; Chaplin's sets, often an eclectic mixture of architectural styles and influences, further emphasized this notion. The Little Fellow displayed such universal characteristics as kindness, vulnerability and a love of humanity that wasn't the exclusive domain of any one people. He wasn't just somebody, he seemed to be partly everybody, and audiences the world over responded favorably to those traits. Charlie was, as Chaplin liked to think of him, a citizen of the world.

The Barber is cut from the same cloth, but lacks the Tramp's worldliness. The Barber's dress, so similar to that of Charlie's, is merely consistent with the plot device of the Barber's amnesia. When he returns to the barber shop he is without a clue as to the amount of time he has spent in the hospital or the changes that have occurred within Tomanian society and his dress reflects this element of being out-of-touch. Thus, it is entirely plausible for such an old-fashioned character to be placed within the narrative of the film.

Two other factors also keep the Barber distinctly different from the Little Fellow. First, and most obvious, is the fact that the Barber speaks, whereas Charlie was limited to a sole gibberish song in *Modern Times*. By comparison to the other characters, the Barber says relatively little, and speaks only when he needs to. Chaplin here is still relying on his skills as a pantomimist to convey feeling and manner, certainly a throwback to the Tramp, but the mere act of speaking creates a different perception of the Barber in the minds of the audience.

Second, it is not the Barber, the Tramp-like character, who drives the narrative action in *The Great Dictator*, but Hynkel. Consistent with his role as a dictator, Hynkel's actions push the movie forward, while the Barber mainly reacts to events in Tomania. When this happened to the Tramp in earlier films, the Little Fellow often found ways to take control, or at least affect his own destiny, as with attempting to earn money for the Blind Girl in *City Lights* or return to the comforts of jail in *Modern Times*. Here, the Barber appears as a rather quiet, timid character in comparison to Hynkel, and is thrust into his speech-making at the end of the film by pure accident.

Perhaps the distinction between the two characters would be more clear if Chaplin hadn't relied on some element of confusion to attract audiences to the picture. With *The Great Dictator*'s twist of mistaken identity, the similarity between the Barber and the Tramp allowed Chaplin break with his old persona in the sense of characterization, but to capitalize on him in a visual sense. The similar nature of the Tramp and Barber characterizations may have been an effort by Chaplin to maintain his popularity with filmgoers, many of whom by 1940 had never seen a silent picture during the silent era. Chaplin may have created a new character from the old, but he nonetheless counted on the Charlie persona to bring audiences into the theaters for his first foray into sound, and his boldest political statement to date.

V. *THE GREAT DICTATOR* AS PROPAGANDA

As I sat listening to [George Bernard Shaw], my mind was forming judgment. I like him and admire his intellect, but perhaps that's what disconcerts me. Wasn't he quoted as saying that all art should be propaganda? To me, such a premise would restrict art.[33]
— Charles Chaplin —1933

Some people have suggested that I made this picture for propaganda purposes. This is far from the truth. I am not interested in propaganda as such — most propaganda is didactic and dull. I made *The Great Dictator* because I hate dictators and because I want people to laugh.[34]
— Charles Chaplin —1940

The Great Dictator was certainly the most overt political statement of Chaplin's film career, and its timeliness made it one of the most anticipated motion pictures of all time. During the First World War, Chaplin's war-inspired projects *Shoulder Arms* and *The Bond* were distributed very close to the end of hostilities in Europe. Even then, *Shoulder Arms* was considered risky for its treatment of war as a humorous subject. With *The Great Dictator*, Chaplin took a very aggressive and very public stance against Fascism, even before America and many other countries considered such overt statements acceptable.* Despite his hatred of dictators and stated desire only to be humorous, there was little doubt as to what the artist strove to achieve: To show the people of the world, through satire, that Hitler and his Nazi forces were a terrible menace to individual freedom and global peace, and that the Fascist dogma was a direct threat to humankind everywhere. The foundation of the Third Reich, in Chaplin's words, was far too "anti-people" for him to sit by and witness such inhumane policies without commentary.[35]

Before the end of the opening credits for *The Great Dictator*, Chaplin has

---

*Charles Silver noted that at the time of the film's premiere, there had been no less than six anti–Nazi films produced in Hollywood, including Alfred Hitchcock's Foreign Correspondent. (Charles Silver; Charles Chaplin: An Appreciation; page 44.) None of these pictures, however, dared make the type of bold anti–Fascist statement Chaplin made with The Great Dictator.

already begun in this vein. The credits introduce two parallel worlds existing in Tomania, that of the ruling class, introduced as the "People of the Palace," and those who are the victims of their political aims, the "People of the Ghetto." Thus, before the action even begins, the stage is already set for a story that will depict the highest and lowest levels of Tomanian society, a negative contrast that accentuates the abuses that ultimate dictatorial power can bring. By cross-cutting throughout the picture between the Barber, an honest and virtuous man, and Hynkel, the power-hungry dictator, the schism between the two worlds and the values each represent is further emphasized.

For instance, as we are introduced to the Barber on the front lines, he is set to fire the ultimate secret weapon, the cannon "Big Bertha." Its target, the voice-over claims, is the Cathedral of Notre Dame. Undoubtedly Chaplin designed the scene to highlight both the desperation and ruthlessness of the Tomanian political and military hierarchy. What strategic use could the Cathedral serve? The voice-over in the scene does not specify any particular interest that the Tomanian command may have in destroying the monument, leaving only its religious, humanitarian and historical significance to designate it as a worthy target of destruction. (The scene foreshadows Hitler's use of rocket attacks on England, which also served the Third Reich largely as a tactic of psychological terror.) The Barber, whose role is to make the machinery work, exemplifies the sort of common soldier who is thrown on the front lines to carry out the intentions of an elite few.

Later, Hynkel is introduced in the midst of making the sort of speech characteristic of Der Führer. Sounding cold and abrasive, it certainly reminds one of newsreel footage of such events. (Newsreels, in fact, were one of the main resources for Chaplin in mimicking the German leader. He would watch them over and over, studying in detail Hitler's mannerisms and personal traits.) Through the voice-over of an official translator, Hynkel spits and snarls with genuine rage, his tirade extolling the virtues of the Aryan race and making an impassioned plea for more children, because the need for soldiers to serve the Double Cross is growing.

After the most lengthy, ugly and violent oratory of the speech, the voice-over calmly [and without going into details] indicates that Hynkel "has just referred to the Jewish people." Afterwards, Garbitsch and Hynkel converse in the limousine over the effectiveness of the rhetoric. Although noticeably violent to the audience, the speech, Garbitsch claims, was soft on the Jews. It is also through this brief conversation that Chaplin introduces us to the duality of Hynkel's character — publicly strong and foreboding, yet weak and almost incompetent in private. Hynkel utilizes his capacity as dictator to instill terror and animosity on the one hand, while hiding his character flaws from both the people of Tomania and the world on the other.

Vanity is yet another character trait that Chaplin exploits. For instance, images of Hynkel adorn nearly all of Tomania and the Palace, and especially in his own office. On the desk sits a large bust of himself, and the file cabinet behind his desk turns out to be a false front, hiding a double set of full-length mirrors in which Hynkel may gaze at all his greatness. In addition, artisans are located in the room adjacent to his office, ever-ready to sculpt and paint in the few moments that their leader can leap in the room and model. But Hynkel's vanity is no more evident than when Garbitsch maniacally fantasizes about the beauty of an all–Aryan Tomania; the dictator, filled with perverse emotion, begs his advisor to leave the room because he "wants to be alone," à la Garbo.

Chaplin's portrayal of Hynkel clearly points toward the abuse of political power, showing that any fool can play a dictator while only a few possess the goodness of heart and strength of character to become true leaders of the people. Garbitsch, in fact, seems to serve as the unofficial mastermind of the Palace and the administrator of the Tomanian policies. Hynkel appears led about by his advisors — even at times by the inept Herring. Without the slightest clue on how to effectively govern yet all the while firmly believing that he alone is in charge, Hynkel gives orders with quick and pompous arrogance until more focused minds — usually Garbitsch's — restrain him from his impulses. Chaplin keyed in on this observation he made of Hitler's character, telling *Life* columnist Richard Meryman in 1967 that "... the mere fact that Hitler used those broad gestures — he'd press down, press up, cross himself with his fists, very effective — was revealing that this man was not too sure of himself. He must have a stooge at the back who says, 'You're doing okay, boss. Do it again. You slaughtered them today.'"[36] Hynkel walks, talks and acts with authority but is essentially rendered helpless when left to his own devices, a creature of whims rather than one of reason. "The menace of totalitarianism is not at all funny," John Paul Smead noted, "but Hynkel's exaggerated manners and erratic tempers make him a highly comic figure. His power is awesome, but he is not."[37] And it is "the people of the Ghetto" — Jews such as the Barber, Hannah and the Jaeckels — who do not have access to their own political or social power, who become the victims of Hynkel's totalitarian measures.

But unless we extend Chaplin's satire of the German leader as a commentary on Fascism as a whole, he falls flat in aiming ridicule at that system of government. His obvious fascination with Hitler and attempt to expose him as a buffoon so dominates the film that the broader theme is muddled, despite our awareness of his satiric intentions.

Where he is most effective in his criticism of Fascism is in portraying Hynkel's policies towards the people of the Ghetto. The Jews in Chaplin's Tomania are predominantly kind people, most of whom care only to conduct their workaday affairs among themselves, without outside interference. They are people of modest and simple means. Under the iron rule of Tomania there is a strong feeling of community within the Ghetto, linked to their being contained in one common geographical area and being subjects of persecution. Intentionally, it seems, the principal characters in the Ghetto are portrayed

Der Phooey's expansive office, from *The Great Dictator.*

much older than other players in the film. Jaeckel and the Ghetto elders, including the Barber, cannot resist the steady physical bullying of the Storm Troopers, however much like typical Keystone Cops they may be. This frailty lends sympathy to their plight. Hannah, in fact, stands out as one of the few members of the Ghetto's younger generation.

Chaplin frames these Ghetto sequences in an aura of helplessness, depicting an entire stratum of Tomanian society at the mercy of the leadership's social and political whims. After Hynkel gives the Ghetto a temporary reprieve from his intimidation while he negotiates for money from the Jewish financier Epstein, retribution is swift and decisive when the request is flatly turned down. An entire class of people is made to suffer at the hands of their leader, a depiction consistent with Chaplin's view of Fascism as being anti-people.

The theme is picked up again at the close of the film when Jaeckel, Hannah and the others escape from Tomania to the neighboring country of Osterlich. Though they have been forced from their homeland, Chaplin specifically designs their country life as he did with the Dream House sequence in *Modern Times.* Jaeckel and the others live in a sort of idyllic fantasy — the countryside is serene, their table full of food, and the group is able to enjoy their togetherness. But just as the dream ends in *Modern Times,* so too does the peace in Osterlich. Hynkel's army sweeps down on the family. This time, however, they are not the inept Storm Troopers, but bloodthirsty Tomanian soldiers. The family is rounded up, and Hannah is beaten attempting to resist.

These contrasts, however, do not encompass a large part of the film. The people of the Ghetto are certainly the subject of pathos, as Chaplin intended them to be, although he clearly missed (until the concluding speech) the opportunity to make a strong anti–Fascist statement on the behalf of all people. Instead, Chaplin chose to attack the political philosophy by attacking its leader, a move that, while wickedly on the mark, fails to adequately serve the larger concept of denting Fascism.

Napaloni, for instance, is developed purely as a comic foil to highlight Hynkel's imperfections as a political and military leader. This section of the film is quite well done, but Jack Oakie's performance does not dwell on his own imperfections (aside from an enlarged ego) and serves, inadvertently, to boost Napaloni's stock in light of the comedian's focus on Hynkel's ineptness. "Hitler, to me," Chaplin was once quoted as stating, "beneath that stern and foreboding appearance he gives in news reels and news photos, actually is a small, mean and petty neurasthenic. Mussolini suggests an entirely different character — loud, noisy, boastful, a peasant at heart."[38]

It seems clear that Chaplin's intention was to level criticism at Fascism as a whole yet he only successfully demonstrated the arrogance and danger to be associated with ultimate dictatorial power. What is to be learned about the ills of the Fascist system must be inferred from the words and actions of Hynkel, and it isn't until the final speech that Chaplin tries to draw a parallel between the actions of Hynkel and all (including Fascist) dictatorships.

John McCabe's biography of Chaplin provides an interesting footnote to *The Great Dictator* and its propagandistic qualities. As McCabe tells the story,

> ... in the fullness of time Hitler actually saw the film. Chaplin was told this by an agent who fled Germany after working in the film division of the Nazi Ministry of Culture. The man told Chaplin that Nazi agents bought a print of *The Great Dictator* in Portugal during the war and took it to Germany. Predictably, when Goebbels saw it he raged, denounced it, and decreed it must never be shown. Hitler, however, insisted on seeing the film — alone. The next night he saw the film again, and once more alone. That is all the agent could tell Chaplin. Chaplin, in telling this story to friends, added, "I'd give anything to know what he thought of it."[39]

Though Michael Hanisch has noted that the Reich's foreign minister, Joachin von Ribbentrop, applied to Propaganda Minister Goebbels to view the film in August of 1944,[40] it can never be known for sure if Hitler or members of his staff ever did. Such an occurrence is not mentioned in Chaplin's autobiography, despite its penchant for name-dropping and the fact that Chaplin would no doubt have reacted with the type of enthusiasm McCabe's story indicates.

VI. THE SPEECH

Movement is near to nature — as a bird flying — and it is the spoken word
which is embarrassing. The voice is *so* revealing, it becomes an artificial
thing, reducing everybody to a certain glibness, to an unreality. Pantomime
to me is an expression of poetry, comic poetry. I knew that in talking pictures I would lose a lot of eloquence.[41]

— Charles Chaplin — 1967

By far the most controversial and critical aspect of *The Great Dictator*,
both then and now, is the final speech, in which the Barber steps into Hynkel's
shoes and addresses the newly-conquered people of Osterlich, as well as the rest
of the world. Chaplin, quite intentionally and without regard to potential criticism, abandons the character of the Barber in this scene to make a direct appeal
to the audience himself. In doing so, Chaplin not only challenged stylistic
norms in shooting such a scene, but personally took an overt and bold political stance unlike audiences had ever seen before in one of his films.

Chaplin was prepared to make his anti–Fascist views public with the mere
contemplation of the picture. The pressbook for *The Great Dictator* openly
played up the controversial angle of the film to critics and exhibitors; Charlie
Chaplin had returned, not only in his first full-talking feature, but with a plea
for humanity as well.[42] In conceiving *Modern Times*, Chaplin consciously
backed away from exploiting the controversial aspects of his narrative, leaving
the struggle of man in the age of machinery a loose and relatively even-tem-
pered portrayal of what he saw as constituting "modern times." Fascism, however, was a topic too timely and too important for Chaplin to address ambigu-
ously. In an America that seemed rather tentative about becoming involved in
the escalating European conflict, even with the threat that Hitler posed to both
European and American interests, someone had to speak out for the Barbers,
the Jaeckels and the Hannahs of the world. In the concluding moments of *The
Great Dictator*, Chaplin appointed himself as that speaker.

The speech, of course, conceptualized many of Chaplin's concerns regarding Fascism. As put forth in a nutshell by Garbitsch in his speech before the
Barber takes the rostrum, Fascism advocated that human needs were subservient to those of the state, and that it necessitated the subversion of individual
freedoms for ordinary citizens. In terms of thematic discussion and its placement within the narrative, reaction to the Barber's oration has been argued
extensively by critics, from the film's initial release to the present day. Most have
acknowledged its awkward placement at the end, its clear break of character
from the Barber and, even supporters concede, the passage's lack of grace and
stature. Even so, it would become the most controversial passage of dialogue
from all of Charlie Chaplin's films.

Writing in *My Autobiography*, Chaplin reprinted the entire text of the
speech, and proudly boasted that Archie Mayo had it reprinted on his Christ-

mas cards for 1940. That he addressed the speech specifically in his memoirs was not uncommon — his autobiography is filled with passages regarding public statements, events or film dialogue that drew public and private criticism. It is as if, in printing the Barber's impassioned plea for humanity, Chaplin hoped that time would ultimately look favorably upon the content and appropriateness of his words.

I'm sorry, but I don't want to be an emperor. That's not my business. I don't want to rule or conquer anyone. I should like to help everyone — if possible — Jew, gentile — black men — white.

We all want to help one another. Human beings are like that. We want to live by each other's happiness — not by each other's misery. We don't want to hate and despise one another. In this world there is room for everyone. And the good earth is rich and can provide for everyone.

The way of life can be free and beautiful, but we have lost the way. Greed has poisoned men's souls — has barricaded the world with hate — has goose-stepped us into misery and bloodshed. We have developed speed, but we have shut ourselves in. Machinery that gives us abundance has left us in want. Our knowledge has made us cynical; our cleverness, hard and unkind. We think too much and feel too little. More than machinery, we need humanity. More than cleverness, we need kindness and gentleness. Without these qualities, life will be violent and all will be lost.

The airplane and the radio have brought us closer together. The very nature of these things cries out for the goodness in man — cries out for universal brotherhood — for the unity of us all. Even now my voice is reaching millions throughout the world — millions of despairing men, women, and little children — victims of a system that makes men torture and imprison innocent people. To those who can hear me I say: "Do not despair." This misery that has come upon us is but the passing of greed — the bitterness of men who fear the way of human progress. The hate of men will pass, and dictators die, and the power they took from the people will return to the people. And so long as men die, liberty will never perish.

Soldiers! Don't give yourselves to these brutes — who despise you — enslave you — who regiment your lives — tell you what to do— what to think and what to feel! Who drill you — diet you — treat you like cattle and use you as cannon fodder. Don't give yourselves to these unnatural men — machine men with machine minds and machine hearts! You don't hate! Only the unloved hate — the unloved and the unnatural!

Soldiers! Don't fight for slavery! Fight for liberty! In the seventeenth chapter of St. Luke, it is written that the kingdom of God is within man — not one man nor a group of men, but in all men! In you! You, the people, have the power to create machines. The power to create happiness! You, the people, have the power to make this life free and beautiful — to make this life a wonderful adventure. Then — in the name of democracy — let us use that power, let us all unite. Let us fight for a new world — a decent world that will give men a chance to work — that will give youth a future and old age a security.

By the promise of these things, brutes have risen to power. But they lie! They do not fulfill the promise. They never will! Dictators free themselves but they enslave the people. Now let us fight to free the world — to do away with national barriers — to do away with greed, with hate and intolerance. Let us fight

for a world of reason — a world where science and progress will lead to the happiness of all. Soldiers, in the name of democracy, let us unite!
Hannah, can you hear me? Wherever you are, look up! Look up, Hannah! The clouds are lifting! The sun is breaking through! We are coming out of the darkness and into the light! We are coming into a new world — a kindlier world, where men will rise above their greed, their hate and brutality. Look up, Hannah! The soul of man has been given wings and at last he is beginning to fly. He is flying into the rainbow — into the light of hope. Look up, Hannah! Look up![43]

As with any sort of political statement, criticism naturally arose from commentators with differing ideologies, or those fearful of the Ideology such words may be advocating. Further, placement of the speech and its context within the film are not only unorthodox stylistically but completely out of character for the Barber. Chaplin appeared to some reviewers as no better than Hynkel himself, mounting his own soapbox at the picture's conclusion and ranting with naive fervor. Paramount in much of the criticism was the comedian's break in character. The Jewish Barber, who quotes the Bible in his speech, never demonstrated throughout the film the skill or courage to deliver such a message, especially when his words are spoken in the midst of the enemy. Anyone viewing *The Great Dictator* knows this is not the Barber; this is Charles Chaplin. Employing shots of up to two full minutes of screen time without a cut, he purposely keeps the audience focused on his face, and thereby his words, in order to bring home his message for humanity.[44] Originally, Chaplin planned to overlay the speech with a montage-like sequence, some of which was shot (and discarded), in which the people of the world tossed their arms aside to join in the Barber's call for "universal brotherhood."[45] Chaplin dispensed with the idealistic visuals, leaving the scene powerful in its simplicity but giving considerable weight to the dialogue itself.

The speech remains controversial even today for reasons of appropriateness and content. In some respects, Chaplin's efforts have been more easily justifiable since the film's release. Historical hindsight has amplified Chaplin's statements and lent an eerily prophetic tone to the film's conclusion, especially in light of Nazi atrocities. Nonetheless, many film historians have found the speech lacking in both literary and ideological distinction, and its delivery too contrived and unbelievable for the simple Barber to communicate. "[T]he abstractions of language, the poetic failure of the words to add up to the grand concepts they attempt to express, represent a severe stylistic disruption in the film," Gerald Mast observed. "... The concepts are so abstract — Marxism sweetened by American idealistic clichés ..."[46] Walter Kerr concurred, noting "... the speech is dreadful. It is a hoary collection of disorganized platitudes, belligerently delivered. Not only the barber has disappeared. Chaplin the artist has disappeared. The film has disappeared."[47] Roger Manvell, yet another critic of the passage, has added rather perceptively that those who should have been its intended audience, the citizens and soldiers of Fascist Germany and Italy, most certainly would have never been allowed to see the film nor absorb the context of its humanitarian message.[48] Since *The Great Dictator* was originally released in countries generally sympathetic to England, France and America, Chaplin was preaching to the choir.

Others have come to Chaplin's defense, however, and several writers, while certainly not overlooking the film's (nor the speech's) inherent flaws, have been more sympathetic, arguing that Chaplin's naked sincerity may exonerate the thematic and structural weaknesses of the dialogue. David Robinson, for one, noted that the speech has not lost its power despite being, at the time of his writing, nearly half a century old.[49] John McCabe commented that "[t]he last speech, despite its strident clichés, is ultimately moving not only because it is beautifully acted but also because, like any good homily, it makes sense. And more. It is in retrospect a haunting reminder that because there was no little Jewish barber to deflect them [the] Germans set forth to erect Auschwitz, Buchenwald, and Treblinka. It is worth listening quietly for six minutes to remind ourselves of that."[50]* French critic André Bazin felt similarly. "In this interminable, yet (in my view) too short scene I remember only the spell-binding tone of a voice and the most disconcerting of metamorphoses. Charlie's lunar mask disappears little by little.... Underneath ... the face of Charles Spencer Chaplin [appears]. The photographic psychoanalysis of Charlie, as it were, remains certainly one of the great moments in world cinema."[51] Francis Wyndham made another keen observation, writing in his introduction to Chaplin's book *My Life in Pictures*, when he noted that the speech is merely a verbal repetition of themes expressed visually in the balloon globe sequence, which was universally praised, often by the same critics who claim to loathe the speech.[52]

Despite its predominantly maligned status, the speech is perhaps most reflective of Chaplin's idealism and humanist philosophy. Moreover, perhaps no other Hollywood star would or could have attempted such a moment. Only Chaplin, with more than two decades of personal and artistic success world wide behind him, could reach out to the citizens of the world as the Barber attempted to. It may lack distinction, force him to break character, and promote ideals far too simple or idealistic to achieve, but it is delivered passionately and honestly from Chaplin's heart — qualities that may not have played well with the critics of 1940 or later, but which certainly connected with audiences both then and now.

To this end, at least one review captured that sort of spirit. In *The Complete Films of Charlie Chaplin*, authors Gerald McDonald, Michael Conway and Mark Ricci quote the reactions of the Young Reviewers of the National Board of Review in 1940: "... [C]hildren felt the picture was excellent. They

---

Here is an example of the heightened impact that history has brought to the critical discussion of The Great Dictator.

approached it with understanding, and liked best of all Chaplin's final message. One nine-year-old boy described it as 'his speech to be kind to everyone.' Another boy, 13 years old, said, 'I liked the picture because it was down to earth and shows the suffering of the people in Europe, and it shows Charlie Chaplin's true character.'"[53] Though Chaplin had always been concerned with the reactions of critics and intellectuals, he no doubt would have been proud that his work could connect so positively with young people.

VII. RESPONSE TO *THE GREAT DICTATOR*

So, the Jewish minority in the U.S.A. is not disturbed in making game of the leader of a great foreign nation. Some days ago a regulation was laid down that prohibited despising foreign heads of state. When will America stick to these fundamental social conventions in international relations in order to prevent such effronteries as the Jew Charlie Chaplin has up his sleeve?[54]
— From the German magazine *Film-Kurier*, November, 1938, on Chaplin's decision to create a motion picture satire based on Hitler

The Great Dictator may not be the finest picture ever made — in fact, it possesses several disappointing shortcomings. But, despite them, it turns out to be a truly superb accomplishment by a truly great artist — and, from one point of view, perhaps the most significant film ever produced.[55]
— Bosley Crowther

"I'm praying, son, that this picture will have a good message and maybe help mankind a bit," he said to me suddenly one day. But he wouldn't have been my father if he hadn't added a humorous aside, "I'm also praying it will be a big hit, because I've spent a lot of money on it."[56]
— Charles Chaplin, Jr.

American critics had mixed overall feelings about *The Great Dictator*, recognizing its historical significance even if it did not match the quality, perhaps, of Chaplin's earlier films. Depending largely on their own philosophical leanings, many critics felt the film was either too weak or too heavy-handed an indictment of Hitler.[57] But even those who found serious faults acknowledged the sincerity and courage Chaplin had demonstrated in bringing it to the screen. European critics were generally more favorable to the film, including the speech, perhaps because they were more directly influenced by the military advances of the Third Reich. Not surprisingly, German newspapers reported the film to be a complete flop, playing to minuscule audiences. Additionally, the Chaplin Studios, which had received hate mail throughout the film's production, was again inundated by Nazi sympathizers worldwide after the motion picture was released.

Rarely had a motion picture garnered so much anticipation and excitement with the general public as *The Great Dictator*, and news of events from overseas brought an uncanny and timely realism to its debut. With the involvement of Great Britain in the war and, later, the fall of France and the violation of the Nazi-Soviet Nonaggression Pact, the film's arrival seemed to coincide with the American public's awakening to the world threat posed by Nazi Germany. Two public sneak previews in September 1940, confirmed this, allowing Chaplin not only to make some necessary cuts but get a clear indication of the type of public enthusiasm that the film would likely garner.

In light of the seriousness of such an international threat, the topical subject of the film provided a publicity of its own in addition to the extensive campaign devised by Chaplin and United Artists. As a result, the public flocked to view *The Great Dictator* despite the technical and substantive shortcomings expressed by many critics. The very hostilities that made it a popular and financial risk in the beginning were now, ironically, creating sustained interest in the film and the comedian himself. It would become Chaplin's largest grossing film to date, netting over $5 million in box office receipts worldwide and playing to audiences for the duration of the war, sometimes opening in countries shortly after their liberation from Fascist control.

Popular and financial successes were not the only accolades garnered by the film. Chaplin won the award for best actor from the New York Critics Circle, an honor which he turned down; as the writer, director, composer and actor, he was incensed that only part of his contribution to *The Great Dictator* was to be honored. The Academy of Motion Picture Arts and Sciences nominated the film in five Oscar categories: Best Picture; Chaplin for Best Actor; Jack Oakie (as Napaloni) as Best Supporting Actor; Best Original Screenplay; and Best Original Score, an honor Chaplin shared with Meredith Willson. The film had been a truly impressive (and long overdue) debut in talking pictures, but the comedian and his film were shut out at the Oscar ceremonies.

But awards were not Chaplin's ultimate concern. The world over, people were waking up to the belligerence of the Third Reich, and *The Great Dictator* helped become an international focal point for those in resistance to the Axis powers. As a result, especially in the United States, Chaplin soared to new levels of popularity. President Franklin Delano Roosevelt was given an exclusive screening at the White House — his comments afterwards to Chaplin were rather nondescript, that reaction to the film was causing some minor civil unrest in Argentina. Chaplin was, however, invited to read the final speech of the film to a radio audience of over 60 million. The program went over well despite Chaplin's obvious nervousness, which disrupted the presentation midway through.

Perhaps in order to continue publicity for *The Great Dictator*, Chaplin became very open in discussing his new political cause. As a revered celebrity, he was soon one of America's most visible critics of Fascism. Several organizations, sharing similar views, even sought him for speaking engagements, affording him an increasingly public platform on which to promote his film and express his anti–Fascist views.

Such attention to the picture, however, proved to be a double-edged sword in the long run. While the popularity of *The Great Dictator* was in some respects unparalleled in his spectacular career, it would in retrospect firmly link him with a progressive ideology that would eventually fall out of favor in the United States. Further, as Chaplin carried his personal anti–Fascist crusade to public speaking engagements, he began to cultivate antagonism among the more conservative elements in American society, many of whom were concerned that he was making an overt effort to get the United States involved in yet another dangerous war overseas. Chaplin's willingness to air his views certainly boosted the financial prospects for *The Great Dictator*, Chaplin's popularity, and his anti–Fascist cause, but it would have rather unfortunate personal consequences for him in the future.

Monsieur Verdoux

Favorable box-office reaction to *The Great Dictator* brought immense personal satisfaction to Chaplin. The film showed sustained public enthusiasm, making it a financial success and alleviating any remaining doubts he may have had about working with sound technology. The support was particularly gratifying in light of the film's topical and controversial content, not only proving to Chaplin the public's growing distaste for the likes of Hitler and Mussolini, but perhaps validating his own political instincts as well. Chaplin was on top of the world; not even the pestering of government tax authorities could bother him. In February of 1941, a court of law held that Chaplin had actually overpaid the government by nearly $25,000.[1]

The Oscar that had eluded Chaplin for *The Great Dictator* was soon made up for. In June of 1941, Chaplin, together with Rollie Totheroh, began to prepare a reissue print of his silent classic *The Gold Rush*. This would be the first of many official reissues Chaplin would make throughout his career, celebrating a classic age of cinema and introducing the Little Fellow to a new generation of movie-goers. The reissue, however, was not exactly a true silent. Utilizing his composing skills, Chaplin worked with James Fields to add a soundtrack, which the Academy of Motion Picture Arts and Sciences honored as the Best Sound Recording of 1942. In this case, embracing sound technology carried critical as well as financial rewards.

For the reissue version, Chaplin also replaced the title cards with his own spoken narrative which today, at points, seems inadvertently comical due to Chaplin's heavy dramatization.* Some simple sound effects were also added, though they form only a minimal enhancement to the film. The ending was also edited, the most notable of several minor cuts, having the Tramp merely walk off with Georgia Hale, rather than the pair kissing during a photo shoot (and "spoiling the picture," as the double-entendre on the title card originally read). James Agee, then a critic for *The Nation* and nearly always sympathetic

---

*To a privileged few, however, the effect was not unusual. Charles, Jr., recalls that his father enjoyed screening his films for family and friends, and nearly always narrated the pictures for his audience with a similar enthusiasm. (Charles Chaplin, Jr.; My Father Charlie Chaplin; pages 92-93.)

to Chaplin's work, tabbed the reissue as his best picture of 1942 in his year-ending column.[2]

But despite such popular and financial success early in the 1940s, the decade would eventually prove to be quite destructive to Chaplin. His difficulties began shortly after the entry of the United States into World War II. With an Army directive to intern citizens of Japanese ancestry, Chaplin lost virtually all of his trusted household staff to the internment camps.*

Soon, servants weren't the only regular faces missing from the Chaplin mansion. While in New York for two different premieres of *The Great Dictator*, Chaplin made a public reference to "his wife, Paulette," the first outright announcement of their relationship — a disclosure thought by some as an attempt to mend the rift between them. Shooting *The Great Dictator* came at a particularly fragile point in their relationship. The role of Hannah did not offer Paulette nearly as many opportunities to display her talents as had the Gamin in *Modern Times*, although she worked dutifully on the long and arduous shoot. But Chaplin's perfectionist drive took its toll on Paulette — during filming he could often be hardest on those closest to him — and she was reduced to tears on several occasions. At times, her dual role as wife of a famous star and romantic lead in his production was too much. Though they appeared together at the two New York premieres, they travelled there separately, and Paulette departed alone shortly afterward. She left the Chaplin household for good after the debut of the picture, quietly filing for divorce in Mexico on June 4, 1942, following a lengthy estrangement. "It was inevitable that Paulette and I should separate," Chaplin would later rationalize. "We both knew it long before *The Great Dictator* was started, and now that it was completed we were confronted with making a decision. Paulette left word that she was going back to California to work in another picture for Paramount, so I stayed on for a while and played around in New York. Frank, my butler, telephoned that when she returned to the Beverly Hills house she did not stay but packed up her things and left. When I returned home to Beverly Hills she had gone to Mexico to get a divorce. It was a very sad house."[3]†

Unlike with Lita Grey, however, the pair were able to agree on a divorce settlement, and their marriage ended as quietly as it had begun.

Shortly before the divorce decree, Chaplin would take part in an event that he would deem, upon reflection, as the "moment my troubles began." On May 18, 1942, Chaplin agreed to speak to a large gathering in San Francisco on behalf of the Russian War Relief, an organization dedicated to promoting

---

*Alistair Cooke recalled encountering Kono, Chaplin's longtime personal assistant until shortly after the comedian's marriage to Paulette Goddard, at an internment camp in California during the war. (Alistair Cooke; Six Men; page 38.)

†The passage, ironically, is virtually identical to Chaplin's own summation of his marriage to Mildred Harris. Similarly, Paulette's exit, as described by Chaplin, seems eerily similar to the emptiness of the Millionaire's house in City Lights.

American and Russian unity in the face of the common enemy, Nazi Germany. Former United States Ambassador to Russia Joseph Davies, the scheduled speaker, had become ill shortly before the event and bowed out. Chaplin, on the basis of his celebrity status and the success of *The Great Dictator*, was asked to fill in. Though he hadn't had the best results with public speaking on previous occasions (Chaplin's voice breaking while reciting the Barber's final speech to a national radio audience, for example), the ongoing acceptance of the film and the popular accolades he was receiving had perhaps instilled him with the courage necessary to face the large crowd.

At the time, Hitler's army was moving swiftly across the Russian frontier with, some were arguing, only the Russian people to stop him from overrunning all of Asia. If the Soviet Union fell, they contended, Hitler would be increasingly difficult to defeat militarily. Popular sentiment began to emerge by 1942 for America to join the other Allied nations in opening a Second Front in Russia in order to deny the Third Reich a foothold in Eastern Europe and Asia.[4] Several prominent political and military leaders openly called for the establishment of this Second Front. Chaplin, with his intolerance of Fascist political philosophy, sympathized with the plight of the Russian people and eagerly accepted the opportunity to speak on their behalf. The Russians, Chaplin felt, while admittedly strange bedfellows in the Allied cause, were nonetheless working to achieve the same ends as the United States, and deserved both moral and military support.

Despite popular approval for the Second Front concept at the time, not all of America was rallying to the defense of the Russian people. Some Americans, mainly some conservatives, found the prospects of the Germans combating the Russians — enemy versus enemy — to be an unexpected benefit from the conflict in Eastern Europe. "Let them both bleed white," Chaplin would disdainfully recall their propaganda saying, "then we'll come in at the kill."[5] Capitalizing on the suffering of others was a trait of Fascism that Chaplin had rallied against — now, it seemed, a few in the United States wanted to twist humanity for similar ends. While this was certainly a minority attitude, it was one that no doubt strengthened Chaplin's resolve to speak out.

The San Francisco rally, however, was considerably tame in its support for Russia. Recognizing the awkwardness of praising the Soviet Union after years of frigid relations, most of the introductory speakers tactfully avoided taking a strong stance either in support of the Russian people or the Second Front concept. Chaplin responded to such timidity in his speech, overcoming his accustomed nervousness, speaking extemporaneously for nearly 40 minutes and whipping the crowd into a frenzy of excitement. "Stalin wants it, Roosevelt has called for it," Chaplin pitched at the finality of his speech, "so let's all call for it — let's open a Second Front now!" For nearly seven minutes, Chaplin recalled, the house roared with approval.

So direct was his support for the Russian War Relief in San Francisco that invitations to similar gatherings began to deluge him almost immediately. A July 22 speech via telephone to a gathering in Madison Square Garden was eventually published in pamphlet form; Chaplin reprinted portions in *My Autobiography.* "On the battlefields of Russia democracy will live or die," his address began. "The fate of the Allied nations is in the hands of the Communists. If Russia is defeated, the Asiatic continent — the largest and richest of this globe — would be under the domination of the Nazis. With practically the whole Orient in the hands of the Japanese the Nazis would then have access to nearly all the vital war materials of the world. What chance would we have then of defeating Hitler?"[6]

Chaplin continued speaking for almost 15 minutes to the enthusiastic New York crowd, yet within his opening passage can be found the shreds of what would become a widespread antagonism toward his political views during the Cold War era. "I did not wish to be valorous or caught up in a political *cause celebre*," Chaplin would rationalize later. "I had only spoken what I sincerely felt and thought was right."[7]

What Chaplin failed to realize was that his widely publicized comments, from at least six large rallies over a period of ten months, often took on an air of being more pro–Russian than anti–Fascist or anti–Nazi.[8] Public support for a Second Front dwindled during the early months of the War, especially after the Allies became involved in North Africa, but the success of *The Great Dictator* and his Second Front speeches made Chaplin an outspoken proponent of the issue. At a time when the American people (including many notable celebrities) were rallying behind our own troops with morale-building endeavors such as the USO, Chaplin was seen as promoting the cause of the Soviet Union throughout the United States, and he began to receive criticism; *Life*, for instance, ran an article on the Russian War Relief effort in the August 24, 1942, issue unflatteringly titled "Hollywood Goes Russian." Gracing one page is a large photo of Chaplin in the midst of one of his Second Front speeches, a fiery pose that makes him look distinctly similar to the image of Hynkel spouting his twisted Aryan policies.[9] Public opinion was changing, but Chaplin wasn't; he would find that his persistence in conveying "what he felt was right" would ultimately work against him. Over time, he lingered too long in his support of the Soviet Union in the eyes of many, while seeming to ignore the plight of American men fighting abroad. His passionate humanistic philosophy appeared increasingly as a concern only for the Allies' more suspicious member.

I. JOAN BARRY

By late February of 1943, as Chaplin's Second Front activities were winding down, another problem affecting Chaplin's public persona was just beginning.

In early June 1941, while estranged from Paulette, Chaplin confidant Tim Durant introduced him to a young woman named Joan Barry,* then 22, who had come to Hollywood some years earlier with the hopes of becoming an actress. He was immediately taken with her.

At the time, Chaplin was interested in a work entitled *Shadow and Substance* by playwright Paul Vincent Carroll, and had purchased the film rights for $20,000. It was an Irish tale with a strong female role, Brigid, that would need to be filled for the project to move forward. Barry, though not overly attractive, caught Chaplin's eye as not only a possibility for the role, but eventually as a romantic interest as well.

Barry, it seems, had found Hollywood less glamorous than she originally thought after her arrival some years earlier. Like many would-be screen stars, she found the realities of the film industry were far more harsh than she had imagined. Parts were hard to come by and odd jobs rarely provided any sort of long-term stability. Struggling under such conditions, she had been arrested on minor shoplifting charges in 1938.

But what she may not have found in the motion picture industry, Barry did find in the company of several prominent men with whom she began to associate. For a short while she was known to the police as the mistress of a prominent Los Angeles businessman who had put her up in a local apartment. Later she was linked to oilman J. Paul Getty. It was through this connection that she finally got a break into show business, receiving a letter of introduction to Chaplin's friend Durant through A.C. Blumenthal. Durant, in turn, introduced her to Chaplin at one of the comic's weekend tennis parties (the center of social activity at the Chaplin mansion following Paulette's departure).

Chaplin took Barry to his Studios, where he arranged to do some preliminary testing of her acting ability. The tests, he felt, went astonishingly well. By June 23, 1941, Barry was an employee of the Chaplin Studios, signing for the part in *Shadow* for $100 a week. In addition, the studios fronted the bill for acting lessons at Max Reinhardt's school. Meanwhile, Chaplin set out to adapt the play into a film script.

Though Chaplin predictably maintains innocence in his memoirs, claiming Barry as the aggressor, the two were soon more than just employer and employee. However, as the relationship progressed slowly through the summer of 1941 (somewhat hampered by Chaplin's work on the *Shadow* script), Barry began to display an alarmingly different side to her personality. She had become increasingly obsessive in regard to her relationship with the actor, and showed characteristics of psychological instability, which didn't go unnoticed by others. On numerous occasions she arrived at the mansion drunk and highly emotional, demanding to see Chaplin.

Barry's real name was Mary Louise Gribble.

Chaplin, of course, was greatly disturbed by her irrational behavior. Eventually, not only did he wish to distance himself from Barry's amorous advances, but her behavior had become a danger to the studios — many felt that it was only a matter of time before her antics would be reported in the press. Further, she had not been fulfilling her obligations at the Reinhardt school, despite Chaplin's insistence. The contract with the Chaplin Studios, as a result, was canceled on May 22, 1942, by the mutual consent of both parties. The termination agreement allowed her to continue being paid through September of that year as well as receive an additional sum, ostensibly to go toward paying off some of her debts. Accordingly, Chaplin began to see less of Barry through the summer and fall.

But agreement or no agreement, Barry was not easily put off. She would still aggressively pursue him on occasion, leaving Chaplin and his associates very distressed over her behavior. In early October of 1942 Chaplin, in New York to give one of his final Second Front speeches at Carnegie Hall, found that the Waldorf-Astoria where he was staying had been besieged by calls from Barry, for whom Chaplin had purchased train tickets so that she and her mother could visit the city. According to Chaplin, he was tempted to disregard the young woman's messages altogether, but he finally relented to Durant's suggestion that he meet briefly with Barry in an attempt to stop her persistent hounding. The two met in his hotel room for roughly 30 minutes. He then escorted her back to the elevator, and the pair traveled the same way they had come to New York — separately.

But no amount of placating the girl, it seems, could bring a halt to her activities, and by Christmas of 1942 Barry had become literally uncontrollable. Several drunken appearances in the late evening hours were highlighted when she once crashed her car in Chaplin's driveway. Not done yet, on December 23 she broke into the Chaplin mansion at 1:00 A.M., gun in hand, threatening to kill herself in despair. According to Chaplin, who had both his sons staying with him at the time, it took all night to convince the troubled woman to relinquish control of the weapon.*

It had become quite clear by then that Barry was a great liability to the entertainer, and he resolved to inform the police if she created another disturbance, despite the rash of adverse press he might garner in the process. Only a week passed before Chaplin found the opportunity; Miss Barry was back at the mansion again, drunk and emotionally as fragile as ever.

Shortly thereafter, on January 1, 1943, Joan Barry was discovered in her apartment after a botched suicide attempt — an overdose of barbiturates. She recovered, and was given probation for failing to pay her apartment rent for a

---

*Biographer Theodore Huff reported a different scenario in his book, one more consistent with Barry's later assertions, citing that Chaplin "was more amused than frightened, for then and there he wooed and won her again." (Theodore Huff; Charlie Chaplin; page 282.)

number of months previous. Two days following her sentencing, Barry packed her things and left Los Angeles for New York.

For the time being, the Barry predicament seemed to have solved itself. Chaplin was now casting for another young woman to play the role of Brigid in *Shadow and Substance*, and in early 1943 was introduced by agent Minna Wallis to Oona O'Neill, daughter of playwright Eugene O'Neill. Oona was a captivating young woman of 17 whose warmth, humor and maturity quickly won Chaplin over. Her acting experience at that point was limited, but she impressed him with subsequent screen tests. Quickly, however, preparation for *Shadow and Substance* was taking a back seat to the budding romance between the two, despite an age difference of almost 38 years (both she and Charles, Jr., were born in May of 1925) and the fact that a host of Chaplin's confidants feared another Joan Barry-type situation. The plan, according to Chaplin's memoirs, was for them to wed following the filming of *Shadow.*

But while Chaplin's personal and professional life seemed to be heading upward toward the middle of 1943, Joan Barry decided to return to Los Angeles on May 7. She attempted unsuccessfully to see Chaplin, and settled for telephoning the mansion to announce matter-of-factly to one of the household staff that she was several months pregnant. Chaplin wanted nothing to do with her and did not return her call.

Rebuffed, Barry, accompanied by her mother, went into consultation with a pair of Hollywood gossip columnists, Hedda Hopper of the *Los Angeles Times* and Florabel Muir of the *New York Daily News*. Hopper, at the time perhaps the most influential of all the "sob sisters of the press" (Chaplin's characterization), had not exactly been friendly toward Chaplin in her columns. Hopper's conservatism directly clashed with his progressive opinions and, like many conservatives, she had been openly critical of his involvement with the Russian War Relief.* Further, as the traditional press had long been at Chaplin's fingertips, he arrogantly looked down upon her position as a gossip columnist.

---

*Hopper would often refer to Chaplin in her columns as "Little White Feather," a derogatory reference to the World War I practice of giving white feathers to men who refused service because of their pacifist beliefs. Chaplin had come under great scrutiny during World War I because many felt he should have enlisted with his native country of England. His normal influx of fan letters suddenly became more hostile in tone, and were often accompanied by a white feather. Chaplin never did serve, though he was active in raising money for the third Liberty Loan drive, making several public appearances along with Douglas Fairbanks and Mary Pickford — not to mention his completion of the promotional short The Bond in 1918, which was distributed free of charge to exhibitors throughout the United States. Chaplin claimed that he had failed the physical exam for the armed forces and was never allowed to serve. Corroboration of such a physical exam had never been found, and is open to some speculation. Privately, Chaplin confessed to Alistair Cooke that a popular tune of the World War I era, "The Moon Shines Bright On Charlie Chaplin," which concerned his being sent to the battlefields, "scared the hell out of him." Accordingly, he threw his efforts behind the Liberty Bond drive. (Alistair Cooke; Six Men; pages 28-29.) Nonetheless, many citizens (and even soldiers active in the European theater) felt that Chaplin contributed enough to the war effort by continuing to produce his films, many of which were shown to the troops overseas to boost morale.

Hopper was ready to exploit the Barry story against, in her view, the un-American and egotistical comedian.

Following Barry's consultations with Hopper and Muir, her story now directly named Chaplin as the father of her unborn child, and a paternity suit was quickly assembled to assert the same in court. Aware that Chaplin would contact the police should she resume her uninvited visits to the mansion, Barry was (according to the comedian) instructed by the columnists to go there and get herself arrested. Deft at public relations, Hopper and Muir knew how to frame a story to gain widespread interest and to evoke sympathy. Later in the ordeal, after charges had been filed and Barry was the object of numerous press reports, Muir would personally arrange a brief vacation for Barry and her mother when it became apparent that the young woman's problems with alcohol were becoming noticeable. Thus, it is conceivable that the columnists helped plan elements of the Barry story before either had reported it.[10]

Although Chaplin was not aware of any potential setup at the time, he was determined to rid Barry from his premises. The timing of the girl's arrest, coinciding with the filing of legal papers naming Chaplin as the father of Barry's child, caused a flurry of sensational press reports. Chaplin's lawyers issued a short statement of denial which also claimed that Barry had demanded payment of $150,000 when she announced her condition over the phone in May.

Thus, Chaplin's newfound interest in completing *Shadow and Substance* with Oona O'Neill came to an abrupt halt and, in a very untimely decision, the pair quickly made arrangements to be married on June 16, 1943, shortly after Oona's 18th birthday. By that time she was legally free to wed without parental consent, which her famous father would have undoubtedly withheld. The pair traveled secretly to the tiny city of Carpinteria, California, where the justice of the peace allegedly ended the ceremony in just enough time for the couple to escape a horde of journalists who had been tipped off to the event. Their honeymoon, in nearby Santa Barbara, provided six weeks of virtual anonymity.

Harry Crocker, the Tramp's romantic rival in *The Circus* and thereafter a member of Chaplin's studio staff, not only arranged the quiet marriage but also handed the exclusive details to Hollywood gossip columnist Louella Parsons. Parsons, a former scenarist for Essanay during Chaplin's year-long stint there, had been far more sympathetic in her treatment of Chaplin and was one of the few gossip queens whose popularity rivaled Hopper's. No doubt the obvious snub (due purely to "unfortunate circumstances," Hopper was later told) only fueled her anger toward Chaplin.

With the filing of the paternity suit on June 4, 1943, Chaplin's public image, already beginning to sag from his outspoken support of the Russian war effort, quickly plummeted to an all-time low, as ongoing coverage of the paternity trial brought questions about Chaplin's morality, in addition to the lingering concerns about his personal politics, to the front pages of many newspapers.

II. THE COURTS

Despite his continued contact with Barry after her release from the studio contract, Chaplin was convinced of his innocence in the fathering of Barry's child. He was so sure, in fact, that as trial preparations began, his attorney, celebrity lawyer Jerry Geisler, was able to arrange with the opposing counsel an agreement to verify the father through blood testing, even though the odds of exonerating Chaplin were one in 14 due to his and Barry's respective blood types. The results of such testing were inadmissable as evidence in the California judicial system at the time. Nevertheless, Barry's lawyers agreed to drop the suit should the tests prove Chaplin's innocence. But the opportunity to get tested was a costly one. A series of agreed payments from the comedian to Barry for her and her child's support, spread over a number of months before and after the blood tests, would exceed $16,000.[11]

Since testing could not take place until a few months after the birth of the child (a girl, Carol Ann, would be born on October 2, 1943), the paternity trial was postponed until well into 1944. In the meantime, however, the federal government had become involved, and a Grand Jury investigation was launched to explore two specific issues. One alleged that Chaplin (along with Tim Durant and several members of the Beverly Hills Police Department) had conspired to deny Barry her civil rights during her arrests in both January and May of 1943, the other that Chaplin had violated the Mann Act. (Yet another allegation, that Chaplin had arranged for two illegal abortions for Barry, was discarded early in the investigation as being without merit.)

The second charge become the backbone of the government's case against Chaplin. The Mann Act prohibited the transport of women across state lines for the purpose of sexual relations. Enacted decades earlier to combat interstate prostitution, the act, now an archaic piece of the legal code, had remained on the books. Investigators focused on Chaplin's Second Front speech at Carnegie Hall on October 16, 1942, when Barry, traveling with her mother at Chaplin's expense, was known to have visited him in his suite in the Waldorf-Astoria. Chaplin claimed to have grudgingly met with her, but Barry alleged that the two engaged in sexual relations. The circumstantial evidence was more than enough to warrant further investigation.

The Federal Bureau of Investigation was brought in to gather pertinent facts and located a number of individuals helpful to their investigation. Two very willing sources were found in Hedda Hopper and Florabel Muir. Based on the testimony of Barry, Hopper, Muir and several FBI agents, four indictments were handed down against Chaplin on February 10, 1944. One concerned the Mann Act violation and the others pertained to the alleged violation of Barry's civil rights.

Four days following the indictments, Chaplin was fingerprinted and photographed, a supposedly hushed affair that was forever immortalized in a syndicated photograph of the displeased comedian which found itself, among other places, in the February 28, 1944, issue of *Life*. The full-page print won *Life*'s "Picture of the Week" award.[12]

Just two days following Chaplin's arraignment, the outcome of the blood tests were announced. Three doctors, one hired by Chaplin, one by Barry, and one remaining independent, concluded that Chaplin could not have been the father: Carol Ann's blood type, B, could not have been the offspring of Chaplin (type O) and Barry (type A). But the results failed to garner the type of prominent press coverage that the Chaplin indictment had. (Hedda Hopper, whose stinging articles on the case continued throughout Chaplin's troubles, also failed to report the blood test outcome in her column.[13]) From Chaplin's perspective, however, the results, publicized or not, had vindicated him. But it was only a temporary victory, considering he still had the federal charges to contend with.

On March 21, 1944, Chaplin went to trial on the Mann Act violation, with the other civil rights violations to be treated at a later court date. Though there was plenty of evidence to suggest that Chaplin *could* have had sexual relations with Barry on that October night, the case ultimately came down to which of the principal characters the jury chose to believe. And, to further cloud Barry's case, it had to be proved that Chaplin had brought her to New York with the specific intention of having intercourse, to which there was considerably less evidence. Both Barry and Chaplin were called to the stand during the trial — Jerry Geisler considered Chaplin the best witness he'd ever seen in court — and each, of course, came armed with greatly opposing versions of the night in question. In defense, Geisler capitalized on the ludicrous notion that Chaplin would have purposely transported Barry to New York for a single, brief tryst during his visit. "I still don't believe that Chaplin," he wrote later, "who could have had Miss Barry's [sic] favors in Los Angeles for as little as 25 cents car-fare, would pay her fare to New York, plus her expenses as a guest at the Waldorf Towers, so that she could be there for improper purposes for one occasion only."[14]

The argument was convincing, for on April 4 the jury of seven women and five men took but three hours to find Chaplin not guilty. The most serious of the four indictments, it was a clear victory for Chaplin, and it looked as if the burdens of Joan Barry were once and for all lifted from him. With favorable blood test results in the paternity suit, an acquittal on the Mann Act charges, and with the rest of the federal case dropped in early May of 1944, the future was definitely looking brighter for Chaplin and his new and now-pregnant wife Oona. But the Barry entourage had other plans. Though her lawyers had begun preliminary arrangements to drop the paternity suit following the outcome of the blood tests, some ingenious legal maneuvering allowed the case to continue despite the agreement, and without refund of Chaplin's considerable financial outlay.

Barry's original lawyer, John Irwin, refused to carry on with the proceedings, and in his place was put Joseph Scott, a stodgy Republican with high moralistic values and a fervent devotion to prosecuting wrongdoers. At the time, blood testing was considered only corroborative, not conclusive evidence of paternity under California law, and in order to bypass the blood testing agreement and reopen the case, Scott arranged for the guardianship of Carol Ann to be transferred from Barry and her mother to the court system, which in turn could sue Chaplin on the baby's behalf. When Chaplin's counsel for the paternity case, Loyd Wright, filed for dismissal, the case's newly-appointed judge denied the order on the grounds of Carol Ann's new custody status, and ruled that there was sufficient cause for the issues to be fairly resolved through the trial process.

Chaplin described the court ordeal for the Mann Act trial as "like a Kafka story," but he should have perhaps made that characterization for the turmoil of the paternity suit that followed.

When the trial opened on December 13, 1944, Chaplin had rid himself of the services of Jerry Geisler, with whom he was unhappy, relying instead on the more cerebral defense of lawyer Charles Millikan. It seems that Chaplin was persuaded to change counsel on the advice of others who, from a publicity standpoint, felt that the high-profile Geisler gave Chaplin the perceived advantage of "purchasing" the best lawyer available. A lawyer of less notoriety, it was reasoned, would help detract from any bias creeping into the heads of either the jury or the public at large. It was an argument that made sense to Chaplin. During the Mann Act trial he had hired a press agent, Casey Shawhan, to put an appropriate spin on the events as they unfolded. To many journalists, including Hedda Hopper, this expensive luxury seemed to signal that Chaplin had something to hide, and needed an extra measure of damage control.

While Millikan was competent in his defense, his style was no match to the flamboyancy of Joseph Scott. Incensed by the charges against the famed comedian, Scott let loose with tactical verbal barrages that many times made him more of a press spectacle than the trial itself. "Cockney cad" and "Pickadilly pimp" are just a few of Scott's antagonistic references to Chaplin, which continued unabated throughout the proceedings and at one point provoked an outburst from Chaplin in defense of himself. Scott's tactics were shrewd, since they created a lose-lose situation for the comedian. To do nothing was to accept the defamation of character, even though his private life to that time had been relatively discreet by Hollywood standards. To fight them tooth and nail would put Millikan and his client on the defensive, expending a tremendous amount of effort to fight simple allegations rather than the actual charges. Millikan took the more prudent approach, opting to concentrate on the faltering case of the prosecution and convince the jury that whatever impression they may have formed of his client in light of Scott's assaults, it was immaterial considering the facts being presented.

On January 4, 1945, after almost five hours of deliberation, the jury announced that it was deadlocked at seven to five for Chaplin's acquittal. Offers by the judge to arbitrate a verdict were promptly refused by Chaplin, who would accept nothing less than a complete release on all charges. His stubborn sense of justice facilitated the need for a retrial, consequently increasing the amount of negative press in the process.

Beginning on April 7, 1945, Chaplin and Millikan went head to head with Scott again in a court of law, but faced a much more pleasant counselor.[15] J. Paul Getty, whom Barry had visited in Tulsa, Oklahoma, close to the time of Carol Ann's estimated conception, provided testimony, as did some additional men with whom Barry may have had relationships. Again Chaplin's counsel pointed to the flaws in Scott's legal arguments, but on April 17 the defense entered the courtroom to receive an entirely different verdict — guilty. With blood testing results inadmissable, by a vote of eleven to one the jury found that Chaplin was indeed the father of Carol Ann. "I came into this court determined to see that the honor of American womanhood was upheld," said the jury's lone dissenter, Mary H. James, following the case, "... but after what I heard here I couldn't vote for that girl."[16] Chaplin would appeal the verdict early in May, only to have the motion for retrial denied a month later.

Despite the negative outcome, the judgment against Chaplin was extremely lenient in light of Barry's demands. Joseph Scott's request for $50,000 in legal expenses and $1,500 per week in support were flatly denied, offering Chaplin perhaps his only reprieve in the guilty verdict. Instead, a lump payment of $5,000 was made to Barry, with a weekly stipend of $75 (which could be slightly adjusted to Carol Ann's needs) to be made until the girl turned 21. More important than the favorable terms, perhaps, was the consolation that the entire issue had finally been laid to rest. Chaplin could exorcise Barry from his life once and for all.

III. THE AFTERMATH

Few men in or out of the public eye have suffered from greater injustice than Charlie Chaplin. Time and time again during my 16 years with him he was the target for baseless accusations.[17]

— Carlyle Robinson

... the trial of Charlie Chaplin carried with it the heaviest weight of public loathing for a client I've ever had anything to do with ...[18]

— Jerry Geisler

Chaplin was so identified with the Tramp that audience members reacted to the actor as the character. This is a partial explanation of the strong effect revelations about Chaplin's personal life had on his career; some members of the audience were unable to accept Chaplin as the innocent Tramp when they discovered Chaplin himself was not innocent in spirit.[19]

— John Paul Smead

Following the heights that Chaplin had achieved artistically and financially with *The Great Dictator* and the re-release of *The Gold Rush*, the following period saw him fall to the lowest point of his career. Chaplin's work with the Russian war relief effort and the appearance of pro-Soviet sympathies in his Second Front speeches had helped tarnish his public image. The Barry trials contributed to the fall of that image so significantly that it would be nearly three decades before Chaplin would regain the public favor of his adopted homeland.

But however unjust one may deem the repercussions of the Second Front speeches and the various trials, it is also clear in retrospect that a good portion of Chaplin's troubles were aided by his approach to these controversies. He had long been considered the greatest of Hollywood's artists, a man whose celebrity status had secured for him a lifetime of wealth, access to the famous and powerful throughout the world, and a large and seemingly undying flow of public adoration. He had become accustomed to this status, had grown more confident in his convictions, and enjoyed his freedom to do and think as he pleased. All of this was reinforced by the ongoing success of his films and the accolades that were bestowed upon him. He was infected with a classical malady, hubris. "The only one of us [silent film comedians] who listened to and accepted the role of genius intellectual critics thrust upon him was Chaplin," Buster Keaton recalled in his autobiography. "Sometimes I suspect that much of the trouble he's been in started the first time he read that he was a 'sublime satirist' and a first-rate artist. He believed every word of it and tried to live and think accordingly."[20] Additionally, by lifting himself from his impoverished Victorian roots to the heights of stardom, Mary Pickford theorized, Chaplin had gained a powerful sense of idealistic righteousness.[21] These traits, viewed by many as simple vanity and arrogance, clouded his ability to assess how much damage he was accruing as a result of his prolonged troubles.

The Barry case was a prime example. Much of Joseph Scott's oratory was certainly slanted, yet appeared to much of the public as a fitting description of Chaplin's personal life. With all four of his marriages, Chaplin was drawn toward a very young woman which, given his age and celebrity status, helped create a negative perception. Alistair Cooke observed Chaplin's tendency to be totally smitten by someone which, coupled with a degree of idolatry from the other party, must have made his various relationships very intense for the women involved.[22]

With this pattern — young wives and young starlets — it was not surprising that Chaplin's romantic interludes could appear as the typical casting-couch scenario, a point that did not go unnoticed by Scott, who referred to Chaplin at one point as "a little runt of a Svengali." Parker Tyler argued that "Chaplin, more or less deliberately, must certainly have counted on this double-edged aspect of his reputation to act both ways, to help him find the right actresses and the right companions. That some women earned both positions at once seems only plausible."[23] It's a feeling that must have lingered, for Charles, Jr., years later, felt the need to write, "My father's artistic integrity has always been the foremost thing in his life, as those who have worked with him will testify. No girl ever got into any of his pictures by way of a boudoir promise. She had to have real potentialities before he would invest time and money in her."[24] Nonetheless, the perception of Chaplin's nature wasn't excusable with the moralistic American public in the 1940s; Chaplin had never considered that his association with younger women might become an issue, and conducted his personal affairs as he pleased.

Chaplin's stubborn insistence to seek full vindication also worked against him. While he concentrated on the trial, which he ultimately believed would clear his name with the public, he seemed almost oblivious to the tremendous amount of adverse press that he was receiving, despite employing a press agent during the Mann Act trial.

In April of 1944, *Time* reported on the federal charges by noting that the correspondent for the *London Daily Express* was required to file two different accounts of the trial events — one version sympathetic toward Chaplin, for publication in Britain, and one "tough and realistic" for publication in the *Express'* Australian copy.[25] The California daily newspaper *The Hanford Sentinel* announced in its February 21, 1944, editorial that it was launching a drive to purchase the actor a one-way ticket back to England.[26] Two months later, *Newsweek* reported that Chaplin had been recently honored in Moscow with a special screening of *The Gold Rush*, with prominent Russians using the occasion to denounce Chaplin's legal troubles in America and praising, among other things, "the tremendous ideological content" of both *City Lights* and *Modern Times*.[27]

Throughout the Joan Barry affair, sensational developments in the trial grabbed headlines, while events such as the blood testing results and Chaplin's Mann Act acquittal received significantly less attention.[28] (It was perhaps the death of Franklin Delano Roosevelt, which occurred during the course of the second paternity trial, that kept Chaplin's guilty verdict from being reported more prominently.) The host of similar news items was indicative of the growing resentment toward Chaplin as a result of his Second Front activities and legal troubles.

One of many interesting points in Charles Maland's study of the print media during the Barry trial was the role played by Hedda Hopper and Florabel Muir, whose sometimes vicious columns kept Chaplin as a prominent figure. Their work during the Barry trials found them not only soliciting damaging information against Chaplin, but then providing the prosecution with some of this intelligence. This was part of a two-way street of information flowing between the Hollywood gossip press and the FBI (on top of information supplied to the FBI by other governmental agencies, including the Immigration and Naturalization Service and tax authorities). In return for their help, it seems, Hopper and Muir were given access to exclusive developments regarding the FBI investigation and court proceedings.[29] Sometimes, Maland notes, such information was dubious indeed. Hopper once relayed to investigators a telephone conversation she had with a woman who dreamt that Chaplin's jury had been bought off by the comedian. (It was a tip the government chose not to pursue.[30])

But it was Chaplin's demand to be vindicated on all counts that dragged out the trial for nearly two years. Tim Durant had initially urged Chaplin to settle the matter as quietly as possible, recognizing that the story had the potential to get out of hand. This advice the comedian ignored. Later, Chaplin's refusal to arbitrate following the first trial, coupled with his willingness to undergo a third trial following the guilty verdict, certainly indicated that he was not willing to let the issue die until his name was cleared. From a public relations standpoint, he was doing himself in with his obstinate ways; the mounting criticism only seemed to strengthen his resolve to fight on. Eventually these personal traits would play a significant role in the troubles that plagued him in the early 1950s.

Completing the exhausting trial left Chaplin with enough time to fully devote himself towards the many other aspects of his life. Oona had given birth to the couple's first child on August 1, 1944, in the midst of preparation for the first paternity trial; a girl, Geraldine Leigh Chaplin. This was not only Chaplin's first daughter (he had hoped that Sydney would be a girl) but the first child that he had the luxury of being close to. Unlike the period in which his two boys were born, this was a time when Chaplin was in a happy relationship and not pressed to move forward with film after film.

Other events pointed toward a swift recovery. Late in 1944, Dwight Eisenhower personally requested a dubbed version of *The Great Dictator* and a print of *Shoulder Arms* be forwarded to France immediately following its liberation from Nazi hands. Also, soon after the judgment was rendered in the Barry trial, during the summer of 1945, the couple would learn that Oona was expecting a second child. A boy, Michael, was born the following March. But most importantly, Chaplin was able to retreat as much as he could from the scrutiny of the public eye for the first time in nearly four years, giving him time to relax and perhaps begin work on another film project.

IV. *LANDRU*

Chaplin's Second Front speech at Carnegie Hall was not only eventful in that it served as the basis for the Mann Act charges leveled against him, but also in conceiving the idea for his next film.

Among the other speakers that evening was Hollywood's newest Wunderkind, Orson Welles. Chaplin recalls that Welles approached him a short time later, while he was still working on *Shadow and Substance*, with a motion picture proposition for them both. Welles' idea involved a documentary-style film on the celebrated "Bluebeard" Henri Désiré Landru, guillotined in 1922 for committing ten murders-for-profit that had shocked France. Welles, it seems, felt that Chaplin would make the ideal Landru in the adaptation, while he served at the director's helm.

Welles' offer, however, was politely refused. Aside from an occasional cameo appearance in the silent era, Chaplin had not worked under another's direction since his days at Keystone, which likely turned him off to the proposal. As was evidenced by his negative reaction to the New York Film Critics' award for Best Actor in *The Great Dictator*, Chaplin was sensitive about being perceived as only a performer; turning Welles away was consistent with Chaplin's efforts to remain wholly responsible for almost every aspect of his films.

While Welles may not have made any headway with Chaplin, the idea of a Bluebeard script became firmly imbedded in the comedian's mind. Twisting the scenario from a documentary to that of a dark comedy offered tremendous possibilities for Chaplin—perhaps he saw in himself the same qualities that Welles had. Chaplin eventually offered Welles $5,000 for simply suggesting the idea, an offer that was no doubt spurred by a lingering suit over the genesis of *The Great Dictator*, filed by Konrad Bercovici.* Welles accepted on the condition that, should the film be completed, he would have the option of taking screen credit for suggesting the idea.

By late 1942, Chaplin had begun tinkering with his next film project, initially under the title of *Landru*. As with many of his other periods between productions, Chaplin would work intensely on the project, only to toss it aside when his interest waned or yet another opportunity arose. Such was the case when he met Oona in mid–1943. He felt he had finally found his perfect female lead for *Shadow*, and his interest in that project flared once again.

When Oona became the fourth Mrs. Chaplin and opted to be a wife and a mother rather than an actress, Chaplin began to devote himself fully to the completion of the Bluebeard script. Though David Robinson cites the lack of materials in the Chaplin archives documenting the evolution of the *Landru* script, we do know that Chaplin appears to have worked fairly steadily on the project, even in the midst of his legal troubles. By late 1945, *Varnay*, the film's new working title, gave way to *Verdoux*, and the Chaplin Studios once again

---

Bercovici, a one-time confidant to Chaplin, contended that he was partly responsible for the idea of a Hitler parody. The plagiarism suit was eventually settled out of court, very quietly, shortly after the resolution of the Joan Barry affair. Chaplin would be troubled by a number of small suits regarding his film work, including one filed against Modern Times, which contended that the conveyer belt scene was lifted from René Clair's 1931 film A Nous la Liberté. That suit was dismissed in 1939, two-and-a-half years after it was filed. Later, Clair reportedly made the self-serving remark that he was honored to have his film serve as inspiration for the great Charles Chaplin.

geared up for production. By June of 1946, almost a month into principal shooting for the film, the eventual title, *Monsieur Verdoux*, was selected.

The picture, released in early 1947, proved to be the most intriguing and cynical film in Chaplin's repertoire. "I saw a great chance to take a tragedy and satirize it," Chaplin told a journalist prior to the film's debut, "as I did with the fatal Donner expedition in *The Gold Rush* and with Nazi Germany in *The Great Dictator*."[31] It would mark the pinnacle of his transformation towards broader social and political themes, mining a darkly ironic vein of the humanist philosophy he toyed with in *Modern Times* and openly pleaded for in *The Great Dictator*. But instead of taking on the Fascist system of government, Chaplin would cast his critical eye toward traditional capitalism and big business — themes that, in a blossoming Cold War America, would not be received enthusiastically. The victim of increasing antagonism towards Chaplin's moral and political practices, *Monsieur Verdoux* would be as eagerly lynched by the American public as *The Great Dictator* had been embraced.

This was partly due to Chaplin's inability to avoid controversy even after the Barry debacle — helped, no doubt, by the new and different attitude the general press had toward Chaplin. Unlike earlier, when journalists were often quick to praise him or come to his defense (as was the case during the Lita Grey divorce when her legal team turned to character assassination), a more critical view of the man was emerging. Instead of being portrayed as a figure of world importance, Chaplin was now depicted as a symbol of wealth and arrogance, a notion hammered into the minds of many Americans, particularly through the reporting of the Barry trials.

Despite Chaplin's progressing work on the *Verdoux* script, which largely removed him from the public eye, he was still under scrutiny by America's conservative-leaning press. In May of 1946, for instance, Chaplin's reportedly derogatory remarks to several United States Customs officials were widely circulated.[32] On the evening in question, Chaplin had attended a screening of the Soviet film *The Bear* on a Russian ship anchored in Long Beach Harbor. Following the film, guests were shuttled back to shore, where they were promptly met by Customs officials seeking to ensure that no dutiable items came with them from the event. According to press reports, Chaplin openly referred to these officials as the "American Gestapo." Regardless of his degree of seriousness in making the off-hand remark, it seemed quite a contemptuous comment toward the country and the institutions that had served him as a resident alien for nearly 30 years. The incident was a minor one, but it did generate negative publicity and helped reinforce the resentment against what seemed to be Chaplin's ungrateful posture toward the United States.

Ultimately, this negativism would be reflected in the reception of *Monsieur Verdoux*. Whatever heights he had scaled as a film star, particularly in light of the public success of *The Great Dictator*, Chaplin was unprepared for the critical and sometimes openly hostile response that *Monsieur Verdoux* received.

Naively unrecognized by him was the amount of artistic, moral and political disapproval the preceding seven years had generated against him. Post-World War II America was not the same country that Chaplin had become accustomed to. The United States, on the whole, was beginning to undergo a radical change in national philosophy — a change that Chaplin not only failed to recognize but didn't understand as well. Such a large breach between the star and his public would not only be felt at the box office, but would also set in motion events that would again touch his private life as well.

V. THE NARRATIVE OF *MONSIEUR VERDOUX*

Using a technique Billy Wilder would later immortalize in *Sunset Boulevard,* the film opens with a grim shot of a gravestone — Henri Verdoux's, with Chaplin's cheery overdubbed voice introducing himself to the audience and detailing the predicament of his character during the Great Depression, all from beyond the grave.

In light of his untimely dismissal from a job as a bank clerk, his voice calmly explains that he had gone into the Bluebeard profession as a "strictly business" opportunity, and he proceeds to recite his story.

The scene moves to the home of the Couvais family, a group of wine merchants in the north of France. While preparing a meal, the combative bunch discuss their sister Thelma. She recently married a rather mysterious gentleman and had not contacted her family in nearly three months, which was very unlike her. To the door comes the postman, delivering a response from the National Bank of Paris, where the family had inquired as to Thelma's whereabouts. They are informed that she abruptly withdrew her money and left no forwarding address. They talk of Thelma's mysterious suitor and, as comic coincidence would have it, they produce a picture of the mysterious man, Verdoux, for all to see.

In a villa in the south of France, Verdoux is seen clipping roses in the garden. Behind him, an incinerator is burning fiercely. By overhearing two neighbor ladies, we learn that it's the third straight day of burning. Verdoux leaves for the house but, in doing so, is quick to avoid a caterpillar in his path, not wanting to harm one of God's little creatures. Rushing to answer a ring at the front door, he finds the postman looking to deliver a parcel for a Mrs. Varnay, whom Verdoux casually announces is in the bathtub; he offers to bring the slip upstairs for her to sign. While out of sight, he pauses to sign the paper himself, all the while manufacturing a conversation with a person who is obviously not there.

Upon the postman's departure, Verdoux rushes to open the parcel. It is money withdrawn from the National Bank of Paris; he counts the stack with the lightning speed and dexterity that only a former bank clerk could possess.

He is then quick to call his stockbroker, leaving a message where he can be reached.

A temporary maid arrives to start the task of cleaning and packing at the estate. Verdoux's stockbroker calls, and Verdoux promptly spends the sum on a 20 percent margin.

Later, at a police office, the Couvais family conveys their suspicions concerning the fate of Thelma. After they leave, the two officers discuss the allegations. Inspector Morrow (Charles Evans) notes the story's similarity to 12 other disappearances in France over the previous three years.

Back at Verdoux's villa, a local real estate agent shows a Madame Grosnay (Isobel Elsom) about the home. Instantly, Verdoux is captivated — not by her beauty or manner, but by her apparent wealth — and sets about attempting to gain her affection. He operates with great haste; left alone for but a moment, he pledges his undying love for his guest. The pitch is cut short however, with the agent returning to their company and Madame Grosnay appalled by Verdoux's strange romantic overtures.

We shift to a sidewalk café, with Verdoux looking over the various females in his vicinity. He makes contact with one who smiles his way, but finds that she is actually sending her affection toward a gentleman over Verdoux's shoulder, a replay of Charlie's first meeting with Georgia Hale from *The Gold Rush*. Verdoux is joined by a gentleman who knew him earlier as a bank clerk. They exchange pleasantries before Verdoux departs, leaving his former acquaintance to recount for a friend the sad tale of Verdoux losing his job at the bank when poor economic conditions forced a cut in the staff.

When Verdoux arrives at his apartment above a furniture warehouse, his stockbroker telephones to demand another 50,000 francs, the amount needed to make his margin call. Undaunted, Verdoux merely reaches for his black book, selects his next victim, and figures he can arrive just in time to pull his scam before the banks close for the day.

The woman, however, Lydia Floray (Margaret Hoffman), is less than pleased to see her husband. He seems to have left unannounced some three months earlier, with nary a word as to his whereabouts. Verdoux explains that, as an engineer in Indo-China for the past quarter year, his letters may not have reached her yet. He is home, he claims, because the impending financial crisis had halted work on his bridge project. Intrigued, yet not entirely convinced, Lydia inquires as to the nature of the so-called crisis, giving Verdoux the opportunity to persuade her to withdraw all of her savings immediately, an amount of 70,000 francs. With some trepidation, this is done.

The pair later retire to bed, with Verdoux slinking after Lydia and her strongbox like a cat to its prey. The city backdrop in the hall window behind them changes from darkness to light, and Verdoux triumphantly emerges from the bedroom alone, box in hand. Again he counts his prize with great dexterity, and leaves a phone message with his broker, noting that the money has been obtained. He begins to set the table for two and, realizing his folly, removes the extraneous place setting. The broker returns the call to the house and Verdoux promises to wire the cash. He then sits down to a solitary breakfast.

We next see Verdoux approaching a modest home, unlike the villas and apartments we have seen before, where he is met by an enthusiastic young boy. They sneak into the garden, where they are able to surprise the mother who sits alone, confined to a wheelchair. This is Mona (Mady Correll), Verdoux's true wife and the mother of his son Peter.

Verdoux has arrived on the day of their tenth wedding anniversary. As a gift, he brings the deed to their home. It is something, he claims, "they can never take away from us." She laments his hard work and the amount of time he must spend away from his home and family, and Verdoux expresses his wish to continue in the cold and ruthless world of business for only two more years or so, and then be in a position to retire. He looks forward to spending more time with the family, since they are "all that I have on this earth."

Later in the evening, Verdoux scolds Peter, who has taken to tormenting the cat. The boy has some sort of cruel streak, he contends, and lectures him that violence begets violence. The scolding is soon interrupted, however, as their dinner guests, the local pharmacist Maurice Bottello (Robert Lewis) and his wife Martha (Audrey Betz), arrive for supper.

Later, a short train ride away, Verdoux arrives at the home of Annabella Bonheur (Martha Raye), who playfully greets her love and introduces him to her guests to her husband, Louis Bonheur. To Annabella, Verdoux, alias Bonheur, is a cargo ship captain who is in port only briefly while his vessel is being repaired.

After the guests depart, Verdoux is very suspicious of their motives. He becomes infuriated when he finds they have sold Annabella what she thought was a cache of hot diamonds, which turn out only to be glass. To compound their argument, Annabella informs him that she was forced to let go of the maid shortly before he arrived. Verdoux is incensed at her ability to throw away her fortune, won in a lottery, on petty schemes and two-bit crooks. He argues that she should leave her financial matters to a much more responsible party — namely, himself.

Frustrated to the point of bitter anger, he resolves to stay but a short time with Annabella. His mind is swayed, however, when Annabella lets slip that she has transferred the title of her large home to Bonheur's name and in order to prevent the attachment of her bank account by creditors, she has withdrawn all her money and put it in safekeeping. Suddenly, Verdoux's resolve to leave weakens.

After an evening out, Annabella appears to have nodded off to sleep, and Verdoux readies some chloroform at the foot of her bed. Suddenly, the downstairs door opens and the maid returns, claiming to have nowhere else to go. Annabella, awakened, promptly hires the maid back and returns to bed. Verdoux's plan is temporarily foiled.

The scene changes back to Verdoux's apartment, where he rapidly flips through the telephone book attempting to locate Madame Grosnay. Posing as her dressmaker, he telephones and discovers that she will be returning from her daily errands soon, and resolves to "accidentally" run into her. His scheme works, for he later sees the woman outside her Paris flat, where she grudgingly acknowledges their previous meeting. She again spurns his advances and rushes inside the building.

Verdoux enters a nearby flower shop and places a large order for Madame Grosnay, which is to be repeated several times over the coming weeks, even though the cost will be high. "Oh well, these things have to be done," he laments, for flowers are just another business expense for the successful Bluebeard.

We move back to Verdoux's family home, where yet another dinner party with the Bottellos is in progress. Verdoux maneuvers the conversation toward the pharmacist's work with a new and humane form of poison designed for veterinary treatment. The government halted his experiments, Bottello explains, because the poison was virtually undetectable in a dead body. It would give the appearance of a heart attack, which makes it a potentially dangerous weapon if utilized by evil hands. Verdoux is captivated, and fantasizes out loud that they themselves could perform an experiment on a derelict to see if it indeed is mistaken as a heart attack when an autopsy is performed. Verdoux is chided by the group for dreaming up such an awful proposition. Nonetheless, he has secretly copied the chemical formula for the mixture on a piece of paper hidden from the group's view.

Back in his apartment, Verdoux finishes mixing the fatal elixir and, adding it to a bottle of wine, he sets out to find a suitable guinea pig. After a short walk on the streets, he comes across a young prostitute (Marilyn Nash) whom Verdoux invites back to his apartment.

In the process of fixing her a hot meal, he finds that they share much in common. She has been holding a kitten in her jacket, shielding the innocent creature from the cruelties of the outside world, much like Verdoux has been doing for Mona and Peter. Over the meal of scrambled eggs, toast and a glass of poisoned wine, she also reveals that she was recently released from jail, having been interned for larceny. Her husband, it seems, had been left an invalid following an injury received during the First World War, leaving her to fend for the both of them. As she toys with her yet unsipped glass of wine, she recalls the need to steal merely to keep them alive. She has been all alone since he died during her stay in jail.

As the prostitute tells her story, Verdoux is clearly moved by its similarity to his own. He quickly removes the wine from her hand, claiming to see some cork in it, and replaces the glass with a fresh, untainted drink, laughing to himself at his uncharacteristic show of clemency. Once she has finished her meal, Verdoux gives her a sizable amount of money to get her off the streets and sends her on her way, wishing her luck in the future.

Even though Verdoux failed to test the poison on the girl, an opportunity to utilize it presents itself rather soon. Inspector Morrow, one of the policemen to whom the Couvais family had relayed their concerns, arrives at the furniture shop to ask Verdoux a few questions. Verdoux courteously offers him a glass of wine. Morrow refuses, though Verdoux does pour a glass for himself — perhaps to throw off suspicion, perhaps anticipating the end of his own business endeavors.

He has been tailing Verdoux for some time, the Inspector says, and relates his theory about Verdoux and his wife-killing, though revealing that his suspicions have not yet been made known to police headquarters. Although no bodies have been located, Morrow is confident that the police can hold Verdoux on charges of bigamy long enough to produce the gruesome evidence. Verdoux has no way out, and Morrow is confident that he has finally cornered his man. He is so confident, in fact, that he pours himself a glass of wine in quiet celebration. Verdoux, whose glass had once neared his lips, now rejects his drink, as it is no longer of use to him. To buy some time for the poison to work, Verdoux agrees to confess in full, but only if Inspector Morrow will allow him the privilege of seeing his wife and child one last time. Morrow agrees, and the pair embark for a train ride to Verdoux's real home.

After leaving Morrow peacefully "asleep" on the train, Verdoux is seen at a roadside café gleefully reading an article on the Inspector's strange death, which the coroner ruled a heart attack. With the experiment completed, he immediately sets off for Annabella's, determined to duplicate the formula's success.

At Annabella's, Verdoux casually requests that the maid be let go for the day so the couple can spend the evening alone together. Annabella hastily arranges this while Verdoux sneaks off with a bottle of wine to the bathroom, where he plans to administer the poison from the peroxide bottle in which it is contained. But he must return downstairs for a corkscrew, and during his absence the maid, using her free time to bleach her hair, borrows the peroxide, only to accidentally break the bottle by dropping it on the floor. To cover her mishap, she replaces Verdoux's bottle with an actual bottle of peroxide, which he proceeds to mix with the wine. Accordingly, the seemingly indestructible Annabella shows no effects from the mixture after consuming almost the whole bottle herself, much to Verdoux's visible dismay.

Later, both Annabella and Verdoux retreat to the country for some needed relaxation. The two embark on an excursion in a rowboat where, Verdoux hopes, he can toss a rope around her neck attached to a rock (an obvious throwback to the Millionaire in *City Lights*). While Annabella is occupied in a futile attempt at fishing, his intentions are continuously foiled by her antics, and Verdoux even inadvertently chloroforms himself when the boat rocks violently. Just as it looks as though he may finally be able to accomplish his devious goal, a group of yodelers appear at the water's edge, spoiling Verdoux's chances of

Verdoux with the indestructible Annabella Bonheur (Martha Raye), from *Monsieur Verdoux.*

an undetected crime. Adding insult to injury, Annabella finally sways the boat enough to send Verdoux tumbling overboard.

Verdoux returns to Paris and checks up on his progress with Madame Grosnay, who has been receiving flowers at a regular clip. She has left a kind message for him with the florist, and Verdoux jumps at the opportunity to visit her at her flat, though he mistakes both the maid and one of Madame Grosnay's visitors as the object of his advances, since he cannot remember what the real Madame Grosnay looks like.

The romance takes off, and the narrative leaps forward to their wedding day, a large, elaborate ceremony, despite Madame Grosnay's (and obviously, Verdoux's) wish for a private ceremony. While Verdoux is paraded before the multitude of guests, he overhears the familiar laughter of an obnoxious woman — Annabella Bonheur, a guest at the ceremony. Verdoux quickly feigns illness in an attempt to plan his next move, though he can think of nothing but fleeing. Verdoux is last seen at the ceremony vaulting the fence, à la Douglas Fairbanks, rather than be revealed as a bigamist.

Later, back at the police office, the Couvais family is now joined by Madame Grosnay in piecing together the Bluebeard mystery, with the police beginning to close in on the identity of the deadly Romeo.

The film moves into a montage of historical events, as the bottom falls from the stock market and chaos erupts worldwide. Banks are overrun, stockbrokers are committing suicide and dictatorial regimes rise in Europe. Verdoux is seen frantically attempting to reach his own stockbroker during the crisis, only to find out that all of his holdings have been wiped out. His face is filled with terror — knowing, perhaps, that he will be unable to rebuild his financial stability. The cruel world has beaten him again, this time permanently.

When we return to him again at the familiar roadside café, it is a distinctly different Verdoux than we have seen before. He is clad in uncharacteristically dark clothing, as though he is in mourning, and his slow shuffle — much like Charlie at the end of *City Lights*— indicates a tired and defeated soul.

He is beckoned to a passing limousine by a woman who, as it turns out, is the prostitute Verdoux had helped some years before. She is now the wealthy mistress of a munitions manufacturer, a business that Verdoux cynically notes should soon be very profitable. As the roles of fortune are now reversed, the girl shows her kindness to Verdoux by inviting him to dine with her, returning the compliment from years before. Verdoux gladly accepts.

The pair talk of their experiences since their first meeting over dinner. The girl has done quite well for herself, but is concerned for Verdoux who, she remarks, seems to have lost his zest for life. Verdoux agrees, and reveals that since the loss of his wife and child shortly after the economic collapse, he has not had much to live for. Although he knows they are much happier away from the cruelties of the world, Verdoux has given up the fight himself.

The pair continue their conversation when, at the opposite end of the cabaret, Jean and Lena Couvais enter. Verdoux is quickly recognized by the pair, and they scramble to contact police and have him arrested. Verdoux takes notice of the commotion; feeling he can no longer run from his past, and without the will to do so, he bids the girl goodbye and stays at the cabaret awaiting his apprehension.

Through a flurry of passing newspaper headlines, we learn that Verdoux has been tried and found guilty of his offenses, and is expected to be guillotined. But before the sentence is handed down, Verdoux is allowed a brief moment to address the court. With this opportunity, he chastises the hypocrisy of condemning his individual actions while society condones warfare and the continued production of weaponry for mass killing. War-mongering political leaders and big business are as cold-blooded as any of his own crimes, Verdoux contends, and by sentencing him to death they are, in actuality, sentencing all of society to the same fate. "I shall see you all ... very soon," comes Verdoux's parting shot.

Moments before execution, Verdoux is visited in his cell by various reporters, all seeking some final words. Verdoux remains philosophical to the end, maintaining that in a world of organized and acceptable forms of killing, his actions were unfairly singled out. "One murder makes a villain; millions a hero. Numbers sanctify, my friend. As a mass killer, I am an amateur by comparison." Verdoux is no less remorseful to the priest who enters the cell to ask him to make peace with the Lord before leaving the earth. "My conflict is not with God," comes Verdoux's reply, "it is with man."

As one last bit of earthly pleasure, Verdoux is allowed to drink some rum before he is escorted to his death, a drink he has never tasted before. In shackles, he is then led by the guards from his cell to the courtyard, where the film ends with Verdoux shuffling slowly into the distance toward his death.

VI. CASTING AND PRODUCTION

It is interesting to note that Chaplin's work in casting *Verdoux* followed a much different path from what was typical for him. With *City Lights, Modern Times* and *The Great Dictator*, Chaplin relied primarily on his trusted staff and associates, though certainly *Dictator* drew upon character actors for its many supporting roles, not to mention a host of new faces on the crew as required by union regulations at the time. For *Verdoux*, Chaplin seems to have charted two alternate courses with respect to his casting choices, one that capitalized on older (but not always the usual) collaborators, and one that brought fresh, new character actors into the studio.

Tops on the list of newcomers was Martha Raye as Annabella Bonheur. Raye, who had made a name for herself with her outlandish personality and performances while touring with the USO, was the ideal match to play Verdoux's indestructible wife. She once likened the request from Chaplin to act in the film to getting a phone call from God, and considered the opportunity one of the highlights of her life, a role that she would have done for nothing.[33]

The comedian wrote Annabella as an unusually domineering female role, and Raye amply filled the part — both onscreen and off. Slightly intimidated by working for the likes of Chaplin, she took to nervously calling her boss "Chuck," to which the comedian humorously responded by calling her "Maggie" (she was born Margaret Reed). The pair became quite friendly, and Raye eventually even had the nerve to begin to call lunch on behalf of the entire cast and crew, to which Chaplin, remarkably enough, consented. This playful chemistry between Raye and Chaplin shows onscreen; theirs are by far the best performances in the film.

But while Raye scored a direct hit with her part, one newcomer that is almost universally reviled is that of Marilyn Nash as the prostitute/munitions mistress. Her performance in this very limited role is rather drab, and is certainly not one of Chaplin's better casting selections. Nash's detractors probably would have given the actress scant attention if Chaplin had not prominently trumpeted her as his new find; a spread in *Life* proclaimed the comedian's newest protégée and featured her rehearsing with the comedian in a three-quarter page picture.[34] Her actual screen time is quite limited for such a budding "starlet," and how much Chaplin's sagging reputation helped derail Nash's chances for an acting career can be argued. At any rate, in *Monsieur Verdoux* she did not demonstrate the promise that Chaplin vigorously touted.

For older collaborators, Chaplin reached back to his early days in the entertainment business. In the role of Madame Grosnay, Chaplin cast veteran actress Isobel Elsom, a chorus girl on the English vaudeville circuit during the time when he was touring with Karno. It is not the only instance where the Karno name surfaces, either. Among the guests at Verdoux's wedding to Madame Grosnay is a "Monsieur Karno," a cameo for Fred Karno, Jr., the son of Chaplin's former employer.

Some of Chaplin's original casting ideas are also interesting to note. Henry Bergman, the loyal Chaplin staffer since 1916, was to have a cameo as the judge in the courtroom sequence. However, Bergman passed away in mid-1946 after a lengthy illness, and his role was not replaced in the film's final cut. A successful restaurateur in Hollywood during his later years, Bergman more or less maintained a symbolic place on the comedian's staff during the sound era, a sort of talisman and reminder of Chaplin's early successes.

Interestingly, Martha Raye, though so appropriate for the role of Annabella, was not Chaplin's original casting choice. Chaplin assistant Jerry Epstein recalled that the comedian originally offered the role to comedienne Fanny Brice[35]; David Robinson's research does not corroborate this, though he notes that Brice originally figured into an early draft of *The Great Dictator*, declining a rather risqué role as Hynkel's sex-starved (and Jewish) wife.[36]

Also under consideration was Chaplin's brother Sydney for the role of Inspector Morrow. Syd, however, had no desire to return to film. He had appeared in many of the Tramp's comedies through the early 1920s, and had established a modest film career of his own. After rejoining his brother's staff for *The Great Dictator*, Syd's second wife Gypsy apparently felt uncomfortable about even a cameo appearance by her husband (Syd still tended to worry a great deal about Charlie's productions at hand), and he deferred to her wishes. This is unfortunate, for *Monsieur Verdoux* could have had the macabre plot twist of Chaplin, in character, poisoning his own brother, also in character.

But by far the most significant consideration from the perspective of Chaplin's old collaborators was the possible return of Edna Purviance, Chaplin's perennial leading lady from 1915 through 1923, to play the role of Madame Grosnay.

Though Edna's film career had come to an end shortly after *A Woman of Paris*, the opportunity to work opposite Chaplin again was tempting. Of late she had fallen on hard times financially, and had grappled with a succession of health problems. Edna arrived at the Studios on March 18, 1946, having no set foot on the grounds nor seen Chaplin in over 20 years, and the reunion was quite emotional for both. She would spend roughly four weeks on the lot testing and rehearsing for the role of Madame Grosnay, until it became apparent to Chaplin that she would not be the ideal actress. It pained him greatly, but Chaplin was forced to let Edna go, though the parting was cordial and Edna seemed grateful for the opportunity. It would be their last face-to-face meeting before her death in 1958.

On the whole, however, the comedian's eventual choices for many roles never seem to work effectively onscreen. Compared to Chaplin's obvious excitement with scripting the parts of Verdoux, Annabella and, to a lesser extent, Madame Grosnay, the remainder of the roles are written and performed with little color. When *Monsieur Verdoux* was revived in New York during the early 1960s, Dwight MacDonald, in assailing the film, was particularly critical of its characters beyond Verdoux and Annabella (he thought Raye brilliant), as the rest of the cast were "not even good as extras."[37] MacDonald's attack on the film was indeed harsh, but his assertion that the cast was a letdown is a valid point.

By the time Chaplin decided to undertake *Monsieur Verdoux*, he had come to accept the production code changes that caused him so much trouble on *The Great Dictator*. As with his stubborn resistance to sound technology, he ultimately reconciled himself with the changing industry, but as he would also do with sound, he was apt to rhapsodize about how efficient and pure the early days of movie-making were.

On April 7, 1946, during pre-production for *Verdoux*, longtime studio manager Alf Reeves passed away at the age of 70. Reeves had known Chaplin longer than any other member of the studio staff (he had selected Chaplin to tour America while serving as the organizer of Fred Karno's troupes in the United States in 1910). During his stint at the Chaplin Studios, he had become one of the integral members of the business staff, and apparently one of the few employees who could freely speak his mind to the comedian.

Chaplin, realizing that Reeves was in failing health, had already taken steps to locate a replacement; John McFadden was hired by the studio the day following Reeves' death. But virtually from the start, McFadden could not endear himself to the rest of the studio staff, most notably cameraman Rollie Totheroh, who had some very unflattering recollections of him.[38*] McFadden was determined to move the comedian and the studios into a new age, establishing an audience wholly distinct from the ones who had enjoyed the silent comedies that brought Chaplin his fame. Many at the studio were critical of McFadden's

---

*Totheroh's importance to the Chaplin Studios, however, was slowly declining during the sound era, which may account for some of his antagonism toward McFadden. Totheroh, Chaplin's principal cameraman since his days at Mutual, may have been viewed as outliving his usefulness; the employment of Karl Struss to shoot The Great Dictator and Limelight supports this. Totheroh likely felt threatened by the younger generation of cameramen and studio managers on whom Chaplin was growing more reliant.

methods which included, according to Totheroh, the destruction of many of Chaplin's vintage film outtakes. Chaplin was even forced to call the staff together on at least one occasion to make peace during the production.[39]

Ultimately McFadden would remain at the studio for only the production of *Verdoux*. Though his brief stint was marked by bad feelings, he nonetheless introduced a new wrinkle to Chaplin's filmmaking repertoire — strict adherence to a production schedule. Whereas Alf Reeves had learned to take a hands-off approach to Chaplin's creativity, a method which led to obscenely lengthy productions on *City Lights* and *The Great Dictator*, McFadden plotted the production of *Monsieur Verdoux* with pinpoint accuracy. With a total shooting time of 80 days, *Verdoux* was shot in one-half the time it took for *The Great Dictator*.[40] Though the script for the picture placed a good deal more reliance on verbal wittiness, with perhaps fewer opportunities for the comedian to experiment or improvise on the set, the swift production was nonetheless an overdue and beneficial product of McFadden's tenure.

Additionally, McFadden helped keep the studio financially stable by renting space to other productions, an economic necessity considering the mounting costs associated with keeping a studio up and running during the 1940s. Though Chaplin was slowly becoming more economical and practical on his own, McFadden can be credited for helping bring about a number of changes that made the comedian's filmmaking and studio management much more efficient.

Other staffing problems seemed to surface during the production as well. Chaplin had chosen to employ one assistant director, Rex Bailey, as well as two associate directors, the comedian's half-brother Wheeler Dryden and Robert Florey. Florey, himself an accomplished director (1932's *Murders in the Rue Morgue*, among many others), leapt at the opportunity to work with Chaplin, about whom he had authored a short work in 1927. As Chaplin had done with his other French-locale production *A Woman of Paris*, several additional assistants were employed to help provide background continuity and authenticity.

However, Florey's own background left him unprepared to accept the subordinate role of a Chaplin assistant, whom, we have seen, the comedian used as sounding boards rather than as integral collaborators. Jack Spears, in the unflattering article "Chaplin's Collaborators," noted Chaplin's vindictive and jealous attitudes toward Florey, even asserting that he purposely billed Dryden ahead of Florey in the final credits in a malicious attempt to spite him.[41*]

---

*It should be noted that Spears was an admirer of Florey's screen work, and contributed an article to the April, 1960, issue of Films in Review specifically praising elements of his long career. Though "Chaplin's Collaborators" covers the whole of the comedian's career to that date, Spears devotes ample space to Florey's situation on Verdoux as exemplifying Chaplin's extreme arrogance and inability to deal with criticism. Monsieur Verdoux is not a perfect film, but it is ludicrous to assert — as Spears wants to — that accepting more of Florey's advice could somehow have transformed what the author otherwise saw as a flawed production.

Spears argues that throughout his career, Chaplin summarily dismissed the advice of his assistants, which many times proved a detriment to the quality of his work. This, in his opinion, was particularly true during his sound era productions. "... [I]n the non-tramp comedies and so-called dramas —*Monsieur Verdoux* and *Limelight*— Chaplin was in over his head. Sound advice and guidance, at least in the technical aspects of those pictures, could have minimized the errors and forestalled some of the loss of Chaplin's prestige."[42]

The gist of Spears' criticism makes a valid point. William K. Everson, for instance, noted the rather ineffective use of French settings, despite Chaplin's employ of technical advisors.[43] Foster Hirsch concurred:

> Visually as well as vocally, then, the film is largely unsatisfactory, self-defeating. The insertions of the Eiffel Tower to let us know we're in Paris; the banal reliance of train wheels to signal Verdoux's restless movement; the documentary insertions of Hitler and Mussolini and the stock market crash, which introduce a sense of the real world, and of historical specificity, not supported by the rest of the film — all indicate Chaplin's awesome lack of interest in the small, tedious necessities of filmmaking, in any facet of the film other than Verdoux himself.[44]

Though the film is not as disastrous as Spears or perhaps Hirsch would assert, their remarks are well taken in the respect that Chaplin's main concern — as had been the case since his early days at Keystone — was the film's central character. Visual realism, from supporting characters to the film's backdrops (Rollie Totheroh characterized the bulk of them as "the lousiest sets I ever saw"[45]), often took a back seat to Chaplin's focus on character, plot and — in this case — social message.

VII. CHAPLIN'S DARKER SIDE

Behind the gaiety and romance of Chaplin's personality — and by no means distracting from the glamour of his company — there lies a strong awareness of violence and horror. Certain subjects both repel and fascinate him.[46]
— Francis Wyndham

... *Monsieur Verdoux* was more of a mission with my father. I feel that this picture served to objectify for him all the mingled fascination and horror he had felt throughout his life toward violence and the macabre ... [and] especially for the destructive grief my father felt in the presence of the dark undercurrents of the human psyche. It was as though he hoped, with burlesque, to lighten the grimness inherent in life and to project it outside himself.[47]
— Charles Chaplin, Jr.

Chaplin's fascination with the darker elements of human nature had never come to the forefront of one of his films as it did in *Monsieur Verdoux*. Previously, the slapstick foundation of his work had helped soften some of the grimness, particularly when dealing with issues of starvation (*The Gold Rush, Modern Times*), homelessness (also *Modern Times*) and the abuses of dictatorial power (*The Great Dictator*). *Monsieur Verdoux* does seem, however, to fit a pattern of Chaplin's interest in the macabre.

In his memoirs, Chaplin recalled an event from his childhood, imparted to H.G. Wells, that shows early indications of a *Monsieur Verdoux*-type story. The young Chaplin was thirsty one day and stopped at the Crown Public House on London Bridge Road to get some water. The boy's thirst was quickly forgotten, however, when he became mysteriously spooked by the gentleman who served him the drink. He darted from the establishment at the first opportunity, while the man's back was turned. Some two weeks later, that same bartender, George Chapman, was arrested for poisoning five of his wives with strychnine. With dramatic flair, Chaplin added that the final victim was languishing in the very building where the young boy received the glass of water from the killer.[48]

Factual or not, the story is one of many indicators of Chaplin's interest in criminal or macabre elements. Sculptor Claire Sheridan related a story of finishing a bust of Chaplin, and upon viewing it for the first time, he wondered aloud, "It might be the head of a criminal, mightn't it —?" He then explained his reaction by noting the similarities between the mind of a criminal and that of an artist.[49] Even *The Gold Rush*, perhaps the most beloved of all Chaplin's films, stemmed in part from his grim fascination with the Donner Party incident, manifesting itself in the cabin scenes between Chaplin and Mack Swain in which Charlie magically transforms into an edible chicken before Swain's eyes. More recently, *Modern Times* owed its inspiration to the starvation and hardship of the Depression years. Even aside from filmic references, Michael Chaplin recalled his father's enjoyment in telling "Nice Old Man" bedtime stories, the sort of yarns where the elderly babysitter employs various creative methods of in the "disposal" of naughty children.[50]

Perhaps because of his perceived similarities between the artist and the criminal, Chaplin seems to have held a compassionate view regarding some crimes, as in the way he depicted the workers who broke into the department store in *Modern Times*. Like Verdoux, they were not motivated by material gain but by mere subsistence, driven to crime not by evil intention but by necessity. But *Monsieur Verdoux* is not as overtly comic as *Modern Times*; moreover, such a sympathetic view was out of step with the dominant values of the day. At a time when America would tolerate it least, Chaplin produced a film that appeared critical of accepted social norms. To Henri Verdoux (and Chaplin as well), society was morally corrupt; the majority of society, on the other hand, could only see Verdoux as corrupt.

Part of the picture's ultimate failure was the presentation of such themes throughout the film. With *The Great Dictator*, Chaplin utilized virtually every scene as an overt denouncement of Hitler and, though less straightforwardly, of Fascism. By the time the Barber rises to make his speech in the finale, the viewer has been inundated with verbal and visual evidence of Hynkel's brutality. We can anticipate, then, the gist of the Barber's words even before he speaks them.

Chaplin strives unsuccessfully for something similar at the end of *Monsieur Verdoux*. Consistent with Verdoux's parting comments in the courtroom, Chaplin did have a specific though grim theme to present in his picture. "Von Clausewitz said that war is the logical extension of diplomacy," Chaplin said prior to the film's release. "Monsieur Verdoux feels that murder is the logical extension of business."[51] Yet until Verdoux's concluding speech, the motion picture deals only indirectly at best with this topic. Though he is thrown out of work by a pair of economic crises, Verdoux's tirade against war, mass killings and the ruthlessness of big business had not been reinforced throughout the film, and his words thus fail to have the same impact on an audience as did the Barber's speech in *Dictator*. The Barber's moment on the podium seemed an honest, humanistic reaction to the social and political chaos around him; Verdoux's moment doesn't connect on this level, and both the director and the character appear to be straining to explain his actions. Again, Chaplin approached the end of his film with a loaded gun, ready to fire his social message at the audience. But unlike *The Great Dictator*, where Chaplin's concluding speech seemed to connect with general audiences, the same was not true for *Monsieur Verdoux*. Many saw the picture as a thinly-veiled criticism of American society, which was not only ill-timed but (given Chaplin's recent troubles) self-serving as well.

VIII. CHAPLIN AS THE REAL HENRI VERDOUX

I am not a hero worshipper of criminals and bad men. Society must be protected ... [b]ut we can at least treat them intelligently, for, after all, crime is the outcome of society.[52]

— Charles Chaplin — 1921

The present Chaplin make-up was assembled by degrees, but it hasn't been changed much for a year or two because the public resents any change. My friends won't have me in any sort of character but the one in which they first adopted me. Once I appeared in my own person — a dress-suit and all that. There was such a frost that I shall never forget it.[53]

— Charles Chaplin — 1918

I left the screen because I didn't want what happened to Chaplin to happen to me. When he discarded the little tramp, the little tramp turned around and killed him.[54] *

— Mary Pickford — 1965

---

*Pickford's statement here is somewhat inaccurate, since she last appeared on the screen in 1933, before the Tramp had been fully abandoned as a Chaplin character. Also, (continued on next page)

Following the public vilification that haunted Chaplin after the Second Front and Joan Barry proceedings, the general narrative of *Monsieur Verdoux* held many potential pitfalls for him and his public image.

Foremost, casting himself in a Bluebeard role immediately after the Joan Barry trial was not the best move Chaplin could have made.[55] Though it's likely that the plot had been conceived (at least in a primitive form) before the Barry affair hit the press, it seems extremely odd that Chaplin would continue to move forward with the project when he was being portrayed as a "lady killer" throughout the trial coverage. Chaplin should have foreseen the association that *Verdoux* would have to his own private life; especially in his next two projects, he specifically encouraged an autobiographical reading of each narrative. But perhaps he was not fully aware of the public's identification of Chaplin with the screen characters he played, a popular image ingrained through the exploits of the Tramp.

In at least one sequence, he seems to use his own troubles as inspiration, as he had done previously in *Modern Times*. During Verdoux's planned experiment of the poisoned wine on the prostitute, the pair engage in a probing conversation on the nature of love. Verdoux's attitude is quite cynical about the female species, a trait that the girl immediately notes. "How little you know about women," she comments. A knowing, ironic sparkle comes across Verdoux's face as he responds: "You'd be surprised." The reply, clearly double-edged in nature, carries over from the film to Chaplin's own private life, and reveals a type of romantic distrust that Chaplin had never before displayed in his filmography.

But the comedian must have felt the volatility of the film's content was of little concern. Chaplin had already been through the messy divorce proceedings of the Lita Grey marriage, with similar kinds of moral charges having little to no effect on his celebrity status or public reaction to his next film, *The Circus*. In all likelihood Chaplin was confident that history would repeat itself, and that a quality motion picture, as he believed *Monsieur Verdoux* to be, could wipe away any bitter feelings held by the public, even when the situation surrounding its lead character had a vague resemblance to his own experiences.

In addition to the personal aspects of the *Verdoux* narrative, the political aspects of the film also remained controversial. His work had become increasingly topical following his world tour of 1931, and the ideas he was expressing were beginning to fall from favor in an increasingly intolerant American society, particularly after his "pro–Russian" Second Front speeches and the "American

---

(continued) *though the pair were still business partners in United Artists, relations between the two had become frosty over the years. Chaplin was almost always a vocal minority in the affairs of United Artists, proving a consistent thorn in the side of the more business-astute Pickford. Regardless of her feelingsabout Chaplin, however, Pickford did attend the premiere of* Monsieur Verdoux *as his guest, which is perhaps an indication of how much the financially-troubled United Artists was banking on the film to be a hit.*

Gestapo" comment garnered widespread (and negative) press coverage. His humanist philosophy, idealistic and rather comforting in the Depression era, now appeared rather threatening in the budding Cold War era. As a political statement, *Monsieur Verdoux* is considerably less bold than *The Great Dictator*. However, *Dictator* was far more in touch with the changing American consciousness, whereas *Verdoux* openly challenged the same.

The history of Chaplin's career seemed to promise that the public would continue to attend his films and make them highly profitable; art, at least according to the comedian's experiences, would prevail. In hindsight, we can see indications that *Monsieur Verdoux* would not hold to this tradition.

As the release date of the film approached, Chaplin may have had an inkling of the potential problems associated with its subject matter. "I was fascinated by the idea of a man having several wives — and trying to get rid of them ... [i]t is not as easy as people think ..." he told *Colliers*, in an article printed one day after the film's premiere. But he thought to add, almost as a disclaimer, "One's work is one's work ... one's private life is one's own. I believe the two should be kept separate. I have been given a great deal of unfavorable publicity — and, like everything else in this industry, it had been amplified out of all proportion to the truth."[56]

Ultimately, though, Chaplin saw his character in ironically heroic terms, while audiences could not. At the core of Verdoux's motives, Chaplin saw the human and rather courageous struggle for survival. Employing the devices of age and economic chaos as active factors in losing his livelihood, Verdoux is portrayed as the victim of societal forces out of control. Like Charlie in *Modern Times* or the Barber in *The Great Dictator*, Verdoux strives to achieve the most basic and fundamental human needs; such is Chaplin's device for pathos in the film. But this time, his enemy is not the Great Depression or a totalitarian leader; instead, it is society — which many interpreted as American society — that will devour him unless he can take what he needs. In the comedian's view, men like Verdoux, the Barber and the Tramp are humble men at the mercy of conditions that are often times beyond their individual control.

In this sense, Verdoux is certainly fashioned from the same mold as the department store burglars from *Modern Times*. But Chaplin was perhaps jaded by mounting public criticism against him throughout the mid–1940s and was, as theorized by Parker Tyler, "caught up in the mechanism of the contingent social morality that capitalistic democracy too is a big, bad machine, the only valid attitude towards which is to attempt to master it (like Verdoux) through guile at any price."[57] Certainly no one, including Chaplin, would condone Verdoux's arbitrary disposal of aging, moneyed women, regardless of how many negative personal characteristics they may have. But many felt that he was indeed looking favorably on Verdoux's lifestyle as a method of surviving in a new social age. Foes of the picture saw Verdoux as a man cornered by larger forces (as Chaplin, based on his memoirs, clearly saw himself during the

Barry trials) who lashes out, utilizing his ruthless psyche to seek social revenge. Chaplin himself contributes to this argument with the Verdoux line, "This is a ruthless world and one must be ruthless to cope with it."

The comedian did make unsuccessful efforts to soften the edges of his character throughout the narrative. For instance, Chaplin carefully constructs the narrative so that only actual murder — committed offscreen — takes place. He also labors to show Verdoux's essentially modest lifestyle. Although he is a sharp dresser, as one would expect a Bluebeard must be, Verdoux does not display the sort of material excess one would anticipate from a wealthy, extravagant individual. When Verdoux arrives on his tenth anniversary, his only present to his wife Mona is the deed to their small home, which helps to solidify the future of his family. Though his methods are horrific, Chaplin attempts to identify his character as a simple man of modest means. His comments to Mona indicate his personal disapproval of "the business," and that he looks forward to the point when he can retire and spend time with his family.

It is problematic that the viewing audience is bombarded with mixed messages concerning Verdoux. Elements of his character seem to point towards a sympathetic individual, but his actions make him monstrous. On the one hand we sympathize with his situation and the ends he is looking to achieve, yet at the same time we are repulsed by his means of getting there. Verdoux is both a martyr and a villain. "As with the character of Alex in Stanley Kubrick's *A Clockwork Orange*," Charles Maland aptly noted, "audiences simultaneously abhor Verdoux and empathize with him because his society seems even more corrupt than he is."[58]

Though we know that society should protect the individual from criminal activity, Chaplin would turn the tables by asking who should protect the individual from society. Verdoux has been a victim in losing his bank position. He nearly regains his security, only to have it plucked away from him again, this time along with, we assume, his wife and child.* The paradoxical question Chaplin asks is: Can we really blame people such as Verdoux for crimes that the larger society does not always apply to itself? We do, he asserts, because we have created an infrastructure that punishes individual acts of inhumanity, while tolerating the same when conducted for the larger good. As Verdoux rationalizes in his cell, "Despair is a narcotic; it lulls the mind into indifference." Chaplin sees Verdoux as no more ruthless or vicious than society itself, yet the indifference of an individual is punishable by law, whereas the indifference of a corporation or a nation perhaps may not be.

---

*Chaplin neglects to elaborate in the film as to the fate of Mona and Peter, merely indicating that he had "lost" them after he was financially ruined. It's unclear what he was aiming for by keeping this point vague. Is their absence intended to help frame Verdoux's loss of hope at the end of the film, signified by his slow shuffle and dark clothing, as with Charlie's tired and tattered appearance at the end of City Lights? Or is Verdoux lamenting his ultimate decision to spare both his wife and son from the cruelties of the world by poisoning them, as he did his many wives?

It is a case where the legacy of the Tramp was working against Chaplin. Prior to the 1940s, when his public image was in much better shape, the comedian's characteristics were largely associated with his screen character — kind, funny, thoughtful and genuine. Now, hostile critics often did the same for Verdoux. Chaplin's departure from Charlie or a Charlie-like character coincided with the plummeting of his public image. Whereas the Little Fellow was viewed as a warm, caring optimist, Verdoux, appearing at Chaplin's lowest point, was simply bitter and cynical. Many of those viewing the film continued to make the association of the screen Chaplin with the real Chaplin.

Just as commentators could not agree about the Barber's speech at the conclusion of *The Great Dictator*, the character of Henri Verdoux also received many differing treatments. Parker Tyler, writing shortly after the release of the film, found the character of Verdoux to be a parody of Adolphe Menjou's Pierre Revel in *A Woman of Paris*.[59] Roger Manvell, contributing to Donald McCaffrey's *Focus on Chaplin*, offered that "Verdoux is ... the natural man dehumanized by the unnatural cruelties which are slowly strangling the civilized world."[60]

Helping define not only Verdoux's appeal to Chaplin but the film's failure to capture the American audience, French critic André Bazin has argued that the character embodies the natural antithesis of Charlie.[61] Whereas the Tramp appeared tattered and worn in appearance, Verdoux is polished and mannered. Both are at odds with social forces; Charlie was often its hapless victim, while Verdoux makes the same system work to his advantage. Additionally, Charlie longs for the sort of romantic companionship that Verdoux regularly attains, even when the Bluebeard is merely using them for financial gain. It was a stark departure from the Charlie character, and heightened the negative reaction to Henri Verdoux. "[Chaplin] was out of character," Rollie Totheroh remembered. "It was a change that the public wasn't used to, and they didn't care so much for him when he was out of character. I could see it coming.... [H]e became old by his contact with the people who were deep thinkers, not the average public. He drifted away from that little character; he didn't want to use it anymore because it was more or less old crowd. It wasn't the character that he wanted to be. He wanted to be distinguished Chaplin now. I really couldn't blame him, but it did hurt his pictures and got him into trouble with the public, his masses."[62] Additionally, Charles Maland has suggested that the absence of a Tramp or a Tramp-like character allowed Chaplin to more fully address the film's political themes, which also played a contributing factor in Verdoux's and the picture's negative reception.[63]* Creating a character who

---

At a press conference held to promote the film (to be discussed later), Chaplin responded to a question regarding the increasing importance of messages, rather than comedy, in his films: "As you get older — as one gets older we are not just satisfied with the same old line. We have to get excited by something before we can arouse our energy to do something. And so I suppose it is one of my indulgences. I'm sorry." (Charles Chaplin; "Charlie Chaplin's Monsieur Verdoux *Press Conference" [introduction by George Wallach], from* Film Comment, *Winter 1969; page 39.)*

was the polar opposite of the Little Fellow, coupled with Chaplin's own personal troubles and changing American values, greatly endangered the prospects for the success of *Monsieur Verdoux*, at least in his adopted homeland.

Though the script for *Monsieur Verdoux* was rejected outright upon its submission to the Breen Office,* primarily in response to the issues of linking business to mass killing and references that clearly indicated the Marilyn Nash character to be a prostitute. After a few compromises, the film went forward as planned. Nonetheless, even in its censored form, *Monsieur Verdoux* would spark controversy among an American populace growing more and more conservative. Its politics would look dangerous, its morality loose, and comedic value appeared virtually nil. Many felt he had created another rostrum to preach from, as he had done at the end of *The Great Dictator* and with his Second Front speeches. Thus, while Chaplin was moving to a distinctly different type of film narrative and style, many were not prepared for the change.

Perhaps some of the fallout could have been mitigated, Chaplin felt, if audiences had responded to the film's comedic situations. But they did not. Audiences looking to see the gag-oriented comedy of the Tramp or broad satire like *The Great Dictator* were to be disappointed. With *Monsieur Verdoux*, Chaplin created a more subtle, intellectual type of picture. Only a small part of the film's humor is derived from action, the rest from dialogue; this, of course, was a distinct break in the comedian's traditional style.

The absence of substantial physical humor makes the pace of *Monsieur Verdoux* slower than previous Chaplin films. Instead, the humor is derived from witty exchanges, which often contain ironic double meanings for elements of Verdoux's life.[64] While on the one hand this offered an opportunity to further utilize dialogue as a narrative device as well as alter the treatment of themes, it may also have caught critics and some loyal fans offguard with its departure from the type of comedies Chaplin had produced in the past. The absence of strong, traditional slapstick elements put the actions of Verdoux on a level of realism that made the film appear largely uncomedic, and which may have encouraged the audience to make the association between Verdoux's actions and Chaplin's personal character. "In *Monsieur Verdoux* [Chaplin] plays a killer," John Paul Smead observed, "but he still wants the audience to be on his side. He treats the audience as a band of co-conspirators.... The unwillingness of American audiences to empathize with a murderer may partially account for the film's cool reception."[65]

Release of *The Circus* had helped rescue the comedian's floundering public persona following the Lita Grey divorce, so Chaplin had high hopes that the

---

*Verdoux *posed his first actual run-in with the Hollywood's moral authority — though, as we have seen, he may have had problems with the subplot of the Gamin and the Convent in one of the original drafts of* Modern Times. *Chaplin was no doubt offended by the changes he was forced to make in his script — he devoted a good portion of his memoirs to the original material in *Verdoux, *even comparing his dialogue with the Breen office's stated objections.*

release of *Monsieur Verdoux* would have an equally positive effect. "Although I had gone through periodic qualms about my career, I never faltered in my belief that a good comedy would solve all my troubles," he wrote in his memoirs. "With this resolute feeling I completed *Monsieur Verdoux*."[66] Regardless of his sagging public perception, surely the people could distinguish the quality of his art from the personal troubles that had plagued him.

Unfortunately for Chaplin, he had severely underestimated the public's willingness to forgive. Additionally, the political climate in the United States had changed so dramatically since the release of *The Great Dictator* that his ideological views, now that *Dictator* and his Second Front Speeches had made them very public, seemed more and more threatening. Unbeknownst to the comedian, his complacency in judging the reaction of the general public would cost him severely.

IX. PROMOTION & RESPONSE TO *MONSIEUR VERDOUX*

We [Chaplin and assistant Chuck Reisner] are both sour on the world and its hypocrisies. It's a great little game panning the world so long as you don't let your sessions get too long or too serious.[67]
— Charles Chaplin — 1922

For the purpose of a play it is consistent enough with life that an unprincipled character, through roguery and deceit, eventually gains worldly goods. But this will annoy many people, even though the sheer irony of the success of weakness may be the subject matter of the play. They will be aroused to such a state of antagonism that they will forget that their emotions have been played upon and that the whole has been very real to them. All this turmoil has been created within the spectators, and yet they will swear that it has not been entertainment at all.[68]
— Charles Chaplin — 1924

I believe that *Monsieur Verdoux* is the cleverest and most brilliant film I have yet made.[69]
— Charles Chaplin — 1964

Charles Maland's study of the promotional campaign for *Monsieur Verdoux*, backed by similar evidence from Tino Balio in his studio history of United Artists, is proof positive of Chaplin's failure to fully understand the scope of how revelations about his off-screen activities had affected his ability to be an on-screen draw. With both *City Lights* and *Modern Times*, films that ran the risk of losing audiences due to the absence of full-fledged sound, the promotional campaigns were extensive, emphasizing what was attractive and traditional about the comedian's work.[70] Most of all, the advertising schemes emphasized the image of the Little Fellow — a conservative move which, consistent with the style of film and comedy presented in *City Lights* and *Modern Times*, drew effectively on the reputation of Chaplin's previous works. For *The Great Dictator*, the film's timeliness and historical importance, in addition to Chaplin's cinematic reputation, helped promote it to box office success. Given *Dictator's* anticipation by critics and the public alike, its promotional campaign remains somewhat of an anomaly from that of the average Chaplin film.

But beginning with *Modern Times*, Chaplin kept his cards very close to his chest during productions, closing his sets to most outsiders and carefully limiting the amount of information released to the public. It seems that for *Monsieur Verdoux*, instead of holding only the press at bay with minimal information, he also kept the United Artists publicity staff in the dark as well. Hence, the picture approached a release date with comparatively little promotion to his earlier releases (an issue which writer Philip K. Scheuer specifically raised in a promotional article appearing in *Collier's* shortly before the film's debut[71]).

Events of the preceding years should have been a tip-off to the comedian that the film required special promotional attention. While Chaplin may have been bankable as a box office draw immediately following the release of *The Great Dictator*, he did not embark on an immediate follow-up project. Instead, almost all the public attention showered upon him for nearly five years had been related to his questionable political views, moral values and increasing scrutiny regarding his status as a non-citizen resident in the United States. Second, Chaplin was finally making the move away from any semblance of the Tramp character in portraying Verdoux.

The comedian, approaching age 60, could not physically play the Little Fellow forever, but Chaplin's timing of the move and, more importantly, the type of character he had created in Verdoux posed serious problems. Given the fact that such a dramatic shift from the traditional Chaplin character and narrative traits was taking place, perhaps the comedian should have approached the promotion of the project with the same care and intensity that he had with his previous three films. He did not.

Thus, United Artists found itself in a promotional bind as the opening approached. Due to the lack of information Chaplin supplied them regarding the production, their efforts in promoting the New York opening were indeed lackluster. The day of *Monsieur Verdoux's* premiere, for instance, a half-page advertisement for the film ran in the *New York Times*. As with earlier promotional campaigns, it focused on Chaplin and his character, though this time he was dressed as the dapper Verdoux rather than Charlie. The ad also lists several "facts about Charlie Chaplin and *Monsieur Verdoux*" which, in part, seem geared towards preparing the potential New York audience for something quite different from the comedian. First, it notes that Chaplin had abandoned the Tramp costume; second, it explains that the narrative of *Verdoux* was quite unlike that of his previous films; third, it announces that the picture introduces his newfound acting talent, Marilyn Nash; and fourth, it notes that the picture was "five years in the making," which included Chaplin's work as a writer, director, producer and composer.[72]

Chaplin would recall that an earlier, advance preview of *Monsieur Verdoux*, had been a miserable experience.

> There was an uneasy atmosphere in the theatre that night, a feeling that the audience had come to prove something. The moment the film started, instead of the eager anticipation and the happy stir of the past that greeted my films, there was nervous applause scattered with a few hisses. I loathe to admit it but those few hisses hurt more than all the antagonism of the press.
>
> As the picture progressed I began to get worried. The laughter was there, but divided. It was not the laughter of old, of *The Gold Rush*, of *City Lights* or *Shoulder Arms*. It was challenging laughter against the hissing faction of the theatre. My heart began to sink.[73]

It became clear that night that, for the film to gross even near what Chaplin and United Artists wished, a quick and highly effective publicity campaign would have to be mounted.

Accordingly, the company arranged a large press conference in New York on April 12, 1947, at Chaplin's insistence, at which the film star personally addressed the press corps. It was an unprecedented move for Chaplin, the first such gathering of its type in his career. As advance word began to filter back to the United Artists publicity people, it looked to be a potentially risky one, too. It was feared that many reporters would be hostile and, worse, that their concerns had little to do with *Monsieur Verdoux* but the many issues surrounding Chaplin's status as a citizen, his morals and his links to alleged Communists. Still, Chaplin dug in his heels and insisted on meeting the hungry press himself.

When Chaplin went before reporters on April 12, the day following the New York *Verdoux* premiere, true to the rumors United Artists staffers had been hearing, the film was the furthest topic from the press' minds. Chaplin had met with representatives from several European papers only the day before without incident, but his reception with American reporters was much different. Characteristically, Chaplin had not bowed to the pressure of those who sought to disparage his work. In the Grand Ballroom at the Gotham Hotel in New York, Chaplin marched into the fray defiantly, enticing the reporters to "proceed with the butchery." And that they did.

Transcript proceedings of the press conference clearly indicate that Chaplin had fallen out of favor with the mainstream of Cold War America.[74] The press cornered the entertainer, forcing him to defend himself in a mock trial that he could not win.

Questions about his political beliefs surfaced immediately, and Chaplin adamantly denied he was a Communist. But when the question was rephrased to inquire whether he held Communist sympathies, his answer was softer and, perhaps, less satisfactory in a political climate critical of the Soviet Union. "I don't know what you mean by 'Communist sympathizer,'" Chaplin responded. "I'd say this—that during the war, I sympathized very much with Russia because I believe that she was holding the front, and for that I have a memory and I feel that I owe her thanks. I think that she helped contribute a considerable amount of fighting and dying to bring victory to the Allies. In that sense, I am sympathetic."[75]

Shortly thereafter, James W. Fay, representing the Catholic War Veterans, took aim at the artist. Fay questioned Chaplin's contribution to helping the war effort, his political beliefs and his friendships with suspected Communists. Fay specifically objected to Chaplin's lack of United States citizenship, despite having resided in America for over 30 years. "I'm objecting to your particular stand that you have no patriotic feelings about this country or any other country," Fay blasted. "You've worked here, you've made your money here, you went around in the last war [referring to World War I] when you should have been serving Great Britain, you were selling bonds, so it stated in the paper that I read, and I think that you as a citizen here—or rather a resident here—taking our money should have done more!"[76] In response, Chaplin noted that over two-thirds of his income had come from overseas showings of his films, which the United States was allowed full taxation on. But almost nothing he could say on his own behalf stirred sympathy for him. Well-paying guest or not, Cold War America was finding too much not to like about Charles Spencer Chaplin.

Only one individual in the ballroom that day spoke up on Chaplin's behalf—James Agee, film critic for both *The Nation* and *Time*. His voice trembling and barely audible in the large hall, he nonetheless spoke out against the steady invectives launched at the comedian by his colleagues.

> What are people who care a damn about freedom—who really care for it—think of a country and the people in it, who congratulate themselves upon this country as the finest on earth and as a "free country," when so many of the people in this country pry into what a man's citizenship is, try to tell him his business from hour to hour and from day to day and exert a public moral blackmail against him for not becoming an American citizen—for his political views and for not entertaining troops in the manner—in the way that they think he should. What is to be thought of a general country where those people are thought well of?[77]

Chaplin thanked the critic for his kind words, but while Agee tore into what he perceived as petty expectations and posturing by the others in the room, he was nonetheless the only pro-Chaplin voice in a sea of negativism.

Consequently, perhaps, as a lingering epitaph from the Gotham Ballroom "massacre," reviews of *Monsieur Verdoux* in the American press tended to be mostly negative. Many critics either hinted or outright stated that they longed for the Charlie of old, some on logic similar to André Bazin's Verdoux/Tramp character contrasts, and found the film's statement about the cruelty of society particularly distasteful. Chaplin "occasionally proves that he is still one of the screen's great pantomimists," went the review for *Life*, "[b]ut he also proves that he can be one of its most confusing moralizers." The film's ending was a "fiendish courtroom speech ... [with] a silly comparison between his small-scale killings and the mass homicide of modern war."[78] Though he lamented the picture as slow with an ineffective mix of comedy and seriousness, Bosley Crowther's review in the *New York Times* respectfully noted that "[t]here is no doubt that a lot of controversy will be created by *Monsieur Verdoux*, but it is plain that Mr. Chaplin is still in the game — and hitting hard."[79]

James Agee, seemingly Chaplin's only vocal supporter at times, was particularly favorable in authoring reviews for two publications (he ran a three-part series on the film in *The Nation*, in addition to his review for *Time*). But symptomatic of Agee's comments at the press conference, he was one of few American reviewers who separated Chaplin the man from Chaplin the screen character. While not overlooking a number of flaws in the picture, most notably his belief that Chaplin "overexerted" himself writing the screenplay, Agee noted, "If it had no other virtues — and it has many — the film is a daring individual gesture, dared in an era when such acts are rare."[80]*

Some Chaplin detractors had more on their minds than just assailing the film in print. Convinced of his Communist ties and questionable morals, patriotic groups such as the Catholic War Veterans and the American Legion began to organize boycotts against the film, sometimes threatening theater owners with an extended patronage blacklist if they refused to pull it from their screens. Unfortunately for all — Chaplin, United Artists and the public — many owners bowed to this type of pocketbook pressure (a "hate campaign of frightening proportions," according to United Artists historian Tino Balio).[81] Ultimately, *Monsieur Verdoux* showed in so few theaters that turning a profit and providing a financial boost to United Artists, as Chaplin hoped the film would do, was an impossibility. Whereas the public had embraced *The Great Dictator* despite its controversial message and mixed reviews, the public avoided *Monsieur Verdoux* because of them, a move that was aided substantially by citizen efforts to suppress the film across America.

Unlike any Chaplin film before, the picture was pulled from circulation in the late spring of 1947 after completing its New York run. It had only grossed $325,000 in the United States, as opposed to $1.5 million abroad, where both

---

Agee's reviews didn't go uncriticized; Dwight MacDonald, reflecting on the film and its history in the April, 1965, issue of Esquire, *was deeply critical of what he observed as Agee's overpraising of Monsieur Verdoux. "[T]o call a badly flawed movie great because of its theme and its creator's intentions is like saying an orator is eloquent but inarticulate — only on the hypothesis that they are really interested in something else, something outside my province as a film critic, something that doesn't appear on the screen." (Dwight MacDonald; "On Chaplin,* Verdoux, *and Agee," from* Esquire, *April, 1965; page 34.)*

critics and audiences were more appreciative of Chaplin's new cinematic direction. It would resurface in the United States during the fall of 1947 with a new promotional campaign (a more controversial and aggressive approach, characterized by posters of Verdoux surrounded by the slogan "Chaplin Changes!; Can You?"), although United Artists' financial situation allowed only selected cities to be targeted. The campaign produced positive results in those areas (including, among others, Washington, D.C.[82]), but the efforts were not duplicated nationwide, and officials at United Artists eventually wrote off *Monsieur Verdoux* as a loss. In essence, America's general perspective had changed, and Chaplin had not kept up. American society had little tolerance for criticism of its policies or institutions. *Monsieur Verdoux* took too broad a swipe at what was perceived as American ideals. During this period the most successful films and filmmakers looked to reinforce traditional values rather than challenge them; nowhere was this more evident than in the Academy Award recipients for 1947. Chaplin's script for *Monsieur Verdoux* was nominated in the category of Best Original Screenplay (one of three writing categories that year, the others being Best Original Story and, simply, Best Screenplay). As with *Dictator*, Chaplin went away empty-handed, losing to the comedy *The Bachelor and the Bobby-Soxer* starring Cary Grant and a teenage Shirley Temple. Likewise, the two other writing awards went to the Christmas film *Miracle on 34th Street*. Clearly, America was in no mood for an introspective look at its problems, but rather studio films that emphasized a sense of optimism instead. With both the industry and the public moving in a different direction from Chaplin's changing narrative interests, *Monsieur Verdoux* had little chance of succeeding upon its initial release.

6

Limelight

Though Chaplin would like to have retreated back to his family and friends following the humiliating American reception of *Monsieur Verdoux,* outside political forces continued to dog the entertainer through the ensuing months. Congress, beginning its investigation of Communist influence in the film industry, began their work just as criticism of Chaplin, still one of the industry's most recognized figures, was beginning to percolate.

"In part because of the government's cooperative efforts with film-makers," Charles Maland noted, "exemplified by the fictional war films or such documentary films as the *Why We Fight* series, elected officials [in post-World War II America] also came to believe in the power of movies. In addition to being pleased that films could affirm traditional American values, however, some officials became concerned that the opposite could also be true: that films could contain disruptive or 'subversive' material that could erode dominant values."[1] Though set in France, *Monsieur Verdoux*'s social criticism was interpreted by many as a direct show of contempt toward American society and further evidence of Chaplin's undesirability as a resident in the United States.

On June 12, 1947, two months following the release of *Verdoux,* Representative John T. Rankin, a Republican from Mississippi, strode to the floor of the House and demanded that the Truman Administration begin deportation proceedings against Charles Chaplin. Rankin's request was an overt call for governmental action, though it was not the first of its kind to be proposed; some three months earlier, a request came from the Senate asking that the Justice Department formally investigate Charles Chaplin's political ties and sympathies.

With reasoning analogous to James W. Fay's comments at the *Verdoux* press conference, Congressman Rankin felt that Chaplin had demonstrated an intolerable scorn for America and American institutions, and thus the government was obliged to act forcefully against him as a non-citizen resident.

Elsewhere in the Capitol, the House Un-American Activities Committee (HUAC) was gaining steam. Though the Committee had its origins even before

189

America's entry into the Second World War*, the nation's new Cold War mentality was fueling its growing importance, which would eventually culminate
in the Communist witch hunts during the early 1950s. Chaplin, long acquainted
with several known Communists and appearing sympathetic to so-called Communist causes, was a likely target for the Committee.

Chaplin was apparently under consideration by HUAC as early as December of 1946, but it wasn't until the summer of 1947, when Chaplin and United
Artists were attempting to salvage *Monsieur Verdoux* with the second promotional campaign, that rumors began to circulate regarding his imminent
appearance before the Committee. Some in Hollywood, including Chaplin's
friend, composer Hanns Eisler, had given testimony previously to the Committee in a special session held in Los Angeles. In July of 1947 it was reported
that Representative J. Parnell Thomas, chairman of the HUAC Committee, had
indicated that Chaplin would be subpoenaed shortly; on September 22, 1947,
The Hollywood Reporter printed a list of film industry personalities (including
Chaplin) slated to be called by HUAC during its October hearings.[2] Unlike
Chaplin, some were being called by the Committee as friendly witnesses,
including Gary Cooper, Adolphe Menjou and Ronald Reagan.

Chaplin had no knowledge of the Committee's intentions, and was surprised and angered by receiving the news through the general press. In a terse
response, Chaplin cabled the Committee regarding the press speculation.

> From your publicity I note that I am to be quizzed by the House Un-American
> Activities Committee in Washington in September. I understand I am to be your
> single "guest" at the expense of the taxpayers. Forgive me for this premature
> acceptance of your headlines newspaper invitation.
>
> You have been quoted as saying you wish to ask me if I am a Communist.
> You sojourned for Hollywood for ten days not long ago, and could have asked
> me the question at that time, effecting something of an economy, or you could
> telephone me now — collect. In order that you may be completely up-to-date on
> my thinking I suggest you view my latest production, *Monsieur Verdoux*. It is
> against war and the futile slaughter of youth. I trust you will not find its humane
> message distasteful.
>
> While you are preparing your engraved subpoena I will give you a hint on
> where I stand. I am not a Communist. I am a peacemonger.[3]

An official subpoena would arrive in late September of 1947, only to have
the Committee postpone Chaplin's testimony on three successive occasions.

---

*In 1941, Chaplin was rumored to be on the prospective testimony list of the Senate's HUAC counter-
part, which sought in the course of its investigation to identify his intentions in making* The Great
Dictator. *Some perceived the film as an open call to war at a time when America's stand was officially
neutral on the conflict in Europe. Premature anti–Fascism, many felt at the time, was a front for Communism, particularly following the violation of the Nazi/Soviet Nonaggression Pact in 1939. Pearl
Harbor, however, caused a permanent delay in Chaplin being subpoenaed by the Senate Committee.
(Charles Maland;* Chaplin and American Culture; *page 184.)*

Finally, "I received a surprisingly courteous reply to the effect that my appearance would not be necessary, and that I could consider the matter closed."[4] And, for the time being, Chaplin did just that.

Even so, Chaplin's public troubles were destined to continue. In November of 1947 he attempted to enlist the help of Pablo Picasso, a known Communist, in protesting deportation proceedings then underway against Eisler. Chaplin, it was reported, asked Picasso to organize a demonstration of artists before the United States Embassy in Paris, coinciding with a protest that Chaplin would ostensibly help organize within the United States. Though Charles Chaplin, Jr., would downplay his father's request as an attempt only to gather support for another artist in need, the notion of appealing to a known Communist to stir up anti-American sentiment abroad struck many as dangerously subversive.[5] Gradually, the rationale behind Representative Rankin's call for Chaplin's deportation some six months earlier began to strike a chord with conservative-leaning public officials, with Chaplin's lack of foresight only fueling this angry sentiment.

As during the Joan Barry trials, Chaplin at first made no effort to distance himself from these controversial issues, treating his private affairs as wholly exclusive from his work. The presidential election of 1948 saw Chaplin lending public support to candidate Henry Wallace, a liberal Democrat who had made cooperation between the World War II victors, including Stalinist Russia, one of the cornerstones in his foreign policy platform. Wallace's progressivism no doubt appealed to the same rationale Chaplin had used to support the Second Front concept earlier, and the entertainer was thus drawn toward Wallace's candidacy. The public, however, was either unable or unwilling to embrace the universality of Wallace's proposals. His bid for the Democratic nomination never struck much of a chord with Americans, in part due to Wallace's openness toward the Russian people. Chaplin also lent his name during this period in sponsorship to several international peace conferences, designed to bring citizens and representatives of the world's peoples together for the betterment of the future. To some government officials and mainstream Americans, these types of gatherings were viewed as Communist-influenced, and looked upon with a great deal of suspicion. By lending his public support to such gatherings, Chaplin was again linking himself to America's Cold War enemy.

Even the comedian's social contacts contributed to the growing suspicion surrounding his nature. During his period, Chaplin often associated with many of the Hollywood émigrés that had populated the Los Angeles area during Hitler's reign in Europe. Like him, many of them were also at odds with America's prevailing political climate, and Chaplin speaks fondly of them in his memoirs.[6] Some were declared Communists, most were artists, and all, like Chaplin, had relocated to America, and hence viewed events with the perspective of an outsider. Unlike many others in Hollywood, they had proven supportive and loyal to Chaplin and his family during the Joan Barry and *Monsieur Verdoux* ordeals. In turn, Chaplin would defend them as well when some found themselves targets of the government's Communist hunting. While his loyalty seems quite honorable, too many aspects of his character were being linked to people or causes that a growing number of Americans viewed as suspect.[7]

It may have taken his own interrogation for Chaplin to finally realize that scrutiny over his professional and personal relations had not subsided following *Monsieur Verdoux*. In the spring of 1948, Chaplin wished to take Oona and their two young children, Geraldine, two, and Michael, one, back to his native England. As with any other non-citizen looking to travel abroad and return, Chaplin was required to make arrangements though the U.S. Immigration and Naturalization Service (INS), applying for a re-entry permit as he had done before previous overseas trips. Oona had never been to England and, together with his growing family, Chaplin had hoped to rekindle memories of his past as he developed his next film project, a story set in the old London music halls tentatively titled *Footlights*. But while arrangements for his previous trips had been a mere formality, these were different times for the INS, and Chaplin was viewed in a much less positive light than in years past.

He was asked to call on INS headquarters in Los Angeles, where he was met not only by a gentleman from the department but one f.om the FBI as well, accompanied by a stenographer poised to record Chaplin's responses to several pointed questions. While researching his book *Chaplin and American Culture*, Charles Maland published excerpts of the meeting in the Winter 1986 edition of *Cineaste*; he characterized the interrogation as "offering a vivid testimony of the Cold War mentality prevalent in the U.S. at the time."[8]

At the meeting, Chaplin was specifically quizzed regarding his membership in and/or contributions to several organizations, all of which the government must have considered suspicious. These groups ranged from known Communist and Socialist organizations to the Screen Actors Guild. (Chaplin's response to a question on possible contributions to the Guild: "… Yes, possibly, but I may not have … I think I have to belong to an Actors Guild in order to work …"[9]). Many questions dealt with Chaplin's sympathies towards Russia, as well as those designed to confirm his participation in events that the government deemed Communistic in origin.

Employing the McCarthyist reasoning of guilt by association, most of the interview seems an attempt to bully Chaplin into divulging the type of shady connections that probably never existed in the first place. He could give officials no damaging testimony, though some of the questions would nonetheless foreshadow his later troubles.

> Q: It is further reported that you [stated]: "I am not a citizen and I don't need American citizenship papers. Citizenship papers don't mean anything. I am a patriot of humanity. I am a citizen of the world."

A: The first part of that is not correct.

Q: You mean you did not make the statement, "I am not a citizen and I don't need American citizenship papers"?

A: I did not make that statement.

Q: As a matter of fact, Mr. Chaplin, you are not a citizen of the United States, are you?

A: I am not.[10]

Later, as Chaplin responded to another question regarding his citizenship, he noted the irony of his financial position as a movie star in America, just as he had responded to James W. Fay at the *Verdoux* press conference.

> Seventy-five percent of my revenue comes from Europe, you see, and this country enjoys one hundred percent of its taxation. My last picture which they didn't release here [indicating *Monsieur Verdoux*], the whole of the income comes from abroad. It comes into this country and the United States gets the full taxation on that.[11]

Chaplin was allowed to add some final comments after the interview was completed.

> ... I want to get on record and say I am not interested in any subversive movement to overthrow the American government or any government, and I am not a politically active person.... My only object is to preserve democracy as we have it. I think there are certain abuses to it, like everything else. I think there has been a great deal of witch burning. I don't think that is democratic. I know it seems very strange and rather bewilders me why I should be considered a Communist. I have been here 35 years and my primary interest is in my work and it has never been anti-anything ... maybe a critical comment, but it was always been for the good of the country. I don't like war and I don't like revolution. I don't like anything overthrown. If the status quo of anything is all right, let it go. In my sense of being a liberal, I just want to see things function in harmony. I want to see everybody pretty well, happy and satisfied.[12]

The reference to the Federal taxation on his films is interesting because, with his history of tax troubles, the Internal Revenue Service, probably acting on a tip from the INS, suddenly became interested in Chaplin's planned departure as well. Fearing that he may be leaving the country for good, they demanded that he put up a bond of over $1.5 million if he chose to travel abroad.

Though Chaplin did manage to get approval from the INS following the interrogation, he instead opted to stay stateside.[13] Along with the financial obstacle created by the Treasury, perhaps he recognized his need to keep a lower public profile, which would be hard to do while traveling abroad for the first time in nearly two decades. Despite his belief in progressive causes and the freedom of the individual, the government's badgering had finally prompted him to succumb to one of the many antagonistic pressures placed on some individuals in Cold War America.

I. THE ATTEMPTED TURNAROUND

As Chaplin continued preliminary work on another film project, he began to back away from the public spotlight. Not only was the damage being felt by the film star personally, but also by United Artists, which was then suffering financial difficulties.

Chaplin's public forays into politics dwindled following the presidential election of 1948, and he also made a concerted effort to disassociate himself from potentially damaging political causes. Notably, Chaplin took action to block a benefit showing of *The Circus* by the leftist San Francisco newspaper *The Daily People's World* in July, 1950, an indication that he was aware of the sort of adverse press (or, more appropriately, guilt by association) that could befall him if he allowed the benefit screening to continue.[14]

Even though the Tramp would not appear on behalf of *The Daily People's World*, Charlie would be put to work in an effort to salvage some of Chaplin's sagging public acceptance. Following a well-received screening for daughter Geraldine's private school, Chaplin decided to dust off one of his classics for reissue. On April 8, 1950, *City Lights* began a small revival at the Globe Theatre in New York, followed by a modest re-release tour that enabled some movie fans to reacquaint themselves with the Little Fellow. Like *The Gold Rush*, re-released eight years earlier, *City Lights* played to small but enthusiastic crowds and excellent critical reception. "Silence had indeed proved golden," John Montgomery commented of the reissue, "for the Chaplin of 1930 has proved a greater comedian than any of his rivals of 1950."[15] In the postscript to his 1951 biography of Chaplin, Theodore Huff added, "*City Lights*, wiping away any possible bad taste left by *Verdoux*, confounded the Chaplin detractors who in 1947 predicted that the public had permanently soured on him. Moreover, a new generation that had grown up without ever having seen Charlie Chaplin took *City Lights* to their hearts as if it had been made only yesterday."[16]

Though the re-release was small, the critical raves were nonetheless welcomed by Chaplin. Still, the film alone could not wipe away the feeling among certain sectors of American society that Chaplin was a danger to the country. Late in 1950, *Variety* reported that Joseph Fehrenback, active in a New Jersey chapter of the Catholic War Veterans (the group James W. Fay represented at the *Monsieur Verdoux* press conference), was actively pushing the national organization to call for a ban on Chaplin's works both in theaters and on television. Fehrenback personally took credit for the removal of the revived *City Lights* from four New Jersey theaters. His rationale for the action included the fact that

Chaplin "appears to be guilty" of Communist leanings, and that an investigation on un–American activities in California felt that the comedian had "followed or appeased some of the Communist party line program over a period of time."[17] Similarly, public officials in Memphis, Tennessee, banned *City Lights* from playing their jurisdiction, deeming Chaplin as an "enemy to Godliness in all its forms."[18]

On a national level, Chaplin's name had also been surfacing in the testimony of several witnesses before the House Un-American Activities Committee, and even though nothing concrete was being alleged, this helped perpetuate a general view that would, over time, appear persuasive enough for people to believe that he was an outright Communist. Screenwriter Bess Taffel, for example, who was called before the Committee on the basis of her connections in Hollywood, recalled the delicate line one walked during the hearings by invoking the Fifth Amendment, which supposedly would protect the witness from self-incrimination. Using Chaplin for her illustration, her comments note how careful a witness had to be when making statements to HUAC.

> A particularly exasperating aspect of the Fifth is that you can implicate others without naming names simply, ironically, by the very act of using the Fifth. For instance, what if they ask you about someone like Charlie Chaplin? I knew that Charlie had never been a Communist, nor a member of any organization. It was against his basic philosophy. But the Committee won't let you say that; you have to answer, as always, "I refuse to answer on the grounds that it might tend to incriminate me," and thereby make it seem as if Chaplin were a Red. I lived in dread that I might, thus, be forced to add to the troubles of a dear friend and a good human being.[19]

To that point, though the government had been investigating Chaplin's activities off and on since his early motion picture days, no substantial evidence had been gathered against him. But although the *City Lights* revival was a triumph in its limited release (aided by an off-year for screen comedy in 1950), even the good-natured Tramp could not stop this kettle from eventually coming to a boil.

Coinciding with the positive critical response to *City Lights'* re-emergence, the remarks of writers such as Montgomery and Huff were also indicative of a new historical appreciation of Chaplin's contribution to the film industry going on at the same time. As antagonism against the comedian mounted during the 1940s to the highest point of his career, a number of journalists and authors rallied in support of his comedic legacy. Along with Huff's 1951 documentation of Chaplin's life, for many years the definitive work on the comedian, many other biographies and critical interpretations hit the bookstands as well: *Chaplin, Last of the Clowns* by Parker Tyler, 1948; *The Little Fellow: The Life and Work of Charles Spencer Chaplin* by Peter Cotes and Thelma Niklaus, 1951; Robert Payne's *The Great God Pan*, 1952; and *Chaplin: The Immortal Tramp* by R.J. Minney, a friend of Sydney Chaplin's, in 1954.

Books were not the only mode of written adulation showered upon Chaplin during the assaults on his character and reputation. One of the most notable pieces of journalism about silent comedy appeared during this period, authored by James Agee, Chaplin's lone defender of *Monsieur Verdoux* at the New York press conference. His article, "Comedy's Greatest Era," appeared in the September 5, 1949, issue of *Life* magazine. An homage to the forgotten art of silent comedy, the work lauds Chaplin for his skills as a pantomime artist, particularly his inflection of mood and his unique and masterful use of pathos.[20] The piece hailed slapstick as a lost art, and no doubt gave a temporary boost to Chaplin's public image, reaffirming his status as a great figure of cinema. But the comedian wasn't ultimately the primary beneficiary of Agee's work. The article was partly responsible for reviving Buster Keaton's stagnant career as well as placing Harry Langdon's name among those of the other comedy greats.

With the exception of Agee's article, however, such accolades may have done little to help Chaplin's public image. None of the books sold particularly well at the time, even though their appearance, at the very least, indicates that Chaplin had remained a popular figure and that he was not without his defenders.[21] Regardless of the reassessment of his character in print, he forged ahead on his new motion picture, one which backed away substantially from the politicized narratives of *Modern Times, The Great Dictator* and *Monsieur Verdoux*, and one in which the comedian attempted to emphasize pathos in order to reconnect with the audience that seemed to have abandoned him.

II. *FOOTLIGHTS*

The excellent reception given the re-released *City Lights* no doubt rekindled Chaplin's confidence to a degree. But he was still disturbed by the way in which the United States seemed to have suddenly turned against him. Just five years prior to the release of *Verdoux*, Chaplin was considered one of America's most widely recognized and best-loved entertainers. By the end of the 1940s, though his personal beliefs and accomplishments in world cinema had changed very little, he was now commonly looked upon as somewhat of a scoundrel by the very public that had once adored him.

Thus, it perhaps seems natural — even appropriate, in some respects — that Chaplin, a sensitive artist, would reflect inward for the inspiration for his next project, a motion picture that would evolve into a work both deeply personal and in some respects deeply moving as well.

Such was the birth of *Footlights*. In the wake of the failed *Monsieur Verdoux*, beginning in the early months of 1948, Chaplin began to lay the outline for a film that would play very close to his own history and heart, despite his lukewarm denials of such. Whereas all of Chaplin's previous features held a bit of their creator's identity in them, *Limelight* (the film's eventual title) as well as *A King in New York,* five years later, would be an explicit autobiography of the comedian.[22]

The original idea is apparently one that Chaplin had conceived shortly after *The Great Dictator,*[23] but one which now, in the midst of his personal controversies, was becoming increasingly topical to him. Setting the story in the vaudeville music halls of turn-of-the-century London, Chaplin looked to return to the origin of his fame during perhaps the lowest point yet of his career. The plot, as it was originally conceived, would center on the relationship between two entertainers — a young ballerina on her way up, Terry Ambrose, and an old comic on his way down, Calvero.* The transformation of popularity from one generation to another, and of public acceptance of an artist, would serve as the focal points, and would also pave the way for Chaplin to use the type of pathos so distinctive of his earlier features, particularly *City Lights.* As was often the case with the Little Fellow, Calvero's fate is structured in such a way that sentiment is conferred onto the character's creator, Charles Spencer Chaplin.

But in addition to the personalization of the story, *Footlights* would also receive some unconventional treatment in the process of constructing its narrative.

Most peculiar in the script's gestation was Chaplin's "novelization" of the original story line, some excerpts from which are reprinted in David Robinson's biography of the comedian.[24] In it, Chaplin wrote elaborate passages detailing the background stories for both Terry and Calvero, which were to be utilized through a number of flashback sequences. The finished picture would not depict such extensive material, though a flashback sequence introducing Terry's romance with a struggling composer is employed. Instead, backstories are established through verbal exchanges between Terry and Calvero. This structure was highly unusual for Chaplin. Not only was the comedian proposing an abundance of dialogue, but — initially, at least — he contemplated departing from the type of linear plot lines that had characterized his work. Also, since the narrative of *Limelight* reverted back to the music halls of his youth, it was clear that Chaplin created characters based upon his own personal experiences, moreso than in his previous films. Thus it is no coincidence that the character of Terry bore resemblances to Hetty Kelly, a young girl who was Chaplin's first love during his music hall days, as well as to his mother Hannah. Likewise, Calvero has distinct similarities to Chaplin's own father.

---

*"Calvero, Tramp Comedian" is the title adorning an old billing poster hung in Calvero's modest apartment. It would serve as one of an innumerable number of references to Chaplin and Chaplin's film career that unmistakably suggest that the picture is a dramatic parable of his own downfall as an esteemed entertainer.

Yet another oddity was Chaplin's concentration on the musical portions. While music had always been important in his sound era features, *Limelight*'s score had an elevated role. Chaplin set to the task of completing the musical portions before actually finalizing the script. Normally, he would compose following the assembly of a rough cut of the film, well into the post-production period. Director Robert Parrish, however, who had played one of the pea-shooting newsboys in *City Lights* as a youth, recalled accepting an invitation from Chaplin to listen to portions of the score for *Limelight* prior to the film being shot.[25] Further evidence of the importance of *Limelight*'s score to the comedian comes from André Bazin's comment that three-quarters of the English pressbook for the film was devoted to the music alone.[26]

While Chaplin's early scoring of the picture does present an oddity, the nature of the plot gives some insight as to why he may have felt it a necessity. The story required an inordinate amount of musical accompaniment, from spirited and humorous jingles for Calvero's stage acts to a 12-minute ballet for Terry's stage finale, *The Death of Columbine*,* in addition to the traditional film score that Chaplin needed to compose. For the songs of Calvero's act, Chaplin undoubtedly found inspiration in his many years on the vaudeville circuit, and we can be reasonably assured of his authentic attempts at recreating this forgotten art form. The ballet sequence posed a challenge for Chaplin. Dancers André Eglevsky and Melissa Hayden were brought in to consult with Chaplin on the musical score, which they felt was adequate to create a proper dance segment, and to help choreograph the piece. In addition, the pair would return later to film their creation.

Photographically, too, *Limelight* would mark somewhat of a departure. As he had done with *The Great Dictator*, Chaplin engaged Karl Struss, after it was apparent from early shooting that Rollie Totheroh's work was lacking. Totheroh would stay on the production, earning the credit of photographic consultant, though his role was clearly diminished. One commentator has suggested that *Limelight*'s higher degree of realism, as opposed to Chaplin's traditionally comical settings, may have necessitated the switch as much as any technical aspects to shooting the film.[27]

Limelight would show Struss' influence in terms of lighting, camera tracking and image composition, although his style had only a small impact on the film and even less so on Chaplin's future work. Though Struss was certainly more skilled with respect to modern camera techniques than Totheroh, Chaplin was evidently not taken with the results, for the comic's final two films revert back to the predominantly stationary camerawork of Chaplin's past. "*Limelight* was slightly the more interesting of the two films photographically," Struss later recalled. "I wanted to use two cameras for every shot, which we

---

The ballet was apparently intended for this length, but only a small portion is seen in the finished film.

had done on *Dictator*, but [Chaplin] wouldn't let me do that the second time. I thought I'd help him, give him something to cut, because he had no knowledge of camera direction, his films where completely 'theater'. It was routine work with him; you'd just set up the camera and let it go and he and the other actors would play in front of it."[28]

Despite outside pressures, the unorthodox scripting, the additional musical burden and the demotion of Totheroh (by then the last of his old staff), Chaplin remarked in his autobiography, that overall, "... I had fewer qualms about [*Limelight*'s] success than any other picture I had ever made."[29] This was perhaps because the story of Calvero was so similar to what he perceived to be his own. Instead of building a narrative from bits and pieces of inspired funny business, as he had often done in the past, Chaplin was writing exclusively from his own experience to make a motion picture both deeply personal and unique. Few people viewing the film during its 1952 release could mistake the parallels between the fate of Calvero, the former star whose brightness was fading, with the fate of Chaplin, the veteran film artist.

III. THE NARRATIVE OF *LIMELIGHT*

On a summer afternoon in London, 1914, we enter the room of a young girl (Claire Bloom), seemingly asleep on the bed. However, as the camera moves closer, the distinct outline of a pill bottle can be seen in her hand. Further, the oven in her room has been left open and the gas on, with the base of the door stuffed with a towel to prevent the vapors from escaping.

Out on the street, Chaplin stumbles into the frame, noticeably drunk. He arrives at his brownstone apartment house, yet is so impaired that he has trouble negotiating the key into the doorlock. Behind him, three small street urchins watch his antics with amusement. (The children are the comedian's own — Geraldine, Michael and the toddler Josephine). Once inside, he is nearly overcome by the smell of gas from the apartment, and looks through the keyhole to survey the premises. Realizing the gravity of the situation, he breaks into the girl's room, removes her to the hallway and staggers off to find a doctor.

He returns with help, and on the orders of the local doctor (played by Chaplin's half-brother Wheeler Dryden), the girl is moved upstairs to the drunkard's modest room for rest and fresh air under his watchful eye. The drunk picks up a violin to pawn, giving him enough extra money to purchase the necessary provisions for his unexpected guest.

When he arrives back at the brownstone, he is confronted by the landlady Mrs. Alsop (Marjorie Bennett), who is upset with the condition of the girl's apartment. Attempting to help the still-inebriated Chaplin, whom she addresses as Calvero, by carrying his groceries to his room, she discovers the girl there, and is unmoved by the story of her attempted suicide. Instead, she is concerned with the rumors that will circulate, and advises him to get rid of her as soon as possible. Once alone, Calvero gathers a blanket and retreats to the couch across the room to nap underneath several pictures and billboards featuring himself—Calvero, Tramp Comedian.

In a dream, we see Calvero take the stage to perform one of his acts. Dressed as a circus ringmaster, he enters into the song "I Am an Animal Trainer," in which he eschews all other of nature's beasts in favor of training fleas. He follows the tune with his flea act, pantomiming the acrobatic contortions of his flea circus as they perform death-defying twists and acrobatics between his outstretched hands.* Unfortunately, his prize flea Phyllis escapes, and the persistent bites from another of his "pupils" chase Calvero from the stage to tumultuous laughter. But returning for his final bow, the laughter fades away, as does the expression on Calvero's face. As he squints outward toward the seats, he realizes that no one is there. Suddenly, we return to the couch were Calvero is now awake, upright in the darkened room, with the same gloomy expression he had in his dream.

In the morning, the young girl is awakened by the entering housemaid, who informs her that her "husband" is temporarily out. Calvero returns and continues the charade while the maid is present, much to the bewilderment of the groggy young girl. Once left to themselves, Calvero is able to explain that for the sake of appearances, they must feign marriage until she has fully recovered, so she is not to worry about the deception. "I've had five wives already," Calvero explains, "one more or less makes no difference to me. Moreover, I've reached the age where a platonic friendship can be sustained on the highest moral plane."

He is curious to learn the girl's story. She introduces herself as Terry Ambrose, a former dancer with the Empire Ballet. Calvero is excited since he too used to work at the Empire long ago, and is heartened that Terry recognizes him as *the* Calvero. She goes on, adding that her parents have passed away and that her only sister is in South America and has not been heard from in years. Following a severe bout of rheumatic fever, Terry has come to despair

---

*The piece harkens back to an earlier, uncompleted Chaplin film, The Professor (begun in 1919), the only known surviving portion of which is contained in the documentary Unknown Chaplin. Discarding the Tramp character altogether, Chaplin plays Professor Bosco, a flea trainer down on his luck, forced to bunk down for the evening in a flophouse. In the existing 450 feet of edited film, Chaplin systematically performs the exact routine that Calvero renders here in Limelight. Interestingly, David Robinson cites that the flea circus routine also found its way into the artist's working notes for both The Circus and The Great Dictator. (David Robinson; Chaplin: His Life and Art; pages 301, 490.) Chaplin must have been very partial to the gag, for he later lamented to an interviewer his inability to utilize the entire scenario, including the flophouse, as he had originally conceived it. (Charles Chaplin to Margaret Hinxman; "An Interview with Chaplin," from Sight and Sound, Autumn 1957; page 77.)

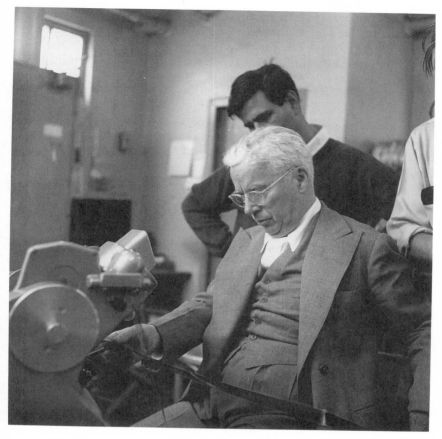

Chaplin cutting *Limelight*. Jerry Epstein stands in the background.

the sadness and apparent futility of life, though Calvero optimistically attempts to change her grim outlook.

In yet another dream, Calvero takes the stage in his shabby costume, one which seems a derivative of the Tramp's. He finds a flower, admires its beauty, then makes it a suitable meal with a quick dash of salt. He then enters into a song, extolling the virtues of spring and the love that blossoms during that season, at the conclusion of which Terry enters in her ballet costume. The pair engage in lively and flirtatious banter, with Calvero humorously reciting an "Ode to a Worm" on her behalf. As the two walk offstage together, again we hear the thunderous applause of Calvero's dream audience.

In the morning, Calvero awakens to find Terry crying. She is hysterical because she has become convinced that she will not be able to walk again. Calvero, not persuaded her ailment actually exists, recounts the miraculous things that can be done with the mind, the greatest of all man's gifts. He continues to probe and begins to sense that something else is ailing her and keeping her from dancing.

Calvero recounts for her his own disease — drinking — that made him a cripple as well. He started on the bottle to loosen up prior to performing, but the habit became so steady that it affected the quality of his shows, and led to his speedy decline as a vaudeville draw. With the theater being the only happiness he had known, he despondently took to further drinking to ease his pain — a vicious cycle that only compounded his troubles. He longs for a comeback, yet is weary of fickle public reaction. Once they had loved him dearly, but he is unsure of his ability to accept their continued rejection.

A telegram from Calvero's agent arrives, advising that a theater stint may be in the works. Despite his earlier doubts, Calvero leaps at the opportunity, confident that his new material can carry him. "Those [theater] managers have been holding out on me," Calvero vengefully remarks, "trying to break my morale. But now they want me, and now I'll make them pay — pay for all their contempt and indifference."

But at his agent's office, his enthusiasm is quickly dampened. Calvero has been offered only a week's engagement at the Middlesex Theatre, a venue where he used to headline, for a minimal salary and without his former star billing. Worse, his agent explains that the name of Calvero still carries the stigma of his failed and drunken escapades, and that the Middlesex engagement has come only as a reluctant favor from the ownership. "I've been talking Calvero to those managers for six months," he explains. "Your name is poison to them; they don't want to touch you." Calvero is indignant, clinging to his honor and star reputation. Despite what he deems as shabby treatment, he accepts the offer, but will perform under an assumed name, since his own is apparently no longer tolerable either with the management or the public.

Upon arriving back home, Calvero recalls the local doctor to examine Terry once again. He can find nothing wrong with her physically, but deduces privately that there could be some sort of psychological ailment that is preventing her from using her legs. With this in mind, Calvero returns to Terry to discover the true reason for her affliction.

Once confronted, Terry further elaborates on the story of her sister Louise, who had raised and cared for her in the absence of their mother and father. It was Louise who paid the bills, with what little that remained going toward developing Terry's talent as a dancer. One day as Terry and some of her friends were leaving the theater early, she realized how Louise had supported them for so long: They spied her prostituting herself so that Terry could pursue ballet. Terry recovered from the initial shock of discovering this truth, but it haunted her again later at the Empire, when one of the dancers who had accompanied her on that fateful day joined the company.

Calvero changes the subject to falling in love. Terry recounts her one true romantic encounter in a flashback. Taking a job at a stationery shop, she had become interested in a young patron (Chaplin's son Sydney) who frequented the shop to buy musical sheets for his compositions. Although their conversations were never more than a simple business transaction, she was nonetheless moved by his struggle to compose music while on the brink of obvious poverty, a situation that she herself, as a budding artist, identified with. Once, when she realized that he was foregoing food to pay for his music sheets, she purposely refunded more change than was due him, and the young man graciously accepted the gift. The store owner, however, discovered her charity and dismissed Terry immediately. Later, she claims, she saw the young composer from afar in the gallery of a theater. His opera was debuting and was being hailed as a success. She never saw him again.

Calvero is moved, and rhapsodizes over the scenario, as he envisions a later meeting between the two—she a gifted ballerina, he a great composer. He elegantly weaves a tale of their reunion, as they dine together on a balcony overlooking the Thames River. Once they become aware of the identity of the other, both profess their love for the other on the moonlit balcony. Terry bursts into tears, as she believes that her useless legs will prevent the dream from ever coming true, but Calvero implores her to keep fighting. Calvero leads Terry through rehabilitation. Gradually, her ability to get around improves, and she is soon awkwardly moving about the apartment under her own power.

Many evenings later, Calvero talks with Terry about his impending engagement at the Middlesex, now postponed until further notice. He speaks with the utmost confidence, expressing his full expectation of making a tremendous comeback. A notice arrives at the apartment—Calvero's calling to the Middlesex—but he declines to share the information with Terry, an indication of his private doubts about recapturing his former success.

When Calvero next takes the stage, he is not dreaming, but at the Middlesex. He painfully attempts to muster his talent, making his way through the song "The Life of a Sardine." But his act is far from polished, and his uneasiness is compounded by a cruelly cold response from the audience. They begin to exit the theater in the middle of his performance, and Calvero can do almost nothing to salvage the act. When a heckler suggests that Calvero exit the stage, he does, abandoning the bulk of his performance on opening night. Later, left to himself in the dressing room, he stares despondently in the mirror, and realizes that his former glory days are over. He is washed up.

Calvero returns to Terry and reveals that he had gone onstage that evening without telling her. As she hears of the disaster, she attempts to console him as he did her, but it is no use. His week at the Middlesex, supposedly Calvero's new beginning on the stage, has lasted no more than that half a performance; he informed the manager he will not fulfill the remainder of his engagement. "They walked out on me," Calvero laments of his hostile reception. "They haven't done that since I was a beginner. The cycle is complete."

Although Calvero blames his soberness for the poor showing, Terry will not tolerate such excuses. She rises in anger, attempting to instill in him the fiery will to persevere that Calvero had employed to help Terry believe in herself. Suddenly she stops her scolding and breaks into tears. In the heat of her anger, neither had noticed that she was standing without help, something Terry had convinced herself she could never do again.

After the passage of time, the pair are seen taking a moonlight walk on the banks of the Thames, where Terry reveals her plans. She will get a job performing, she says, bringing in the money that will support the couple. She uses the word "us" poignantly, and Calvero realizes that her bond to him has grown into something stronger than a platonic friendship.

Six months pass, and Terry has found a position as a chorus dancer at her old haunt, the Empire Theatre. Telephoning Calvero, she relays the good news of the day: Not only was she asked to audition for the lead in the Empire's upcoming ballet, but she has arranged a tryout for Calvero to play the role of a clown in the production as well.

When she arrives home at the apartment that evening, Calvero is playing the violin accompanied by several street musicians, all of whom are quite drunk. Before realizing that Terry has entered, the band strikes up a new tune under Calvero's drunken cue — "Proceed with the butchery." They halt when Calvero notices Terry. Mrs. Alsop staggers in, even more inebriated than the musicians themselves. However, Terry's arrival, not to mention the lack of remaining alcohol, has signaled an end to the festivities, and Calvero bids his guests farewell. Afterward, Terry and Calvero talk of his potential role in the ballet, which he is reluctant to take after the bitter experience at the Middlesex. Terry implores him to try.

At the Empire, Calvero enters the stage where Terry is rehearsing with the news that he has been hired to play the clown. Luckily, he has arrived in time to watch Terry's audition. Following introductions to the owner of the Empire Theatre, Mr. Postant (Nigel Bruce), Terry is introduced to pianist Ernest Neville, who is the same starving composer she had helped at the stationery shop. Though Neville is quick to recognize her, Terry struggles to be cold and detached, denying any feelings she still holds for him. She dances marvelously, and as she concludes her audition, Calvero sits quietly by himself as the group leaves the stage, mesmerized by Terry's youthful grace and talent, which only serves to drive home the futility of a continuing relationship between the two.

When Terry returns to the stage to report that she has landed the part, Calvero lauds her abilities as a ballet dancer. Impulsively, she professes her love for him. Calvero scoffs at the idea of a life together, as he knows he would only prove a burden to her and hamper her bright career.

As they prepare to leave the theater, Calvero sends Terry ahead for lunch, since he still has costuming needs to attend to. By coincidence, she enters the same restaurant as Neville and respectfully agrees to dine with him. Although

Neville is shy, he insists that they have met before, and Terry reluctantly reveals herself. They share recollections of their meetings, and Neville gives every indication that he shares the same romantic memories that Terry had previously related to Calvero. Struggling with her feelings, she announces to Neville that she will be marrying soon. Neville is taken aback, but politely expresses his happiness for her.

Later, as rehearsals begin for the ballet, Bodalink (Norman Lloyd), coordinating the Empire's production, begins to describe the setting to the dancers as the scene moves into the actual performance, and we see Columbine, played by Terry, lying on her deathbed, surrounded by clowns who attempt to raise her spirits with their comic business. However, it is no use, and as a last dying wish, the clowns carry her bed closer toward the window so that she may have one final look outside. When the bed is returned, Columbine has already passed away. The following scene shows Columbine's lover before her gravestone, attempting to resurrect his lost love with the help of a magic wand. Just as he loses hope of ever seeing her again, Columbine's spirit appears, and the lovers are able to share one last romantic dance together.

We next move to opening night of the ballet, and as the finale nears, Terry is suddenly seized with fear, claiming once again that her legs will fail her. Calvero, realizing that drastic measures are called for, scolds and slaps her, and she obediently takes the stage, giving a final dance that caps a brilliant performance. To the deafening roar of the Empire crowd, Terry races offstage in tears and into the arms of Calvero, her savior who has brought her — finally — to this moment of personal glory.

At the post-performance dinner, however, Terry is unable to locate Calvero, who opted instead to drink in a nearby bar, leaving her to socialize with, among others, Neville. He accompanies her to the modest brownstone and, as the young couple part at the front door, he implores Terry to recognize the futility of her devotion to Calvero, that he can only be an encumbrance to her and her budding career. Although Neville will soon be forced to leave for service in World War I, he expresses his deep love for Terry; she is torn, her resolve to love Calvero obviously weakening. Yet Terry remains devoted to the old comedian, and resists the temptation to be with Neville. Neither is aware that Calvero passed out from drink directly inside the front door of the brownstone, and has awakened in time to overhear the conversation. Quietly, he stumbles back to the apartment so that Terry will not know of his presence.

The following day, Calvero reads the glowing reviews of Terry's performance aloud from the paper, yet Terry is distant and musters only tears in response. In a seemingly last-ditch effort she begs Calvero to run away with her to marry — hoping, perhaps, that this will firmly exorcise her growing affection for Neville. Calvero, now aware of the identity of the young composer, reminds her of the romantic interlude he had earlier predicted.

Meanwhile, back at the Empire, Mr. Postant expresses his great satisfaction with the ballet, but wishes to make a minor alteration: Replacing one of the clowns with another actor. "I don't care if he's Calvero himself, he isn't funny." When it is revealed that the clown *is* Calvero playing under another name, Mr. Postant reconsiders; he is sympathetic to the obvious hard times that the once-famous comedian must be facing. Since Postant had already contacted the casting agency, he quickly phones them again to save the replacement actor the futile trip to the Empire.

He is, however, too late. Later that day, as Calvero leaves through the stage doors, he runs across an old friend and fellow music hall veteran named Griffin. Without knowing he is talking about Calvero, Griffin explains the reason for his visit to the theater, noting the inadequacy of the actor currently playing the clown. Calvero is polite, hiding the sadness of his setback, and wishes his old friend the best of luck during his audition. A failure now at too many endeavors, Calvero makes the decision to leave altogether, with only a note left behind to explain his absence to Terry.

Time passes, and we next see Calvero plying his trade with the street musicians seen previously in his apartment. Clad in an outrageous suit, complete with tails and a top hat, he wanders into the saloon outside of which he had been playing for donations. One patron is Neville, recently returned from military service. Pleasantries are exchanged, but predictably the conversation leads to Terry. Neville reveals they have been seeing much of each other, and Calvero seems pleased that the two are fulfilling his earlier prophecy. Mr. Postant arrives in the saloon to meet Neville, and is also taken aback by Calvero's meager profession. Calvero, however, is unashamed. "All the world's a stage; this one's the most legitimate ... there's something I like about the streets — it's the tramp in me, I suppose." Calvero takes leave of the two, but not before instructing Neville to conceal their meeting from Terry so as not to upset her.

This he does, but it is not long before Terry spots Calvero from a passing car. They reconcile, with Calvero noting that his absence had actually been a blessing for her. She is unsuccessful in persuading him to return, but piques his interest in performing onstage one last time, at a benefit performance in his honor at the Empire. Although shunning the idea at first, since Calvero knows the crowd would be patronizing, he realizes that it would provide a good opportunity to present some new material he has been working on. Terry sets out to secure Calvero a position at the Empire once again.

On the night of the benefit, Terry expresses her nervous anticipation to Mr. Postant. Surely another failure would break Calvero for good. But he assures her that the audience will be sympathetic, for they are interested in celebrating Calvero's long career and will be quite generous with their applause.

Nestled in the dressing room with his comedic partner, played by fellow silent comedian and real-life music hall veteran Buster Keaton (in their only

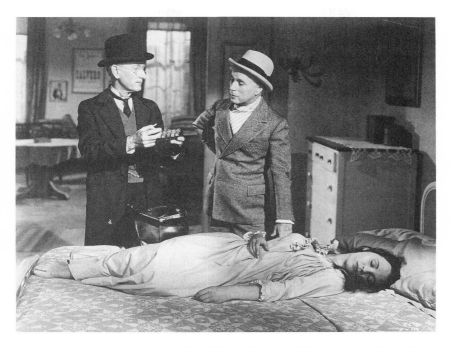

Calvero with the local physician (Chaplin's half-brother Wheeler Dryden) and Terry, from *Limelight.*

screen appearance together), Calvero readies himself for the upcoming performance. Person after person enters to wish them luck and remind the pair of former days; the constant stream drives Buster from the dressing room in order to keep his sanity. Left alone, Calvero retrieves a hidden liquor bottle, again displaying his lack of confidence. Terry enters to wish him luck, and Calvero is not afraid to admit to his drinking. Although she is dismayed, she too feels the anxiety of the evening and chooses to watch his performance nervously from the wings. Just as Calvero makes his entrance, she is overcome with emotion and tearfully races to her dressing room, unable to bear the suspense.

Like his earlier dream, Calvero begins with the flea circus and "I Am an Animal Trainer," this time receiving much more than imaginary applause. Terry, unable to resist the temptation, peers from her quiet dressing room long enough to hear the theater's enthusiastic reaction and returns to her seat, crying out in a cathartic release of relief and happiness.

After Calvero finishes the tune "The Life of a Sardine," which had so badly bombed at the Middlesex, it appears that he will be forced to shorten his performance; he has gone three minutes over schedule already. Over the thunderous applause out front, Calvero heatedly protests in the wings of the Empire that he is not being give the opportunity to present his entire act. It is only an angry phone call from Mr. Postant demanding that Calvero return to the stage for an encore that Keaton and Chaplin are allowed to engage in their act, a dual game of comic one-upsmanship.

The pair enter the stage for a musical number, Calvero a grotesquely stout violinist and Keaton a near-sighted pianist, complete with Coke-bottle glasses. The pair start by tuning their instruments, though difficulties befall them both; the enormity of Calvero's false stomach gives the illusion that one of his legs is miraculously shrinking in length.

Keaton, meanwhile, is engrossed with his own problem of attempting to keep his musical sheets together long enough to perform. Then the piano wires spring apart, requiring an investigation by both comedians, which results in Keaton inadvertently crushing Calvero's violin underfoot. All is not lost, however, as Calvero simply pulls another instrument from his trousers.

Their song finally begins, working itself into a feverish pitch of musical dexterity (though Chaplin himself played the violin, this tune was dubbed into the film). But the number ends violently for both comedians — Keaton is thrown from his piano stool and Calvero falls into the orchestra pit, his backside lodged in a drum. Calvero is lifted from the stage to the wings of the theater, all to the enthusiastic applause of the capacity house.

It is only when the drum is set down that the crew realizes that Calvero has a problem which, he remarks, must be his back. He is lifted back to the stage to thank his appreciative audience, but is quickly shuttled to a nearby room, where the crew removes the drum and places him on a prop couch. Mr. Postant arrives to congratulate Calvero, only to find a doctor explaining that the problem is not Calvero's back at all — he has had a heart attack. Postant, flanked by Neville and Terry, rush to Calvero's side.

Calvero implores Terry to take the stage and complete her performance. Sadly but obediently, she follows his instructions. He then asks Neville and the surrounding stage hands to bring the couch into the wings so that he can watch Terry dance. Paralleling the "Death of Columbine" ballet seen earlier, the couch is transported to grant his dying wish, but Calvero is unable to cling to life long enough to see Terry complete her performance. As Terry dances before the audience, Neville and the stage hands gently place a sheet over Calvero's head. Finally, as *Limelight*'s introduction proclaimed, old age has given away to youth.

IV. LIFE THROUGH THE LENS

If a hundred years from now we come across *Limelight* and no record of either Chaplin or his works, that face of his, the deep melancholy of those eyes, would still be enough to tell us that from beyond the grave a man is

talking to us about himself, and that he is calling us to witness his life
because it too is life, our life.[30]
— André Bazin

Asked whether or not the new picture is autobiographical, Chaplin smiles.
"Everything is autobiographical," he says with an eloquent movement of
his small hands, "but don't make too much of that."[31]
— Chaplin to Richard Lauterbach — 1950

Limelight was a compendium of personal and emotional experiences for
Chaplin. Page after page could be devoted to a discussion of the autobiographical references and influences alone. *Limelight* is simply, and most
straightforwardly, the most introspective work that Chaplin undertook
throughout his career. Following the failure of *Monsieur Verdoux*, *Limelight*
proves beyond a doubt that Chaplin had taken to reassessing the bulk of his
cinematic career and his prospects for remaining a star. *Limelight* was the vehicle in which Chaplin put his personal, and perhaps final stamp upon the trajectory of his cinematic career, celebrating his role as a creator and, through
the screen conduit of Calvero, evoking sympathy for the unfair persecution he
felt he was enduring in a conservative United States.

That there are connections between the film and Chaplin in real life is
obvious. The question is how much of the material is directly associated to
Chaplin's own experiences. Initial press regarding *Limelight* found Chaplin
downplaying such correlations, as with his comments to journalist Richard
Lauterbach above.

It's a thin facade that Chaplin maintained for the rest of his life. Even in
his memoirs, *My Autobiography*, Chaplin insists that the true inspiration for
the film came from the tragic downfall of former vaudeville comic Frank Tinney, whom Chaplin had seen early in his own vaudeville career.[32] Upon their
last meeting, some years later, Chaplin noted that Tinney had become very
self-conscious as a performer, and had lost the comic inspiration that catapulted
him to fame. So, too, is the scenario similar to Chaplin's recollection of the
vaudeville clown Marcelline, whom Chaplin claims to have seen years later as
a virtually unknown performer in a traveling circus.

But *My Autobiography* contains an even more telling reference to Calvero's
inspiration. As a young boy performing as a clog dancer in the Eight Lancashire
Lads, Chaplin recalls dancing in a benefit similar to the one Calvero performed
in, this one also on behalf of an aging, alcoholic music hall veteran — his own
father, Charles Chaplin, Sr. "The night of the benefit," he recalled, "my father
appeared on the stage breathing with difficulty, and with painful effort made a
speech. I stood at the side of the stage watching him, not realizing that he was
a dying man."[33] Like Postant did for Calvero, the music hall industry had gathered around one of its own to celebrate the talents of a down-and-out colleague.
The similarities between Calvero and Charles, Sr., are quite clear, and as the
comedian seems to have held only fond memories of his father, despite the

many less-than-stellar traits that kept him out of young Charlie's life, it seems consistent that he would treat the decline of his screen vaudevillian with the dignity with which he wished to perceive Charles, Sr.'s, final days. Chaplin's memory of his father almost certainly had a strong influence in the development of the tragic, alcoholic film character.

But aside from the vaudeville backdrop and the alcoholism of Calvero, there is certainly no mistaking the fact that Chaplin's own life, moreso than the experiences of Tinney, Marcelline or his father, played the most pivotal role in the shaping of Calvero. In his memoirs, Chaplin described Calvero as a man who "grew old and introspective and acquired a feeling of dignity, and this divorced him of all intimacy with the audience."[34]* The assertion carries obvious relevance to the comedian's own personal situation, especially considering his move away from traditionally comic themes in his pictures, and into topics of a more serious political and social nature.

Other factors demonstrated how personal *Limelight* was. The presence of Chaplin's son Sydney as Neville, Charlie, Jr., as one of the clowns in the ballet, Geraldine, Michael and Josephine in the opening sequence and even Oona (who doubled for Claire Bloom during a few retakes when the actress was unavailable) perhaps signaled some sort of visible closure to Chaplin's career. Though he had often spoken of retiring from the screen, even Charles, Jr., seemed to sense that perhaps his father was more serious this time when he privately expressed that *Limelight* was to be his last picture.[35] For all involved, from Chaplin's closest associates to the audience themselves, it was clear that they were seeing something very intimate, very personal, and — at this moment in time — very Chaplin.

More a tragedy than comedy, *Limelight* was Chaplin's effort to be critically and popularly accepted once again. Reporters at the *Verdoux* press conference vocally lamented the demise of the Little Fellow as a screen character. Though Chaplin could not bring him back to life, at least with respect to a new film, he could detail the experiences of the Tramp's creator. *Limelight* was Chaplin's attempt to return to his glory of old, not by employing the Tramp, but by placing the film's appeal partly on the comedian's own cinematic legacy, and partly on the recent destruction of his own stardom. As André Bazin noted, "... Calvero exists 'only for the others'. He knows only himself as reflected through the public mirror. Chaplin ... assert[s] only that the artist is incomplete without his public ..."[36] Given Chaplin's withdrawal from the public spotlight late in 1948, *Limelight* serves as the celebration for a notable entertainment figure, perhaps much in the fashion of the benefit performances for Charles, Sr., or for Calvero.

---

*"As a man gets on in years he wants to live deeply," Calvero expresses in the film. "A sad feeling of dignity comes upon him, and that's fatal for a comic.... [Eventually] I lost contact with the audience — I couldn't warm up to them."

V. A RETURN TO OLDER THEMES

Unlike *Modern Times, The Great Dictator* and *Monsieur Verdoux,* films that departed from Chaplin's traditional thematic structure, *Limelight* offers the return to a more recognizable and, to the critics of 1952, perhaps more tolerable form of Chaplin feature. With *Limelight,* he comes the closest to fulfilling Charles Maland's aesthetic contract since *City Lights.* The Tramp is absent, yet what remains is nonetheless closely linked to the Little Fellow and his misadventures on the silver screen.

Foremost, *Limelight* exhibits Chaplin's most overt use of pathos in two decades. Calvero is clearly designed to capitalize on the memory of Charlie and Charlie's creator, whose contributions to comedy and the performing arts, like Calvero's, had been seemingly forgotten with the passage of time. Where once he had commanded top billing and top dollar, Calvero now cannot escape the effects of the latent evil — alcohol (or perhaps in Chaplin's case, scandal), which seems to have irreparably damaged his career. The magic of his creative youth may have escaped him and, though he continues to create comic scenarios, he does so knowing the public has proven unreliable. Considering the negative comments of his theatrical agent, Calvero seems to be equally as infamous for his downfall as he was famous for his performances. Naturally, he feels that his art will rise above his tarnished persona (hence the willingness to play at the Middlesex and the Empire, even under an assumed name), yet must still overcome the burdens that have been placed upon him, with little guarantee that his public reconciliation will be embraced.

Thus, we cannot escape Chaplin's use of Calvero as an emotional surrogate. As many reviewers and scholars have noted, *Limelight* overflows with a melancholy aura, seeking to extract unabashed emotion concerning an artist's struggle to compete against the fickleness of the general public, where the loved can become the unloved virtually overnight. Chaplin wants to cash in on his many years of public adulation in order to shame his current critics and reap (at least what he felt to be) his just due as an artist. For all he has offered the world through his film work, Chaplin seems to say, there should be a more appropriate exit than the humiliating decline he was then enduring in his adopted country.

Yet despite creating pathos for himself through the story of Calvero, the situations of Chaplin and his new film character reveal that they weren't exactly parallel — a fact not missed by hostile critics, who viewed the film's melodramatic nature as another display of the comedian's egotism. Whereas Calvero was clearly desecrated as a man — penniless, hungry and without much hope of regaining success in the only trade he knew — certainly no one could say the same of Chaplin himself. He may have lost touch with the bulk of the American public, but he was certainly not penniless, hungry or without his ardent supporters worldwide. Nearly a decade of negative press had taken its toll, certainly, but Chaplin clearly was not a ruined man in the sense that Calvero was. Further, many of Chaplin's critics were not about to soften their feelings on him simply through the premise of the film.

Aside from pathos, romance, too, found a more prominent role in *Limelight* than in his previous three releases. Specifically, the blossoming love between Terry and Calvero seems to mesh more closely with the Little Fellow's romantic constructions from both *The Circus* and *City Lights*. And, as he did previously in *Modern Times*, Chaplin's story not only fashioned a coupling based on mutual dependence, but allowed him to even address some of his more publicly-known misconceptions about his own morality as well.

Chaplin felt that the role of Terry necessitated the selection of a near-perfect actress, which led him to interview several possible candidates from February to late August of 1951. Playwright Arthur Laurents recommended stage actress Claire Bloom, then only 20 years of age, who was already earning a number of excellent notices in London for her stage work. In late April, Bloom flew to New York to meet with Chaplin for a week's worth of rehearsals, accompanied by her mother. "He had insisted I bring my mother as chaperon," Bloom later recalled. "He didn't want any more trouble in the press regarding another young actress — which was very nice for me and extraordinary for her."[37]

Chaplin affectionately recounted the narrative of *Limelight* for her during the auditions, as well as many recollections from his boyhood in London and on the English Music Hall circuit; she could tell these memories had a deep and significant meaning for him. Following her week with Chaplin, she departed for England with the knowledge that she would hear back from the Chaplin Studios shortly.

But she didn't. Chaplin was taken with her audition, but he continued to interview other young women as well, looking for the perfect fit for the part. Finally, after months without a word, Chaplin finally decided on Bloom, and she and her mother flew to Los Angeles in late September of 1951 to commence her work at the Chaplin Studios. *Limelight's* significance owes a great deal to Bloom's strong performance in the role of Terry which, next to Paulette Goddard's Gamin in *Modern Times*, is one of the most well-developed female characters in all of Chaplin's filmography.

As for Bloom's character, Terry's situation invites comparisons to both *City Lights* and *Monsieur Verdoux*. Like the Blind Girl and Verdoux's wife Mona, Terry is afflicted by a crippling ailment which Chaplin's character feels compelled to nurse. Calvero's pawning of a violin to support the girl finds a parallel in Charlie's attempts to earn money to aid the Blind Girl, as it does in Verdoux's "work" to support his wife and son. Both relationships have been built upon the willingness of Chaplin's character to help within his capacity, an element of a greater inner bond that Charlie, Verdoux and Calvero feel toward their particular love interests. Although Mona would eventually become a casualty of Verdoux's cynical world, both the Blind Girl and Terry are able to benefit from this care and attention, and find a new and prosperous life outside of their temporary ailments.

But Chaplin's construction of the relationship between Terry and Calvero is somewhat different than in films past. In the case of the Blind Girl, Charlie's efforts to raise money for her leads him down an uncertain romantic path, leaving the final outcome of their "face-to-face" meeting in mystery. Similarly, Verdoux's relationship with Mona is not in the pursuit of love, but focuses on the lengths an individual will go to support and nurture love though unstable times.

With Terry, Chaplin makes overtures to shun love rather than encourage or maintain it. The romance in *Limelight* carries similarities to the love scenes in *The Circus*; specifically the capitulation of the Chaplin character from pursuing love into playing the role of matchmaker between the girl and Chaplin's rival. In *The Circus*, this was Rex the tightrope walker, and in *Limelight*, Neville the composer.[38]

Yet another significant scene in *Limelight* that links it with *The Circus* is Chaplin's use of an "overhearing" scene: Calvero, behind the door of the brownstone, listens while Terry and Neville talk of their relationship directly outside. In a similar scene in *The Circus*, the Little Fellow learns the "dark, handsome stranger" a fortune teller predicted Merna would marry is not himself, but Rex. The situation is slightly altered in this case — whereas the Tramp actively worked to unite Merna and Rex, Calvero's method of help is to disappear from Terry's life altogether.

While Calvero no doubt is attracted to Terry and her youthful vibrance, deep down he also realizes the foolishness of pursuing that desire, and the inevitable failure that would follow. There is no doubt that the prospects of nurturing Terry back to health and helping her in her career was very appealing to Calvero. His second dream sequence contains ample evidence of his growing affections for her, considering the nature of their flirtatious banter. The very nature of the dream is two-fold; Calvero longs to see himself and Terry performing again, and no doubt wishes he could engage in a romance with the young girl. But Calvero also knows that such thoughts are merely a selfish reflection of his own desires. What he recognizes (and what Terry tries so valiantly to hide) is that their relationship could never be idyllic. Though he has cared for her, nurtured her through her illness and played an integral part in her return to the Empire Ballet, they have reached the apex of their relationship. Terry has the entire world at her doorstep — her skills and talents as a ballerina will carry her to lofty heights, if only, Calvero recognizes, she will let go of her burdensome attraction to the old comedian's kindness. Again, the romance depicts themes previously developed in *City Lights*, for when the nurturing roles are reversed, leaving Chaplin's character the worse off, each girl seems to feel an obligation to offer help and encouragement.[39] In this case, however, the Chaplin character will have none of it; Calvero recognizes that Terry and Neville could have the type of loving relationship that would be

Chaplin as vaudeville performer, from *Limelight* (1952). With Buster Keaton.

impossible between himself and the girl, and he is not about to spoil the fulfillment of her dreams.

One interesting note in the Terry/Calvero relationship is the incongruence between the romantic themes onscreen and Chaplin's offscreen lifestyle. Though it is widely regarded that Oona was an extremely stable and positive influence during the remainder of Chaplin's life, their personal relationship bears a striking similarity to the sort of relationship Calvero seeks to avoid in the film. Once a budding actress, Oona quickly gave up her desire to perform after marrying her 54-year-old husband, finding solace in devoting herself to being a wife and mother to the couple's rapidly growing family. However, it is nonetheless interesting that Calvero would find such a liaison futile, while Chaplin himself would not.

In terms of comedy, Chaplin only marginally embodied the characteristics of his past films. Since discarding the character of the Tramp, he had evolved his comedic style uniquely to fit his subject matter, a change that contributed to many critics' longing for the Charlie Chaplin of old. *The Great Dictator* worked its comedy from pure satire, yet remained closely rooted to the slapstick style Chaplin had produced in the past. With *Monsieur Verdoux*, Chaplin moved from outright satire to a more dark, ironic and witty use of verbal humor. While *Verdoux* is certainly a comedy, its underlying social fabric had distanced itself from the sort of comedic style one could have expected from an earlier Chaplin feature.

Limelight, in yet another gentle twist, found much of its humor stemming from pathos, or the tragic elements of the story, and therefore the picture appears hardly comic at all. The segment featuring Chaplin and Keaton is the most overtly comedic sequence, though its appeal was in the type of humor that Calvero/Chaplin had created in the past.* But Chaplin's clear emphasis in the film, much to the chagrin of some critics, was the tragic overtones of Calvero's story, stressing the pathos (and to a degree, even the romance) of the narrative rather than create a film with a prominent comedic feel.

Calvero's vaudeville performances, the most distinctive places for Chaplin to inject comedy into the film, underscore this point. He clearly utilizes the scenes to emphasize the narrative's tragic circumstances, particularly Calvero's dream sequences in which his acts fail so miserably. These scenes bring to mind Walter Kerr's commentary on *The Circus*, where Chaplin emphasized a comedic storyline requiring the Tramp to be patently unfunny as a circus clown, but humorous when not performing.[40] In *Limelight*'s similar treatment, Chaplin must perform authentic comedic sequences designed not so much to make the audience laugh but empathize the degree to which Calvero has fallen. It is not until the film's final moments in the benefit performance at the Empire (namely the Chaplin/Keaton sequence), that Calvero's stage presence becomes energized and his shenanigans take on a particularly funny appearance. So as far as comedy was concerned, Chaplin's use of humor is significantly absent in *Limelight*.

Part of the problem with this final stage act, in fact, may have been Chaplin's decision to leave it virtually silent. The sequence is a derivative of one Chaplin previously used in his 1916 Mutual film *The Vagabond*. In that two-reeler, the Little Fellow is a traveling musician playing his violin for money in saloons, as Calvero does late in *Limelight*. One day out in the country he comes upon an abused gypsy girl (Edna Purviance) and for her enjoyment plays a frenzied piece of music that ultimately sends him tumbling into a nearby barrel.

That scene in *The Vagabond*, of course, relied on the comic antics of Charlie to generate laughter. He utilized the same principle when building upon the situation for *Limelight*, despite the fact that the comic song is being performed before a packed theater audience onscreen. "During dubbing," Jerry Epstein remembered, "Charlie refused to put any audience reaction to the Chaplin-Keaton scene. I couldn't understand why. He said the real audience watching the film would supply the laughter. 'What if the film's showing at a matinee to a half-empty house?' I said. 'Won't it sound strange, playing the scene in complete silence?' He looked at me peeved. But that was Charlie. He was law unto himself. He made the rules, and he enjoyed breaking them."[41] Epstein's

---

Keaton, too, was a veteran of the vaudeville circuit, having travelled with his mother and father for many years as a knockabout troupe called "The Three Keatons."

comment highlights Chaplin's unwillingness to gear *Limelight*'s comedic elements, generally the main attraction in every one of his releases, for the audience. Naturally, his assumption was that the film would be playing to packed houses everywhere.

Ironically, the Chaplin/Keaton sequence, perhaps the film's most memorable comedic moment, has been the subject of some debate. Discarding Chaplin's newfound working methods, improvisation seems to have been brought back onto the set, as the two comedic virtuosos each expanded on Chaplin's comic outline. Disputes have risen on exactly how much of Buster's performance was cut from the film. Keaton biographer Tom Dardis quotes James Agee's wife Mia (who was on the set with her husband) as saying that most of Buster's antics found their way to the cutting room floor.[42] Co-star Claire Bloom also alludes to the fact that many of Keaton's gags were cut, though she seems to feel that Chaplin was right in not including all of Buster's material in the final print.[43]

Chaplin biographers have tended to be more sympathetic toward the editing of this sequence. Jerry Epstein has a unique perspective on the event, since he was present in the cutting room at the time:

> I was with Charlie the entire editing of the film; I never left his side. On that sequence, we must have had enough footage to release at least five complete pictures. The problem was weeding out and making sense of the best things in both their performances. Of course, Charlie cut some of Keaton's gags. If he didn't, the picture would have run forever. But he cut just as many of his own best laughs ... [Chaplin] said, "You've got to keep the narrative going. You can't stop the picture for this one scene."[44]*

It is interesting to note that Chaplin makes no reference in his memoirs to Buster's presence in *Limelight*. Likewise, Keaton does not discuss the sequence in his autobiography, instead concentrating on Chaplin's negative comments about television, the medium that was helping to bring about Keaton's resurgence as a comedian.[45]

Many of Keaton's antics may have never seen the light of day in the finished film, but the scene is designed not only to recapture the lost art of vaudeville comedy, but to demonstrate the type of routine that first brought Calvero his fame. The context of its placement, during the benefit performance, naturally lent itself to showcase Calvero's talent as opposed to that of his partner's. Epstein's account of the cutting (with Chaplin's remarks) may not satisfy fans

---

Chaplin may have a point with this comment. Brownlow and Gill's Unknown Chaplin *series, Volume III — "Hidden Treasures" is devoted almost exclusively to material Chaplin shot but never used. The second version of* City Lights *opening, the flea circus act from* The Professor *that later became part of* Limelight *and a hilarious shadow pantomime of the Little Fellow's military exam from* Shoulder Arms *are among the many inspired pieces summarily discarded by Chaplin — all, ostensibly, based on logic similar to this.*

of Keaton's talents, but it does recognize the dramatic intent of the sequence. Since *Limelight* has often been characterized by Chaplin's detractors as an egotistical homage to himself, certainly an observation not altogether unwarranted, the Chaplin/Keaton comedy routine has often served as a key element in this argument.

But aside from the pairing of the two comedic greats, there are few instances of vintage Chaplin comedy within the film. One is when Calvero seeks a pressed pair of pants early in the film; he has no further to go than between the mattresses of his bed, where his trousers remain perfectly pressed under the occupant's weight. At another point, during Calvero's whimsical pantomime for Terry's amusement, he imitates a Japanese bonsai tree, another playful moment out of Chaplin's comedic past. However, the treatment of the material differs from earlier films, and renders both gags almost invisible in the greater context of each scene. Chaplin breathes no energy into retrieving his trousers, treating Calvero's actions as merely an aside, with no effort to milk the comedic potential. And though his pantomimed imitations are certainly amusing, they are — as with similar gags — lost in the maze of establishing dialogue during the first quarter of the film. Chaplin's emphasis on tragedy and pathos, dependent on this lengthy set-up, distinctly undermined the comedic aspects of the film, a point which many critics found disconcerting.

VI. PROMOTION & RESPONSE TO *LIMELIGHT*

At the moment talkies are popular. But in my productions, the spoken word will always be held to a strict minimum. Sounds, exclamations — yes. They express better than anything else the real and the natural. But the least possible amount of useless talk.[46]

— Charles Chaplin — 1932

The ideal talkie has not been made yet; it won't be until we discover the *limitations* of sound. We can't say the formula is less talk and more action, or more talk and less action, or anything else. It depends on what the subject matter calls for.[47]

— Charles Chaplin — 1947

What sets *Limelight* completely apart from the Chaplin tradition, and what damages it most seriously, is not its pretentious flirtation with weight, but its hopeless capitulation to words.... From the first reel of *Limelight* it is perfectly clear that Chaplin now wants to talk, that he *loves* to talk, that in this film he intends to do little *but* talk.[48]

— Walter Kerr

In gearing for the release of *Limelight*, Chaplin took greater care in addressing promotional aspects than he had with *Monsieur Verdoux*. Perhaps recognizing his earlier mistake, *Limelight* more closely followed the pattern of Chaplin's early films through *The Great Dictator*.

Advance word focused on the sentimental aspects of the story. There was an immediate linkage between the trajectory of Chaplin's own career and the plight of Calvero, one which Chaplin sought, often unconvincingly, to downplay. As with his so-called resistance to sound, Chaplin's public statements and the reality of his professional work were sometimes two very different things.

The build-up to the release played off the belief that *Limelight* could be Chaplin's last film — one that would bring closure to his long and distinguished career. It was a distinctly different type of anticipation than for any other of Chaplin's works during the sound era. Previously, with *Monsieur Verdoux, The Great Dictator*, and *Modern Times*, the political and/or social aspects of each project tended to dominate early press reports. With *City Lights*, the film which *Limelight* resembles the most thematically, interest was piqued by Chaplin's refusal to embrace full sound technology. But with *Limelight*, for the first time during the sound era, a Chaplin film contained no controversial aspects technically, politically or socially.

Part of this may be due to the softening of Chaplin's image following *Monsieur Verdoux*, particularly with respect to the re-release of *City Lights* in 1950. As we will see later, re-releasing his older films provided him both with a handsome revenue source and an excellent public relations tool. Not only could the films attract new fans, but they could also divert the hostility of vocal critics. Though the re-release of *City Lights* appears not to have been an intentional move with respect to promoting *Limelight*, it nonetheless served an important service in reminding some audiences of Chaplin's rich cinematic history.

In the print media, Chaplin was even more overt in attempting to redefine his public image prior to *Limelight*'s release. One magazine article is particularly worthy of note. *Life* did an eleven page photographic spread in its March 17, 1952, edition, entitled "Chaplin at Work." Primarily taken during the production of *Limelight*, the pictures highlight Chaplin's working methods at the time, particularly his hands-on method of acting out every part for his cast personally. Several photos were also taken at the Chaplin mansion on Summit Drive, in the company of Oona and their family.[49]

The photos are significant for two reasons. First, the look into *Limelight*'s production helped emphasize his role as an artist. The photos highlighted his creative drive and vision in producing the film, with the depiction of his working methods demonstrating his perfectionist drive. Given the general secrecy that surrounded the shooting of *Modern Times, The Great Dictator* and *Monsieur Verdoux*, the photos also signify a new openness by the comedian which had as much to do with its autobiographical nature of the picture as the necessity for Chaplin — and United Artists — to avoid another publicity fiasco like *Verdoux*.

Second, the photos taken at Summit Drive portray Chaplin as a family man. After his marriage to an 18-year-old Oona, followed shortly afterward by the lengthy Joan Barry trials, the purpose here was clearly to align himself with the more conservative values of the early 1950s. Unlike many of the comedian's previous relationships, the bond between Oona and Chaplin had grown exceptionally strong, and his newfound domesticity was a welcome respite from the troubles that had plagued him. "If only I had known Oona or a girl like her long ago," he once remarked to Charles, Jr., "I would never have had any problems with women. All my life I have been waiting for her without even realizing it until I met her."[50]

Despite their wealth and status, the Chaplins appeared on the pages of *Life* as having the same concerns as all parents: That their children — Geraldine, Michael, and newest editions Josephine (born March 28, 1949) and Victoria (born May 19, 1951) — were brought up in a safe, loving environment, with the best their parents could provide for them. In this sense, the photoshoot attempts to dispel notions about Chaplin's high lifestyle or immorality. Judging from the magazine spread, he was, for all practical purposes, just a man devoted to his family and his career, who just happened to be one of the world's most famous entertainers as well.

Despite these efforts, however, critical reaction to *Limelight* was somewhat mixed. Walter Kerr's observation of Chaplin's newfound penchant for dialogue was a typical bone of contention; commentators of the 1950s and today have lamented the film's many talkative sequences. The abundance of dialogue in *Limelight* was a sharp contrast to anything Chaplin had produced in his career, including *Monsieur Verdoux*, which relied primarily on verbal humor. Not only was the film essentially a tragedy, almost devoid of comedy, but it was prolific with words, particularly in the opening reels while establishing the backgrounds of Terry and Calvero. Like the Barber and Verdoux, Chaplin's Calvero seemed to have something to say to the audience, but instead of mounting a rostrum at the end of the film, he brought his speeches to the screen soon after the opening credits.

Though most reviews were mixed to good, respectful of Chaplin and his intentions, even the most sympathetic critics found the picture's talkiness a detriment.

Several reviewers felt the whole of Chaplin's accomplishment and its importance to the body of his work outweighed the obvious flaws. J.L. Tallenay was one:

> [*Limelight's*] construction involves instances of ineptness: the entire first part of the film is broken up by long monologues on the part of Calvero, and the dramatic action takes too long to get under way. Finally, although it is fictitious, the film has a number of sequences that sound a personal and autobiographical note which may strike some people as discordant.

But despite these seeming weaknesses, and perhaps even because of them, *Limelight* is a major work of extraordinary richness and unprecedented originality.[51]

André Bazin would make similar observations.

Almost everybody praises the second half, but many deplore the *longueurs* of the first half. However, if one were truly responsive to the last 24 minutes of the film, in retrospect one could not imagine a different opening.... I have seen *Limelight* three times and I admit I was bored three times, not always in the same places. Also, I never wished for any shortening of this period of boredom. It was rather a relaxing of attention that left my mind free to wander — a daydreaming about the images.... I see that this phenomenon and the special nature of periodical boredom have a common cause, namely that the structure of *Limelight* is more musical than dramatic.[52]

Generally, American reviews of *Limelight* (where it opened in New York during October of 1952 prior to a wider release scheduled for January 1953) emphasized what Charles Maland called the "great artist" approach.[53] This was that *Limelight*, or any Chaplin release for that matter, was significant due to Chaplin's status as a world-renowned artist, and that its heavily autobiographical nature (noted by virtually all reviewers regardless of their relative like or dislike of the picture) vaulted the film to importance. The emphasis on tragedy may have caught many commentators offguard; supporters like Bosley Crowther of the *New York Times*, for one, in a somewhat tentative review, called the film moving, but stopped short of calling it great.[54] Others didn't hesitate to attack the comedian's latest project. "... [The] real vitality of Chaplin is absent from much of the film," Eric Bentley maintained, and "instead we have the *ersatz* of sentimentality. He can't see for the crocodile tears."[55] (Published almost a month after the picture's debut, Bentley's comments, as we shall see, show how changing events in Chaplin's personal life just prior to the release of *Limelight* had a profound effect on how the film was received in America, and to some extent, in Europe, where Chaplin would tour as he had with *City Lights*.)

Most critics, even those who disliked *Limelight*, recognized that it was to hold a special place in Chaplin's filmography. The film did not feature the Charlie character, as some had hoped for following the release of *Monsieur Verdoux*, but had certainly departed from his recent trend toward charged political and social themes. While the Tramp didn't return, it seemed that Chaplin the artist had, and even though some considered it a flawed effort, it was nonetheless greeted with respect.

What is clear today is that *Limelight* attains its importance due to the presence of Chaplin and the personal troubles he was facing at the time. "*Limelight*," Gerald Mast shrewdly observed, "is probably a better film in light of the 40 year career that went before it and the public animosity that Chaplin was himself suffering at the time than it is as a single work of art. It is one of those reminders that the totality of Chaplin's work is more impressive than any individual film."[56]

Unfortunately, the public animosity Mast refers to was not yet over for the comedian. Though the picture, in some respects, can be considered part of a public reconciliation, *Limelight* would end up being a casualty of the continuing furor surrounding Charles Chaplin.

7

A King in New York

Chaplin first previewed *Limelight* on August 2, 1952, to an enthusiastic crowd of Hollywood luminaries at the Paramount Theatre in Los Angeles. The timing of the preview was unusual, as the film wasn't slated for wide-scale distribution in the United States until January of 1953. Chaplin, however, was readying himself for an earlier round of premieres, the first to take place in the heart of Calvero's world — London.

As he had wished to do some four years earlier, the comedian made preparations to travel to Europe accompanied by his family. Oona and the children had never been to England, and Chaplin was eager to show them the place that had so influenced him as a youth.

Also, as *Limelight* was not a typical Chaplin film, with its emphasis on tragedy rather than comedy, touring was perhaps his best method of generating enthusiastic public response to the picture.[1]

In July of 1952, Chaplin formally applied to the Immigration and Naturalization Service for a re-entry permit, as he had previously done in 1948, disclosing the reason for his trip, his intended length of stay and the like. Surprisingly, the effort to secure the necessary paperwork went much more smoothly than it had four years earlier. In fact, when the date of his departure arrived, Chaplin's sole inconvenience may have been his need to avoid a process server at the New York docks. Lawyers for United Artists had advised Chaplin to board the *Queen Elizabeth* very early in the morning so as to avoid the possibility of being served with papers in an expected lawsuit against the company.

The ship left New York for England on September 17, 1952. James Agee, who had become a close friend, had come to see the Chaplin's off, but was unable to locate him from his vantage point onshore. Chaplin would recount that he and Oona waved frantically from respective portholes in an effort to catch Agee's attention, but they were unsuccessful. It would be the last time Chaplin would ever see his ardent supporter, for Agee would pass away unexpectedly of a heart attack some two years later.

I. CLOSING THE DOOR

My love for humanity is a fundamental deep-seated instinct, but my love for the crowd depends on my mood. At times they are inspiring, at other times frightening, for I instinctively sense that they are capable of either loving or lynching.[2]   — Charles Chaplin — 1933

I remember getting in a taxi one morning to go to work [on *Limelight*] and telling the driver to go to the Chaplin studios. "Is that goddamned commie still working in our country!" said the driver. After that, I learned to just give the street address.[3]   — Claire Bloom — 1992

[My father's] chief fault in the political field is perhaps that of being an idealist in this age of expediency ...[4]   — Charles Chaplin, Jr.— 1960

On September 19, 1952, the attorney general for the Truman administration, James McGranery, announced to the press that Chaplin would be required to submit to a formal inquiry upon his return to America, at which time the Justice Department would determine the merit of allowing him to resume residency. At the time of the announcement, McGranery was reluctant to discuss the specific reasons the government had in subjecting Chaplin to such scrutiny, either because, in the government's view, it may have aided Chaplin in his defense, or, as some later surmised, because the United States government at the time had little in the way of firm evidence on Chaplin's suspicious activities.[5] However, his comments seemed to indicate that the move was part of a planned action against the comedian.

It was not until September 30 that McGranery became more specific: Chaplin was being formally charged with being a member of the Communist Party, with exhibiting indecent moral behavior and with maintaining an offensive and mocking attitude toward the United States. Though the American government could not substantiate its case against Chaplin during the earlier Mann Act trial, though the HUAC Committee had previously found that Chaplin's testimony would "not be necessary," and though his political and personal appearances had significantly dwindled in recent years, suddenly the comedian was considered threatening once again. Coming in the midst of McCarthyism in America, McGranery's tactful neglect of specific information in his original announcement could be overlooked, especially in the case of a celebrity non-citizen whose problematic social and political life had been played out in the press. Since Chaplin was due to be overseas until the spring of 1953 touring with *Limelight*, the government had time following McGranery's announcement to build and substantiate the charges while he was away.*

---

*Author James P. O'Donnell theorized that the government's extensive investigation of Chaplin was about to be leaked; therefore McGranery was forced to make an announcement to the press before the government was actually prepared to make its case. In his article, O'Donnell (continued on next page)

Chaplin recalled that publicity man Harry Crocker became white as a ghost as he read the news to his boss. To further complicate matters, the wire services had inundated the *Queen Elizabeth* with requests for a statement from the comedian.

> Every nerve in me tensed. Whether I re-entered that unhappy country or not was of little consequence to me. I would have like to tell them the sooner I was rid of that hate-beleaguered atmosphere the better, that I was fed up with America's insults and moral pomposity, and that the whole subject was damned boring. But everything I possessed was in the States and I was terrified they might find a way of confiscating it. Now I could expect any unscrupulous action from them. So instead I came out with a pompous statement to the effect that I would return and answer the charges, and that my re-entry was not a "scrap of paper," but a document given to me in good faith by the United States government — blah, blah, blah.[6]

Chaplin's concern with his financial holdings in the United States was valid. In almost every major contention between himself and another party, whether it was the Lita Grey divorce, the Joan Barry/Mann Act trials, or the application for his re-entry permit in 1948, the government had been quick to assert its tax claims coinciding with these matters. The fact that the majority of his personal wealth was tied up in his adopted homeland, including his studio, certainly weighed heavily in tempering Chaplin's public response to the crisis on this European tour, despite the ill feelings he was undoubtedly harboring.

The European press, generally more enthusiastic about Chaplin's recent film releases and certainly more supportive concerning his personal troubles in the United States, welcomed him in droves upon his arrival in England. Europe seemed to mobilize in defense of its native son, many journalists denouncing not only the unfairness of Chaplin's predicament but McCarthyism as a whole. Surely his contributions to art and humanity outweighed the sort of "suspicious" activities he was alleged to have been involved in.

In this respect, Chaplin's political troubles served him well during the European tour. Spurred by McGranery's announcement, Chaplin's arrival in various countries was met by not only by a tremendous amount of fanfare, but also a slew of reporters eager to capture his reaction to the charges. Chaplin tactfully avoided lengthy comments about the situation, but the extra attention nonetheless had a beneficial impact on the scheduled showings of *Limelight*.

(continued) *cites "a close friend in London" who claims that Chaplin had fathered another child out of wedlock — hence the moral charges — who had now become a famous starlet (the author neglects to name names). O'Donnell also alleges that Chaplin, a notorious impersonator of famous people at Hollywood parties, had a particularly naughty version of First Lady Bess Truman attempting to launch a battleship which got the government's goat. O'Donnell adds, however, that President Truman himself disavowed that story in a letter to the author. (James P. O'Donnell; "Charlie Chaplin's Stormy Exile," from* The Saturday Evening Post, *March 8, 1958; page 96.)*

Whether truthful or not, the allegations against Chaplin had heightened attention to the European premieres of the film, especially in light of the picture's
autobiographical elements. Even writer James O'Donnell, who contributed a
largely unflattering portrait of Chaplin in exile to *The Saturday Evening Post*
in 1958, recognized the positive value the emerging scandal had with European
audiences. "Triumphant was the word for Charlie," O'Donnell wrote. "Of all
the turns in an amazing career, this razzle-dazzle tour of Europe was his most
remarkable conquest. The Little Fellow had pitted his personal prestige against
the dignity of the United States Government. He had won, hands down, precisely because he was the Little Fellow."[7]

Chaplin was big news wherever he went. The October 23, 1952, screening
in London was a benefit for the Royal London Society for Teaching and Training the Blind, and the event was broadcast live on British television, a first for
any film premiere in England. Princess Margaret, in a move that may have
appeared as a mild denouncement of the United States' position, was an honored guest at the gala affair. Her attendance that October evening, coupled
with the introduction of Chaplin and Oona to the Queen a few days later, once
again fueled rumors that Chaplin would be knighted, as had been speculated
on both of his previous visits. Of course, he was not knighted on either of
those visits, nor would he be knighted on this one. Even if the Royal Family
had overcome their phobia of conferring such honors on "a mere motion picture comedian," as had been one rumor in 1931, they surely would not have so
clumsily stumbled into the middle of an international dispute over Chaplin and
his alleged political ties.

As it was released, reviews of the picture were largely favorable; Europe
would warmly embrace Chaplin's film. Critics were particularly keen on the
similarities between Chaplin and Calvero, noting the many autobiographical
references, and found the picture a moving celebration of a world renowned
artist. "When I say I wept," André Bazin wrote of the Paris premiere, "I am
not exaggerating. As the lights went up, they revealed 400 directors, screen-
writers, and critics choked with emotion, their eyes as red as tomatoes."[8] Chaplin would go on to open the film in many other European cities as well, each
time garnering high praise and enthusiasm (save for some minor protests over
the comedian in Italy). Individually, the governments of France and Italy formally feted the comedian. Swedish film critic Olof Lagercrantz even proposed
that Chaplin receive the 1952 Nobel Peace Prize. Overall, Chaplin and Europe
reaffirmed their love affair with each other.

But stateside, the events of late 1952 conspired not only to further tarnish
Chaplin's battered reputation, but also to dash any hopes that *Limelight* might
succeed there. The actions of the United States government had effectively
squelched public support for the picture. Many Americans felt after media
speculation surrounding Chaplin's abrupt departure that the Truman Administration would not have taken such an action were it not warranted. There were

few voices trumpeting the injustice done to Chaplin personally or the historical significance of his artistry, either from the general public or from within the
film industry. Perhaps Chaplin proved too controversial, or the nature of his
craft too trivial in light of the popular apprehension toward the Communist
threat. At any rate, the United States government continued to gather information to aid their case, watching and waiting for Chaplin to make his next move.

Though Chaplin would not reveal his future plans until well into 1953, it
seemed abundantly clear that he was making preparations to make Europe his
permanent home. Uncharacteristically, Chaplin may have given up the fight
precisely when he had a very solid case to prove the government wrong[9]; Alistair Cooke recalled that the Solicitor General for the Eisenhower Administration, Simon E. Sobeloff, told him in 1954 that he felt the government essentially had no constitutional grounds to deport Chaplin, let alone enforce it.[10]
In fact, both the INS and FBI were frantically preparing for Chaplin's return
hearing, but in all that time, they could find little that would have conclusively
supported such a ban.[11] But the common perception of Chaplin's decision to
remain in Europe perhaps looked to be, in effect, an admission of his guilt. To
many, he may have appeared to be fleeing.

Much of this, of course, occurred in the months preceding the scheduled
national release of *Limelight* in the United States, which effectively doomed its
financial and, at least to some degree, its critical success. United Artists officials
found themselves in an increasingly precarious position, having to promote a
film whose maker was held in growing disregard throughout the United
States.[12] United Artists was committed to distribution efforts, though eventually pressure from reactionary groups — shades of the fate that befell *Monsieur
Verdoux*— threatened to spill over and affect the company's other releases, making it a virtual no-win situation for the company.

Though Chaplin had moved away from controversial political posturing
within the film, as he had done in his personal life during his final years in his
adopted homeland, groups such as the American Legion, the Catholic War Veterans and the Veterans of Foreign Wars showed no clemency. The ban on Chaplin's re-entry to the United States had suddenly imbued the film with political
overtones, and incited powerful forces to rally against it.

On October 12, 1952, the National Executive Committee of the American
Legion passed a resolution to urge exhibitors to withhold showing *Limelight*
until Chaplin's re-entry permit had been legally issued by the government. In
accordance with this national directive, local chapters of the Legion prepared
to picket and boycott theaters showing the film when it premiered. What these
local chapters accomplished was nothing short of pure intimidation, utilizing
their organizational capabilities to threaten lengthy boycotts of local movie
houses unwilling to comply with their demands. Failure to do so carried not
only the threat of a direct drop in ticket sales, but also the onus of being looked
upon as an endorser of what Chaplin supposedly represented — a non–American

resident who was a Communist sympathizer. At the time a minority view-point, William Murray characterized the situation in March of 1953 accord-ingly:

> Theatre Owners of America and the Allied States Association, the two leading exhibition organizations, adopted a hands-off policy regarding Legion picket lines and refused to protect local theatres. Since the two associations comprise the majority of theatres in the country, a strong stand on their part would have done much to off-set local pressure. Instead, they released a pious statement pointing out that the local managers and owners would have "to live with the people to whom they show their films." ... By now *Limelight* in the normal course of events should have been shown in approximately 2500 theatres throughout the coun-try. On February 15 it had been shown in only about 150. The power of an igno-rant and irresponsible censorship has been demonstrated.[13]

The Legion struck with little or no warning in communities all across America, at the last possible moment, often leaving retaliatory measures difficult. Where such protests could be effectively opposed, such as in Wash-ington, D.C. (where a *Washington Post* editorial rallied in defense of Chaplin's work), *Limelight* played to larger and generally more receptive audiences. More often than not, however, theater owners buckled and thus most communities would never see the film during its original run. This included Los Angeles, not only the center of the film industry but the single most important booking on the West Coast. In New York, where the film premiered three months before the national release date, the picture played well until the organized boycott effort got up and running.

The American Legion, the most militant and active in their efforts against *Limelight*, certainly was not the only organization that hurt the picture and its star. The movie industry, too, itself under scrutiny for Communist influences, made efforts to keep Chaplin's troubles at a safe distance. Fox and Loew's, for instance, two critical exhibitor chains for the film, balked at showing the film early in 1953. When RKO emerged to pick up some screenings, millionaire Howard Hughes, then chairman of RKO Theatres Corporation, wrote the Legion assuring the group that he was personally making efforts to force RKO to drop all of its scheduled bookings.[14]

Accordingly, *Limelight* was never given a chance to stand on its own mer-its. "No one in Hollywood was willing to take the highest chance on anybody or anything," David A. Cook noted of the period. "The industry had its fill of trouble and wanted no more of it. Safety, caution and respectability were the watchwords of the studio chiefs, and controversial or even serious subject mat-ter was to be avoided at all costs. Thus, vitiated, frightened, and drained of cre-ative vitality, Hollywood experienced in miniature what the whole of American society was to experience during the McCarthy-era witch hunts — intellectual stagnation and moral paralysis."[15]

Sympathetic commentary such as William Murray's, at least in America, was hard to come by for Chaplin. When it became apparent that *Limelight* would not receive a fair chance to find its audience, Chaplin had it pulled from circulation in the United States.[16] It was clear that the era of McCarthyism, coinciding with nearly a decade of almost continual bad press, had made the Chaplin name both tiresome and unwelcome in the United States. Though some had rallied to his defense through books, articles and interviews, the general public had soured on hearing any more about the tired and fading actor, despite the fact that he had made a decidedly uncontroversial film for the first time in over 20 years. To the bulk of a now conservative-leaning American public, Chaplin was one less nuisance, and there was little opposition to the government's action against him. How could the public, after all, relate to *Limelight*'s pathos, with its obvious autobiographical elements, when the object of such sympathy was popularly reviled? *Limelight* would have to find its audience, as James Agee had felt of *Monsieur Verdoux*, in Europe. At least in America, Chaplin's so-called final picture was dead on arrival.

II. THE EX-KING COMES HOME TO EUROPE

Despite public statements to the contrary, privately Chaplin must have felt from the moment he received the *Queen Elizabeth* cable that his life in the United States was over.* When his European tour with *Limelight* was nearing an end, toward the fall of 1952, Chaplin began to take actions that would seem to signal his intention of not returning. At the Paris premiere of the film, for instance, he took the opportunity to dine in his hotel room with Pablo Picasso, Jean-Paul Sartre and Louis Aragon, leftist dinner companions whom Chaplin certainly would not entertain (even privately, as he did) if he was worried about unfavorable reaction back home, a point not lost on staffer Harry Crocker. "Stalin will be joining us later," Chaplin joked to his trusted advisor, who failed to see any humor in the comment.

Come November of 1952, Chaplin arranged for Oona to return to the United States, entrusted with the job of collecting his finances and wrapping up any unfinished business in Hollywood. She left London on November 17, and Chaplin agonized the entire ten days she was away. When she returned,

---

Charles Maland has theorized that Chaplin's comments in response to the Queen Elizabeth *cable were in fact an effort at reformulating his political views to a position more tolerable to Cold War America. (Charles Maland;* Chaplin and American Culture; *page 80.) This, however, assumes that Chaplin was intent on returning home to fight the government's charges. It seems more likely that Chaplin's conciliatory manner was a calculated effort not to offend United States officials, especially in light of all his financial ties to the country. Gradually, Chaplin became more openly critical of the government's actions as he was able to extricate his property holdings in the United States.*

her account of the journey was indeed harrowing. Upon arrival at their mansion on Summit Drive in Hollywood, she was informed that the FBI had already made two separate visits to the house, each time to interrogate Chaplin's household staff as to his daily activities, acquaintances and connections, and to gather any other information that could be useful in their investigation.

Others were being questioned as well. The Chaplin-Paulette Goddard divorce records were reviewed to locate possible indiscretions or moral charges. Lita Grey was asked to recount the sordid details of their marriage and 1927 divorce proceedings before officials of the Immigration and Naturalization Service (she gave them no help).[17] Wheeler Dryden, too, was often a target of FBI men, and became so distraught over the probing that he spent the rest of his life (he died in 1957) suffering from mild paranoia.[18]

Prior to leaving America, Chaplin had placed most of his cash and valuables in a safety deposit box which Oona was instructed to take possession of. Though the clerk at the Los Angeles bank took a suspiciously lengthy amount of time in locating the valuables, she was able to travel back to England with what she had come to retrieve. Later, in early 1953, Rollie Totheroh would be hard at work salvaging what he could on behalf of his employer. The bulk of Chaplin's post-1919 films were shipped from California for storage in Europe, and Totheroh himself personally accompanied the transport of Chaplin's famous cane, derby and trousers across the Atlantic.[19]

Chaplin also began to search for a suitable home for his family, as Oona, then pregnant with the couple's fifth child (Eugene Chaplin would be born in August, 1953), wished to find a permanent residence for the family. Shortly after the first of the year, the Chaplins began renting the Manoir de Ban in Switzerland, a 37 acre estate in Corsier, a suburb of the resort town of Vevey, nestled between the larger cities of Lausanne and Montreaux on the shores of Lake Geneva. They would purchase the Manoir in February. There, they felt, the children could comfortably adjust to their new life in Europe, and Chaplin could also enjoy the financial benefits the country had to offer. Ironically, though Charles, Jr., would recall that his father had long admired the beauty of Switzerland, Chaplin wrote of his previous visit there (during the 1931 world tour and his stay with Douglas Fairbanks at St. Moritz): "I've never been intrigued by Switzerland. Personally I dislike all mountainous country."[20] Now, at least, in the relative quiet of the Swiss countryside, Chaplin could devote more of his time to his growing family and perhaps shun the spotlight.

The family settled in at the Manoir, but Chaplin still had to rid himself of his Summit Drive mansion, which had been extensively remodeled during the production of *Limelight* to accommodate his growing family. Both it and the Chaplin Studios would go up for sale in March of 1953; the studio was sold at a substantial loss in October for only $700,000. Later, in March of 1955, Chaplin relinquished his half-ownership in United Artists, also accepting what he felt was less than market value.

With most ties to the United States severed by the spring of 1953, Chaplin formally turned in his re-entry permit in London on April 10. In a brief statement, Chaplin let his true feelings be known, ones that he had no doubt been harboring ever since learning of the Attorney General's announcement some seven months earlier.

> I have been the object of lies and vicious propaganda by powerful reactionary groups who, by their influence and by aid of America's yellow press, have created an unhealthy atmosphere in which liberal minded individuals can be singled out and persecuted. Under these conditions I find it virtually impossible to continue my motion picture work, and I have therefore given up my residence in the United States.[21]

Although the government's immediate problem had been solved by Chaplin's decision to remain in Switzerland, he remained a popular lightning rod for controversy in the U.S. long after his departure. In the years following his exile, headlines continued to appear in the "American yellow press" regarding the comedian's activities, many of which seemed to reinforce the wisdom of barring his re-entry.

Chaplin's acceptance of a peace prize from an allegedly Communist-influenced world peace organization in mid-1954, for instance, was heralded as yet another indication of his commitment to subversive politics, and also provided generous fodder for an antagonistic American press (*Newsweek*, for instance, reported the incident under the heading "Little Man and a Plot"[22]). Accompanying the honor of winning the prize was a cash allotment of £5000, which Chaplin eventually distributed to several charities. Many American journalists, capitalizing on what many regarded as Chaplin's fascination with material wealth, reported that he seemed more interested in the money than in the actual honor itself. Similarly, in July of 1954, Chaplin had lunch with Chou-en-Lai, China's Communist leader and a point of concern surrounding the United States military involvement in the Korea. Arrogantly, Chaplin downplayed the incident in his memoirs. "During the Korean crisis," he wrote, "when the world held its breath over that extremely dangerous brink, the Chinese Embassy telephoned to ask if I would allow *City Lights* to be shown in Geneva before Chou En-lai, who was the pivotal center around which the decision of peace or war was to be decided."[23] Whether or not *City Lights* saved the world from an impending disaster is, of course, highly debatable, but Chaplin's eagerness to accommodate the Chinese leader was interpreted by some as another sign of his Red-leaning tendencies.

The American press would further deride Chaplin in the fall of 1954, following a cable sent by the comic to a "Cultural Salute to Paul Robeson," honoring the black activist and artist whose freedom of movement was being restricted by the U.S. government. "After living in the United States 40 years," *The Saturday Evening Post* editorialized on the event, "Chaplin has openly joined our enemy, the Soviet slave masters.... The purpose of the affair, as the Communist Party explained, was 'to launch the campaign for [Robeson's] right as an artist to travel abroad.' What this really means is the alleged right of a nominal American citizen, who at heart is a Soviet subject, to go abroad in what is practically wartime in order to help our enemy."[24] With the peace prize, Chou En-lai and Paul Robeson incidents, the American media largely represented to its public a classic example of McCarthyist tactics: Guilt by association.

Eventually, Switzerland, too, began to form its own share of antagonism toward Chaplin. A little over a year following his arrival in Vevey, Chaplin was sued by Isobel Deluz, who had briefly been engaged at the Manoir as his personal secretary and script typist. She had quit her position and was seeking three months' back wages and vacation pay.

Later, Deluz recounted her experiences in James O'Donnell's exposé on Chaplin in *The Saturday Evening Post*. Her story highlighted what many people had come to perceive: Chaplin was a temperamental, self-important little tyrant, whose public kindness and generosity were masking a privately-displayed short temper, an unreasonable stubbornness and a volatile disposition. Chaplin, she claimed in the suit, was quite hard on both his family and his hired help, requiring Deluz to type and re-type scenes from several ongoing projects while never indicating which idea went with which script, and almost always dissatisfied with her efforts. "Most of the time he was just brooding and mooching about, and then he was a neurotic terror," Deluz commented. "I was just beaten down by his tantrums — his first-rate clowning, his second-rate manners and his sixth-rate philosophy."[25]

Deluz would win her case, though not without Chaplin's full commitment to clear himself (it seems the Joan Barry lesson was forgotten) and not without creating a wave of gossip and newspaper headlines throughout the small town of Vevey.

Shortly after the outcome of the Deluz case, Chaplin was again at the center of a dispute, but this time with the city as a whole. The Manoir was situated close to the town's firing range, on which generations of men from Vevey and the neighboring communities had fulfilled their yearly marksmanship obligation for Switzerland's militia. In 1955, almost three years after his arrival in Vevey, Chaplin filed suit against the city due to the noise coming from the range, despite genuine efforts by city officials to keep use of the area to a minimum. While eventually the noise suit was more or less resolved — never completely to Chaplin's satisfaction — he had quickly become not only Vevey's most celebrated resident, but one of its more controversial ones as well. These traits would not endear him to everyone in the city. In some respects, his situation seemed akin to the close of *The Pilgrim*, where Charlie straddles the U.S. and Mexican border as he makes his way into the distance, neither country proving a safe haven for the Little Fellow.

Yet despite Chaplin's brief trouble with his hired staff and the city of Vevey, the peacefulness of the Manoir provided him with an excellent opportunity to concentrate on his motion picture career, which he fully intended to continue.

As Isobel Deluz recounted for *The Saturday Evening Post*, Chaplin never missed a beat planning a return to the big screen, immediately delving into several potential projects after settling into the Manoir. Although numerous ideas were being bandied about, including those that would become his next film, 1957's *A King in New York*, Chaplin initially began to focus on a previous interest. Having been put on hold due to the Joan Barry incident, he began to pursue *Shadow and Substance* once again, dusting off the old script and setting out to refine its narrative. For a brief period the *Napoleon* script was also toyed with, though it was inconceivable that Chaplin, given his age, would allow such a plum role to go to another actor, especially after his many years of yearning to play it himself. (Also, such an undertaking would certainly have been compared to *The Great Dictator*, which may have already satisfied Chaplin's own Napoleonic ambition to make a picture on the subject of political and military power.)

The idea that would evolve into Chaplin's initial European film project was first publicly suggested late in 1953, when Chaplin announced that he was looking for a 12-year-old boy to play a critical role in it. Six months later, in May of 1954, the title of *The Ex-King* was announced, the story of an exiled monarch who escapes a revolution in his own country and flees to New York. Armed with atomic plans that will bring peace and comfort to the world, the character finds the harshness of Cold War America too much to endure, and ultimately returns to the more tolerant continent of Europe. Oddly, at the time of the announcement, Chaplin seems to have been considering filming *The Ex-King* as a musical, though the production never took such a form.[26]

The picture, as Chaplin eventually filmed it, would prove a vicious portrait of all the characteristics he found distasteful about America. As he had done in *The Great Dictator*, he sought to utilize his skills as a satirist to poke fun at many traits of the modern United States — in particular, its intolerance of different ideas, which had helped trigger the events that led to Chaplin's own exile.

III. THE NARRATIVE OF *A KING IN NEW YORK*

The film opens in the mythical country of Estrovia, home to King Igor Shadov (Chaplin), where hundreds of civilians are seen storming the gates of the royal palace. They are shouting down the monarchy (one even hanging an image of Shadov in effigy) and are seeking to capture their leader. Once they burst into the palace, they are outraged to find it empty. Fearing the worst, the mob rushes straight to the Treasury. Not only has Shadov escaped, but he has taken the wealth of the nation with him.

We next see King Shadov's plane taxi into New York amid much press and fanfare. Triumphantly alighting, Shadov is immediately met by his Ambassador to the United States, Jaume (Oliver Johnston), and chuckles over his narrow escape from Estrovia. Amid flashes of press photographers and media microphones, Shadov is initially concerned with the location of the absconded securities which, to his dismay, have been placed in the name of Shadov's Prime Minister (Jerry Desmonde), of whom Shadov is most suspicious. He is more polite, however, when the Prime Minister suddenly arrives to shuttle the King through the mass of people.

Once inside the airport terminal, Shadov is obliged to pose for some press photos — one of which finds Shadov, asked for a serious pose, slipping his hand inside his vest and scowling, à la Napoléon. They pause for an impromptu press conference, moderated by the Prime Minister, in which the subject of Estrovia's fortune is quickly brought up. The Prime Minister attempts to skirt the issue, but Shadov orders him to disclose the information so that both the press and the King may learn of its location.

Shadov is also asked to elaborate on his atomic plans, which played a significant role in his overthrow. Although his advisors wanted to use Estrovia's atomic technology for the production of nuclear weaponry, Shadov explains, he insisted that it be used domestically for peaceful purposes. The hard line faction of his government was poised to exploit the military applications of Estrovia's nuclear capabilities, and Shadov claims to have brought his plans with him so that he can unveil them to America's Atomic Commission and hopefully bring about a utopia on Earth.

Shadov is then funneled through Immigration officials, who process his papers while he ironically extols the virtues, kindness and generosity of America for the benefit of neighboring reporters. "I am deeply moved by your warm friendship and hospitality," Shadov exclaims while being fingerprinted much as Chaplin had been at the beginning of the Joan Barry ordeal. "This big-hearted nation has already demonstrated its noble generosity to those who seek a refuge from tyranny."*

On arriving at the Ritz Hotel, Shadov is eager to assume control over Estrovia's fortune and, since the bank has closed for the day, instructs the Prime Minister to make himself available the following morning at 10 A.M. to complete the transfer. Then, wishing to escape the troubles that have besieged

---

*"This odd fellow," James O'Donnell commented in his Saturday Evening Post series, "chose to immortalize one of his most wretched moments." (James P. O'Donnell; "Charlie Chaplin's Stormy Exile," from The Saturday Evening Post, March 22, 1958; page 110.)The scene, however, is reminiscent of the red flag sequence in Modern Times, when Chaplin overtly satirized rumors about his own political beliefs.

him over the previous days, Shadov goes out for the evening to relax in the pleasures that New York has to offer.

Unfortunately, King Shadov quickly finds that there is little relaxation in the bustle of the Big Apple. He and Jaume escape the crowded and noisy street by ducking into a movie theater, only to find it overrun by rambunctious dancing teens; the King is forced to step over the swooning bodies of several girls in the aisles. When the excitement dies and the film begins, the coming attractions are ludicrous enough to drive Shadov from the theater. The first, *A Killer with a Soul*, seems to have similarities with Chaplin's own *Monsieur Verdoux;* "You'll love him — he'll creep into your heart," the caption reads. "Bring the family!" This "killer" fires three shots at his victim from point blank range, only to miss altogether.

The next attraction is entitled *Man or Woman*— shades of Ed Wood's *Glen or Glenda*— in which the voices of the male and female characters are reversed, lampooning their implied sex change. *Terror Rides Again*, the final attraction, plays like a bad 1950s western: The hero enters the saloon, guns down five people, and with only one bullet left, continues to fire a volley of shots at the remaining outlaw. The heads of the audience snap back and forth across the wide screen format, as if they were watching a tennis match. Shadov decides he can no longer witness this travesty of entertainment. He and Jaume withdraw to a local club.

There, they feel they can finally enjoy a pleasant atmosphere. Seated near the front of the stage with his back to a pianist, Shadov peruses the menu. Unbeknownst to him, however, the stage with the pianist rotates out of view to reveal a pop band, with the drummer's cymbal directly over the King's head. Accordingly, Shadov is pummelled when the band suddenly begins to play. To make matters worse, both Shadov and Jaume are unable to communicate their order to the waiter over the noise, leaving Shadov with no choice but to pantomime the order of some caviar and turtle soup. (It is ironic that Chaplin, who so long had used pantomime to overcome the "barrier" of silence in his early films, in this case must utilize the same skills to communicate over the noisy excitement of the modern world.)

The following morning, Shadov awakens to find his worst fears materialized — the Prime Minister has disappeared and with him, Estrovia's fortune. His atomic plans are now all that Shadov has to his name, although Jaume points out that the public continues to believe that Shadov has absconded with all the funds. "Just as well," Shadov explains. "I would sooner be thought of as a successful crook than a destitute monarch."

A phone call announces the arrival of Irene Shadov, the Queen of Estrovia. She enters, and the two are very cordial, although it is quite clear that their relationship is no closer than that. She has just arrived in New York from Paris, where she had heard of the revolution in Estrovia, and only plans to stay briefly before returning to France. The pair are quickly interrupted by another phone call; Jaume announces that it is a woman named Cromwell, wishing to invite the King to her home for dinner. Shadov flatly refuses.

The King takes lunch in his hotel room with the Queen, and the couple reminisce as though they have been separated for quite some time. We discover their marriage had been arranged by the state and, although they initially had some feelings toward each other, they mutually concluded that they did not love one another and parted amicably. Now they have lost the throne, the last bond between them, and talk of divorce. But because she can only stay briefly, they must part without clearly resolving the issue of their marriage.

Shadov is interrupted in his efforts to ready a bath by a melodic female voice from the adjoining bathroom, luring both the King and Jaume to the key-hole for a better view. Suddenly, the girl cries out in rather calculated distress that she has fallen in the tub, twisting her ankle. Shadov enters to help the girl, though he accidently falls into her tub in the process. Anne Kay (Dawn Addams) is the woman's name, and Shadov is immediately captivated by her beauty. In the midst of their conversation, she is less than casual in dropping the name of Mrs. Cromwell, whose dinner party she will be attending that evening.

Shadov, determined to get to know Anne better, reconsiders the invitation to dine at Mrs. Cromwell's. As he retires to his own bath, Jaume takes another telephone call which, conveniently, is "that Cromwell woman again," insisting that the King accept her invitation. His opportunity at hand, Shadov instructs his associate to accept the offer.

Later that evening, the dinner guests at the Cromwell residence are eagerly awaiting the arrival of the King. Anne Kay arrives, boasting proudly about her entrapment of Shadov. It is not long before the King arrives for the festivities, and Anne is able to slip away to the dining room while the King goes through the formality of greeting the other dinner guests. Anne, it turns out, is an advertising executive, and has concealed cameras throughout the dining room to capture the King during the meal. She plans to televise the proceedings in order to help pitch the products of the show's sponsors, unbeknownst to Shadov.

At the meal, Shadov is clearly more interested in Anne than anything else around him. In the midst of seemingly harmless flirtation, Anne, prompted by a buzzer, oddly utilizes one of Shadov's last words — fresh — to launch into a monologue on anti-perspirant, leaving Shadov visibly confused and uncomfortable. It is only after consulting with Mrs. Cromwell on his right that he learns of Anne's profession, and attributes her strange outburst to her occupation.

Following Anne's sudden pitch, she implores the King to recite Shakespeare, for she has heard of his performances at similar dinner parties. Shadov is obviously flattered, and dramatically launches into a scene from *Hamlet* much to the delight of the guests (and the hidden cameras). Jaume, nearly

King Shadow attempting to pantomine his order for turtle soup over the rumble of the nearby orchestra, from *A King in New York* (1957).

asleep in front of the television back at the Ritz Hotel, awakens to witness the horrifying public humiliation of Shadov.

Having finished with his performance, King Shadov returns to his place next to Anne, only to endure her sudden launch into another sales pitch, this time extolling the virtues of Oxytone toothpaste. As before, Shadov is self-conscious, this time about his breath.

Later that evening, upon Shadov's return to the hotel, Jaume reveals Anne's televised deception. Too ruffled to sleep, the pair agree to go to a nearby nightclub to unwind. But Shadov is recognized by several patrons who had seen the broadcast and is inundated for autographs.

By the following day, it's clear to both Shadov and Jaume that the public's reaction in the nightclub was not an isolated incident. Inexplicably, the King's antics, as captured by the hidden cameras, have boosted his popularity, and opportunities to make further product endorsements come flowing into the hotel.

Anne arrives carrying a letter from Mrs. Cromwell. Shadov, still reeling from her trickery, defiantly shreds the contents of the letter — though he pauses momentarily when Anne informs him that the envelope also contains a check for $20,000, a gratuity for the King's role at the Cromwell function.

Nonetheless, Shadov has other business to attend to, and Anne is sent on her way.

Because the check has piqued Shadov's interest in money, he asks Jaume about the state of their own finances, and learns that they are virtually depleted. Shadov is quick to leap towards the trash can, attempting to reassemble the torn check while instructing Jaume to send a kind thank-you to Mrs. Cromwell. Given the sorry state of his finances, Shadov has no false modesty in accepting the money and, given the fact that the Atomic Commission has been slow in responding to the King's request to review his plans, it will be needed.

Later that day, Shadov and Jaume embark on a venture to the Queen's County School, a progressive learning institution for young boys. While touring, the King is told that the curriculum allows each child to excel at the activity that best captures his attention. All the while the King is being pelted by several pea-shooting boys, reminiscent of the mischievous newsboys of *City Lights*.

Left alone temporarily, Shadov becomes acquainted with one youngster, Rupert Macabee (played by Chaplin's son, Michael), editor of the school's magazine on world issues, who is currently passing his time by reading from the works of Karl Marx. "Surely you're not a Communist?" asks Shadov. "Do I have to be a Communist to read Karl Marx?" comes Rupert's rhetorical answer.

Taken aback, the King engages the young boy in a political conversation which, once underway, Shadov has great difficulty participating in. The boy is skeptical of America's so-called "freedom," noting that no political system allows freedom in the most pure sense of the word. Government has created a web of entangling rules and regulations that keep the individual from exercising true freedom, and "political despots" have limited citizen's freedom of thought and association. All the while, the King is attempting vainly to inject a thought or two into the conversation, only to have Rupert escalate his feverish rhetoric and drown out Shadov's words. Ultimately, the headmaster is able to rescue the King from the boy's tirade, though not before he has been verbally assaulted.

The King and Jaume return to the hotel, where they continue to be showered with endorsement opportunities while, strangely, social invitations seem to be in short supply. Jaume feels that the King himself is to blame; Shadov's vision of a world "Utopia" under his atomic plans is an unpopular notion given the American political climate, where paranoia and fear toward such idealism predominates.

Under the door is slipped an envelope which, Jaume realizes, contains the bill for the hotel room. Being over $11,000 in debt to the Ritz and with barely a cent to their names, Shadov begins to reconsider the endorsement offers coming to him.

Rather conveniently, an ad man for Royal Crown Whiskey suddenly darts into the room, offering the King $50,000 for a single commercial. Shadov agrees to the offer. Unfortunately, the live commercial goes badly. Having never tasted whiskey before, the King chokes violently before an audience of millions.

However, the work puts Shadov's financial troubles temporarily behind him. Anne again returns to the hotel with the unlikely news that the King's likeness has become even more popular with the American public than before, despite the whiskey ad. Shadov can have his choice of further endorsements.

Anne arranges for a brief photo session with Shadov for an intended promotion plugging the use of hormones. Shadov, however, is much more interested in being left alone with Anne than taking photographs, and his aggressive advances are interrupted by a young studio helper as he wrestles her unwillingly to the floor. Flustered but not ready to abandon the shoot, Anne hits upon the idea of Shadov getting a facelift — providing a "before" and "after" photo approach to the hormone campaign. Although skeptical, Shadov allows himself to follow through on her advice.

At the surgeon's office, Shadov's bandages are unwrapped to reveal a hideous face. Horrified, Shadov departs for the hotel with instructions not to stretch his skin too much, as the stitches need time to heal and gain strength. When Anne arrives, she is also shocked at the work of the plastic surgeon. She insists that they cannot continue with the ad with Shadov's new face and will request that the doctor undo his work as soon as possible. Shadov is overcome with shock and disbelief and staggers about the hotel room. As a consolation, Anne takes him out for dinner and a show, reminding Shadov that everything will be righted shortly.

At the club, Shadov is quite uncomfortable with his new look. Unable to smile or even to drink through a straw, he suffers through the entertainment and looks forward to returning to the hotel where he can be alone. Anne finally consents, but not until they have stayed for the comedy act.

Understanding the care he must take in nursing his stitches, Shadov cringes when the comedians take the stage, knowing he cannot laugh at the proceedings. The act, a variant of the old Keystone pie-throwing gags, involves a bowler-hatted paper hanger who "inadvertently" gets into a spat with another player, supposedly a member of the audience. Hostilities quickly escalate, with both participants engaging in a game of one-upsmanship in dousing the other with paper glue. The audience roars with laughter, and Shadov, despite his desperate attempts otherwise, finally lets out a similar burst. His stitches break, and Anne follows him in rushing from the club. The following day, Shadov returns to the surgeon, and is relieved that the doctor is able to restore his former looks.

Back at the Ritz, Shadov is leaving a car when he happens upon young Rupert — wet, cold and wandering the streets alone. The King, though despising the boy from their earlier meeting, cannot allow him to remain outside, and invites him up to his room for some food and a hot bath.

While Jaume phones room service for some lunch, Shadov asks Rupert why he left his school. He ran away, he replies, because "they" wanted to question him about the political ties of his parents. Jaume, fearful that the King could be linked with Communism should the boy be found in the hotel room, implores Shadov to rid himself of Rupert. The King, however, is furious with Jaume's insensitivity. "Should the boy freeze to death just because his parents are Communist?" Shadov queries.

Given a place to stay for the time being, Rupert is allowed free run of the hotel room while the King and Jaume are away. Since a strange young boy has suddenly appeared in the suite, hotel security arrives to question Rupert. Not wishing to reveal his true identity to the authorities, he claims to be Shadov's young nephew. When the King returns, he reluctantly confirms the boy's version of the relationship. About to be disciplined for his shenanigan, Rupert is saved by a phone call to the room. Although it is a bad connection, Jaume announces that the Atomic Commission is planning to arrive in New York either that day or the next, intent on reviewing the King's touted atomic plans. With the date of their arrival in question, both Shadov and Jaume rush out to retrieve the plans from the safety deposit box in which they are held, again leaving young Rupert alone in the room.

As one set of elevator doors close on Shadov and Jaume, the others open to reveal the members of the Atomic Commission. Rupert, introduced as the King's nephew, is left to entertain the gentlemen while they await Shadov's return. What starts as small talk with the boy, however, soon becomes a heated political discussion and begins to resemble Shadov's first meeting with Rupert at the Queen's County School. The boy fluently speaks of his progressive, if not openly Communistic, views. Although Shadov returns shortly into young Rupert's speech, the damage has already been done with the distinguished gentlemen of the Atomic Commission. Shadov is able to present his atomic plans, but to a group already reeling from bad feelings.

Later, as he plays a game of checkers with Rupert, Shadov reports to the boy that the Commission was not interested in his designs after all, since they claim to have similar plans for atomic technology. Though his own prospects have been dashed, Shadov is nonetheless intrigued to learn more about Rupert's troubles.

Their conversation is interrupted by the televised Communist hearings. The event of the day, the announcer notes, concerns a pair of schoolteachers — the Macabees, Rupert's parents — and their unwillingness to testify against others associated with the Communist Party of America. Braving charges of contempt of Congress, they each face two years in prison for their non-cooperation with the Committee. Shadov turns to the boy, who begins to cry.

Their somber moment is broken by a knock at the door: A United States marshall, tipped off to Rupert's whereabouts, has arrived to take the boy away. Assured that he is only being returned to the Queen's County School, Shadov allows the official to escort Rupert from the suite.

Just as Jaume had feared, the linking of Rupert to the King prompts a swirl of media attention regarding Shadov and his political sympathies. Television reports, claiming to have undeniable proof that the deposed monarch is part of a Communist plot involving his touted atomic plans, help fan the fires of mistruth about the King's activities. Shadov obtains the services of a lawyer who advises his client to come to his office immediately, though disguised so as to avoid a forthcoming subpoena from the United States government.

Shadov and Jaume exchange coats and hats for the journey, although a suspicious-looking man in the hallway spots the deception and starts after the King. As it turns out, the man is nothing more than an autograph hunter, and soon a crowd of fans are surrounding Shadov, all shoving papers to sign in his face. Unfortunately, after signing one such paper, its owner declines to take the document back, and Shadov realizes he has inadvertently accepted the subpoena. The scene cuts to show several newspaper headlines announcing that Shadov will appear before the government committee, and that Rupert has undergone an interrogation upon returning to his school.

Eager not to be late for the Congressional hearing, Shadov and his lawyer scurry to an elevator intent on catching a cab. Having forgotten his briefcase, Shadov is urged by his lawyer to hail a cab while he returns to his office. In the lull of the ride to the building lobby, the King absentmindedly places his finger inside the nozzle of the elevator's fire hose, only to find that he cannot remove it. Shadov and his lawyer are thus forced to depart for the hearings with the hose in tow.

Shadov bounds into the hearing room just in time to hear his name called before the Committee. However, outside in the hallway, where the tail end of the hose lies, security guards mistakenly assume that there is a fire in progress. Attaching Shadov's hose to an extension, they pump water towards the nozzle. Such pressure is enough to free the King's finger, though it also douses the entire Congressional Committee, as well as members of the press, the audience and even Shadov's own lawyer.

Again through a succession of newspaper headlines, we learn that the King's testimony has cleared his name, and one even reports that he is to receive Congress' highest honor for his help. But Shadov and Jaume are nonetheless making preparations to leave America, feeling that they can find a better life for themselves in Europe. Anne arrives at the Ritz to see them off, and Shadov laments that the pair may never see each other again. She shrugs off their so-called romance, but wishes the King would reconsider and stay stateside. "Don't judge by what's going on today," Anne implores, "it's just a passing phase. Very soon it will be all over."

"Quite so," retorts Shadov. "In the meantime, I'll wait it out in Europe."

A telegram arrives from Shadov's wife Irene, indicating that she does not wish to divorce. The two are quite content carrying on separate lives as they do, and there is no sense spoiling an amenable situation.

Later, on his way to the airport, the King has one final errand to run, paying a visit to the Queens' County School. While awaiting Rupert's arrival, the headmaster proudly informs Shadov of the boy's commendable actions, disclosing for government investigators the names of the Communist organizers that his parents would not, gaining suspended sentences for both of them. "A hero and a patriot," the headmaster deems the boy.

But when Rupert enters it is apparent that he is not the same child the King came to know. The sadness over his face indicates the degree of humiliation to which he has been subjected. He has violated the principles both he and his parents believed in, with the Congressional Committee using the boy as a political toy to achieve its own paranoid, selfish ends. Rupert chose to save his own parents, yet it is clear from his face that saving them may have devastating effects on him personally.

Shadov attempts to comfort Rupert, but the boy cannot help but sob. The King promises to one day invite both him and his parents to come visit, but the kind offer seems to give Rupert little comfort.

Thus, Shadov and Jaume make their way out of the country, returning to the European continent from which they came.

IV. SATIRIZING THE UNITED STATES

This was the most angry and bitter film Chaplin ever made — and indeed one of the most ferocious feature films an artist ever created out of his own experience.[27]

— David Robinson

Anxiously, [Chaplin] wanted to know what we thought of *A King in New York*. "Did you think it was so anti-American, as they say it is? *Did* you?" For a while he gave a fair imitation of a man who didn't care that it had been ignored by America. "Of course; it will never be shown there." But from the way he worried the point you felt that he did care, desperately.[28]

— Margaret Hinxman

[Chaplin's objects of ridicule] may be American but they are not America; they do not touch reality. In the King's ambiguous attitude towards them, his amused and skeptical condescension, one feels that Chaplin is saying not, as in the past, "laugh at this — this is the human condition" but "laugh at this — it is merely laughable."[29]

— Penelope Houston

In many ways, *A King in New York* was as deeply personal a film as *Limelight*. Like its predecessor, the film clearly depicts aspects of Chaplin's life that had been a tremendous influence on his personal character; King Shadov, the deposed monarch, like Calvero, is unmistakably Charles Spencer Chaplin, the deposed king of screen comedy. Yet unlike *Limelight,* where sympathy for the central character was quite notable, *A King in New York* is a rather clumsy attempt to achieve something similar. For such a legendary screen genius, *A King in New York* was a tremendous letdown from the Chaplin the world had come to know.

As with *Limelight,* there was no mistaking the parallel situations between Chaplin and the character he played. Both had been at the pinnacle of success in their respective countries, only to be cast out by so-called angry mobs — a notion that was not entirely accurate in Chaplin's case, although he certainly perceived it as such. Similarly, the Communist hearings that Shadov is inadvertently drawn into, based on his friendly association with Rupert, bear a resemblance to Chaplin's own Communist links through friendships with composer Hanns Eisler and others. Scenes from Shadov's arrival in New York — the King's speech on liberty while being fingerprinted, coupled with Shadov's Napoleonic pose for the benefit of press photographers — also highlight the film's more personal touches. But however autobiographical Chaplin had created the film, the object of *King* was not as much to focus attention on the actor himself, as had been the case in *Limelight,* but to lash out at the United States as a whole.

Chaplin's cultural critique of American society in the 1950s is clearly where the film scores its most satisfying satirical points. Indeed, Chaplin utilizes his narrative to skewer a number of developing trends and institutions that would forever change the face of American society.

Topping that list (and being the most personal to the film's creator) were the Communist hearings themselves. In introducing the hearings, Chaplin is quick to depict what the television announcer deems as their "lighter side," showing the make-up, prep work and production aspects of broadcast programming that drew one of early television's first mass audiences. Like Calvero in his dressing room, the House Un-American Activities Committee members delicately doub on their make-up, while in their minds they rehearse the dialogue for their upcoming performance.

Chaplin's scene is both amusing and lighthearted, but his specific thrust is much deeper. Rather than protect the public, he felt, the government of the United States was essentially victimizing members of its own citizenry simply for having different, or in some cases unorthodox views. Caught in the middle of this powerful frenzy were people such as the Macabees, schoolteachers whose freedom of association was being severely restricted. Thanks to their exploitation by opportunistic public officials, they became the inadvertent focus of popular scorn. Like Bess Taffel's comments about the perils of taking the Fifth Amendment at the HUAC hearings, the Macabees' catch-22 is symptomatic of the era: They are asked to name names, defiance of which constitutes contempt of Congress, acceptance of which borders on incrimination of themselves and possibly others. Rather than betray their beliefs and their friends, the Macabees refuse to give in and are unjustly, Chaplin seems to assert, sent to jail.

Not content with the elder Macabees, however, it is the government's destruction of young Rupert Macabee where Chaplin attempts to most dramatically present the destructiveness of McCarthyism. It is Rupert who proves the main focus of *King*'s pathos rather than Shadov. Since the audience may find some of Rupert's political views narrow and repugnant, as Shadov does on their first meeting, Chaplin relies more on the emotional breakdown of the boy to generate this sympathy. Political powers, cloaked in their righteous pursuit of truth and justice, think nothing of exploiting a young boy to suit their own purposes.

Though the Communist hearings and associated scenes contain the bulk of the film's formal criticism of American society, Chaplin also takes shots at other aspects of the United States he found equally distasteful. Commercialization, for instance, finds itself a second prominent target in Chaplin's vitriolic attacks. The televised dinner party at Miss Cromwell's, a thoroughly unbelievable plot device, was nothing more than an extended promotional gimmick, with Anne Kay's trickery of Shadov helping to feed America's consumption of goods.

In some respects, Anne and her advertising counterparts resemble the Un-American Activities Committee in their selfish motives. Shadov is sought out to be exploited by such individuals, for the returns on the use of his image would clearly make themselves and their clients a fortune. After all, why shouldn't a king be pitching Royal Crown Whiskey?

When such ads prove successful, defying both Shadov's and certainly common logic, they are besieged with similar requests, for everyone is looking to make a fast buck from the King. Shadov is thus placed in a similar position (though hardly as sympathetic) as Rupert, being a springboard for the opportunistic use of others.

This is personified in Anne Kay, whose depiction throughout the film suggests her interest in Shadov certainly does not extend farther than the next photo shoot or promotional deal. In almost every way, Chaplin's so-called love interest falls distinctly short of the romanticism that had prevailed in his earlier films. Instead of portraying romance or love as a human need, Chaplin brings Shadov and Anne's relationship down to the level of the society he is attempting to satirize. Both characters are wanting to exploit the other — she to further her career, he for a brief romantic tryst — and neither are ultimately shy about their respective motives, as their amicable parting before Shadov's return to Europe demonstrates. Perhaps Chaplin sought to portray the demise of the idealized romantic encounter, or perhaps he failed to grasp or fully develop the romantic aspects of the film as he had hoped.

While some of Chaplin's pointed criticism of American society may have been effectively depicted, his efforts are clearly overshadowed by the film's altogether sloppiness in narrative structure. Biographer David Robinson was not amiss when he commented that the film shows "a general air of shabbiness," citing the poor quality of the sets, the flimsy characters and lifeless action as uncharacteristic in light of Chaplin's previous motion pictures.[30] In a critical sense, Chaplin's desire to attack the United States with *A King in New York* came at the expense of formulating and executing a well-crafted story. Aside from a few individual satirical barbs, the picture fails in pushing the narrative forward, stopping at several points while its creator dabbles in his various political and social denigrations. Considering that Charles, Jr., felt that the script had been considerably toned down from the original draft, its quite clear that *A King in New York* had as much — if not more — to do with revenge than it did with continuing Chaplin's legacy on the screen.[31]

Chaplin refused to allow the film to be released in the United States (it would not be widely seen until a 1973 re-release), a move that significantly hurt it financially and denied it to the very audience that Chaplin would have wanted to see the film. The two main satirical points, the Communist witch hunts and commercialization of American society, would not have as much impact in other countries as they would have had within the United States. Also, McCarthyism (but not anti-Communism) was a failed movement in America by 1957. Though much of the world was familiar with the changes in the United States and with Chaplin's troubles with its government, his pointed criticisms would hardly carry the same impact outside the country. The thrust of the film was not an overly familiar subject, especially in European countries where a broad spectrum of political thought had long been accepted.

In addition to his refusal to show the film in the U.S., Chaplin also made errors in several other areas while constructing the film's narrative which precluded it from having an impact on an audience, even if it had been released stateside. With the characterization of Shadov, for example, Chaplin evidently failed to consider a number of character nuances that would actually have the opposite impact on an audience from what he had intended. For example, placing himself in the role of a deposed monarch, thus allying his own situation with that of royal personage, Chaplin ran the risk of placing too much emphasis on the plight of his political troubles with the United States, and it appeared arrogant and egocentric. Whereas Calvero, and even Henri Verdoux for that matter, had been the innocent victims of tragic circumstances, Igor Shadov is certainly not constructed from the same mold, even though Chaplin would have us believe so.

For those who were adamantly opposed to Chaplin and what they felt he stood for, the Chaplin/Shadov connection was nothing more than a confirmation of all the traits they reviled: A wealthy, arrogant and egotistical man who demanded far more respect and reverence than he deserved. Whereas Charlie and Calvero had been sympathetic creations, ones who had capitalized on thoughtful human traits — the hopes and fears that come with the pursuit of love, acceptance and human compassion — few could sympathize with Shadov, a king who arrogantly regarded the revolution that took his throne as a "minor annoyance,"* who seemingly cares nothing for the land he has been forced to abandon, and who furthermore had looted the entire treasury during his getaway. ("Ah, ha! We fooled them!" Shadov gleefully announces to Jaume as he steps from the plane in New York.) From the outset, Chaplin had inadvertently made Shadov more repugnant than compassionate. This absence of compassion in Shadov (his humanistic traits are only evident in responding to Rupert's plight, in addition to his stale comments on wanting to use atomic energy "only for peaceful purposes") provides a blemish in the very premise of *A King in New York* and inhibits a warm relationship between the audience and the Estrovian monarch.

Flawed, too, was Chaplin's use of pathos. Though Shadov and Chaplin are undoubtedly meant to be the indirect recipients of sympathy throughout the film, it is the character of Rupert who is designed to evoke much of the direct pathos from the film. But like Shadov, this character too poses a serious problem. While Rupert's fate highlights the destructive aspects of the Communist witch-hunts, one cannot overlook that Chaplin was also using an innocent boy to further his own political designs. Embarrassingly, he himself gives up the speechmaking that had figured in the finales of *The Great Dictator* and *Monsieur Verdoux*, and instead expresses his thoughts through the mouth of Rupert.

The effect is only heightened by the fact that Chaplin cast his own son Michael (just 10 years old) as Rupert. Though not much of an actor, Michael was able to carry the role off adequately. Originally, when Chaplin announced the film as *The Ex-King* in May of 1954, he noted that he was in the process of searching for a young actor to portray the part of Rupert. Michael, it seems, was originally intended to take a bit role in the film — that of a young boy baking pastries at the Queen's County School who is unable to keep from placing his finger in his nose during the process.† As work on the script slowly progressed, however, Michael arrived at approximately the correct age for Rupert that Chaplin had envisioned, and the role was his.

But from the moment of the audience's introduction to Rupert Macabee, he fails to exude any sort of sympathetic charisma that would make him a natural figure for pathos. We are assured that the boy is an extremely gifted thinker for his age, but Rupert's dialogue throughout the film lends itself less

---

*In the opening of the film, Chaplin inserts a superimposed title that reads "One of the minor annoyances of modern life is a revolution" as we see the citizens of Estrovia storm the castle and hang their former king in effigy. The comedian's sarcasm is duly noted, but not only does the title convey both Chaplin and Shadov's views of their respective oustings, but seriously downplays the threat that a revolution poses — a point that, considering the ongoing concern with the spread of Communism throughout the world, would not have played well with many audiences.

†The gag, a throwback to the sort of vulgarisms of Chaplin's music hall and early film work, remains, immediately preceding Shadov's first encounter with Rupert.

to the boy's intellectual abilities than it does to suit the needs of the film's creator. Even in their initial meeting at the school, the boy mounts his soapbox, delivering a cold and staccato monologue that's deliberately written to Chaplin's personal advantage.

> SHADOV: And what's that you're reading?
> RUPERT: Karl Marx.
> SHADOV: Surely you're not a Communist!?
> RUPERT: Do I have to be a Communist to read Karl Marx?

Later in the conversation between the pair:

> SHADOV: Well, if you are not a Communist, what are you?
> RUPERT: Nothing. I dislike all forms of government.
> SHADOV: But somebody has to rule.
> RUPERT: ... And I don't like the word "rule."
> SHADOV: Well, if you don't like the word "rule," let's call it leadership.
> RUPERT: Leadership in government is political power, and political power is an official form of antagonizing the people....
> SHADOV: ... Politics aren't necessary.
> RUPERT: Politics are rules imposed upon the people.
> SHADOV: In this country rules are not imposed, they are the wish of all free citizens.
> RUPERT: Travel around a bit, then you'll see how free they are!
> SHADOV: Yes, but you didn't let me finish ...
> RUPERT: (over Shadov's attempts to interject) They have every man in a strait jacket and without a passport, he can't move a toe....In a free world they violate the natural rights of every citizen. They have become the weapons of political despots! And if you don't think as they think, you are deprived of your passport. So leaving the country is like breaking out of jail, and entering the country is like going through the eye of a needle.... It's incongruous that in this atomic age of speed we are shut in and shut out by passports.... And free speech does not exist ... and free enterprise? Today it's monopoly ... monopoly is the menace of free enterprise.... And the atomic bomb. It's a crime that when the world cries for atomic energy, you [indicating Shadov] want to make atomic bombs!

Though we are supposed to feel the humor of seeing King Shadov outdueled by such a young boy, one simply cannot separate Chaplin's own political troubles from Rupert's dialogue. However, strong Chaplin's need to lash out at his enemies, it appears to viewers both arrogant and obnoxious to have such personal grievances aired through the mouth of this innocent young boy — a boy who, like the character he was portraying, had become the political puppet of those around him. "London critics assailed him as a ventriloquist," James O'Donnell would remark, "spitting through the mouth of his own child."[32]

Michael, who at his young age published his own memoirs shortly before his father did, commented very little on his first major acting role, simply offering that his father advised him to act "as natural as possible."[33] It was apparent that Michael had little training and felt uncomfortable before the camera. Having a father who was not only one of the world's most famous comedians, but both his acting partner and director undoubtedly contributed to Michael's apparent uneasiness. With this in mind, perhaps, biographer David Robinson generously dubbed the performance as merely admirable.[34]

Unfortunately, Chaplin's memoirs also reveal very little about *A King in New York*, an oversight most likely attributable to the film's cold reception; Chaplin, in fact, probably spoke volumes on his dissatisfaction with *King* with his silence concerning the film in his autobiography, the next major endeavor he would undertake. It was only after many years that Chaplin comfortably discussed the picture. Jerry Epstein recalled a playful argument between Charlie and Oona over who gave the best screen performance, Michael or Jackie Coogan in *The Kid*, as Chaplin was composing an original score for his silent classic in the early 1970s.[35] Ever the protective mother, Oona insisted that Michael possessed the better acting ability and because they could come to no logical consensus, the pair had dropped the matter altogether. Later, with the publication of Chaplin's *My Life in Pictures* in 1974, in which he occasionally expounded on passages made previously in his original memoirs, Chaplin cited Michael's work as excellent — bowing, perhaps, to Oona's persistence.[36]

Personal and political issues aside, *A King in New York* concentrates more on comedy than *Limelight* before it, though with distinctly less success. Chief among the film's comedic sequences are Shadov and Jaume's attempt to enjoy a relaxing evening on the town, Shadov's night out with Anne following his plastic surgery and, of course, Shadov's exploits before the Congressional Committee. All display an uncharacteristic flatness and often a lack of originality.

Shadov and Jaume's New York experiences form the most satisfying comedic sequence of the film, and the theater previews are the highlight of their evening out. Though B-movies had long been a financial boon for Hollywood studios, Chaplin apparently found them, and their popularity, based on his depictions, insulting to established filmmakers such as himself.

But this section of the film, along with the other two notable comedic sequences, do not come close to the ingenuity or quality of Chaplin's previous film efforts. The paper-hanging sketch in the cabaret is a typical Keystone-type scenario, with the inevitable sloshing of glue being the prime joke exercised over and over. It's a throwback to Wal Pink's vaudeville sketch *Repairs* from 1906, the two-reeler *Work* (1915) and a similar scene from *The Circus*, with the inclusion of a fictitious audience member in the act reminiscent of Chaplin's drunk in the Karno sketch *Mumming Birds*.

The scene, however, is exactly the type of broad slapstick that Chaplin

With co-star Dawn Addams in *A King in New York.*

looked to distance himself from at Keystone. While the sequence may be mildly amusing, it is inconceivable that a more sophisticated audience of the 1950s would find such an act as humorous as they do in the cabaret scene. It is far more amusing to watch Shadov in his vain attempts to avoid watching the sketch, thereby not breaking the stitches of his facelift, than it is watching the actual performance. Since there's no indication that Chaplin was satirizing the audience of the cabaret — which would be inconsistent with the scene — one must conclude that the comedian was more concerned with recording the actions of Shadov than he was in the stage action. For a man who had devised some of the most memorable comedy scenes ever put onto film, the paper-hanging sketch seems like a convenient and easy solution rather than a finely crafted piece of comic business. It was a factor noted by a number of critics, including Penelope Houston, who disparagingly called it "as embarrassing a miscalculation as any comedian has given us since Lubitsch tried to crack jokes about concentration camps."[37]

Similarly, Chaplin's business with the firehose and the Congressional Committee is also below par. Placing one's finger in a firehose may be consistent for a child's character, but seems wholly out of place for a distinguished royal figure. Biographer David Robinson cites an interview in which Chaplin boasted that if he had actually been called before the House Un-American Activities Committee, he would have arrived in his old Charlie outfit, and would have stockpiled "all sorts of comic business to make a laughing stock of the inquisitors."[38] Yet when Chaplin did get an opportunity to confront the United States government in *A King in New York*, the result is a dismal letdown. Admirer Charles Silver has made a strained analogy equating Chaplin's use of low comedy with the government's own "low comedy" of the McCarthy hearings,[39] but this seems more an effort to explain away Chaplin's obvious lapse in judgment.

The strain of Chaplin's latest project was felt during its production. "*Limelight* had been such a happy experience," recalled assistant Jerry Epstein. "[W]ith *A King in New York*, the atmosphere was frosty and strained."[40] Chaplin, for the first time in nearly 35 years, did not have the comfort of utilizing his own studios and staff in producing a motion picture. While England's Shepperton Studios provided an adequate space, Chaplin had to forgo many of his customary luxuries. The studio was rented, an expensive proposition which required Chaplin not only to strictly adhere to a shooting schedule (May 7 to July 28, 1956, the shortest period for any of Chaplin's features), but to temporarily uproot his family from their home in Vevey. This was no doubt a strain on Chaplin both creatively and financially; indeed, the personal cost of undertaking a new motion picture in a rented, modern studio may be partly responsible for some of the film's lackluster quality. To this end, a comment Chaplin made in the 1930s is revealing. "Europe pleases me," he responded to a question during his world tour, "and I have often wanted to come here to work. But just think: if in Hollywood I need tomorrow 30 lions, 200 pretty girls, and a crowd of 3,000 people, I have only to make three telephone calls. In less than 24 hours I find in my studio the 30 lions, 200 pretty girls, and 3,000 people. Besides, my numerous assistants know my needs and are accustomed to working with me (I am not always very accommodating). Where in Europe could I find such service?"[41] At Shepperton, Chaplin tried unsuccessfully to recreate the atmosphere of his old studio, though the results were not what he hoped for.

V. RESPONSE TO *A KING IN NEW YORK*

> If *A King in New York* does not sound funny in the telling, it must be said it is not very funny in the viewing. There are some marvelous moments ... (b)ut the writing is perfunctory ("To part is to die a little") and the physical production is at times dowdy or inappropriate ... [But] *A King in New York*, in spite of its failings, must be seen — at least once.[42]
> — John McCabe

Early screenings of the film before foreign audiences and critics made clear that *A King in New York* was not one of Chaplin's better releases. Some may have sympathized with Chaplin's plight with the United States, but that sympathy alone could not lift the picture from its numerous problems. By and large, most reviewers (European, at least) greeted the film with lukewarm commentary, positive only in the sense of recognizing Chaplin's stature in film history. But *A King in New York* also was Chaplin's least impressive feature film to date. Its importance stemmed not from the fact that it was a well-made picture — for it wasn't — but that Chaplin was important as a figure of cinema, and hence the picture garnered far more attention than the average film of similar quality. Though *New York Times* critic Bosley Crowther would note in a 1960 interview with Chaplin that reaction abroad to *A King in New York* was "generally popular,"[43] it was clear that very few moments in the picture measured up to the Chaplin of old.

Since Chaplin expressly forbade the film to be shown in the United States, reaction to the picture there was indeed limited. Some commentary did come from critics overseas, though occasionally an American writer would file a commentary after viewing the film abroad. One such critic, writing under the pseudonym "Paul Lee," submitted his opinion to the magazine *America*. Although largely sympathetic with Chaplin as an artist, the author nonetheless had little positive to say about his latest work:

> Unfortunately, the new theme of charity and sacrifice that colored *Limelight* and seemed to presage Chaplin films of a more positive vision is lacking in *A King in New York*. Though his genius for comedy and technical effect remains undiminished, the film suffers from the fact that its creator has sold his birthright for a "pot of message." The discretion that marked the films he made from 1914-1932 is gone. In its place is a satire of a most vitriolic sort.... No one can challenge his right to criticize America's mores — a right which Chaplin has, incidently, exercised abundantly and which caused him to refuse naturalization despite more than 30 years residence in the United States. One might justifiably ask, however, whether the sharp blade of caricature and satire which Chaplin wields in his latest film is a surgeon's scalpel, which cuts to heal, or a dagger which seeks only to wound.[44]

Nor has the film gained in stature since its release, as has been the case both for *The Circus* and *Modern Times*. "It is hard to believe," David Robinson wrote in 1972, "that Chaplin could have felt so blandly philosophical about his own situation and future.... He was painfully close to the situations which provided the themes of *A King in New York*; yet the comedy now seemed somehow detached, without the central fiber of serious reality. He attacked his targets with no deadlier weapon than some easy superficial slapstick; the Un-American Activities Committee was dismissed with a fire-hose."[45]

Chaplin appears to have been privately displeased with his efforts. He would begin writing his memoirs shortly after completion of the film, but devotes not a single sentence to *A King in New York* in *My Autobiography*. A pair of stills, in fact, is all that accounts for the film. Only later, in 1975, when

Chaplin published *My Life in Pictures*, a picture book that essentially excerpted comments from his original memoirs, did *A King in New York* warrant some additional commentary. They are reminiscent of Jerry Epstein's remarks on the strained atmosphere at the Shepperton Studios. "... I was disappointed in the picture," Chaplin noted. "I meant it to be quite up-to-date and modern but perhaps I didn't understand it. It started out to be very good and then it got complicated and I'm not sure about the end.... I feel a little uneasy about the whole film. The critics said that it was too serious — but then I've had that complaint made about nearly all my films when they where new. They said it about *The Gold Rush* and *The Circus* and *Modern Times* and *The Great Dictator* and *Monsieur Verdoux*— but later opinions change."[46]

The comedian held out hope that time would turn opinions on *King*, but its flaws were not a matter of changing tastes and differing perspectives. "If Charlie had conceived *A King in New York* in terms similar to those in *Monsieur Verdoux*," Roger Manvell noted, "he might have achieved a social satire on the theme of modern intolerance, and a film of at least comparable stature."[47] Chaplin had the ability to fully exploit his political problems with the United States within the film, yet his passion to seek bitter revenge appears to have gotten the best of him. What was eventually brought to the screen was not only ill-conceived, but in many cases badly executed, promoted and poorly distributed (at least with regard to the film's prohibition on American bookings). Chaplin's efforts to counter the personal affront by the United States took precedence over his filmmaking gifts, and the result is plainly evident onscreen. While critical reassessment may soften our reaction to the picture's numerous flaws, it can't — and the comedian hoped it would — eradicate them. Though Chaplin had dealt with poor reviews before, he was not prepared for the near-universal reaction to *A King in New York*, which was polite at best. Whereas in *Limelight* Chaplin had dealt with personal themes and met with general success (in Europe, at least), *A King in New York* used similar themes quite ineffectively, forming a passionate attack on the United States that led him astray from the type and quality of film that had been his trademark. It was, for all intents and purposes, Chaplin's first feature film to disappoint on almost every level.

Nevertheless, *A King in New York* remains an important production in the filmography of Charles Chaplin. Like *Limelight* before it, the film exhibits a degree of thought and emotion rarely displayed in the work of a major artist. It has some substantial flaws — in its conception, its treatment of themes, in its performances both before and behind the camera — but it nonetheless gives us a fuller picture of its creator at this period of his life. Even more so than viewing the Tramp films, *A King in New York* transcends its own narrative to give viewers a clear window into Chaplin's thoughts and feelings. *King* was a critical and financial failure, and perhaps justifiably so, but remains significant not only because Chaplin created it, but also because he invested much of himself in it.

8

A Countess from Hong Kong

On April 16, 1959, Chaplin's 70th birthday, he announced to press at the Manoir that he would be bringing the Little Fellow back to the silver screen. Chaplin, of course, could not be taken literally on the subject; though he was rather fit for his age, he certainly wasn't suggesting that he was assuming the role of the Tramp for yet another film. Rather, later that year, he and Jerry Epstein set to the task of putting together three of Chaplin's more popular silent shorts—*A Dog's Life, Shoulder Arms* (both from 1918) and *The Pilgrim* (1923)—into one feature film. Musical scores composed by Chaplin were added to each, as were connecting segments spoken by the comedian himself. He still maintained a critical eye on his work as well. As with his re-issue of *The Gold Rush* in 1942, several sequences hit the cutting room floor, most due to the artist's belief that they would not play well with modern audiences. The trilogy, now running slightly over two hours in length, was released in September of 1959 as *The Chaplin Revue*.

This continued a pattern in the timing of re-releases. Although not designed as such, the decision to bring back *City Lights* in 1950 had coincided with increased scrutiny of Chaplin's alleged political and moral transgressions, and was most certainly a help to his sagging public image in the period prior to *Limelight.** Additionally, it softened antagonism by film critics of the period who had vocally lamented his abandonment of the Tramp character. *The Chaplin Revue*, in this sense, could have played a similar role. Critical and public response to *A King in New York* had been disappointing; some even suggested that Chaplin was past his days as an influential artist. However, he could always count on acceptance and high regard for his earlier films, a fact that would lead him at several junctures to capitalize on their popularity both financially and artistically. With a limited release schedule and narrow appeal to filmgoers, *The Chaplin Revue* did not play widely, but helped Chaplin reconnect with many fans and critics following *A King in New York*.

---

*Chaplin's release of The Gold Rush *in 1942 also coincided with the beginning of negativity generated in response to his Second Front activities and the unfolding events with Joan Barry. However, preparations for the film had already been underway during this tumultuous period, and the positive response from the re-release proved merely a stroke of luck for the comedian.*

While the acceptance of his previous film work was a help, the popularity of the Tramp could not always distance Chaplin from the hostility of his final years in the United States. Commentators, some of them very vocal, continued to harbor negative feelings toward the once-adored entertainer. Hedda Hopper, for one, occasionally assailed him in her columns, and James P. O'Donnell wrote a most unflattering three-part series, "Charlie Chaplin's Stormy Exile," in the March 1958 issues of *The Saturday Evening Post*—both indications that the American press had not softened in its stance. Reinforcing popular notions of Chaplin's arrogance, O'Donnell characterizes the private side of the comedian as "paranoid" and a "creature of whims," as a man who possessed the Jekyll and Hyde personality to be warm and engaging at one moment, mean and unreasonable the next. Coming from a large-circulation publication, O'Donnell's *Post* series reemphasized to the United States that Chaplin was a negative figure.

Writers were not the only people seemingly after Chaplin: The Internal Revenue Service still had an outstanding tax bill for the comedian, even though the government had forced him out of the country seven years previous. The IRS wanted to slap Chaplin for taxes on income received on *Limelight* between the release of the picture and the day he officially handed in his re-entry permit, April 10, 1953 —$1.1 million. Chaplin eventually settled the issue, apparently on his own instigation, for less than half that amount. *Newsweek* speculated his motives were familial in nature; if Oona or the younger children wished to enter the United States at some future date with a portion of the comedian's inheritance, the magazine hypothesized that settling the issue assured their freedom from any potential tax liability.[1] The move also cleared the way for re-releases such as *The Chaplin Revue*, which could then play America unencumbered by any outstanding tax implications. Even in his absence, it seemed, Chaplin continued to be a figure of some prominence in the U.S. Out of sight, perhaps, but definitely not out of mind.

While both journalists and the government continued to fuel negative images of Chaplin, Hollywood itself stayed out of the fray, almost in silent endorsement of the status quo. When the idea for the Hollywood "Walk of Fame" came about, Chaplin was not included among the first 100 laid down honoring the film industry's pioneers.* Similarly, occasional Chaplin film screenings at colleges and public theaters continued to be shut down or hindered by public protest against the comedian and what many felt he stood for. His contributions to the industry he helped establish were only grudgingly acknowledged.

Nor was antagonism toward Chaplin the exclusive providence of the United States. When Oxford University decided to bestow him with an honorary

---

*Josef von Sternberg called attention to this oversight in his 1965 memoir Fun in a Chinese Laundry, and alluded to the fact that Chaplin should be included at once. (Josef von Sternberg; Fun in a Chinese Laundry, p. 33.)

Doctor of Letters at its June, 1962, commencement ceremonies, it did so over the vocal objections of historian Hugh Trevor-Roper. While the scholar did not directly take issue with Chaplin's political views, he did object to the degradation of Oxford's academia by conferring such an honor on a mere entertainer.* The episode placed Chaplin at the front of another controversial situation, and the flap was widely reported. Heightening interest in the affair was the presence of Dean Rusk, President John F. Kennedy's secretary of state, at the ceremonies. Chaplin and Rusk were quite cordial during their brief introduction.

Chaplin received the honor from Oxford, making light of the controversy in his address, and later followed this with the acceptance of yet another honorary degree from the University of Durham in Ireland. From there, Chaplin made his way back to Switzerland, where Oona gave birth to another son, Christopher, just a few days later, on the 8th of July. The boy was the last child in Chaplin's burgeoning family. With daughters Jane (born May 23, 1957) and Annette (born December 3, 1959), he now had ten children between his marriages to Oona and Lita Grey.

Creatively, the project that took up most of Chaplin's time during this period was not another film or re-release preparation, but penning his own memoirs. Chaplin began work on the manuscript following the release of *A King in New York*, and took the effort quite seriously. After nearly five decades in cinema and as a major (and sometimes highly controversial) world figure, the time had come to recount his own story, as so many columnists and biographers had attempted to do for him throughout his career.

Chaplin insisted on completing the manuscript himself, and to his own perfectionist standards. With only the aid of a typist, he made daily treks to his study at the Manoir, often spending virtually all day trying to perfect his style, much as he had done in filming his classic comedies. But although he was diligent with his work, he was also quite slow; he told Bosley Crowther of the *New York Times* that his memoirs were just a few weeks from completion in a 1960 interview, though the much-delayed book would not appear in print for another four years.[2]

Eventually, as work on his autobiography continued and an actual release date neared, Chaplin began to organize a re-release schedule for several of his films, capitalizing both on a renewed interest in silent film and the manuscript's upcoming publication date. Since the late 1950s, he had been employing a legal team to assert his right of ownership to several of his First National and United Artists films, since his absence from the United States had made it easier for unscrupulous individuals and companies to distribute films which he owned. (He did not own the rights to his Keystone, Essanay or Mutual films, copies of which were widely available to collectors and enthusiasts.) Owning

---

*The argument mirrors the rumored objections by the Windsors during Chaplin's 1931 world tour, when it was widely speculated that a knighthood might be bestowed upon him during his visit.

his own studio, beginning with his stint at First National, had given him the legal rights to all the films produced therein, the only exception being the 1925 version of *The Gold Rush*. In the midst of his political troubles in 1952, its copyright had expired, as Chaplin's staff had forgotten to renew it.[3]

Proving ownership was also a slow process, but once it had been firmly established, the re-releases moved ahead. In late 1963, the Plaza Theatre in New York began a year-long retrospective that featured a number of Chaplin's works, showing *City Lights, The Chaplin Revue, The Great Dictator, Modern Times* (paired with the sound re-issue version of *The Gold Rush* for most of its run), *Monsieur Verdoux* and *Limelight*.[4] In a sweetly ironic turn, it would be *Monsieur Verdoux*, rejected by the public in 1947, that had the longest and most profitable run at the Plaza.

The retrospective played only New York, but the re-releases were an integral part of what Charles Maland characterized as Chaplin's "guarded restoration" in the United States. Critical response was positive and the public, much less conservative in the early 1960s and by then removed from the scandals that had hounded Chaplin prior to his banishment, was allowed to view the comedian as an artist and not necessarily as a controversial figure. Though playing to a limited market, the re-releases helped to wipe away some of the lingering negativism toward the comedian, opening the door for Chaplin to once again ride atop the Tramp's popularity as a screen figure. The overall success of the small retrospective not only indicated Chaplin's popularity as a figure of cinema, but also helped to bolster interest as the time grew nearer for the publication of his memoirs.

I. THE BOOKS AND CRITICAL REASSESSMENT

A lot of Charlie's autobiography to me is false, because I knew him so well. He's building himself up for a pinnacle I don't think he ever reached.[5]
— Roland Totheroh

I asked [famed biographer Emil Ludwig] what he considered most essential in writing a biography. He said an attitude. "Then a biography is a biased and censored account," I said.
"Sixty-five percent of the story is never told," he answered, "because it involves other people."[6]
— Charles Chaplin

After nearly six years of preparation and much anticipation, *My Autobiography* finally hit bookstores in September of 1964. Interest was very high for the work, dubbed by *Time* as "one of the richest publishing coups of the century," and it appeared in eight different languages simultaneously.[7] Additionally, the manuscript was selected for the Book-of-the-Month Club not only in

America (where it was published by Simon & Schuster), but in similar European book clubs as well. The Russian publication *Izvestia* even bartered directly with Chaplin for an exclusive excerpt — nine pounds of caviar in exchange for the right to publish a mere 1000 words in their magazine.

Reviewers had mixed reactions. Chaplin was almost unanimously lauded for the depiction of his childhood in Victorian England — a "Dickensonian" account to many (Chaplin aids this analogy by referring often to Dickens in the opening chapters) — but criticized for his anecdotes thereafter. Often, he was very selective with his subject matter, and had the tendency to divulge little about important topics while writing several pages on relatively insignificant minutiae. ("Is poor 'Fatty' Arbuckle worth only one paragraph," lamented Bosley Crowther in the *New York Times Book Review*, "while Sir Herbert Beerbohm Tree gets two pages?"[8]) In detailing his Hollywood career, Chaplin concerned himself more with the various luminaries he had met, displaying a penchant for name-dropping that makes his memoirs more of a social roll call than a particularly candid glimpse into his life or his work. Moreover, Chaplin omitted discussions about several notable movie folk (as with Crowther's Arbuckle comment), and said very little about others who had worked directly with him for years, such as Henry Bergman or Rollie Totheroh.

Particularly disappointing for cinema fans were Chaplin's considerable oversights in discussing not only individual films, but his creative methods in general. "If you have questions about the mysterious art of silent film comedy," wrote David Madden in *Film Quarterly*, "plan to seek answers elsewhere. Except for a few elementary and half-hearted passes at what's expected, Chaplin seems less interested in retracing his steps as a movie-maker than fascinated by audience responses and salary and profit escalations."[9]

Jack Spears, no ardent admirer of the comedian or his sound era screen work, was even more direct in pinpointing the manuscript's weakness. "I doubt if Chaplin made any serious effort, while engaged on *My Autobiography*, to analyze his complex motivations and make his total personality understandable. His attitude seems to be that his inner self is his own business, an attitude that is self-defeating in an autobiographer."[10] "We leave the book," concluded Harding Lemay's review in *Life*, "as we approached it: with our own personal image of Charlie Chaplin — and no other — stamped indelibly upon a mental retina."[11]

Even though *My Autobiography* was an overall disappointment to many readers, it served its author well in selectively defending some of the more controversial events of his career; the Second Front speeches, the Joan Barry affair, script changes to *Monsieur Verdoux** and his exile received prominent attention.

---

*In My Autobiography, Chaplin wrote that the Breen office sent him a letter with "a long list of detailed objections" but he had told reporters gathered at the infamous Monsieur Verdoux press conference that there were only a handful of issues to be reconciled, and that he had relatively few problems with getting the script approved. (Charles Chaplin; from "Charlie Chaplin's Monsieur Verdoux Press Conference" [introduction by George Wallach], from Film Comment, Winter 1969; pp. 41–42.)

My Autobiography often proves more revealing when reading between the lines, assessing the comedian's choice of subject matter and tone — *A King in New York*, despite being his most recent film release, isn't even discussed, for instance. The omission of intimate detail surrounding the production of his films in favor of detailing his various social encounters, many felt, seemed to indicate that Chaplin had begun to value celebrity and wealth over the nature the work that vaulted him to prominence.

    Chaplin's version of his life was not the only version circulating during this period; others associated with Chaplin published their own accounts as well. Charles Chaplin, Jr. (with the help of writers M. and N. Rau), was the first to pen such a biography. *My Father, Charlie Chaplin* (1960) was widely regarded as a level, candid and thoughtful depiction of his famous father. Of particular interest is the younger Chaplin's gushingly fond memories of his father's relationship with Paulette Goddard, at the time the only stable mother figure he and brother Sydney had. Charles, Jr., is also able to define his father's weaknesses fairly even-handedly — his stubbornness, occasionally explosive manner and tireless perfectionism. An interesting aside, noted at the beginning of Charles, Jr.'s, book, is a passage that the elder Chaplin contributed to *Woman's Home Companion* about his 1931 world tour on meeting Lord Birkenhead, son of the famed British statesman. "At that time," Chaplin recalled, "he was writing a biography of his father. This was quite a difficult task, I thought, and wondered if a son, in doing such a biography, could sufficiently detach himself from the subject so as to see the deep shadows as well as the highlights which are necessary to a true portrait of a great man."[12] Perhaps his comment was just idle musing, but Chaplin could have been anticipating the inevitable; by most accounts, Charles, Jr., did a fair job with his book. Two other works followed the publication of *My Autobiography*, both in 1966; one by Michael Chaplin, *I Couldn't Smoke the Grass on My Father's Lawn*, co-written with Charles Hambett and Tom Merritt, and one by Lita Grey, *My Life with Chaplin*, co-written with Morton Cooper. Neither was particularly insightful. Aside from detailing her own personal troubles, Lita's work had to make the most of her little contact with the comedian — two years of marriage and sporadic encounters over the ensuing years, virtually all on the account of their boys.

    Michael's contribution provides even less in the way of substance. As a young man, Michael had been estranged from the family and living in London, and in 1965 it was widely reported that he had applied for National Assistance from the British government. Given his distance from the family circle, it was anticipated that his work would take the form of a tell-all exposé, which it did not; it is a product of its time, with a profusion of beatnik lingo, as evidenced by the title of the book alone. Unhappy with the work, Michael eventually resorted to employing his father's legal counsel to threaten to back out of the book deal unless several changes to the text were made.[13] Ultimately, a revised version was agreed upon, and the book moved forward for publication.

The comedian demonstrating for Marlon Brando how to dance with Geraldine Chaplin. Brando's frustrated expression sums up his experience under Chaplin's direction.

Coinciding with the publication of Chaplin's memoirs was an ongoing reassessment of his film work. In general, silent film was becoming more widely recognized as an art form worthy of critical study and preservation. Hundreds of scholars and period enthusiasts began to reassess the nature of silent film and the pioneers of the industry, sometimes challenging long-held contentions about the development of cinema. In the case of D.W. Griffith, for example, attention moved away from masterworks such as *The Birth of a Nation* and *Intolerance* as the artistic highpoints of his career, and more emphasis was placed upon his early work with the Biograph Company as the true technical, artistic and structural foundation for his directorial genius.

Similarly, the nature of silent comedy was also being scrutinized. It was during this reassessment that the work of Buster Keaton, a distant third in popularity behind Chaplin and Harold Lloyd during silent comedy's heyday, began to win over critical experts, primarily due to his inventiveness, timing, acrobatics and technical brilliance. In comparison, some of Chaplin's works, both sound and silent, did not hold up as well to the new analytical examination. Chaplin must have been sensitive to this criticism, for parts of his memoirs adopt a defensive tone against critics of his motion picture accomplishments.

As we have seen, since his departure from the silent format, Chaplin found that both dialogue and the increasing cost of filmmaking forced an end to the improvisational style of working he had employed earlier. Particularly with

Chaplin's introduction of more serious (and hence, less comical) themes in works such as *Monsieur Verdoux* and *Limelight*, a great deal more attention was required to the preciseness of dialogue as opposed to either movement or images to fully convey his artistic intentions. But throughout the sound era there seemed to be an ever-widening gap between Chaplin's creative interests, his working methods and the evolving film industry. Critic Otis Ferguson, shortly after the release of *Modern Times*, prophesied that "if [Chaplin] keeps on refusing to learn any more than he learned when the movies were just learning, each successive picture he makes will seem, on release, to fall short of what went before."[14] Although Ferguson was speculating in the mid-1930s, by the late 1950s and 1960s his observation was becoming a more common view of Chaplin's filmmaking skills. Even sympathetic commentators such as André Bazin recognized the trend in Chaplin's work:

> The only serious formal criticisms that can be leveled against a Chaplin film concern its unity of style, the unfortunate variations of tone, the conflicts of symbolism implicit in the situations. From this point of view the quality of Chaplin's films since *The Gold Rush* has definitely fallen off.... Chaplin [also] has some pretensions to being a social philosopher, and no injustice is done to the artist to find his ideas, though appealing, also an encumbrance.[15]

Similar remarks over the years, particularly regarding the technical aspects of Chaplin's work, did not go without defense in *My Autobiography*. "... [T]he imaginative student should use his own art sense about dramatic effects," Chaplin wrote. "If the amateur is creative he needs only the barest technical essentials ...

"I am surprised that some critics say my camera technique is old-fashioned, that I have not kept up with the times. What times? My technique is the outcome of thinking for myself, of my own logic and approach; it is not borrowed from what others are doing. If in art one must keep up with the times, then Rembrandt would be a back number compared to Van Gogh."[16]

But several key points have detracted from Chaplin's long-term critical reception. The silent film technique which Chaplin learned at the Keystone Studios utilized a fairly immobile camera, allowing the actors to simply play and improvise in front of the lens. Chaplin naturally began his directing by imitating this style, which — combined with his theatrical background — was the only style he was familiar with. But while technical and creative techniques advanced by leaps and bounds during the last 15 years of silent cinema, Chaplin did not always move rapidly to adopt or experiment with these new methods. Because his pantomime and Tramp character were the keys to his success as a film artist, he tended to rely on established cinematic methods that would exploit these characteristics the best, or which could heighten the sense or emotion of a particular scene. His reliance on medium shots, for instance, were probably best suited to capture the Little Fellow's facial and physical movements. But while other directors had learned to heighten dramatic effects by varying shots or scene composition, Chaplin rarely strayed from his proven mode. He gravitated toward those techniques that enhanced his own performance — essential, in his view, since his character was at the forefront of all his films. But in the late silent era, Chaplin still preferred to work more closely with an older style of filmmaking.

As he moved into sound film, Chaplin did adopt some of the industry's evolving lighting and directing techniques, yet never, it seems, to everyone's satisfaction. Terry's audition in *Limelight*, when Calvero is left alone in the theater while the lights are shut off around him, is an exceptional dramatic effect that captures the emotional isolation of Calvero. But such innovations aren't consistently present from film to film. Because of this, Karl Struss often gets much of the credit for the photographic content of *Limelight*, since Chaplin's films before and after fail to show similar influences.

In terms of narrative construction, Chaplin's character-oriented comedy had pitfalls as well. Chaplin, long admired (or to some, reviled) as a tireless perfectionist when it came to shooting and constructing his films, was also subject to some embarrassing glitches — some of which were discussed in the first chapter of this book. Although he was often proud of them, sets could look wholly makeshift (Rollie Totheroh called them the worst he had ever seen), and the continuity in his films was often lacking.

Many of the continuity glitches, as we have seen, are the result of the informal, highly improvisational structure of Chaplin's work routine but others are so conspicuous that they cannot be so easily explained. Often, when confronted with potential problems, it seems, Chaplin could become quite indignant. "[T]hey'll never notice it," Totheroh recalled Chaplin saying of a situation the cameraman had pointed out during the filming of *Sunnyside*, "they'll be busy watching me."[17] It's a belief that Chaplin clung to; some three decades later, Robert Parrish related a similar conversation with the comedian.

> [Chaplin] once asked me to look at some rushes of *Monsieur Verdoux*. There were five takes of a simple shot of Charlie doing a little dance at the foot of some stairs. Charlie was good in all takes, but in take three the camera panned a little bit too far and you could see an electrician leaning on a lamp for about six frames (a quarter of a second). Charlie asked me which take I liked best. I told him take two or take five. He said, "Did you like my dance in take three?" I said, "Yes, but what about the electrician?" Charlie jumped out of his seat and said, "What are you looking at *him* for? You're supposed to be looking at *me*. If you noticed the electrician that means I wasn't holding your attention."[18]

Chaplin's assertion is certainly egotistical, but he also was aware that the audience naturally focused on his character within a particular scene — this was certainly the case with the Tramp, and hadn't necessarily changed, in Chaplin's mind, with his succeeding film efforts. But it is still difficult for historians to reconcile the fact that he could meticulously drill Virginia Cherrill in *City Lights* over such a trivial action as how to present a flower, when in *Limelight* the positioning of pictures in Calvero's apartment changes from shot to shot. David Robinson points out the embarrassing glitch in the finale of *A Dog's Life*, where Scraps the mutt is revealed as the mother of several pups, despite the fact that it was quite obvious throughout the film that Scraps was a male.[19] For the comedian, the improvised ending was merely convenient; the effect outweighed the physical impossibility. While minor imperfections are impossible for any filmmaker to avoid, some of Chaplin's were so blatant that it damaged his reputation for perfection, not to mention the notion of him as one of the genre's premier creative artists.

Two works, both from the early 1970s, capture the critical polarization regarding Chaplin's film work. Writing in the *New York Times Magazine* in 1972, Richard Schickel made a strong argument to debunk the mystique surrounding the whole of Chaplin's films, particularly his sound films, maintaining that the comedian was, and always had been, a silent comic. Entitled "Hail Chaplin — The Early Chaplin," Schickel noted that few could touch his brilliance on the silent screen or approach the worldly appeal of the Little Fellow, yet he felt strongly that Chaplin's silent comedy brilliance could not make up for his deficiencies as a filmmaker, which became more and more apparent as he moved into feature filmmaking, and which truly damaged the quality of his sound era projects. "... [T]he two-reel length of these early comedies was perfectly suited to his gifts," Schickel noted. "... He found poetry in the ordinary, he transcended reality, [and] he extended the range of pantomime to previously unimagined dimensions.... [T]he little films of the Little Fellow were, in effect, solo ballets. As such, they had no more need of plot, of subsidiary characterizations, of great themes than one of Nijinsky's variations did."[20] Moving into feature filmmaking and the utilization of sound brought elements of technical and narrative depth that Chaplin not only used selectively but could never completely master, and hence his successive sound era projects proved more and more disappointing. But Chaplin's early screen success, coupled with his overwhelming popularity nonetheless had the effect of softening many critics, in the author's opinion, who had often been willing to overlook the comedian's filmic shortcomings on account of his celebrated reputation.

Schickel was particularly dismayed with what he felt was Chaplin's infatuation with his own persona, an effort to maintain over the years the "uncomplicated love affair" between the artist and his public that had developed during the silent era, when Charlie was cinema's biggest box-office draw. "One saw that [Chaplin's] art was based not on holding up a mirror to life," he notes, "but up to himself, that our presence, necessary as it was to satisfy his drive for power (which Sam Goldwyn, who knows something about the subject, called the most developed he had ever encountered), was essentially an intrusion on what was, really, a perfect love, that of an artist for his creation — which was, alas, himself."[21]

In contrast to Schickel were scholars typified by Gerald Mast, who argued similar issues in 1973's *The Comic Mind* much differently. He would perhaps find little fault with a number of Schickel's observations, particularly regarding Chaplin's silent film mastery, though Mast held a much higher regard for the bulk of Chaplin's sound era releases.

Because Schickel's article was an overview of Chaplin's screen work and historical legacy, it did not discuss at length a number of the specific technical issues the author perhaps could have cited in support of his arguments; Mast's book had more of an opportunity to reflect on these issues. In terms of camera technique, often lamented by Chaplin detractors as embarrassingly simplistic, he points toward a number of instances where the camera placement was truly inventive. Among Mast's examples were the brilliant "House of Mirrors" episode from *The Circus*, the café sequence from *Modern Times* (shot downwards from a high angle) and the interplay between the foreground and background in the flower shop scene from *Monsieur Verdoux*.[22]

Additionally, Mast argues that because editing naturally implies trickery, Chaplin used editing effects rather sparingly, and only with regard to his character's motivation or the particular action of the narrative. Many additional technical devices were likewise unsuited to Chaplin's artistic needs. On such logic, Mast concludes, Chaplin is not weak cinematically because, in his words, "such a position assumes 'good' cinematic technique is fixed rather than a function of a particular work. It also ignores the greater intimacy of the film medium — and intimacy is at the heart of Chaplin's cinematic method.... [His] technique was perfectly suited to communicate what he wanted. And that is as good as technique can ever be."[23]

While opinions such as Schickel's and Mast's represented very divergent critical discourse, the combined efforts of these and many other scholars have helped better define the comedian's strengths and weaknesses as a motion picture artist. Chaplin's perceived flaws — excessive sentimentality,* technical shortcomings or self-serving narratives — helped diminish the overall view of his artistry, but not his influence on the industry or his astronomical popularity during the silent period. David Cook's comments are typical of this collective assessment. "[Chaplin's] genius was as an actor and a mime. So long as his little tramp character stood at the center of his films, they were masterworks of comedy and pathos. When the tramp disappeared, the limitations of Chaplin's directorial ability became increasingly apparent. With few exceptions, it

---

*"Chaplin's style was profound in its simplicity," Charles Silver defensively noted of the comedian's work, "and he was always too preoccupied with depth of feeling to worry about depth of focus." (Charles Silver; Charles Chaplin: An Appreciation; p. 75; reprinted from Silver's own contribution to Film Comment, Spring 1972.)

was Chaplin's *presence* in his films, rather than anything in their formal structure, that made them interesting, important, and distinguished."[24]

While the critical reassessment of the 1950s, 60s and 70s has helped define and refine our understanding of the origin of cinema and its important figures, in terms of silent comedy, Chaplin's artistic reputation has perhaps suffered the most. Indeed, the comedian's work had been lauded so often for so long that his status was grossly overinflated; once one can strip away Chaplin's popularity as a film star and the image of the Tramp, in many respects an icon of the Twentieth Century, a more realistic picture emerges. Chaplin's true genius was his pantomime, unique characterization and undeniable skill in mixing pathos with comedy — a concoction of humor and sentiment that lifted his comedies to a different level of aesthetic appreciation. For the silent period, Chaplin was an adequate, though never particularly innovative technician, utilizing camera and directorial techniques that enhanced his own performance and avoided tremendous complication.

His work in the sound era displayed these same characteristics, though the gap between himself and other filmmakers grew larger with every passing motion picture project. Coinciding with Chaplin's move away from any semblance of the Tramp character with 1947's *Monsieur Verdoux*, his pictures began to appear less technically astute, utilizing more dialogue and in many cases dispensing with the pantomime that was his greatest performing asset. Many have viewed his projects following *The Great Dictator* as part of the comedian's downward spiral as a filmmaker.

In terms of silent comedy, the genre's top three comics brought very different strengths to their work: Chaplin's was skilled pantomime and near-perfect realization of character in the Tramp; Keaton's amazing ingenuity, dexterity and technical brilliance; and Lloyd's perfection of gag comedy, in addition to his high level of artistic and popular consistency throughout the 1920s.

Each in their own way displayed characteristics that have made their films lasting and distinctive. But of the three, only Chaplin managed to continue his career successfully after the introduction of sound; Keaton's career languished after shooting a number of talking features with Jimmy Durante, and Lloyd, despite several sound projects throughout the 1930s, was never able to regain the audience following he had as a silent star. Chaplin's wealth and popularity were considerable assets to continuing his film work, but the comedian also possessed the ability to create stories that appealed to broad sections of the viewing public. While at first this meant the continuance of the Tramp character, Chaplin still managed to stay at least partially in touch with his audience, slowly evolving in terms of narrative themes and technical accomplishment but nearly always remaining appealing to both critics and filmgoers. To be sure, most of Chaplin's sound era films aren't nearly as innovative, influential or even memorable as his silent work, but the fact that he still managed to remain an important figure in the industry long after the introduction of talking pictures attests to his skill and resourcefulness as a filmmaker.

II. THE RETURN TO FILMMAKING

Though Chaplin had put aside feature filmmaking following *A King in New York*, he never abandoned thoughts of returning to motion pictures. Once *My Autobiography* was behind him, he finally had his chance.

On November 11, 1965, Chaplin gathered with reporters in London's Savoy Hotel to make the formal announcement: At age 76, he was planning to embark on the 81st film of his career. The project, he announced, would be called *A Countess from Hong Kong*—a revamped version of the *White Russian/Stowaway* script that Chaplin had penned for Paulette Goddard shortly after *Modern Times*. For the first time in almost half a century, since the comedian's stint with First National, the picture was not to be produced by Chaplin; a deal had been struck with Universal Studios, who enthusiastically put up the film's $4 million budget. The change seemed to suit Chaplin, who claimed to reporters that he felt liberated from the strain of carrying an entire production on his own shoulders.

Though the picture was some 30 years in the making, the comedian was nonetheless primed to begin work, optimistic (as always) that he was embarking on his greatest film yet. David Robinson attended the Savoy press conference, which was his first opportunity to see Chaplin in the flesh.

> He would not say much about the story except that it was set in the period just after the Second World War, and a lot of the action takes place aboard a ship. It has no political message. Asked to be more precise, Mr. Chaplin said he was sorry but he was tired; which he clearly was not. He would add modestly that, "the situation is riotously funny but justified and believable…. It is not slapstick, but comedy of character, taken from life."
>
> Chaplin said that his son Sydney would play in it. "He's a very good comedian and I think he will contribute to the lilt and hilarity of the screenplay." (Chaplin always chooses his words carefully if sometimes curiously.) Inevitably the columnists asked if his son Michael would play. Chaplin was grave. "I'm not answering any personal questions …" and when the newsman tried to insist, "Don't get smart-alecky with me …" He was not solemn when asked about America. He had no plans to go there unless it happened to be in connection with the picture; but in any case he had no quarrel with Hollywood. "I wrote a book, and I think America came out of it pretty well. I happen to like Hollywood. Anyway, I don't think that's pertaining much to the picture."

Chaplin then left his brief conference in the hands of Universal executives, who gave their perspective on working with one of cinema's legendary talents, but Robinson was quick to notice that some reporters had already found their story angle: "And, incorrigibly, at the telephone in the corner," ends his brief article, "a reporter was already ringing through his copy: 'Charles Chaplin, world famous clown who began life in London's East End, today refused to comment when asked....'"[25]

Working in England again (this time at Pinewood Studios), Chaplin found that the production arrangement was not the only new wrinkle to the film. It would be his first picture in color, and for the first time would utilize established box office talent other than himself. Sophia Loren, whom Chaplin had greatly admired in Vittorio de Sica's *Yesterday, Today and Tomorrow* (1963), and Marlon Brando, one of the greatest dramatic actors of his time, both committed to the project without even reading the script; Chaplin's reputation was enough incentive to put their energies behind *A Countess from Hong Kong*. "I would have acted in the telephone book, with him directing," Brando was quoted as saying.

The adaptation of the original *Stowaway* script went quickly and smoothly; little of the comedian's original work apparently remains in the Chaplin archives, so thorough were his efforts to update and expand the story.[26] Meanwhile, Jerry Epstein, serving as producer of the film in addition to working as Chaplin's assistant, put the production together, which was to begin shooting on January 25, 1966, and ran for 14 weeks.

But even before a single frame of film had been exposed, Chaplin was to experience his first run-in with star egos. According to Epstein, Brando, through his agent, insisted that he receive top billing.[27] He tipped off the Chaplin camp that Carlo Ponti, Loren's husband and chief negotiator on the *Countess* deal, would insist that she receive top billing, but very late in the contract talks—a move he had apparently utilized before. Brando's agent was accurate: After it was brought up, Ponti adamantly maintained that Loren was the bigger international star, and her name should be more prominently featured. Besides, Ponti argued, Brando was not only less of a box office draw, but regularly hindered productions with his erratic behavior, making him a wholly troublesome talent. None of this, of course, sat well with Chaplin. "Who the hell are they?" he angrily remarked to Epstein one day as the billing issue dragged on. "*I'm* Charlie Chaplin!"[28]

Eventually, after the comedian threatened to recast her part, Loren and Ponti backed away from insisting on top billing, and the pre-production problems seemed to be taken care of. As Chaplin and Epstein got ready for the beginning of the shoot, the contractual side of the filmmaking was settled—with both stars in place, all that was asked was for Brando to lose a little weight prior to the January 25 start of production. But how the project was coming together seemed of minor importance. What was important was that Charlie Chaplin was working again, and his tremendous comedic gifts were being put to use directing two of the hottest talents in the film world. With Chaplin's reputation, in addition to a generous amount of publicity generated by Universal, anticipation for the film was high indeed.

III. THE NARRATIVE OF *A COUNTESS FROM HONG KONG*

The film opens, as so many Chaplin films had before it, with an introductory title: "As a result of two world wars, Hong Kong was crowded with refugees."

In a bustling Hong Kong dance hall, where for a price drunks, sailors and the like can dance (and presumably partake in much more) with supposed royalty, an American diplomat, Ogden Mears (Brando), traveling through the Orient en route to Hawaii and the mainland United States, takes the opportunity to dance with one such girl, Natascha (Loren). The son of a wealthy and prominent businessman, Mears is simply out for an evening of pleasure before boarding the ocean liner for his return voyage across the Pacific. The two engage in some pleasant but idle conversation before the diplomat retires for the evening, and Mears leaves the dance hall thinking nothing of his innocent meeting with the beautiful young woman.

Later, when he returns to his state room and the ship departs for Honolulu, he is surprised to find Natascha, who claims to be an exiled Russian countess, hiding in his cabin, armed with a plea for help. She recounts for him her sad past — she fled her homeland when it became too dangerous to continue living there, and had become the mistress to a gangster at the tender age of 14. Now she has been reduced to a lowly dance hall girl, but always held out hope that she could one day begin again in America, where she could escape her dismal existence and partake in its many opportunities. If Mears can hide her throughout the voyage and, utilizing his position as a diplomat, arrange the necessary papers to gain her legal entry into the United States, Natascha can realize the better life she's always dreamed of.

Reluctantly, Mears agrees, but only after hearing her story. The proposition is a risky one for him: He's being considered for an ambassadorship in the Middle East, and any hint of scandal could ruin his chances of receiving the important post. For this reason, his failing marriage has been maintained in order to keep up appearances, though his wife back home (Tippi Hedren) is scheduled to meet the boat in Honolulu, where they plan to discuss their future together. If anyone were to find Natascha in his cabin, the illegality of his actions and appearance of impropriety would likely ruin both his personal and professional lives.

But attempting to hide her from Mears' entourage, not to mention shipboard personnel, proves a daunting task. Day after day, every knock at the door is greeted with anxiety, as Natascha, who boarded with only a single dress to her name and must wear a pair of Ogden's borrowed pajamas as night clothes, leaps from living room to bedroom, bedroom to bathroom with each successive visitor to the diplomat's cabin. Furthermore, she is tremendously bored while cooped up in the room, and at one point risks being caught by escaping from its confines for an evening in the ship's ballroom and lounge, where her beauty grabs the interest of more than a few male passengers.

Despite a number of close calls, the deception manages to stay undiscovered, but it also cannot fool everyone, as Mears' comically somber valet Hudson (Patrick Cargill) and trusted advisor Harvey Crothers (Sydney Chaplin) eventually become accomplices. But the inclusion of more people in the cover-up doesn't insure its success — in fact, it only tends to raise the stakes a bit further. Mears becomes angered and frustrated for allowing such an explosive situation to continue, but gradually the mismatched pair — foes for much of the voyage — begin to fall in love.

Later, as the sea passage nears a close, Mears and his entourage are left frantically brainstorming a method of getting Natascha off the boat and into the United States. Obtaining a passport is an impossibility, and Immigration officials are likely to discover her if nothing is done. However, they do have at least one ace up their sleeves: If a convincing marriage can be arranged between Natascha and an eligible American citizen, her passage into the country will be assured. Ogden is married, as is Harvey. So Hudson, much against his will, is drafted into service. The strange ceremony is performed — with more than a little skepticism — by the ship's captain.

The plan seems to be a sound one, save for Hudson's inability to remember the agreed-upon story, as Immigration in Honolulu will undoubtedly be suspicious concerning such an abrupt courtship. The ship docks in port, and as Ogden readies himself for the reunion with his wife Martha, trouble erupts. The presence of government officials has made Natascha very uneasy, and fearing that she is about to be caught, Natascha makes her own escape by leaping over the side of the ship and into the harbor, where she swims to shore and her freedom.

While Ogden attends to his wife, Harvey is entrusted with locating Natascha. Conveniently, Ogden and Martha agree to part, clearing away the marriage issue from his life. When Harvey and Natascha return to their seaside hotel, she and Ogden pledge their love for each other, with he abandoning his diplomatic career for a life together with the Russian beauty who has stolen his heart.

IV. SHOOTING *A COUNTESS FROM HONG KONG*

According to both contemporary press reports and Jerry Epstein's recollection of the production, *A Countess from Hong Kong* was a relatively easy and pleasurable experience for Chaplin, who clearly relished the opportunity to return to feature filmmaking. In spite of the hassles that preceded the shoot, the production ran from January 25 to May 11, 1966, with very few troubles to speak of.

Yet despite the relative harmony on the set, an image that Universal, obviously, sought to promote, not everything went as smoothly as appearances seemed to indicate. Sophia Loren got along famously with her illustrious director, a feeling that certainly comes through in her performance, and she stayed devoted to both Chaplin and the film long after the production was finished. Brando, however, was another story. The actor was initially awed by Chaplin, a longtime favorite (Brando reportedly pored over his films in preparation), but there soon developed a great rift between director and star.

Filming started on the wrong foot. Asked to lose weight prior to the beginning of production, Brando did not do so. Further, as Carlo Ponti had warned them, Brando disrupted the production schedule almost immediately by failing to appear for the first three days of shooting, forcing Chaplin to work around his absence. Inquiring reporters were told that the actor had suddenly come down with an attack of appendicitis. Eventually, Brando did make himself available for the cameras, but the strain on the set was already being felt.

Chaplin moved forward with his work as if everything was going as planned. But Brando quickly took a dislike to his directorial methods — methods that Chaplin had been employing for decades, but which did not serve Brando's talents well at all. He was particularly at odds with Chaplin's meticulous coaching, which left almost nothing for an actor to do but repeat what he had performed.

Historian Kevin Brownlow, compiling material for his landmark book *The Parade's Gone By*, accompanied Gloria Swanson to the set of *A Countess from Hong Kong*, where he got to see Chaplin directing first-hand.

> Sophia Loren, devastating in her low-cut dress, was joined by Marlon Brando in a blue dressing gown, looking furious. A wave of tension followed him as he shuffled from behind the camera and onto the set.
> Chaplin seemed oblivious. As he directed Loren, and then Brando, I scribbled down the directions verbatim. He tried to work out a way in which Loren could walk over to Brando, holding a glass. He paid no attention to dialogue. I heard him give only one dialogue direction. He may have written words, but he could not remember them. "So-and-so-and-so-and-so etcetera," would be his average line.... It was as exciting as watching a Chaplin film no one ever knew existed; first he played the Brando role, then he skipped over and did the Loren part. One was aggressively masculine, the other provocative and feminine, yet both remained pure Chaplin. It is a real loss to the cinema that Chaplin refused to allow a film to be made about the production.[29]

Swanson was also impressed with the opportunity to see Chaplin at work — she had been an unknown extra at the Essanay Studio in Chicago during the comedian's brief stay in the Midwest some fifty years previous — but she also recognized the challenge of working with him. "You can see why actors find him difficult," she whispered to Brownlow at one point during their visit. "This is a simple scene, and he's making much ado about nothing."[30]

It was the type of direction that Brando was not used to; despite telling Epstein and the steady stream of reporters visiting the set that *Countess* was one of the easiest shoots he had been on, Brando in fact quietly resented Chaplin's unwillingness to allow him to develop his own character, or even choreograph his own movements. "... I was a puppet, a marionette in [*Countess*]," he told an interviewer many years later. "I wasn't there to be anything else because Chaplin was a man of sizable talent and I was not going to argue with him about what's funny and not funny.... He shouldn't have tried to direct it.... He wasn't a man who could direct anybody. He probably could when he was young. But with Chaplin's talent you had to give him the benefit of the doubt."[31]

A good portion of the actor's resentment toward Chaplin stemmed from his treatment of his own son Sydney on the set of *Countess*. As had been the case before, particularly with Paulette Goddard on the set of *The Great Dictator*, Chaplin was often the hardest on those closest to him, as if their performances were somehow a reflection on himself. Jerry Epstein recalled:

> ... Charlie was patient with all the other actors except Syd. In films, you have to come on the set prepared, but Syd needed time to digest his directions. Charlie was impatient. "For Chrissakes, come on Syd!" Charlie would say irritated. "Get some feelings into the lines. You're trying to make Sophia feel better. Show a little warmth!" When Syd didn't respond immediately, Charlie became more agitated. "For Chrissakes, what's wrong with you? Get the lead out of your pants!"
>
> Marlon, watching from the sidelines, became worked up as he saw Charlie hammering away at Syd. He took me to one side: "How can he humiliate his own son like that in front of all these people?" "Marlon," I replied, "Syd knows Charlie is doing it for his own good. He adores his father. So keep out of it — it's between father and son."
>
> But Marlon's anger didn't subside. From that moment on, Marlon, the champion of the underdog, refused to take Charlie's directions. Just two days earlier, Marlon said it was the easiest film he'd ever worked on. Now, whatever Charlie wanted to say to him had to be relayed through me. Charlie wouldn't get intimidated by Marlon's behavior; nothing was going to kill his enthusiasm for the task at hand.[32]

Claire Bloom had similar recollections of Chaplin's treatment of his son on the set of *Limelight*, noting that Syd could be quite animated away from the studio, but around his father he was "nervous and wooden."[33] To Brando, this type of treatment was an outrage. "He was a mean man, Chaplin," he told Lawrence Grobel. "Sadistic. I saw him torture his son.... Humiliating him, insulting him, making him feel ridiculous, incompetent. He played a small part in the movie and the things Chaplin would say to him. I said, 'Why do you take that?' His hands were sweating. He said, 'Well, the old man is old and nervous, it's all right.' That's no excuse. Chaplin reminded me of what Churchill said about the Germans, either at your feet or at your throat."[34]

As a result of the differences with his director, Brando essentially gave up on *A Countess from Hong Kong* in the midst of production. Although he fulfilled his contractual obligation and did so with a minimum amount of disruption, his focus was clearly on getting the film completed quickly and painlessly — even if it meant following Chaplin's sometimes trivial stage direction to the letter. Privately, he regarded the film as a disaster, although it would be many years before Brando would begin to his air negative feelings on working with Chaplin. "I still look up to him as perhaps the greatest genius that the medium has ever produced," Brando recently wrote in *Songs My Mother Taught Me*. "I don't think anyone has ever had the talent he did; he made everyone else look Lilliputian. But as a human being his was a mixed bag, just like all of us."[35]

Even with the underlying tension on the set of *A Countess from Hong Kong*, the picture managed to stay on schedule, and spirits remained relatively light. Much to Chaplin's chagrin, Universal had arranged for a number of journalists to visit the set throughout the shoot. Old acquaintances and friends (such as Gloria Swanson) also dropped in to wish the comedian well. As a result, the set at Pinewood was a good deal more open than the Chaplin productions of earlier years, particularly during the *Modern Times, The Great Dictator* and *Monsieur Verdoux* shoots. Most press reports were fascinated with the question of why Chaplin, who turned 77 during the production, was still eager to work. He once responded to the question by claiming he was but a servant to the muses; other times he was less romantic. "It's all such fun," Chaplin told *Newsweek*'s Joe Morgenstern early in post-production. "Every minute I'm proving something to myself. I don't know what it is, but ... I'm proving that I can do it. I have to have something to do. I have a very comfortable home in Switzerland and I could just as well play around — go skiing and all that nonsense — but I've always been enthusiastic about work. Sometimes I've been more enthusiastic than the work deserved, I suppose."[36]

Many visiting reporters were particularly taken with the sight of Chaplin staging and performing scenes for the cast and crew — planning with meticulous detail every little gesture and movement for a performer, then demonstrating how the others should move or react as well. *Life*'s Dora Jane Hamblin visited the set when Chaplin was filming with Sophia Loren, demonstrating a gag where Natascha becomes comically flustered while attempting to read a book as Ogden directs an icy stare at her:

> Charlie suddenly demonstrates. He picks up a book Sophia is supposed to be reading and settles himself into a chair. He sighs, shrugs, turns the pages. Suddenly a look of consternation ripples over his face. He's forgotten what the last paragraph said. He turns the pages, crosses his legs, adjusts the strap of his gown, and reads on. In silence, total silence. Suddenly, he's frantic, turning several pages

backward, then forward, then backward. Jerome Epstein, an old Chaplin associate who is the film's producer, bursts into laughter.
"*That's* a tricky one," he says.
Sophia gets up and gets into the chair and picks up the book. She copies the
Chaplin gestures, and adds a couple of her own as Charlie chuckles in the background. They do five takes and Sophia struggles off the set exhausted, pleading
for a cigarette.[37]

Chaplin drew more strength from his own family than from the attention lavished upon his latest production. As with *A King in New York*, the
Chaplins uprooted themselves for the picture, and his children, many of whom
were then on their own, were frequent visitors to the set. Oona held a special
position during the production, sitting quietly and unobtrusively out of the
way, but commanding Chaplin's attention nonetheless. "Oona was with me
every day on the set," Chaplin later wrote in *My Life in Pictures*. "I needed her
to be there."[38] Despite his vigor for filmmaking, an element of unassuredness
can be detected in Oona's presence, to whom he would look toward at the conclusion of every successful take. She would nod and smile politely — never
intruding, always reassuring.

V. THE FAILURE

If there was one positive aspect to the stream of reporters filing through
the studio throughout the shoot, it was that the attention was a welcome
reminder to Chaplin that he was still a filmmaker of great importance. Thanks
to the shrewd publicity staff at Universal, *A Countess from Hong Kong* was proving to be his most anticipated film since *The Great Dictator*; not only was he
working with some of the day's biggest box office talent, but in helming the production himself, audiences and critics looked forward to another screen triumph from the former king of silent cinema. After leaving America abruptly
in 1952 and with underwhelming popular and critical reaction to *A King in New
York*, the release of *Countess* found Chaplin poised, at least in his mind, to
regain the good will of filmgoers the world over.
But he did not — reaction to *Countess* was universally awful, and even
sympathetic reviewers had a tough time discussing Chaplin's latest motion picture release. In some ways, *A Countess from Hong Kong* does display vintage
Chaplin touches. The scene Dora Jane Hamblin described, where Natascha
uncomfortably attempts to read a book or, later, Sydney Chaplin's playful
harassment of a nosy passenger in the ship's bar are the kind of whimsical
comic business that Chaplin used to create for himself in earlier films. And
therein, perhaps, lies part of the problem. Despite Sophia Loren's and Sydney
Chaplin's adept mimicry in both scenes, it's a type of physical comedy that

With Marlon Brando preparing for his cameo appearance as a seasick purser, Chaplin's last film appearance, in *A Countess from Hong Kong.*

seems more suited to the elder Chaplin's talents than their own. In fact, given the comedian's directorial methods, it is almost more amusing to imagine Chaplin demonstrating these gags himself on the set than it is to see them performed onscreen. Visualizing Chaplin in such a way is almost an unavoidable reflex when viewing the film, and helps underscore the notion that *A Countess from Hong Kong* suffers without Chaplin's presence before the camera.

Similarly, other elements of the film seem familiar. Occasional bits of dialogue are clearly autobiographical; early in the film, Ogden Mears laments being the son of one of America's most prominent and richest men, noting the tremendous burden this places upon him. Chaplin's irony is having Mears speaking at the time to his trusted advisor Harvey Crothers, the part played by Sydney Chaplin. Natascha's later trouble with Immigration officials, as well as the occasional offhand remark about Communism, are also recognizable elements that pepper the screenplay.

But ultimately its satisfying moments are fleeting, and on the whole, *A Countess from Hong Kong* is a disappointment (though perhaps not as much today as it was when it was first released, when it appeared very much out of synch with popular cinematic trends). The first third of the film is essentially a series of slamming doors and bedroom mix-ups — perhaps effective in the 1930s, when Chaplin penned the original version of the script, but quite dated in the late 1960s. These early scenes create a large hole from which the picture must climb. The last half of the film picks up, though perhaps too late.

The tremendous negative criticism *A Countess from Hong Kong* received was not entirely warranted, though there was plenty to dislike about the film. Aside from the dated screwball-type comedy, the picture often veers sharply toward comic material that Chaplin wants to include — his brief cameo appearance as a seasick porter is a prime example — with only the barest narrative justification for these events. Put another way: In *Monsieur Verdoux,* Chaplin's character counts money with lightning speed and accuracy, wholly consistent with his former profession as a bank clerk. In *Countess,* the seasickness episode is only thinly plausible, and looks like an effort to insert a brief comic diversion into the picture. Chaplin runs into a similar situation elsewhere, in a sequence featuring Margaret Rutherford as an elderly ship passenger who inadvertently becomes the recipient of romantic overtures from a man who believes he is wooing Natascha.

Technical flaws, too, plagued *Countess.* The production lasted for some 14 weeks but has a rushed and distinctly unpolished feel. Many of the film's cost-cutting measures, such as using stock footage of Hawaii, are glaringly apparent. Chaplin encountered a similar problem in *A King in New York,* attempting to integrate actual photography of the Big Apple into a re-creation of the city at Shepperton Studio. Deficient, as well, is a moment set on the beach at Waikiki, which is so obviously recreated on a soundstage that the backdrop proves a tremendous distraction to the viewer.

Many of the performances throughout *Countess* are lifeless, save for Loren, who genuinely looks like she's having a good time with the material, even if it was a little ill-suited to her talents. Brando is particularly wooden as Ogden Mears; the physical comedy early in the picture clearly gave him trouble. Mears is a character with more charm and suaveness than Brando was able to imbue him with. (Cary Grant, whom Jerry Epstein claims was initially interested in the role, seems a more likely candidate to have played Mears successfully.[39]) Despite what he endured on the set, Sydney Chaplin turns in the best performance of the picture, though Harvey Crothers was a relatively small role.

"A major problem with the film was that, in the year of *Bonnie and Clyde, The Dirty Dozen, The Graduate, Weekend* and *Belle de Jour*," David Robinson noted, "a gentle romantic comedy was an almost incomprehensible anachronism."[40] Despite Universal's excitement in working with Chaplin and the press buildup preceding its release, the film would be a disappointment to both the studio and to Chaplin.

VI. RESPONSE TO *A COUNTESS FROM HONG KONG*

People in the know say it is a timeless comedic masterpiece. People in the know also say it is an antiquarian catastrophe. No one but the most brilliant director ever knows anything about a film until all the pieces are pasted together, and even he cannot be sure. "I have to cut just so much and not a bit more or the whole film may be ruined," says Chaplin. "I feel like a rabbi."[41]

— Joe Morgenstern, on visiting Chaplin early in the post-production phase of *A Countess from Hong Kong*

I think it's the best thing I've ever done.... Things like *The Gold Rush*— one, two three, pantry cakey — it's so easy. A situation comedy like *Countess* is much more difficult to keep going.... The humor of *Countess* may not be mechanical, but the situations are excruciating. The critics now are terrified of the old-fashioned, but this picture is ten years ahead of its time.[42]

— Charles Chaplin

... if an old fan of Mr. Chaplin's movies could have his charitable way, he would draw the curtain fast on this embarrassment and pretend it never occurred.[43]

— Bosley Crowther

Though Chaplin had a few defenders in the press when *A Countess from Hong Kong* was released, most critics felt the picture was significantly beneath the par of his other sound films, including *A King in New York*. While Chaplin would maintain that he felt *Countess* was one of his best works, critical and popular response didn't bear this out. However oblivious Chaplin was toward the tension on the set between himself, Loren and Brando, his film reflected these strains. Brando may have been excited by the prospect of working with one of his cinematic idols, but it is quite clear that he found the experience miserable, and one can sense his lack of confidence in almost every scene. In all likelihood, Loren was probably having the same doubts about the film, yet her response was entirely different. She adored Chaplin, and the pair got along extremely well from the moment she agreed to play in *Countess*, and this, too, comes out in her performance. Whereas Brando seemed to retreat from the motion picture, Loren embraced it for what it was — the opportunity to work with one of film's legendary figures — and didn't seem to be overly troubled with the direction of the production.

These star performances were indeed one focal point for jabs at the film, but it was ultimately Chaplin's work as a director and screenwriter that bore the brunt of criticism. *A Countess from Hong Kong* was outmoded by any standard, from the title that opened the film to the closing credits. While Chaplin certainly had the utmost confidence in the picture, his work was so out of touch with mainstream cinema in the late 1960s that most critics regarded the work as an embarrassment to his stature. Critical reception of the film was dismissive, and in some cases even mean-spirited.

The picture was quite unlike anything Chaplin had attempted before; Roger Manvell called it the "least characteristic" of all his works.[44] Critics of Chaplin's camerawork had plenty to lament; while the script played to Chaplin's strengths, moving from room to room aboard the ship and perhaps limiting camera mobility, much of *Countess* is "pure theater." The action on the screen takes precedence — as Kevin Brownlow observed, Chaplin paid little if any attention to dialogue cues — and the comedian was content to simply allow the actors to perform before the camera. Whereas cinema was becoming much less constricted during the 1960s, Chaplin still seemed to be clinging to his stagebound ways.

Nor does *A Countess from Hong Kong* follow the pattern that Chaplin had displayed in creating films in the past, most notably *Limelight* and *A King in New York*. Particularly during the sound era, as we have seen, his choice of subject matter was often directly influenced by developments or observations made from his own life, culminating with *Limelight* and *King*, both of which were heavily autobiographical. While *Countess* was based in part on Chaplin's trips to the Orient and his encounter with May Reeves during his 1931 world tour, there is little within the narrative that specifically reflects Chaplin the man; a distinct break from the trend displayed in his recent films. Issues and themes that had been previous concerns to the comedian no longer asserted themselves forcefully, and what remains comes off as little more than lip service. Ogden Mears' comment on the trouble of being the son of a famous man is a brief ironic aside, while Natascha's concern over Immigration officials in the United States is just a lukewarm reminder of its director's own troubles. Whereas every one of Chaplin's films since *The Great Dictator* carried a strong and identifiable message, the old-fashioned *Countess* seems to be about nothing, a featherweight comedy of little significance, barring the appearance of Brando, Loren, and the return of a motion picture legend. Projection problems plagued *Countess'* London premiere on January 5, 1967, Jerry Epstein recalled, and it was perhaps an omen, for reaction by critics afterward was swift and immediate: The film was a bomb.[45] The British press was so antagonistic, in fact, and Chaplin so hurt by the reaction, that he felt cornered once again, as he had during the height of criticism against him in America; he publicly called London critics a bunch of "bloody idiots." The Paris premiere went much better, with a number of critics even scolding the English press for so coldly bashing the film, but box office receipts from Europe over the coming weeks were clearly less than Universal and Chaplin had hoped.

Unlike *A King in New York*, *Countess* opened in America — his first new release there in 15 years — three months later, in March of 1967, but reaction there was much the same as in Europe; the publicity blitz couldn't right the sinking motion picture. Based on reaction in Europe, Chaplin put on a brave face and helped promote his picture in America but he seems to have known that *Countess* would again be poorly received. "When one is waiting for the opening of a picture," he told Richard Meryman shortly before the New York debut, "it's like waiting for an execution. Depression. Worst damn days — and at my age I don't want to wish the days away.... I've had a lot of assurance that it's good, but you always have your doubts. Perhaps I don't know at all. Perhaps I've been wrong.

"The public will be the ones to judge it, and they unconsciously are so right in the mass. Their rebuffs are very gentle. They merely don't go. A critic gets furious and foams and writes a column about this dastardly thing and how horrible the man is. The public just says, 'Oh, let's don't go. It's not so good.' After a man has sweated blood to give them everything—'It's not so good.' A light indifference. Terrifying."[46]

And Chaplin was right — critics did react unfavorably in America. Jerry Epstein recalled that *New York Times* critic Bosley Crowther had attempted unsuccessfully during the production of *Countess* to obtain an exclusive interview with Chaplin (he had previously done one for the *Times* in 1960), and was later very angered when Universal would not schedule a press screening of *Countess* prior to its premiere. Thus, Epstein contends, Crowther — arguably America's foremost movie critic at the time — was set on panning the film.[47] Calling the picture a "painfully antique bedroom farce" in his March 17 review, Crowther saved niceties only for Chaplin's brief appearance as a seasick porter, as well as Margaret Rutherford's cameo.[48] Overall, he felt, the production showed almost nothing of Chaplin's comedic genius.

Nine days later, in the *Times'* Sunday edition, Crowther again panned the film, in a vicious column that also attacked Orson Welles' *Falstaff* (aka *Chimes at Midnight*), asserting that both artists were damaging their reputations by continuing to produce substandard work. Crowther's characterization of *Countess* had gone from "painfully antique" to "gruesome" in just a few days, and while he found Chaplin largely responsible for most of the picture's deficiencies, both Marlon Brando and Sophia Loren were also targets of criticism. "They surely sensed it was foolish," he lamented, "that they had the most dismal dialogue, that the characters they were acting were barren of even rudimentary charm and fun. I would think that two actors as distinguished and comparatively contemporary as they would have tried to save Mr. Chaplin from this fiasco, which is one of the most humiliating and unnecessary I have ever known to happen in films. To my way of thinking, as a kindly person, they are as much to blame."[49] Jerry Epstein had the unpleasant task of sharing Crowther's comments with Chaplin, who insisted on hearing them. "He sat on the sofa opposite," said Epstein of the moment in Chaplin's living room at the Manoir. "I could barely get the words out. He listened stoically with his arms folded across his chest — his expression never changed. He made no comment. When I finished, he left the room."[50] While Crowther proved one of the most vocal critics assailing Chaplin's film, his opinions were largely shared by others. Brendan Gill of *The New Yorker* wrote a typical review — short and sweet, tinged with a degree of sadness about panning the release. "About *A Countess from Hong Kong*," he wrote, "the less said the better. Indeed, since it marks the nadir of one of the greatest figures in movie history, it would be a natural act of piety on my part to ignore it altogether, but Charlie Chaplin himself insists upon its being taken seriously, and the machinery of Hollywood publicity has made it sufficiently conspicuous among us. At 77, Mr. Chaplin shows us not a trace of his former genius, and his two stars, Marlon Brando and Sophia Loren, are made to suffer innumerable professional indignities under his direction. These days, Mr. Brando often gives the impression of being revolted by having to work in movies at all; in this picture his revulsion nearly succeeds in bringing a silly character to life by killing it."[51]

"Nostalgia itself does not doom a film," Paul D. Zimmerman added in *Newsweek*. "... But at 77, [Chaplin's] old techniques are not simply crusty and conventional, but stiff and clumsy. His camera work is primitive, his control of color uncertain, his plot muscle-bound and labored, his prose lending-library Mandarin, his lavish, aristocratic sets as out of date as a padded cocktail gown of the '30s."[52] *Time* was perhaps the most blunt. "*Countess* is bad enough to make a new generation of moviegoers wonder what the Chaplin cult was all about," wrote their reviewer. "It serves as a melancholy reminder that an important part of being a champ is knowing when to retire."[53]

Unlike the majority of Chaplin's sound era films, *A Countess from Hong Kong* remains largely inaccessible to the general public. Even compared to

A King in New York, also undistinguished in the whole of the comedian's filmography, *Countess* holds even less of an interest to Chaplin enthusiasts because it is so badly dated and executed, and only rarely captures the character of its creator. Based on its critical and popular reception, as well as its inaccessibility to later motion picture enthusiasts, the film has little significance in discussions of Chaplin and his films. Fortunately, most critical notices at the time of its release tended to be brief and dismissive, and the film's demise never garnered anywhere near the amount of publicity lavished upon its production. *Countess* simply slipped away into obscurity; as Chaplin related to Richard Meryman, the public's rebuff was gentle — they merely didn't go.

Ironically, the failure of *A Countess from Hong Kong* may not have totally damaged Chaplin's creative reputation, as both Bosley Crowther and *Time* had speculated. Instead of emphasizing the degree to which he had fallen, reaction to *Countess* may have actually reinforced the enduring qualities of his earlier motion picture work.[54] Whereas most reviewers assailed Chaplin's latest release, the majority recognized it as wholly uncharacteristic of his previous films, and most importantly drew a clear distinction between the Chaplin of 1967 and the Chaplin of earlier screen triumphs. Even though the film fared poorly with the general public, the appearance of *A Countess from Hong Kong* managed to focus attention on the comedian and his body of creative work. In an America far removed from the scandals and Cold War influences that had tainted his earlier reputation, the time was coming for a reconciliation between Chaplin and the country that had shunned him some two decades before.

9

Epilogue

Critical and public response to *Countess* hurt Chaplin deeply; the film grossed just slightly over $1 million in the United States, a pitiful amount in comparison to his earlier successes. Nonetheless, Chaplin was undeterred in his wish to continue creating motion pictures. Following *A Countess from Hong Kong*, Chaplin began developing a new project entitled *The Freak*, created specifically to feature his daughter Victoria. The narrative centered on the story of a young South American girl who possessed the amazing gift of flight, courtesy of an angelic pair of wings sprouting from her back, reminiscent of the Heaven sequence from *The Kid*. She is kidnapped and brought to London, where her captors seek to make a fortune by passing her off as an angel at religious gatherings. She escapes from the grasp of these men, however, and is chased throughout London, where a panicked populace fears the "hideous" creature. The girl is eventually caught and must stand trial to determine whether she is human at all. Jerry Epstein recalled the finale as quite tragic: "Every time I read the ending, I wept; I was convinced it would have the same effect on the audience. To me it was Charlie's best film since *City Lights*. When I saw *E.T.* with Oona, I said to her *The Freak* was a combination of *E.T.* and *The Elephant Man*. She agreed."[1]

Chaplin worked hard on the project, though the ages of both himself and Victoria would ultimately stand in the way. He had survived the rigors of completing *Countess* with only a broken ankle (the result of an accidental fall during post-production), but Chaplin was fast approaching 80 and unable to work at his former pace. Yet another stressful film project, many felt, would be very hard on his fragile health. Then, in 1969, at the age of 18, Victoria abruptly married French actor Jean-Baptiste Thierrée, and began a life away from the Chaplin family. (The couple would later develop their own circus, Le Cirque Imaginaire.) Despite the growing likelihood that *The Freak* would never be realized, Chaplin never relinquished the hope that his film would someday move forward.

On a sadder personal note, Chaplin also lost a number of people close to him during this period. Around the time of the release of *A King in New York*, in the fall of 1957, his half-brother Wheeler Dryden passed away in Hollywood.

Though Chaplin had never been very close to Wheeler, he was nonetheless a devoted member of the comedian's studio staff in the sound era, and had remained faithful throughout Chaplin's final years in the United States. Additionally, in January, 1958, Edna Purviance passed way. Although they never saw each other again following their reunion on the set of *Monsieur Verdoux*, Edna frequently wrote letters, which were forwarded to Chaplin through the studios. Most went unanswered, as he was notoriously terrible at keeping up with his correspondence, even with his closest friends and family. Still, unlike a number of figures from Chaplin's early film career, Edna warrants a number of warm remembrances in *My Autobiography*— Chaplin even ends his memoirs with a pair of letters she wrote shortly before her death, which would seem to indicate some sort of bond between the two that had remained in spite of their non-contact over the years.

Closer to Chaplin's immediate circle was the passing of his older brother Sydney, who died in the south of France the day before his younger brother's 76th birthday, on April 15, 1965. In addition to being Chaplin's business and creative advisor on a number of occasions, Sydney also managed to have a modestly successful film career of his own, appearing in many Tramp comedies and also acting in a number of his own well-received comedy shorts (particularly during a stint with Keystone after his brother's departure). Sydney retired from the film industry early, before the advent of sound, and took up residence in the south of France. Following Chaplin's exile to Switzerland, he had been a regular summer visitor at the Manoir.

Perhaps the most disheartening event, however, was the unexpected death of Charles Chaplin, Jr., in April, 1968; he passed away quite suddenly in the California home of Lita Grey from injuries received following a severe fall. Charles, Jr., had attempted to make a film career for himself following a stint under the command of General George Patton in World War II. Although he played one of the clowns in the ballet sequence from *Limelight*, his career never really got off the ground, as he found the weight of his famous lineage quite cumbersome. Living up to the Chaplin name as a performer was no easy task— it would be Sydney, the more confident and outgoing of the two brothers, who would have the more successful career in show business. Drinking, too, had become a problem for Charles, Jr. Just in his mid–40s, his untimely death was a most disheartening blow to his father.

I. THE RECONCILIATION

With his most prolific creative years behind him, appreciation for the body of Chaplin's work, as well as the work of his contemporaries in silent comedy, grew exponentially during the 60s and 70s. In an effort to respond to this demand, the comedian had been looking for an opportunity to lease his films to an appropriate outside party, giving them maximum exposure and reaping their financial worth. Ultimately, film executive Moses Rothman approached Chaplin with a generous offer to re-release the Chaplin collection, and the comedian, with the help of Jerry Epstein, began to ready most of the old features again for re-release. Chaplin's immediate concern was to compose and record scores for those films which didn't yet have music, with one, *The Circus*, even featuring an original song, "Swing Little Girl," written and sung by himself.

In part to publicize the re-releases, Chaplin also agreed to make a few brief public appearances, as he had done in touring with *The Kid*, *City Lights* and *Limelight* in the past. Part of this effort resulted in Chaplin being honored for his overall contribution to the world cinema at the 1971 Cannes International Film Festival, an event which caught the attention of the United States, this time in a positive way.

When the re-releases became available in America in the fall of 1971, interest in the comedian grew, and in January, 1972, the Academy of Motion Picture Arts and Sciences announced that Chaplin had been formally invited to receive an honorary Oscar at the March ceremonies — the first open hand Chaplin had received from the United States in over three decades. Though Rothman's influence undoubtedly played a large part in securing the tribute, it was certainly an award that was long overdue for the comedian. Silent comic contemporaries such as Mack Sennett (in 1938), Harold Lloyd (in 1952) and Buster Keaton (in 1959) had similarly been honored by the Academy, and by 1972 Chaplin was not only one of the genre's greatest names, but one of its few surviving artists as well. He agreed to attend the awards ceremony, but even so, as the day of his honor grew nearer, Chaplin became increasingly nervous about his appearance after many years of bad feelings between himself and his former country.

Anticipation was high for Chaplin's return to the United States; in March, 1972, on Hollywood's "Walk of Fame," the comedian was finally recognized with his own star, over a decade after many of the industry's pioneers had already been immortalized in such a manner. But the focus of most of the Chaplin activity began on April 2, when Charles and Oona arrived at New York's Kennedy Airport to press and fanfare not unlike that which greeted King Shadov in *A King in New York*. Two full weeks of honors and gala affairs followed, as Chaplin made his way across the country to Hollywood for the Oscar ceremonies. The first was a tribute by the Lincoln Center Film Society in New York, where he received a lengthy standing ovation following screenings of *The Kid* and *The Idle Class*. During his travels there were numerous old faces to greet him: Emotional reunions with Jackie Coogan, Georgia Hale, Claire Bloom and Paulette Goddard, among many other notable well-wishers.

Chaplin was delighted with the tributes to his work, especially the honorary Oscar he received on April 16, 1972, his 83rd birthday. Typically, he was consumed by pre-event jitters; for some reason, he was haunted by the irrational fear that, despite the hoopla surrounding his presence at the ceremonies, no one would attend.

His fears, of course, were completely unfounded. When the time came for his tribute, Academy president Daniel Taradash presented the statuette with a simple yet fitting introduction, citing the "incalculable effect he has had in making motion pictures the art form of the century." Chaplin was overwhelmed, barely managing a few soft-spoken words of thanks. Finally, America had chosen to embrace him once again, as it first had almost 60 years earlier when he was just beginning with Keystone. The stinging memory of two decades in exile was wiped clean for this brief moment, and the country that had formerly loathed him now greeted his homecoming with tremendous enthusiasm. "The tears drenched the audiences 3000 miles apart," Alistair Cooke would write of the moment. "He was very old and trembly, and groping through the thickening fog of memory for a few simple sentences. A senile, harmless doll, he was now — as the song says — 'easy to love, absolutely safe to adore.'"[2]

Richard Meryman, who had last interviewed Chaplin as part of the promotion for A Countess from Hong Kong, accompanied the comedian briefly on the New York leg of his return visit, and again contributed a piece to Life.

> I talked to Chaplin in his hotel room at the Plaza. "I'm tired, exhausted," he said. "I hear the applause and I tighten up. Last night at the Lincoln Center was a terrific thing. So sweet. Like children after they've been slapped down and they're sorry they've done something. The kindness came through. Thought I was going to blubber like a kid...."
>
> So we had arrived — obliquely — at the ugliness of those last years in America. I asked him if there was any bitterness — or sadness — looking back at those times. "No, no. I don't feel anything at all. I felt that when it was over — it was over."[3]

Chaplin was appreciative of the honors laid before him, but as his comments to Meryman reflect, he still harbored some ill feelings toward the United States. "I was very touched by the [Academy Award] gesture," Chaplin wrote later in My Life in Pictures, "but there was a certain irony about it somehow."[4]

II. THE LIMELIGHT

Though Chaplin had only visited America for two weeks, the world-wide press attention spurred a resurgence of interest in the man and his works. Especially following his departure, Rothman's re-releases in the United States (primarily Chaplin's sound and silent features) were playing to new and far more appreciative audiences than Chaplin had enjoyed in a long while. As more and more theaters across the country were screening revival films, Chaplin's pictures attracted a much broader viewership than had attended the year-long retrospective at New York's Plaza Theatre during 1963 and 1964. In fact, an effective case has been made that the re-releases in the 1970s, coupled with his highly publicized return to the United States, may have helped firmly cement Chaplin as a figure of critical importance to the film industry.[5]*

On an interesting note, the re-releases scored the comedian yet another Oscar the following year. Due to the hostility of the American Legion and other reactionary groups back in the 1950s, *Limelight* had been pulled from circulation before it had a chance to make its Los Angeles debut, and an extended run in L.A. was one of the Academy's qualifying criteria for Oscar nominations. As a result of the film's re-release both there and in New York, *Limelight* finally became qualified for Academy consideration, two decades after its original debut. Chaplin's musical score was honored with an Oscar for Best Original Dramatic Score of 1972, claiming for itself a piece of Academy trivia in the process.

Back home in Vevey, Chaplin filled his time with several projects. Filmmaker Peter Bogdanovich sought to produce a documentary on the comedian shortly after his American visit. He abandoned it, however, when his original idea of holding a running conversation with Chaplin on the various aspects of his career fell through. "... [W]hen we got to his home in Vevey," cinematographer Nestor Almendros recalled of the project, "we discovered that Chaplin was no longer Chaplin. He had almost completely lost his memory, he was a body almost without a mind. He could hardly answer the questions; we heard only monosyllables, barely intelligible non sequiturs."[6]

Still, the project moved forward without Bogdanovich's involvement, and only a little of his interview with Chaplin became part of the documentary, released as *The Gentleman Tramp* in 1975. Narrated by Walter Matthau, whose wife Carol was a close friend of Oona's, the film is largely uneventful, though it does include some of Oona's 16mm home movies, taken as the Chaplin children were growing up. These provide a moving glimpse of the comedian as a father in semi-retirement.

In support of this notion is the situation that befell Harold Lloyd. According to biographer Tom Dardis, Lloyd clung tightly to his screen work during his lifetime, assembling no large-scale re-releases (though he did supervise several compilation films). He feared that letting go of his films would find his pictures sliced apart, shown at ludicrously fast sound speed and combined with painfully inadequate soundtrack additions, including sound effects. The relative inaccessibility of Lloyd's pictures may partially account for the loss of prestige to his motion picture accomplishments over the years — Lloyd, the most consistent and profitable of the silent comics in the 1920s, is largely unknown today. Unfortunately, in 1974, three years after his death, Time/Life leased the more famous sequences from a number of his pictures, turning them into the very sort of clips Lloyd sought to avoid during his lifetime. (Tom Dardis; Harold Lloyd: The Man on the Clock; p. 306.)

In 1974, Chaplin published a companion to *My Autobiography* entitled *My Life in Pictures*. Though the book was essentially a photo album, with many pictures never before seen by the public, it was nonetheless an interesting glimpse into an extraordinary life and a form of filmmaking that had long since disappeared. Chaplin also remained active in scoring the remainder of his films, most notably *A Woman of Paris*, which hadn't been seen by motion picture audiences in nearly half a century. One could say that Chaplin never really left the motion picture industry at all, at least in spirit. He was ever attempting to remain active, despite his age and increasing health problems.

As the film industry had honored Chaplin with its highest award, so too would England choose to bestow upon him their own tribute in 1975 — a Knightship, finally, after rumors of the honor had tailed the comedian on all three of his major European tours over the preceding 50 years. Chaplin, too frail to stand during the ceremony, accepted the honor from his wheelchair. The Little Fellow, society's down-and-out loner, had become Sir Charlie.

Chaplin's mind never ceased in the pursuit of another creative project, but he eventually reached an age where his body could no longer follow. It was evident at the time of his Knighthood that public appearances proved exhausting, and his schedule became less and less active. Claire Bloom, often a guest at the Manoir, recalled Oona's loving care for her husband during his periods of ill health. "When I was young," she recalls Oona once saying, "he took care of me. Now I take care of him."[7] Often, Chaplin would simply sit with Oona, enjoying her presence but rarely speaking.

For the most part, the last years of Chaplin's life were spent at the Manoir in the company of friends and family. According to Jerry Epstein, he still enjoyed screening films, both his own and contemporary selections as well. Oona was his primary care giver, though eventually the burden became too much for her alone to manage, what with her other activities both inside and outside the Manoir. Toward the fall of 1977, she was forced to relinquish her dual role of wife and nurse, and a staff of professionals was brought in to care for Chaplin, then virtually bedridden.

Finally, on the early morning of Christmas Day, 1977, Sir Charles Chaplin died quietly in his sleep at Vevey. Though confined to his room throughout the Christmas Eve celebration the night before, he nonetheless left this earth in the midst of his family's love, laughter and togetherness — the very same emotions that he had brought to millions of people the world over through 50 years in motion pictures. The news, of course, captured headlines around the globe, bringing innumerable tributes and condolences from artists, statesmen and ordinary citizens the world over. Two days later, in a private ceremony, his body was laid to rest in a small cemetery a short distance from the Manoir.

As a darkly ironic testament to Chaplin's popularity, the comedian continued to capture people's imaginations even after his passing. Sometime during the night of March 1, 1978, Chaplin's casket was stolen from its gravesite. The world again focused on Vevey and the Manoir as police attempted to track the grave robbers, who indicated through several telephone calls that their ransom was 600,000 Swiss francs. Oona refused to cooperate, though she was terribly concerned when the culprits began to make threats against the safety of the Chaplin children if their demands were not met. As the case stretched into its second week, Swiss police eventually traced the origin of the mysterious calls to common street phones in the neighboring city of Lausanne, and were able to apprehend the criminals when they attempted to make a scheduled call to the Chaplin household.

The perpetrators turned out to be a pair of auto mechanics, Roman Wardas, 24, of Poland and Gantcho Ganev, 38, of Bulgaria, who were attempting to raise money in order to open their own auto repair business. Their plan, the December 1978, trial revealed, was to simply bury the casket a few feet underneath its original position, but poor weather on the night of the crime foiled their scheme. Instead they hastily transported and re-buried the coffin in a cornfield near the city of Noville some 20 kilometers away, and hoped to receive the ransom money before it was discovered. Geraldine Chaplin, who had taken most of the ransom calls at the Manoir throughout the 16-day ordeal, served as the chief witness against the two men. Their bungled plot landed them convictions for extortion and disturbing the dead — Wardas was sentenced to four-and-a-half years in prison, while Ganev received a suspended sentence of 18 months.

* * * * * * * * * *

Raised in poverty, abandoned by a father who died an alcoholic, and by a mother committed to the madhouse, he raised himself to the heights of glory and wealth by his own means. He reversed his fate. In the world's capitals, London, Paris, Berlin, Tokyo, he was welcomed as a king. Everywhere, people sought to honor him for what he had given them. The cockney kid became a nobleman. He was a self-made myth.[8]
— Adolphe Nysenholc

Nothing — not the later movies which failed, not his personal life or the political controversies, not even the prospect of an 80-year-old man living out his life on a country estate in Switzerland — can destroy our image of the little clown. That part of Charlie Chaplin, like great poetry, has stuck on its own.[9]
— Paul Frederickson

Overall, the life story of Charles Spencer Chaplin is certainly impressive. Going from his birth in Dickensonian London to a broken family in extreme poverty, to portraying a character that made him one of the single most recognized and revered men on earth is nothing short of extraordinary. From such impoverished and obscure roots rose a man who came to symbolize and epitomize the grandeur and artistry of early Hollywood, and whose character likeness created laughter, love and hope for a large portion of the world's citizens.

Yet, as Frederickson notes above, it is his silent film image, not his later films nor even the man himself, that has remained memorable. Though creating Charlie as a character was Chaplin's master stroke, the silent comedies for which he is remembered did not mark the whole of his career. Indeed, his artistic creativity extended far beyond the simple Keystone, Essanay, Mutual and First National formats, as his comedic genius spread to feature films and long outlasted the demise of silent pictures. And though we will never be able to separate Chaplin from his famous screen character, there still remains a section of his creative history that is largely overshadowed by our collective memory of him, that of his sound era films.

Chaplin never ceased moving forward as a storyteller. Though he would eventually depart from his cinematic roots, he was an artist unwilling to simply rest on the laurels of his famous creation. In bringing his images to the screen in his later works, Chaplin revealed an artistic metamorphosis, one in which his subject matter was influenced more and more by the driving forces around him. From the moment Hollywood had committed itself to sound technology, the stable world of the silent comedian began to change, and Chaplin went with it, possessing both the popularity and financial means to address new artistic questions, and on his own terms.

With the transition of Hollywood from silent to sound productions, Chaplin dared to do what only a star of his stature could have done — utilize the evolving technology to enhance his own filmic talents, rather than simply adapt his narratives to incorporate the popular new medium. He shunned conventional wisdom, but the public continued to patronize his films; moviegoers trusted the Chaplin of old, with his reputation as a first-rate artist. They knew his product would be high in quality, entertaining, and — sometimes — even thought-provoking, with or without the use of sound technology.

Despite their avoidance of dialogue, both *City Lights* and *Modern Times* serve as a testament to the universal popularity of the Little Fellow. They preserve a measure of timelessness that seems to capture all that the Tramp (and silent comedy) had become. In a period marked by change not just in Hollywood, but in America and throughout the world, both films share a sense of optimism and humanity that perhaps the world needed at the time, and which the Tramp himself certainly symbolized.

Later, as the countries of the world shifted their attention from their economic plights to the threat of Fascism and war, Chaplin too turned his personal thoughts to the dangers of world conflict. Consequently, his films of this period reflected these concerns. In retrospect, *The Great Dictator* is not as unique within Chaplin's filmography for being his first talking picture as it is for the political courage it took him to produce the film, which was begun a full three years prior to the United States' involvement in World War II. Whereas many initially felt that *Modern Times* would play with openly Communistic themes, only to be miffed by the film's political ambiguity, *The Great Dictator* was a full-fledged political statement by Chaplin, dared long before similar statements against the Third Reich were either fashionable or acceptable. As many noted at the time, perhaps only a star of Chaplin's prominence could have success-fully satirized Hitler, which, as we have seen, he accomplished with devastat-ing effectiveness.

Similarly, *Monsieur Verdoux* found Chaplin not only abandoning any sem-blance of a character invoking the image of the Little Fellow, but taking a fas-cinating, if flawed, look at the horrors of war and the scruples of contempo-rary society. What he found were evils that were as equally unpleasant as those in his earlier satire of Hitler. But a conservative-leaning America was not ready to accept such a harsh critique of modern life, especially when Chaplin's social observations came on the heels of nearly five years of hostile press concerning both his Second Front activities and the Joan Barry trials. The comedian's view of the world, and more precisely that of the United States, found him consis-tently on the defensive as post–World War II attitudes and values changed. Assaults on his stature as an artist and as a man came from many directions, and it was arguably only late in his life that he was able to regain some of that respect.

In the final two pictures he wrote, directed and starred in, Chaplin allowed his intensely personal feelings to dominate. *Limelight* saw Chaplin the artist fac-ing the reality of his age and the waning interest of his audience. We are moved by the story of Calvero because it is really the story of Chaplin, a man haunted by memories of what he had once been and, more precisely, all he had known of himself. The narrative, though overly melodramatic at times, touches the basic human need — as well as the artist's need — to be wanted and accepted. Chaplin even fictionalizes his own end on film: Calvero dies on the stage, the only life he has ever known.

A King in New York also capitalized on Chaplin's own experiences, this time focusing more on his personal politics. In doing so, he used his story almost strictly to exonerate himself, while lashing out at the United States. But the film was not the same sort of biting satire that Chaplin had employed in making *The Great Dictator*; rather, it was a simply catharsis of hostile emotions and frustrations. Whereas Chaplin successfully made a mockery of Hitler, *King* never came close to doing the same to the United States. The picture was pure bitterness, more expedient in its criticisms than thought-provoking.

Finally, though *A Countess from Hong Kong* was quite easily Chaplin's worst release of the sound era, its promotional campaign brought attention that reinforced his image as a motion picture figure of tremendous importance. Miscast, badly outdated and in many respects poorly executed, Chaplin's ship-board farce was hardly characteristic of his previous film work, and the public avoided it. *Countess* proved a forgettable film, but the anticipation for its release among filmgoers proved that Chaplin was not a forgettable artist.

As French critic André Bazin noted shortly after the premiere of *Limelight*, Charlie Chaplin has found a unique place in the realm of cinema history. Though he will always remain our "Little Fellow" from the silent era, Chaplin had continued to evolve as an artist long after the introduction of the talking film, and indeed never ceased to find stories to bring to the screen. "Since *Modern Times*," Bazin observed, "the last ... of his virtually silent films, Chaplin has never stopped moving forward into the unknown, rediscovering cinema in relation to himself ... [He] remains an example and a symbol of creative freedom in the least free of arts."[10]

Looking back over the body of his work, Chaplin's projects following the advent of talking pictures never quite matched the skill or brilliance of his earlier silent films. It can be argued, in fact, that *The Great Dictator* was the final popular and critical tour de force of his career. It was his first talking film, but his last to openly employ all the general techniques of his silent film heritage, at least in terms of comedic style, storytelling, camera framing and editing. Perhaps even Chaplin knew his legacy would be his early work. "Lines spoken from the screen are easily forgotten," he said in a 1942 interview. "It's the action that is remembered. Movement is liberated thought."[11]

However, the comedian's sound era films should hold a unique place in the Chaplin story, and certainly merit as much study and analysis as his earlier works. As he moved away from the era of silent pictures, slowly phasing out his Tramp character, his films began to take on a more personal, and in the view of some historians, more auteuristic sense. As writer, director, producer and star, the content of Chaplin's films from the 1930s to the 1960s often touched themes important to the artist himself; an evolving cinematic outlook that confronted changes in technology, politics and personalities. While his impact on the motion picture industry was ingrained long before the premiere of *City Lights*, his ongoing curiosities and concerns never allowed him to rest upon his past achievements. In this sense, Charlie Chaplin was not only a creation of the cinema but a creator of cinema as well. Throughout his career, the background from which he rose, the issues that inspired love or hate within him and the deep regard he maintained for humanity, as depicted in the entirety of his films, changed the motion picture industry. For him, there was no such thing as retirement, as evidenced by his tireless yet futile work on *The Freak*; even at the end of his 1974 book *My Life in Pictures*, when the comedian was long past the ability to undertake another feature film, he still asserted, "I mean to make it one day."[12] There was always one more story to tell.

Since the advent of mass media, arguably no single one entertainment figure has become so renowned, honored or loved as the Little Fellow. As his creator, Chaplin will forever be linked with the image of Charlie. The qualities that Chaplin's screen character seemed to embody — a love of humanity, an honesty and a firm belief in the power of the human spirit — are the same themes Chaplin utilized in his final, less successful motion pictures as well. Though the Tramp eventually disappeared, Chaplin remained a popular figure, the lasting influence of his early screen persona.

Mary Pickford recalled Chaplin as an "obstinate, suspicious, egocentric, maddening, and lovable genius of problem child."[13] Her description does a fair job of capturing the many sides of Chaplin, both as a man and as an artist. But while the comedian's artistic and personal temperament could be widely variable, to the public of his day he appeared quite differently. "... Charlie is something more to the people than a popular comedian," biographer William Dodgeson Bowman wrote in 1931. "He is an institution. They recognize him as one of themselves, as a man of broad human sympathies for whom they have affection and admiration. It may be objected with truth that it is the Charlie of the screen that they love. But a sure instinct tells them that the two Charlies have very much in common ..."[14] We view him now from a different perspective, but in many respects we still view him as his public did back in 1931.

Notes

Preface

1. David Robinson, *Chaplin: His Life and Art*, p. xiv.

1. Prologue

1. Charles Chaplin, *My Autobiography*, p. 18.
2. *Ibid.*, p. 12.
3. *Ibid.*, p. 31.
4. David Robinson, *Chaplin: His Life and Art*, p. 16.
5. Charles Chaplin, *My Autobiography*, p. 76.
6. Harold Manning, edited with notes by Timothy J. Lyons. "Charlie Chaplin's Early Life: Fact and Fiction," from *Historical Journal of Film, Radio and Television*, Volume 3, Number 1—1983, p. 37.
7. Charles Chaplin, *My Autobiography*, pp. 59–60.
8. *Ibid.*, p. 75.
9. *Ibid.*, p. 95.
10. Stan Laurel as interviewed by John McCabe, *Charlie Chaplin*, p. 36.
11. Charles Chaplin, *My Autobiography*, p. 135.
12. Bosley Crowther, "The Modern — and Mellower — Times of Mr. Chaplin," from *New York Times Magazine*, November 6, 1960, p. 55.
13. David Robinson, *Chaplin: His Life and Art*, p. 102. Robinson also cites the inconsistent versions of the telegram's contents over the years.
14. *Ibid.*, pp. 101–103.
15. Charles Chaplin, *My Autobiography*, p. 138. David Robinson also reprints a letter from Chaplin to Sydney in August of 1913, announcing his intention to sign with the Keystone Studios. In it, Chaplin clearly values the amount he is being paid over the type of work he would be performing, as his salary — in his estimation — will afford him a mere five years in the motion picture business before retirement would be possible. (David Robinson, *Chaplin: His Life and Art*, p. 98)
16. David Robinson, *Chaplin: His Life and Art*, p. 87.
17. Charles Chaplin, *My Autobiography*, p. 144–146.
18. Gerald Weales, *Canned Goods as Caviar: American Film in the 1930s*, p. 13.
19. David Robinson, *Chaplin: His Life and Art*, p. 114.
20. Harold Lloyd to Kevin Brownlow, *The Parade's Gone By*, p. 460.
21. Bo Berglund, "The Day the Tramp Was Born," from *Sight and Sound*, Spring 1989, p. 112.

22. From *Exhibitors World*, undated, quoted in Peter Haining (editor), *The Legend of Charlie Chaplin*, p. 203.

23. Charles Chaplin, *My Autobiography*, p. 153.

24. *Ibid.*, p. 150.

25. David Robinson, *Chaplin: His Life and Art*, pp. 121–122.

26. Charles Chaplin, *My Autobiography*, pp. 209–210.

27. Richard Meryman, "Ageless Master's Anatomy of Comedy," from *Life*, March 10, 1967, p. 90.

28. Charles J. McGuirk, "Chaplinitis," from *Motion Picture Magazine*, July/August, 1915, cited by Charles Maland, *Chaplin and American Culture*, p. 9.

29. David Robinson, *Chaplin: His Life and Art*, p. 153.

30. *Ibid.*, p. 150.

31. Charles Chaplin, *My Life in Pictures*, p. 156.

32. *Ibid.*, p. 179.

33. Charles Chaplin, *My Autobiography*, p. 239.

34. David Robinson, *Chaplin: His Life and Art*, p. 296.

35. Charles Chaplin, *My Autobiography*, p. 300.

36. David Robinson, *Chaplin: His Life and Art*, Illustrations Section 4 (between pages 424 and 425). Photograph copyright of the Roy Export Company Establishment.

37. Charles Chaplin, Jr., *My Father, Charlie Chaplin*, pp. 10, 15–17.

38. Eddie Sutherland, interviewed by Robert Franklin, quoted in David Robinson, *Chaplin: His Life and Art*, pp. 271–272.

39. Elsie Codd's comments from *Charlie Chaplin*, by Louis Delluc (translated by Hamish Miles), reprinted in Donald McCaffrey (editor), *Focus on Chaplin*, p. 59.

40. Eddie Sutherland, quoted in *Unknown Chaplin* (Kevin Brownlow and David Gill), Thames Television —1983.

41. *Ibid.*, quote by Virginia Cherrill.

42. Charles Chaplin, *My Autobiography*, p. 188.

43. Charles Chaplin, *My Life in Pictures*, p. 161.

44. Charles Maland, *Chaplin and American Culture*, p. 45.

45. Timothy J. Lyons, *Charles Chaplin: A Guide to References and Resources*, Page 17; see also Charles Maland, *Chaplin and American Culture*, p. 51.

46. Carlyle Robinson, "The Private Life of Charlie Chaplin," from *Great Stars of Hollywood's Golden Age* (Frank C. Platt, editor), p. 72.

47. Timothy J. Lyons (editor), "Interview with Roland H. Totheroh," from *Film Culture*, Spring 1972, p. 275.

48. Kevin Brownlow and David Gill, *Unknown Chaplin*, Thames Television —1983.

49. David Robinson, *Chaplin: His Life and Art*, p. 313.

50. Virginia Cherrill, quoted in *Unknown Chaplin* (Kevin Brownlow and David Gill), Thames Television —1983.

51. David Robinson, *Chaplin: His Life and Art*, pp. 339, 369.

52. Konrad Bercovici, "A Day with Charlie Chaplin," from *Harper's Magazine*, Dec. 1928, reprinted in Peter Haining (editor), *The Legend of Charlie Chaplin*, p. 75.

53. Charles Chaplin, *My Autobiography*, p. 207, 232.

54. David Robinson, *Chaplin: His Life and Art*, pp. 658–659.

2. City Lights

1. Theodore Huff, *Charlie Chaplin*, p. 226.

2. James Agee, "Comedy's Greatest Era," from *Life*, September 5, 1949, p. 77.

3. Charles Chaplin, *My Trip Abroad*, p. 131.

4. Kevin Brownlow, *The Parade's Gone By*, p. 341.

5. *Ibid.*, p. 338.

6. *Ibid.*, p. 569.

7. David Cook, *A History of Narrative Film*, p. 237.

8. Gerald Mast, *A Short History of the Movies*, p. 188.

9. David Cook, *A History of Narrative Film*, pp. 243–245.

10. Charles Maland, *Chaplin and American Culture*, p. 112.

11. Charles Chaplin, *My Autobiography*, p. 324.

12. Tom Dardis, *Harold Lloyd: The Man on the Clock*, p. 209.

13. Charles Chaplin, Jr., *My Father, Charlie Chaplin*, pp. 110–111.

14. James Agee, "Comedy's Greatest Era," from *Life*, September 5, 1949, p. 86.

15. Charles Chaplin, *My Autobiography*, p. 387.

16. *Ibid.*, p. 325. Chaplin's passage here indicates his belief that the blind clown theme was perhaps too sentimental. This is odd, in that the scenario he eventually concocted for *City Lights* would be one of the most sentimental of his career, perhaps second only to 1952's *Limelight*. To be sure, the blind clown scenario carries its share of overt pathos. However, it seems much more logical — despite Chaplin's comments — that the comedian was toying with themes too "unoriginal" in light of his recent releases..

17. *Ibid.*, p. 115.

18. Timothy J. Lyons (editor), "Interview with Roland H. Totheroh," from *Film Culture*, Spring 1972, p. 284.

19. Charles Chaplin, "A Rejection of the Talkies," from *New York Times*, January 25, 1931, reprinted in *Focus on Chaplin* (Donald McCaffrey, editor), p. 63. The article is part of Chaplin's promotional efforts to sell *City Lights* to a public which may no longer embrace a silent film, even one featuring the Tramp.

20. Gerald Mast, *The Comic Mind*, p. 105.

21. Charles Chaplin, *My Autobiography*, p. 226.

22. Timothy J. Lyons, *Charles Chaplin: A Guide to References and Resources*, p. 199.

23. Alistair Cooke, *Garbo and the Night Watchmen*, p. 266.

24. David Raksin, "'Music Composed by Charles Chaplin': Auteur or Collaborator?," from *Journal of the University Film Association*, Winter 1979, p. 49.

25. Charles Chaplin, Jr., *My Father, Charlie Chaplin*, p. 126.

26. David Robinson, *Chaplin: His Life and Art*, pp. 401–402.

27. David Gill, quoted by Leonard Maltin, "Silent Film Buffs Stalk and Find a Missing Tramp," from *Smithsonian*, July 1986, p. 50.

28. Charles Maland, *Chaplin and American Culture*, p. 110, 114.

29. Charles Chaplin, *My Autobiography*, pp. 303–304.

30. Virginia Cherrill, quoted from *Unknown Chaplin* (Kevin Brownlow and David Gill). Thames Television —1983.

31. Charles Chaplin, *My Autobiography*, p. 326.

32. Alistair Cooke, *Six Men*, p. 35.

33. David Robinson, *Chaplin: His Life and Art*, p. 402.

34. *Ibid.*, p. 406.

35. Carlyle Robinson, "The Private Life of Charlie Chaplin," from *Great Stars of Hollywood's Golden Age* (Frank C. Platt, editor), pp. 101–102.

36. David Robinson, *Chaplin: His Life and Art*, p. 407.

37. Gerard Molyneaux, *Charlie Chaplin's City Lights: Its Production and Dialectical Structure*, pp. 187–188.

38. David Robinson, *Chaplin: His Life and Art*, p. 391.

39. Gerald Mast, *The Comic Mind*, p. 113.

40. Richard Meryman, "Ageless Master's Anatomy of Comedy," from *Life*, March 10, 1967, p. 89.
41. Charles Maland, *Chaplin and American Culture*, p. 111.
42. Gerald Mast, *The Comic Mind*, p. 106.
43. David Robinson, *Chaplin: His Life and Art*, p. 413.
44. Alexander Bakshy, "Charlie Chaplin Falters," from *Nation*, March 4, 1931, pp. 250–251.
45. George Jean Nathan, "A Rejection to the Praise Given Chaplin's Artistry," from *Passing Judgements*, reprinted in *Focus on Chaplin* (Donald McCaffrey, editor), p. 81.
46. Mordaunt Hall, "Chaplin Hilarious in his *City Lights*," from *New York Times*, February 6, 1931, p. 11.
47. Charles Maland, *Chaplin and American Culture*, pp. 122–123.

3. Modern Times

1. Charles Chaplin, "A Comedian Sees the World," from *Woman's Home Companion*, September, 1933, p. 7.
2. *Ibid.*, p. 10.
3. Jerry Epstein, *Remembering Charlie*, p. 11.
4. Charles Chaplin, "A Comedian Sees the World," from *Woman's Home Companion*, October, 1933, p. 17.
5. *Ibid.*, pp. 17, 102.
6. David Robinson, *Chaplin: His Life and Art*, p. 434.
7. Charles Chaplin, "A Comedian Sees the World," from *Woman's Home Companion*, December, 1933, p. 23.
8. *Ibid.*, p. 42.
9. *Ibid.*, January 1934, p. 21.
10. Charles Chaplin, *My Autobiography*, p. 372.
11. *Ibid.*, p. 376.
12. David Robinson, *Chaplin: His Life and Art*, p. 458.
13. Charles Chaplin, "A Comedian Sees the World," from *Woman's Home Companion*, January, 1934, p. 86.
14. Charles Chaplin, *My Autobiography*, p. 377.
15. Parker Tyler, *Chaplin, Last of the Clowns*, p. 125.
16. David Robinson, *Chaplin: His Life and Art*, p. 455.
17. Charles Maland, *Chaplin and American Culture*, pp. 127, 132–139.
18. Charles Chaplin, "A Comedian Sees the World," from *Woman's Home Companion*, December 1933, p. 36.
19. *Ibid.*, October 1933, p. 16.
20. "Chaplin Gibes at Leaders," from *New York Times*, June 14, 1932, p. 26.
21. David Robinson, *Chaplin: His Life and Art*, pp. 428, 437.
22. *Ibid.*, pp. 436–437.
23. Charles Chaplin, *My Autobiography*, p. 380.
24. *Ibid.*, p. 380.
25. Charles Chaplin, Jr., *My Father, Charlie Chaplin*, p. 22.
26. Charles Chaplin, *My Autobiography*, p. 360.
27. Charles Maland, *Chaplin and American Culture*, pp. 144–145.
28. *Ibid.*, p. 145.
29. Charles Chaplin, Jr., *My Father, Charlie Chaplin*, p. 119.

30. Charles Chaplin, *My Autobiography*, p. 366.

31. David Robinson, *Chaplin: His Life and Art*, p. 466.

32. *Ibid.*, p. 466.

33. *Ibid.*, p. 466.

34. Walter Kerr, *The Silent Clowns*, pp. 354–355.

35. Charles Chaplin, Jr., *My Father, Charlie Chaplin*, p. 126.

36. Julian Smith, *Chaplin*, p. 88. Even with Smith's observation, it is notable that Chaplin continued to lament the abandonment of silent cinema for the remainder of his life, making public statements even long after he himself had made the jump to sound. Though Chaplin moved forward as an artist, albeit at his own speed, he would fiercely defend not only his own work but his old motion picture medium as well.

37. Charles Chaplin, Jr., *My Father, Charlie Chaplin*, p. 113.

38. Gerard Molyneaux, "*Modern Times* and the American Culture of the 1930s," from *Charlie Chaplin: His Reflection in Modern Times* (Adolphe Nysenholc, editor), p. 109.

39. John Paul Smead, *Five Films by Charles Chaplin: His Transition into Sound*, p. 50.

40. Charles Maland, *Chaplin and American Culture*, pp. 145–146.

41. Kevin Brownlow, *Behind the Mask of Innocence*, p. 437. Brownlow relates that Sinclair also attempted to write a script for D.W. Griffith.

42. Charles Chaplin, *My Autobiography*, p. 380.

43. *Ibid.*, p. 383.

44. Meyer Levin, from *Garbo and the Night Watchmen* (Alistair Cooke, editor), p. 263.

45. Charles Maland, *Chaplin and American Culture*, p. 151.

46. Theodore Huff, *Charlie Chaplin*, p. 255.

47. Charles Chaplin, *My Trip Abroad*, p. 8.

48. Charles Maland, *Chaplin and American Culture*, pp. 147–148.

49. Charles Silver, *Charles Chaplin: An Appreciation*, p. 22.

50. David Robinson, *Chaplin: His Life and Art*, pp. 462–463.

51. Charles Chaplin, *My Autobiography*, p. 347.

52. David Robinson, *Chaplin: His Life and Art*, p. 468.

53. Gerard Molyneaux, "*Modern Times* and the American Culture of the 1930s," from *Charlie Chaplin: His Reflection in Modern Times* (Adolphe Nysenholc, editor), p. 108.

54. William K. Everson, *American Silent Film*, p. 266.

55. David Robinson, *Chaplin: His Life and Art*, p. 473.

56. Charles Maland, *Chaplin and American Culture*, p. 155.

57. Alistair Cooke, *Garbo and the Night Watchmen*, p. 268.

58. *Ibid.*, comments by Otis Ferguson, p. 273.

59. Frank S. Nugent, "Heralding the Return, After an Undue Absence, of Charlie Chaplin in *Modern Times*," from *New York Times*, February 6, 1936, p. 23.

60. Charles Maland, *Chaplin and American Culture*, pp. 157–158.

61. Alistair Cooke, *Garbo and the Night Watchmen*, p. 253.

4. The Great Dictator

1. Jean Cocteau, *My Voyage Round the World*, excerpted from David Robinson, *Chaplin: His Life and Art*, pp. 480–482.

2. Lita Grey Chaplin, *My Life with Chaplin*, p. 287.

3. Charles Chaplin, *My Life in Pictures*, pp. 206–209.

4. Charles Chaplin, "Roles I Would Like to Play," from *Bravo*, circa 1930, reprinted in Peter Haining (editor), *The Legend of Charlie Chaplin*, pp. 193, 196.

5. Charles Chaplin, "A Comedian Sees the World," from *Woman's Home Companion*, October, 1933, p. 106.

6. David Robinson, *Chaplin: His Life and Art*, pp. 473–474. Here, a telegram from Chaplin to brother Sydney indicates his desire to plunge directly into another film project following *Modern Times*, though it does not mention the type of project he envisioned.

7. *Ibid.*, pp. 475–476.

8. *Ibid.*, p. 483.

9. Maurice Bessy, *Charlie Chaplin*, pp. 413–414.

10. Rudy Behlmer (editor), *Memo from David O. Selznick*, p. 176.

11. *Ibid.*, p. 182.

12. Larry Ceplair and Steven Englund, *The Inquisition in Hollywood*, p. 94.

13. *Ibid.*, p. 96; Testimony of James W. McGuinness to HUAC, October, 1947.

14. Charles Chaplin, *My Autobiography*, p. 392.

15. Rudolf Arnheim, quoted by Michael Hanisch, "The Chaplin Reception in Germany," from *Charlie Chaplin: His Reflection in Modern Times* (Adolphe Nysenholc, editor), p. 29.

16. Ivor Montagu, *With Eisenstein in Hollywood*, p. 94.

17. From *Film-Kurier*, October, 1938, cited by Michael Hanisch, "The Chaplin Reception in Germany," from *Charlie Chaplin: His Reflection in Modern Times* (Adolphe Nysenholc, editor), pp. 30–31.

18. Ivor Montagu, *With Eisenstein in Hollywood*, p. 94.

19. Adolphe Nysenholc, "Charles Chaplin and the Jewish World," from *Charlie Chaplin: His Reflection in Modern Times* (Adolphe Nysenholc, editor), pp. 21–22.

20. Charles Maland, *Chaplin and American Culture*, p. 171.

21. Gerith Von Ulm, *Charlie Chaplin: The King of Tragedy*, p. 387, see also Theodore Huff, *Charlie Chaplin*, p. 263. Von Ulm does not give a source for this rumor, though former Chaplin handyman Kono, who was no longer working for the comedian, served as a main source for her book. As Von Ulm's work was being written during the production of *The Great Dictator*, her information at the time was speculative at best. Huff, who for many years held the honor of authoring the definitive version of Chaplin's life, is perhaps only repeating Von Ulm's assertion in his work.

22. Charles Silver, *Charles Chaplin: An Appreciation*, p. 47.

23. Charles Chaplin, *My Autobiography*, p. 392.

24. "Dictator Ruffled," from *Time*, June 24, 1940, p. 52.

25. Charles Chaplin, *My Life in Pictures*, p. 268.

26. Charles Chaplin, *My Trip Abroad*, p. 114.

27. Theodore Huff, *Charlie Chaplin*, p. 263. The quote by Chaplin is from an unnamed source.

28. Charles Chaplin, *My Autobiography*, pp. 392–393.

29. David Robinson, *Chaplin: His Life and Art*, pp. 499–501.

30. John Paul Smead, *Five Films by Charles Chaplin: His Transition to Sound*, p. 135.

31. *Ibid.*, p. 198; See also pages 188–189, 233.

32. Jack Oakie, *Jack Oakie's Double Takes*, pp. 76–77. Charles Chaplin, Jr., would have similar recollections of his father's aggravation with the new production codes. See Charles Chaplin, Jr., *My Father, Charlie Chaplin*, pp. 216–218.

33. Charles Chaplin, "A Comedian Sees the World," from *Woman's Home Companion*, September, 1933, p. 10.

34. Peter Cotes and Thelma Niklaus, *The Little Fellow: The Life and Work of Charles Spencer Chaplin*, p. 76. The quote by Chaplin is from an unnamed source.

35. Charles Chaplin, *My Autobiography*, p. 405.

36. Richard Meryman, "Ageless Master's Anatomy of Comedy," from *Life*, March 10, 1967, p. 94.

37. John Paul Smead, *Five Films by Charles Chaplin: His Transition to Sound*, p. 105.

38. Peter Cotes and Thelma Niklaus, *The Little Fellow: The Life and Work of Charles Spencer Chaplin*, p. 117. The quote by Chaplin is from an unnamed source.

39. John McCabe, *Charlie Chaplin*, p. 197.

40. Michael Hanisch, "The Chaplin Reception in Germany," from *Charlie Chaplin: His Reflection in Modern Times* (Adolphe Nysenholc, editor), pp. 32–33.

41. Richard Meryman, "Ageless Master's Anatomy of Comedy," from *Life*, March 10, 1967, p. 92.

42. Charles Maland, *Chaplin and American Culture*, p. 168.

43. Charles Chaplin, *My Autobiography*, pp. 399–400.

44. Charles Maland, *Chaplin and American Culture*, p. 178.

45. David Robinson, *Chaplin: His Life and Art*, p. 503.

46. Gerald Mast, *The Comic Mind*, p. 117.

47. Walter Kerr, "The Lineage of *Limelight*," from *Focus on Chaplin* (Donald McCaffrey, editor), p. 147.

48. Roger Manvell, *Chaplin*, p. 195.

49. David Robinson, *Chaplin: His Life and Art*, p. 504.

50. John McCabe, *Charlie Chaplin*, p. 197.

51. André Bazin, "The Myth of *Monsieur Verdoux*," from *What is Cinema?*, Volume II (Hugh Gray, editor), pp. 110–111.

52. Francis Wyndham, introduction from Charles Chaplin, *My Life in Pictures*, p. 34.

53. Gerald McDonald, Michael Conway and Mark Ricci, *The Complete Films of Charlie Chaplin*, p. 207.

54. From *Film-Kurier*, November, 1938, quoted by Michael Hanisch, "The Chaplin Reception in Germany," from *Charlie Chaplin: His Reflection in Modern Times* (Adolphe Nysenholc, editor), p. 32.

55. Bosley Crowther, "*The Great Dictator*, by and with Charlie Chaplin, Tragi-Comic Fable of the Unhappy Lot of Decent Folk in a Totalitarian Land, at Astor and Capital," from *New York Times*, October 16, 1940, p. 29.

56. Charles Chaplin, Jr., *My Father, Charlie Chaplin*, pp. 239–240.

57. David Cook, *A History of Narrative Film*, p. 201.

5. *Monsieur Verdoux*

1. David Robinson, *Chaplin: His Life and Art*, p. 511.

2. James Agee, *Agee on Film*, p. 23.

3. Charles Chaplin, *My Autobiography*, p. 406.

4. Gallup poll cited by Charles Maland, *Chaplin and American Culture*, p. 189.

5. Charles Chaplin, *My Autobiography*, p. 407.

6. *Ibid.*, pp. 409–411. Reprinted from a pamphlet published by the Council of the Congress of Industrial Organizations.

7. *Ibid.*, p. 409.

8. Charles Maland, *Chaplin and American Culture*, pp. 193–194.

300 Notes

9. "Hollywood Goes Russian," from *Life*, September 24, 1942, p. 35.

10. FBI telegram dated January 31, 1944, cited by Charles Maland, *Chaplin and American Culture*, p. 211.

11. David Robinson, *Chaplin: The Mirror of Opinion*, p. 138.

12. *Life*, February 28, 1944, p. 35.

13. Charles Maland, *Chaplin and American Culture*, p. 211. Maland also notes, however, that the Chaplin case was getting such prominent coverage in the national media at the time that Hopper may have felt no need to address the issue.

14. Jerry Geisler, *The Jerry Geisler Story*, p. 187.

15. "Father for Carol Ann," from *Newsweek*, April 30, 1945, p. 41.

16. *Ibid.*, p. 42.

17. Carlyle Robinson, "The Private Life of Charlie Chaplin," from *Great Stars of Hollywood's Golden Age* (Frank C. Platt, editor), p. 116.

18. Jerry Geisler, *The Jerry Geisler Story*, p. 182.

19. John Paul Smead, *Five Films by Charles Chaplin: His Transition to Sound*, p. 29.

20. Buster Keaton, *My Wonderful World of Slapstick*, p. 130.

21. Mary Pickford, *Sunshine and Shadows*, p. 231.

22. Alistair Cooke, *Six Men*, p. 25.

23. Parker Tyler, *Chaplin, Last of the Clowns*, p. 97.

24. Charles Chaplin, Jr., *My Father, Charlie Chaplin*, p. 260.

25. "Mann and Woman," from *Time*, April 3, 1944, p. 24.

26. "Chaplin as Villain," from *Newsweek*, February 21, 1944, p. 48.

27. "Modern Times in Moscow," from *Newsweek*, May 15, 1944, p. 42. An accompanying note from *Newsweek* and CBS correspondent James Fleming, who filed the report, alludes that the Soviets may have been praising Chaplin's works in return for his support of the Second Front.

28. Charles Maland, *Chaplin and American Culture*, pp. 207, 213.

29. *Ibid.*, pp. 268–269; see also David Robinson, *Chaplin: His Life and Art*, p. 752.

30. *Ibid.*, p. 212.

31. Chaplin to Philip K. Scheuer, "Rags to Riches," from *Collier's*, April 12, 1947, p. 44.

32. Charles Maland, *Chaplin and American Culture*, pp. 254–255.

33. Martha Raye to Charles Chaplin, Jr., *My Father, Charlie Chaplin*, pp. 313, 318.

34. "New Chaplin Film," from *Life*, April 28, 1947, p. 59.

35. Jerry Epstein, *Remembering Charlie*, p. 44.

36. David Robinson, *Chaplin: His Life and Art*, pp. 490–491.

37. Dwight MacDonald, "On Chaplin, *Verdoux*, and Agee," from *Esquire*, April, 1965, p. 26.

38. Timothy J. Lyons (editor), "Interview with Roland H. Totheroh," from *Film Culture*, Spring 1972, pp. 262–263.

39. David Robinson, *Chaplin: His Life and Art*, p. 537.

40. *Ibid.*, p. 746.

41. Jack Spears, "Chaplin's Collaborators," from *Films in Review*, January, 1962, p. 34.

42. *Ibid.*, p. 36.

43. William K. Everson, "*A Woman of Paris*," from *Film Comment*, September/October, 1972, p. 15.

44. Foster Hirsch, "*Monsieur Verdoux*," from *Film Comment*, September/October 1972, p. 23.

45. Timothy J. Lyons (editor), "Interview with Roland H. Totheroh," from *Film Culture*, Spring 1972, p. 243.

46. Francis Wyndham, introduction from Charles Chaplin, *My Life in Pictures*, p. 33.

47. Charles Chaplin, Jr., *My Father, Charlie Chaplin*, p. 312. Charles Jr. also reveals in his book that *Monsieur Verdoux* is his least favorite of his father's films.

48. Charles Chaplin, *My Autobiography*, p. 351.

49. Claire Sheridan, *My American Diary*, p. 341.

50. Michael Chaplin, *I Couldn't Smoke the Grass on My Father's Lawn*, p. 47.

51. Theodore Huff, *Charlie Chaplin*, pp. 293–294. The quote by Chaplin is from an unnamed source.

52. Charles Chaplin, *My Trip Abroad*, p. 152. Chaplin's commentary was made in recounting the trip he made to Sing Sing prison upon his return to the United States.

53. Charles Chaplin, "How I Broke into the Pictures," from *The Strand*, January 1918, reprinted in Peter Haining (editor), *The Legend of Charlie Chaplin*, p. 38.

54. Mary Pickford to Kevin Brownlow, *The Parade's Gone By*, p. 135.

55. Charles Maland, *Chaplin and American Culture*, p. 234.

56. Philip K. Scheuer, "Rags to Riches," from *Colliers*, April 12, 1947, p. 15.

57. Parker Tyler, *Chaplin, Last of the Clowns*, p. 173.

58. Charles Maland, *Chaplin and American Culture*, p. 232.

59. Parker Tyler, *Chaplin, Last of the Clowns*, p. 147.

60. Roger Manvell, "*Monsieur Verdoux*," from *Focus on Chaplin* (Donald McCaffrey, editor), p. 141.

61. André Bazin, "The Myth of *Monsieur Verdoux*," from *What Is Cinema?*, Volume 2 (Hugh Gray, editor), pp. 105–106.

62. Timothy J. Lyons (editor), "Interview with Roland H. Totheroh," from *Film Culture*, Spring 1972, pp. 284–285.

63. Charles Maland, *Chaplin and American Culture*, p. 233.

64. Jean Paul Smead, *Five Films by Charles Chaplin: His Transition to Sound*, pp. 137–138, 161.

65. *Ibid.*, p. 148.

66. Charles Chaplin, *My Autobiography*, p. 435.

67. Charles Chaplin, *My Trip Abroad*, p. 18.

68. Charles Chaplin, "Can Art Be Popular?," from *Ladies' Home Journal*, October, 1924, reprinted in Richard Koszarski, *Hollywood Directors, 1914–1940*, p. 104.

69. Charles Chaplin, *My Autobiography*, p. 454.

70. Charles Maland, *Chaplin and American Culture*, p. 236.

71. Philip K. Scheuer, "Rags to Riches," from *Colliers*, April 12, 1947, p. 44.

72. Advertisement for *Monsieur Verdoux*, *New York Times*, April 11, 1947, p. 31.

73. Charles Chaplin, *My Autobiography*, p. 453.

74. See "Charlie Chaplin's *Monsieur Verdoux* Press Conference" (introduction by George Wallach), from *Film Comment*, Winter 1969, pp. 34-42.

75. *Ibid.*, p. 36.

76. *Ibid.*, p. 36, comments by James W. Fay.

77. *Ibid.*, p. 41, comments by James Agee.

78. "New Chaplin Film," from *Life*, April 28, 1947, p. 59.

79. Bosley Crowther, "*Monsieur Verdoux*, New Film Starring Charlie Chaplin, Has World Premiere at Broadway," from *New York Times*, April 12, 1947, p. 11.

80. "*Monsieur Verdoux*," from *Time*, May 5, 1947, p. 100.

81. Tino Balio, *United Artists: The Company of the Stars*, p. 214.

82. Charles Maland, *Chaplin and American Culture*, p. 247.

6. *Limelight*

1. Charles Maland, *Chaplin and American Culture*, p. 258.

2. Larry Ceplair and Steven Englund, *The Inquisition in Hollywood*, Appendix 4, p. 439.

3. Reprinted from David Robinson, *Chaplin: His Life and Art*, p. 545. The reference in the telegram inviting the Committee to view *Monsieur Verdoux* is interesting. At the time, the second promotional campaign was underway, with Washington D.C. being one of its targeted cities.

4. Charles Chaplin, *My Autobiography*, p. 449.

5. Charles Chaplin, Jr., *My Father, Charlie Chaplin*, pp. 342–343, 349.

6. Charles Chaplin, *My Autobiography*, p. 434.

7. Charles Maland, *Chaplin and American Culture*, p. 222, 225.

8. Charles Maland, "Are You Now, or Have You Ever Been ...," from *Cineaste*, Winter 1986, p. 11.

9. *Ibid.*, p. 11.

10. *Ibid.*, p. 13.

11. *Ibid.*, p. 14.

12. *Ibid.*, p. 15.

13. *Ibid.*, p. 10.

14. Charles Maland, *Chaplin and American Culture*, p. 276.

15. John Montgomery, "A Brief Overall View," from *Focus on Chaplin* (Donald McCaffrey, editor), p. 25.

16. Theodore Huff, *Charlie Chaplin*, pp. 308–309.

17. "Catholic War Vets Fight Showings of Charles Chaplin Pix," from *Variety*, December 13, 1950, reprinted in "Charlie Chaplin's *Monsieur Verdoux* Press Conference" (introduction by George Wallach), from *Film Comment*, Winter 1969, p. 42.

18. Quoted by Anthony Slide, "The American Press and Public Versus Charles Spencer Chaplin," from *Cineaste*, Winter 1984, p. 7. The quote is from an unnamed source.

19. Bess Taffel, cited by Larry Ceplair and Steven Englund, *The Inquisition in Hollywood*, pp. 384–385.

20. James Agee, "Comedy's Greatest Era," from *Life*, September 5, 1949, p. 77.

21. Charles Maland, *Chaplin and American Culture*, pp. 277–278.

22. *Ibid.*, p. 292.

23. Charles Chaplin, Jr., *My Father, Charlie Chaplin*, p. 246. Charles Jr. reports that his father enthusiastically gave a general plot outline to gossip columnist Louella Parsons.

24. David Robinson, *Chaplin: His Life and Art*, pp. 551–557.

25. Robert Parrish, *Growing Up in Hollywood*, p. 44.

26. André Bazin, "The Grandeur of *Limelight*," from *What Is Cinema?*, *Volume II* (Hugh Gray, editor), p. 132.

27. John Paul Smead, *Five Films by Charles Chaplin: His Transition to Sound*, p. 216.

28. Karl Struss, from Charles Higham, *Hollywood Cameramen: Sources of Light*, p. 131.

29. Charles Chaplin, *My Autobiography*, p. 459.

30. André Bazin, "The Grandeur of *Limelight*," from *What Is Cinema?*, *Volume II* (Hugh Gray, editor), p. 133.

31. Richard E. Lauterbach, "The Why's of Chaplin's Appeal," from *New York Times Magazine*, May 21, 1950, p. 32.

32. Charles Chaplin, *My Autobiography*, p. 261.

33. *Ibid.*, p. 50.
34. *Ibid.*, p. 261.
35. Charles Chaplin, Jr., *My Father, Charlie Chaplin*, p. 325.
36. André Bazin, "The Grandeur of *Limelight*," from *What Is Cinema?, Volume II* (Hugh Gray, editor), p. 133.
37. Claire Bloom, "Charles the Great," from *Vogue*, December 1992, p. 114.
38. Charles Maland, *Chaplin and American Culture*, p. 291.
39. Gerald Mast, *The Comic Mind*, p. 122.
40. Walter Kerr, *The Silent Clowns*, pp. 339–342.
41. Jerry Epstein, *Remembering Charlie*, pp. 96–98.
42. Tom Dardis, *Keaton: The Man Who Wouldn't Lie Down*, p. 262.
43. Claire Bloom, *Limelight and After*, p. 112.
44. Jerry Epstein, *Remembering Charlie*, p. 96.
45. Buster Keaton, *My Wonderful World of Slapstick*, p. 271.
46. Chaplin, as quoted from an article by René Fonjallaz in *La Revue Mondiale* (Paris), excerpted from *The Review of Reviews*, August 1932, p. 49. The quote, no doubt, was part of Chaplin's extensive promotional campaign for *City Lights*, which found him steadfastly defending his decision to remain essentially silent.
47. Chaplin to Philip K. Scheuer, "Rags to Riches," from *Collier's*, April 12, 1947, p. 45.
48. Walter Kerr, "The Lineage of *Limelight*," from *Focus on Chaplin* (Donald McCaffrey, editor), pp. 144–145.
49. Charles Maland, *Chaplin and American Culture*, p. 295.
50. Charles Chaplin, Jr., *My Father, Charlie Chaplin*, p. 295.
51. J.L. Tallenay, "The Tragic Vision of Charlie Chaplin," from *The Commonweal*, February 6, 1953, p. 452.
52. André Bazin, "The Grandeur of *Limelight*," from *What Is Cinema?, Volume II* (Hugh Gray, editor), p. 132.
53. Charles Maland, *Chaplin and American Culture*, p. 296.
54. Bosley Crowther, "The Screen: Chaplin's *Limelight* Opens," from *New York Times*, October 24, 1952, p. 27.
55. Eric Bentley, "Chaplin's Mea Culpa," from *New Republic*, November 17, 1952, p. 31.
56. Gerald Mast, *The Comic Mind*, p. 122.

7. A King in New York

1. André Bazin, "The Grandeur of *Limelight*," from *What Is Cinema?, Volume II* (Hugh Gray, editor), p. 129.
2. Charlie Chaplin, "A Comedian Sees the World," from *Woman's Home Companion*, December, 1933, p. 23.
3. Claire Bloom, "Charles the Great," from *Vogue*, December, 1992, p. 120.
4. Charles Chaplin, Jr., *My Father, Charlie Chaplin*, p. 339.
5. David Robinson, *Chaplin: His Life and Art*, pp. 575, 750–756.
6. Charles Chaplin, *My Autobiography*, p. 465.
7. James P. O'Donnell, "Charlie Chaplin's Stormy Exile," from *The Saturday Evening Post*, March 8, 1953, p. 98.
8. André Bazin, "*Limelight*, or the Death of Moliere," from *What Is Cinema?, Volume II* (Hugh Gray, editor), p. 124.

9. Charles Maland, *Chaplin and American Culture*, pp. 282–287. Like his work in sifting through the legal and government documents surrounding the Joan Barry trial, Maland's work on Chaplin's banishment from the United States (from documents obtained through the Freedom of Information Act) is excellent.

10. Alistair Cooke, *Six Men*, p. 43.

11. Charles Maland, *Chaplin and American Culture*, p. 286.

12. *Ibid.*, p. 308.

13. William Murray, "*Limelight*— Chaplin and his Censors," from *Nation*, March 21, 1953, p. 248.

14. Charles Maland, *Chaplin and American Culture*, p. 304.

15. David A. Cook, *A History of Narrative Film*, p. 410.

16. Jerry Epstein, *Remembering Charlie*, p. 104.

17. Lita Grey Chaplin, *My Life with Chaplin*, pp. 316–321.

18. David Robinson, *Chaplin: His Life and Art*, pp. 580–581.

19. Timothy J. Lyons (editor), "Interview with Roland H. Totheroh," from *Film Culture*, Spring 1972, p. 282.

20. Charles Chaplin, "A Comedian Sees the World," from *Woman's Home Companion*, December 1933, p. 38.

21. Public statement by Chaplin upon handing in his re-entry permit, reprinted by David Robinson, *Chaplin: His Life and Art*, p. 584.

22. "Little Man and a Plot," from *Newsweek*, June 14, 1954, p. 48.

23. Charles Chaplin, *My Autobiography*, p. 485.

24. Editorial, "Double Play: Chaplin to Robeson to Malenkov," *The Saturday Evening Post*, September 4, 1954, p. 10.

25. James P. O'Donnell, "Charlie Chaplin's Stormy Exile," from *The Saturday Evening Post*, April 15, 1958, p. 100.

26. David Robinson, *Chaplin: His Life and Art*, p. 585.

27. David Robinson, *Chaplin: The Mirror of Opinion*, p. 156.

28. Charles Chaplin to Margaret Hinxman, "An Interview with Chaplin," from *Sight and Sound*, Autumn 1957, p. 77.

29. Penelope Houston, "*A King in New York*: A Review," from *Sight and Sound*, Autumn 1957, p. 78.

30. David Robinson, *Chaplin: The Mirror of Opinion*, pp. 156–161.

31. Charles Chaplin, Jr., *My Father, Charlie Chaplin*, p. 360. Charles, Jr.'s, comments seem to indicate that he had not actually seen the finished film at the time of his 1960 book.

32. James P. O'Donnell, "Charlie Chaplin's Stormy Exile," from *The Saturday Evening Post*, March 22, 1958, p. 110.

33. Michael Chaplin, *I Couldn't Smoke the Grass on My Father's Lawn*, p. 62.

34. David Robinson, *Chaplin: His Life and Art*, p. 589.

35. Jerry Epstein, *Remembering Charlie*, p. 220.

36. Charles Chaplin, *My Life in Pictures*, p. 306.

37. Penelope Houston, "*A King in New York*: A Review," from *Sight and Sound*, Autumn 1957, p. 79.

38. Undated Chaplin interview with Margaret Hinxman, quoted in David Robinson, *Chaplin: His Life and Art*, p. 547. Hinxman did interview Chaplin for the Autumn 1957 issue of *Sight and Sound* (which was subsequently reprinted in Andrew Sarris' *Interviews with Film Directors*, 1967), though that text contains no mention of Chaplin addressing the House Un-American Activities Committee.

39. Charles Silver, *Charles Chaplin: An Appreciation*, p. 62.

40. Jerry Epstein, *Remembering Chaplin*, p. 141.

41. Chaplin, as quoted by René Fonjallaz, *La Revue Mondiale* (Paris), reprinted in *The Review of Reviews*, August 1932, p. 50.

42. John McCabe, *Charlie Chaplin*, pp. 232–233.

43. Bosley Crowther, "The Modern — and Mellower — Times of Mr. Chaplin," from *New York Times Magazine*, November 6, 1960, p. 60.

44. "Paul Lee," "Whither Chaplin," from *America*, October 5, 1957, pp. 13, 14.

45. David Robinson, *"A King in New York,"* from *Film Comment*, September/October, 1972, p. 26.

46. Charles Chaplin, *My Life in Pictures*, p. 306.

47. Roger Manvell, *Charlie Chaplin*, p. 215.

8. A Countess from Hong Kong

1. "Why Chaplin Paid Up?," from *Newsweek*, January 12, 1959, p. 39.

2. Bosley Crowther, "The Modern — Mellower — Times of Mr. Chaplin," from *New York Times Magazine*, November 6, 1960, p. 52.

3. Charles Maland, *Chaplin and American Culture*, p. 327–328.

4. *Ibid.*, pp. 329–330.

5. Timothy J. Lyons (editor), "Interview with Roland H. Totheroh," from *Film Culture*, Spring 1972, p. 282.

6. Emil Ludwig to Charles Chaplin, *My Autobiography*, pp. 357–358.

7. "The Little Tramp: As Told to Himself," from *Time*, October 1, 1964, p. 132.

8. Bosley Crowther, "A Moving Picture of the Hero as Himself," from *New York Times Book Review*, October 4, 1964, p. 5.

9. David Madden, *"My Autobiography,"* from *Film Quarterly*, Winter 1965–1966, p. 55.

10. Jack Spears and A.H.W., "Chaplin's Autobiography," from *Films in Review*, December 1964, p. 607.

11. Harding LeMay, "A Tantalizing Look Behind Chaplin's Mask," from *Life*, October 2, 1964, p. 26.

12. Charles Chaplin, "A Comedian Sees the World," from *Woman's Home Companion*, September 1933, p. 87.

13. David Robinson, *Chaplin: His Life and Art*, pp. 617–618.

14. Otis Ferguson, from *Garbo and the Night Watchmen* (Alistair Cooke, editor), pp. 274–275.

15. André Bazin, "The Myth of *Monsieur Verdoux*," from *What Is Cinema?*, Volume II (Hugh Gray, editor), pp. 118–119.

16. Charles Chaplin, *My Autobiography*, p. 254, 255. Chaplin would battle critics of his style for the rest of life. In one of his publicity articles for *Countess*, Chaplin would angerly comment to Richard Meryman: "I think that personality, people, the human equation transcend any acrobatics the camera might do … Hell, anybody can go up the actor's nostrils." (Richard Meryman, "Ageless Master's Anatomy of Comedy," from *Life*, March 10, 1967, pp. 84, 86).

17. Timothy J. Lyons (editor), "Interview with Roland H. Totheroh," from *Film Culture*, Spring 1972, p. 264.

18. Robert Parrish, *Growing Up in Hollywood*, p. 44.

19. David Robinson, *Chaplin: His Life and Art*, p. 229.

20. Richard Schickel, "Hail Chaplin — The Early Chaplin," from *New York Times Magazine*, April 2, 1972, p. 47.

21. *Ibid.*, p. 49.
22. Gerald Mast, *The Comic Mind*, p. 65.
23. *Ibid.*, pp. 65, 67.
24. David A. Cook, *A History of Narrative Film*, p. 203.
25. David Robinson, "Chaplin Meets the Press," from *Sight and Sound*, Winter 1965–1966, p. 20.
26. David Robinson, *Chaplin: His Life and Art*, p. 608.
27. Jerry Epstein, *Remembering Charlie*, pp. 171–172.
28. *Ibid.*, p. 172.
29. Kevin Brownlow, *The Parade's Gone By*, pp. 505, 507.
30. *Ibid.*, p. 506.
31. Lawrence Grobel, *Conversations with Brando*, pp. 74–75, 75–76. Though Brando was at odds with the comedian for much of the shoot, he was not open with his negativity in public. In fact, the reclusive actor respectfully neglected to discuss his true feelings about Chaplin and *A Countess from Hong Kong* until after the comedian passed away in 1977.
32. Jerry Epstein, *Remembering Chaplin*, p. 186.
33. Claire Bloom, *Limelight and After*, pp. 109–110.
34. Lawrence Grobel, *Conversations with Brando*, p. 75.
35. Marlon Brando (with Robert Lindsey), *Songs My Mother Taught Me*, p. 319.
36. Joe Morgenstern, "The Custard Pie of Creation," from *Newsweek*, June 6, 1966, p. 91.
37. Dora Jane Hamblin, "The Passionate Clown Comes Back," from *Life*, April 1, 1966, p. 84.
38. Charles Chaplin, *My Life in Pictures*, p. 310.
39. Jerry Epstein, *Remembering Charlie*, p. 171.
40. David Robinson, *Chaplin: His Life and Art*, pp. 614–615.
41. Joe Morgenstern, "The Custard Pie of Creation," from *Newsweek*, June 6, 1966, p. 90.
42. Chaplin to Francis Wyndham, reprinted in David Robinson, *Chaplin: His Life and Art*, p. 616.
43. Bosley Crowther, "*A Countess from Hong Kong*," from *New York Times*, March 17, 1967, p. 35.
44. Roger Manvell, *Chaplin*, p. 36.
45. Jerry Epstein, *Remembering Charlie*, pp. 192–193.
46. Richard Meryman, "Ageless Master's Anatomy of Comedy," from *Life*, March 10, 1967, p. 82.
47. Jerry Epstein, *Remembering Charlie*, p. 195.
48. Bosley Crowther, "*A Countess from Hong Kong*," from *New York Times*, March 17, 1967, p. 35.
49. Bosley Crowther, "How Hath the Mighty?," from *New York Times*, March 26, 1967, p. 1D.
50. Jerry Epstein, *Remembering Chaplin*, p. 195.
51. Brendan Gill, "The Current Cinema," from *New Yorker*, March 25, 1967, p. 153.
52. Paul D. Zimmerman, "Chasing the Dream," from *Newsweek*, April 3, 1967, p. 90.
53. "Time to Retire," from *Time*, March 31, 1967, p. 95.
54. Charles Maland, *Chaplin and American Culture*, pp. 326, 329, 334–337.

9. Epilogue

1. Jerry Epstein, *Remembering Charlie*, p. 201.
2. Alistair Cooke, *Six Men*, p. 44.
3. Richard Meryman, "Love Feast for Charlie," from *Life*, April 21, 1972, p. 89.
4. Charles Chaplin, *My Life in Pictures*, p. 316.
5. Charles Maland, *Chaplin and American Culture*, pp. 347–348.
6. Nestor Almendros, *A Man with a Camera*, p. 123.
7. Claire Bloom, *Limelight and After*, p. 99.
8. Adolphe Nysenholc, *Charlie Chaplin: His Reflection in Modern Times*, p. viii.
9. Paul Frederickson, "Good-Bye Charlie," from *The Saturday Evening Post*, Summer 1972, p. 58.
10. André Bazin, "The Grandeur of *Limelight*," from *What Is Cinema?, Volume II* (Hugh Gray, editor), p. 139.
11. Chaplin to Al Hirschfield, "A Man with Both Feet in the Clouds," from *New York Times Magazine*, July 26, 1942, p. 29.
12. Charles Chaplin, *My Life in Pictures*, p. 319.
13. Mary Pickford, *Sunshine and Shadow*, p. 236.
14. William Dodgeson Bowman, *Charlie Chaplin: His Life and Art*, p. 118.

Bibliography

Books

Agee, James. *Agee on Film*. New York: McDowell Obolensky, 1958.

Almendros, Nestor. *A Man with a Camera*. New York: Farrar, Straus and Giroux, Inc., 1984.

Asplund, Uno (translated by Paul Britten Austin). *Chaplin's Films*. New York: A.S. Barnes and Company, 1973.

Balio, Tino. *United Artists: The Company Built by the Stars*. Madison, Wisconsin: The University of Wisconsin Press, 1976.

Bazin, André (foreword by Francois Truffaut). *Jean Renoir*. New York: Simon & Schuster, 1973.

Bazin, André (Hugh Gray, editor). *What Is Cinema?, Volumes 1 & 2*. Berkeley, California: University of California Press, 1967.

Behlmer, Rudy (editor). *Memo from David O. Selznick*. New York: Viking Press, 1972.

Bergen, Candice. *Knockwood*. New York: Linden Press — Simon & Schuster, 1984.

Bessy, Maurice. *Charlie Chaplin*. New York: Harper & Row, 1985.

Betz, Albrecht (translated by Bill Hopkins). *Hanns Eisler: Political Musician*. New York: Cambridge University Press, 1982.

Blesh, Rudi. *Keaton*. New York: The Macmillan Company, 1966.

Bloom, Claire. *Limelight and After — The Education of an Actress*. New York: Harper & Row, 1982.

Bowman, W. Dodgeson. *Charlie Chaplin: His Life and Art*. New York: The John Day Company, 1931.

Brando, Marlon (with Robert Lindsey). *Brando: Songs My Mother Taught Me*. New York: Random House, 1994.

Brownlow, Kevin. *Behind the Mask of Innocence*. New York: Alfred A. Knopf, 1990.

Brownlow, Kevin. *The Parade's Gone By*. New York: Alfred A. Knopf, 1969.

Brownlow, Kevin and Kobal, John. *Hollywood: The Pioneers*. New York: Alfred A. Knopf, 1979.

Ceplair, Larry and Englund, Steven. *The Inquisition in Hollywood: Politics in the Film Community 1930–1960*. Garden City, New York: Anchor Press/Doubleday, 1980.

Chaplin, Charles. *My Autobiography*. New York: Simon & Schuster, 1964.

Chaplin, Charles. *My Life in Pictures*. London: Peerage Books, 1985.

Chaplin, Charles. *My Trip Abroad*. New York & London: Harper & Brothers, 1922.

Chaplin, Charles Jr. (with N. and M. Rau). *My Father, Charlie Chaplin*. New York: Random House, 1960.

Chaplin, Lita Grey (with Morton Cooper). *My Life with Chaplin: An Intimate Memoir*. New York: Bernard Geis Associates, 1966.

Chaplin, Michael. *I Couldn't Smoke the Grass on My Father's Lawn.* New York: G.P. Putnam's Sons, 1966.
Cook, David A. *A History of Narrative Film.* New York & London: W.W. Norton & Company, Inc., 1981.
Cooke, Alistair (editor). *Garbo and the Night Watchmen.* New York: McGraw-Hill, 1971.
Cooke, Alistair. *Six Men.* New York: Alfred A. Knopf, Inc., 1977.
Cotes, Peter and Niklaus, Thelma. *The Little Fellow: The Life and Work of Charles Spencer Chaplin.* New York: Philosophical Library, Inc., 1951.
Dardis, Tom. *Keaton: The Man Who Wouldn't Lie Down.* New York: Limelight Editions, 1988.
Dardis, Tom. *Harold Lloyd: The Man on the Clock.* New York: The Viking Press, 1983.
Davies, Marion (edited by Pamela Pfau and Kenneth S. Marx). *The Times We Had: Life with William Randolph Hearst.* Indianapolis: The Bobbs-Merrill Company, 1975.
Eells, George. *Hedda and Louella: A Dual Biography of Hedda Hopper and Louella Parsons.* New York: G.P. Putnam's Sons, 1972.
Eisenstein, Sergei (Jay Leyda, editor). *Film Essays and a Lecture.* Princeton, New Jersey: Princeton University Press, 1982.
Epstein, Jerry. *Remembering Charlie.* New York & London: Doubleday, 1989.
Everson, William K. *American Silent Film.* New York: Oxford University Press, 1978.
Gehring, Wes D. *Charlie Chaplin: A Bio-Bibliography.* Westport, Connecticut: Greenwood Press, 1983.
Gehring, Wes D. *Charlie Chaplin's World of Comedy.* Muncie, Indiana: Ball State University Monograph, Number 30, 1980.
Giesler, Jerry (as told to Pete Martin). *The Jerry Giesler Story.* New York: Simon & Schuster, 1960.
Gifford, Denis. *Chaplin.* Garden City, New York: Doubleday & Co., 1974.
Gifford, Denis (with Mike Higgs). *The Comic Art of Charlie Chaplin.* London: Hawk Books, 1989.
Grobel, Lawrence. *Conversations with Brando.* New York: Hyperion, 1991.
Haining, Peter (editor). *Charlie Chaplin: A Centenary Celebration.* London: W. Foulsham & Co. Ltd., 1989.
Haining, Peter (editor). *The Legend of Charlie Chaplin.* Secaucus, New Jersey: Castle, 1982.
Higham, Charles. *Hollywood Cameramen: Sources of Light.* Bloomington, Indiana: Indiana University Press, 1970.
Huff, Theodore. *Charlie Chaplin.* New York: Henry Schuman, Inc., 1951.
Jacobs, David. *Chaplin, the Movies and Charlie.* New York: Harper & Row, 1975.
Jacobs, Lewis. *The Rise of American Film.* New York: Teachers College Press, 1968.
Kamin, Dan. *Charlie Chaplin's One-Man Show.* Metuchen, New Jersey: The Scarecrow Press, 1984.
Keaton, Buster (with Charles Samuels). *My Wonderful World of Slapstick.* New York: Da Capo Press, Inc., 1987.
Kerr, Walter. *The Silent Clowns.* New York: Alfred A. Knopf, 1975.
Koszarski, Richard. *Hollywood Directors: 1914–1940.* New York: Oxford University Press, 1976.
Koszarski, Richard. *Hollywood Directors: 1941–1976.* New York: Oxford University Press, 1976.
Lyons, Timothy J. *Charles Chaplin: A Guide to References and Resources.* Boston: G.K. Hall & Company, 1976.
McCabe, John. *Charlie Chaplin.* Garden City, New York: Doubleday & Co., Inc., 1978.

McCaffrey, Donald W. (editor). *Focus on Chaplin*. Englewood Cliffs, New Jersey: Prentice-Hall, Inc., 1971.

McCaffrey, Donald W. *Four Comedians: Chaplin, Lloyd, Keaton, Langdon*. New York: A. Zwemmer Limited, A.S. Barnes & Co., 1968.

McDonald, Gerald D., Conway, Michael and Ricci, Mark. *The Complete Films of Charlie Chaplin*. Secaucus, New Jersey: Citadel Press, 1988.

Maland, Charles J. *Chaplin and American Culture: The Evolution of a Star Image*. Princeton, New Jersey: Princeton University Press, 1989.

Manvell, Roger. *Chaplin*. Boston & Toronto: Little, Brown & Company, 1974.

Mast, Gerald. *The Comic Mind*. Chicago: The University of Chicago Press, 1973.

Mast, Gerald. *A Short History of the Movies*. Indianapolis: The Bobbs-Merrill Company, Inc., 1971.

Minney, R.J. *Chaplin: The Immortal Tramp*. London: George Newnes Limited, 1954.

Molyneaux, Gerard Francis. *Charlie Chaplin's City Lights: Its Production and Dialectical Structure*. Madison, Wisconsin: Doctorate of Philosophy Dissertation, University of Wisconsin-Madison, 1976.

Montagu, Ivor. *With Eisenstein in Hollywood*. New York: International Publishers, 1969.

Montgomery, John. *Comedy Films 1894–1954*. London: George Allen & Unwin Ltd., 1968.

Morella, Joe and Epstein, Edward Z. *Paulette: The Adventurous Life of Paulette Goddard*. New York: St. Martin's Press, 1985.

Negri, Pola. *Memoirs of a Star*. Garden City, New York: Doubleday & Co., Inc., 1970.

Nysenholc, Adolphe (editor). *Charlie Chaplin: His Reflection in Modern Times*. New York: Mouton de Gruyter, 1991.

Oakie, Jack. *Jack Oakie's Double Takes*. San Francisco: Strawberry Hill Press, 1980.

Osborne, Robert. *Sixty Years of the Oscar*. New York: Abbeville Press, 1989.

Parrish, Robert. *Growing Up in Hollywood*. New York: Harcourt Brace Jovanovich, 1976.

Payne, Robert. *The Great God Pan*. New York: Hermitage House, 1952.

Pickford, Mary. *Sunshine and Shadows*. Garden City, New York: Doubleday & Company, Inc., 1955.

Platt, Frank C. (editor). *Great Stars from Hollywood's Golden Age*. New York: Signet Books, 1966.

Robinson, David. *Chaplin: His Life and Art*. New York: McGraw-Hill, 1985.

Robinson, David. *Chaplin: The Mirror of Opinion*. London: Secker & Warburg, 1983.

Rollins, Peter C. (Editor). *Hollywood as Historian: American Film in a Cultural Context*. Lexington, Kentucky: The University Press of Kentucky, 1983.

Ross, Lillian. *Moments with Chaplin*. New York: Dodd, Mead & Company, 1978.

Sarris, Andrew. *The American Cinema: Directors and Directions 1929–1968*. New York: E.P. Dutton & Company, 1968.

Sarris, Andrew (editor). *Interviews with Film Directors*. Indianapolis: Bobbs-Merrill Co., 1967.

Sheridan, Claire. *My American Diary*. New York: Boni and Liverwright, 1922.

Silver, Charles. *Charles Chaplin: An Appreciation*. New York: The Museum of Modern Art, 1989.

Sklar, Robert. *Movie-Made America: A Cultural History of American Movies*. New York: Vintage Books, 1976.

Smead, John Paul. *Five Films by Charles Chaplin: His Transition to Sound*. Ann Arbor, Michigan: unpublished Doctor of Philosophy (Speech) Dissertation, University of Michigan —1974.

Smith, Julian. *Chaplin*. Boston: Twayne Publishers, 1984.

Tyler, Parker. *Chaplin, Last of the Clowns*. New York: The Vanguard Press, 1948.

von Sternberg, Josef. *Fun in a Chinese Laundry*. New York: The Macmillan Company, 1965.

von Ulm, Gerith. *Charlie Chaplin: The King of Tragedy*. Caldwell, Idaho: The Caxton Printers, Ltd., 1940.

Weales, Gerald. *Canned Goods as Caviar: American Film Comedy of the 1930s*. Chicago: The University of Chicago Press, 1985.

White, David Manning, and Averson, Richard. *The Celluloid Weapon: Social Comment in American Film*. Boston: Beacon Press, 1972.

Selected Articles and Reviews

Agee, James. "Comedy's Greatest Era," *Life*, September 5, 1949, pp. 70–88.

Bakshy, Alexander. "Charlie Chaplin Faulters," *Nation*, March 4, 1930, pp. 250–251.

Bentley, Eric. "Chaplin's Mea Culpa," *New Republic*, November 17, 1952, pp. 30–31.

Berglund, Bo. "The Day the Tramp Was Born," *Sight and Sound*, Spring 1989, pp. 106–112.

Bloom, Claire. "Charles the Great," *Vogue*, December 1992, pp. 114, 120.

Chaplin, Charles. "A Comedian Sees the World," *Woman's Home Companion*, September 1933 — January 1934.

Churchill, Winston. "Everbody's Language," *Collier's*, October 26, 1935, pp. 24, 37–38.

Crowther, Bosley. "How Hath the Mighty?," from *The New York Times*, March 26, 1967, Section 2, p. 1, 7.

Crowther, Bosley. "The Modern — and Mellower — Times of Mr. Chaplin," from *The New York Times Magazine*, November 6, 1960, pp. 52–60.

Crowther, Bosley. "A Moving Picture of the Hero as Himself," from *The New York Times Book Review*, October 4, 1964, Pages 4–5.

"Double Play: Chaplin to Robeson to Malenkov," editorial in *The Saturday Evening Post*, September 4, 1954, pp. 10.

Fonjallaz, René, article excerpted from *La Revue Mondiale*. "Charlie Chaplin and the Talkies," from *The Review of Reviews*, August 1932, pp. 49–50.

Frank, Waldo. "Charles Chaplin — A Portrait," from *Scribner's Magazine*, September 1929, pp. 237–244.

Frederickson, Paul. "Good-Bye Charlie," from *The Saturday Evening Post*, Summer 1972, pp. 56–59.

Gill, Brendan. "The Current Cinema," from *The New Yorker*, March 25, 1967, Page 153.

Gorney, Jeffrey. "Paulette Goddard Lost Too Many Good Parts," from *Films in Review*, August–September 1974, Pages 401–416, 424.

Hamblin, Dora Jane. "The Passionate Clown Comes Back," from *Life*, April 1, 1966, pp. 79–86.

Hinxman, Margaret. "An Interview with Chaplin," from *Sight and Sound*, Autumn 1957, pp. 76–78.

Hirschfield, Al. "A Man with Both Feet in the Clouds," from *The New York Times Magazine*, July 26, 1942, pp. 12, 29.

Houston, Penelope. "*A King in New York*: A Review," from *Sight and Sound*, Autumn 1957, pp. 78–79.

Kuriyama, Constance Brown. "Chaplin's Impure Comedy: The Art of Survival," from *Film Magazine*, Spring 1992, pp. 26–38.

Lauterbach, Richard E. "The Why's of Chaplin's Appeal," from *The New York Times Magazine*, May 21, 1950, pp. 24–25, 32–33.

Lee, Paul. "Wither Chaplin," from *America*, October 5, 1957, pp. 12–14.

Lyons, Timothy J. "Interview with Roland Totheroh," from *Film Culture*, Spring 1972, pp. 230–285

Lyons, Timothy J. et al. "Chaplin and Sound," from *Journal of the University Film Association*, Winter 1979, pp. 1–50.

Madden, David. Review of *My Autobiography*, from *Film Quarterly*, Winter 1965–1966, pp. 54–58.

Maland, Charles J. "Are You Now, or Have You Ever Been...? — The INS Interview with Charles Chaplin," from *Cineaste*, Winter 1986, pp. 10–15.

Maltin, Leonard. "Silent Film Buffs Stalk and Find a Missing Tramp," from *Smithsonian*, July 1986, pp. 46–57.

Manning, Harold (edited with notes by Timothy J. Lyons). "Charlie Chaplin's Early Life: Fact and Fiction," from *Historical Journal of Film, Radio and Television*, Volume 3, Number 1, 1983, pp. 35–41.

Meryman, Richard. "Ageless Master's Anatomy of Comedy," from *Life*, March 10, 1967, pp. 80–94.

Meryman, Richard (photography and accompanying thoughts by Candice Bergen). "Love Feast for Charlie," from *Life*, April 21, 1972, pp. 86–90.

Morgenstern, Joseph. "The Custard Pie of Creation," from *Newsweek*, June 6, 1966, pp. 90–94.

Murray, William. "*Limelight* — Chaplin and His Censors," from *Nation*, March 21, 1953, pp. 247–248.

O'Donnell, James P. "Charlie Chaplin's Stormy Exile," from *The Saturday Evening Post*, March 8, 15 and 21, 1958.

"The Process of Dissolution," editorial in *The Commonweal*, February 6, 1953, pp. 441–442.

Robinson, David. "Chaplin Meets the Press," from *Sight and Sound*, Winter 1965–1966, p. 20.

Scheuer, Phillip K. "From Rags to Riches," from *Colliers*, April 12, 1947, pp. 15, 44.

Schickel, Richard. "Hail Chaplin — The Early Chaplin," from *The New York Times Magazine*, April 2, 1972, pp. 12–13, 47–48.

Slide, Anthony. "The American Press and Public versus Charles Spencer Chaplin," from *Cineaste*, Winter 1984, pp. 6–9.

Spears, Jack. "Chaplin's Collaborators," from *Films in Review*, January 1962, pp. 18–36.

Spears, Jack, and A.H.W., "Chaplin's Autobiograpy," from *Films in Review*, December, 1964, pp. 606–610.

Tallenay, J.L. "The Tragic Vision of Charles Chaplin," from *The Commonweal*, February 6, 1953, pp. 451–453.

Wallach, George (editor). "Charlie Chaplin's *Monsieur Verdoux* Press Conference," from *Film Comment*, Winter 1969, pp. 34–42.

Video

Brownlow, Kevin, and Gill, David. *Unknown Chaplin*. hames Television —1983.

Index

320 Index